ReFocus: The Later Films and Legacy of Robert Altman

ReFocus: The American Directors Series

Series Editors: Robert Singer, Frances Smith, and Gary D. Rhodes

Editorial Board:
Kelly Basilio, Donna Campbell, Claire Perkins, Christopher Sharrett, and Yannis Tzioumakis

ReFocus is a series of contemporary methodological and theoretical approaches to the interdisciplinary analyses and interpretations of neglected American directors, from the once-famous to the ignored, in direct relationship to American culture—its myths, values, and historical precepts.

Titles in the series include:

ReFocus: The Films of Preston Sturges
Edited by Jeff Jaeckle and Sarah Kozloff

ReFocus: The Films of Delmer Daves
Edited by Matthew Carter and Andrew Nelson

ReFocus: The Films of Amy Heckerling
Edited by Frances Smith and Timothy Shary

ReFocus: The Films of Budd Boetticher
Edited by Gary D. Rhodes and Robert Singer

ReFocus: The Films of Kelly Reichardt
E. Dawn Hall

ReFocus: The Films of William Castle
Edited by Murray Leeder

ReFocus: The Films of Barbara Kopple
Edited by Jeff Jaeckle and Susan Ryan

ReFocus: The Films of Elaine May
Edited by Alexandra Heller-Nicholas and Dean Brandum

ReFocus: The Films of Spike Jonze
Edited by Kim Wilkins and Wyatt Moss-Wellington

ReFocus: The Films of Paul Schrader
Edited by Michelle E. Moore and Brian Brems

ReFocus: The Films of John Hughes
Edited by Timothy Shary and Frances Smith

ReFocus: The Films of Doris Wishman
Edited by Alicia Kozma and Finley Freibert

ReFocus: The Films of Albert Brooks
Edited by Christian B. Long

ReFocus: The Films of William Friedkin
Steve Choe

ReFocus: The Later Films and Legacy of Robert Altman
Edited by Lisa Dombrowski and Justin Wyatt

ReFocus: The Films of Mary Harron
Edited by Kyle Barrett

edinburghuniversitypress.com/series/refoc

ReFocus:
The Later Films and Legacy of Robert Altman

Edited by Lisa Dombrowski and Justin Wyatt

EDINBURGH
University Press

For B.
&
For Patricia Wyatt, Shelagh Heffernan, and Jeffrey Clarke, with love.

Edinburgh University Press is one of the leading university presses in the UK. We publish academic books and journals in our selected subject areas across the humanities and social sciences, combining cutting-edge scholarship with high editorial and production values to produce academic works of lasting importance. For more information visit our website: edinburghuniversitypress.com

© editorial matter and organisation Lisa Dombrowski and Justin Wyatt, 2021, 2023
© the chapters their several authors, 2021

Edinburgh University Press Ltd
The Tun – Holyrood Road
12 (2f) Jackson's Entry
Edinburgh EH8 8PJ

First published in hardback by Edinburgh University Press 2021

Typeset in 11/13 Ehrhardt MT by
IDSUK (DataConnection) Ltd

A CIP record for this book is available from the British Library

ISBN 978 1 4744 7885 4 (hardback)
ISBN 978 1 4744 7886 1 (paperback)
ISBN 978 1 4744 7887 8 (webready PDF)
ISBN 978 1 4744 7888 5 (epub)

The right of the contributors to be identified as authors of this work has been asserted in accordance with the Copyright, Designs and Patents Act 1988 and the Copyright and Related Rights Regulations 2003 (SI No. 2498).

Contents

List of Figures · vii
Notes on Contributors · ix
Acknowledgments · xi

Introduction: Autumnal Altman—Rethinking his Last Quarter Century · 1
Lisa Dombrowski and Justin Wyatt

Part I The Creative Process

1. I Yam What I Yam What I Yam: Altman and the Transpositional Poetics of *Popeye* · 13
   Mark Minett
2. For Real: *Tanner '88*, *Tanner on Tanner*, and the Political Spectacle in the Post-Network Era · 30
   Chuck Tryon
3. Home-makers: Examining the Altmans' Place-based Production Practices in *Cookie's Fortune* · 47
   Nathan Koob
4. A Perfect Couple: The Altman–Rudolph Connection · 65
   Richard R. Ness
5. Unmade Altman: What the Archive Tells Us · 81
   Philip Hallman

Part II Industrial Frameworks

6. Offbeat and Out of Sync: *Popeye* and the Failure of an Auteur-Driven Franchise · 99
   Tim J. Anderson

7 "Here Comes the Hot-Stepper": The Hollywood Renaissance, Indie Film, and Robert Altman's Comeback in the 1990s 117
Yannis Tzioumakis

8 "I Fiddle on the Corner Where They Throw the Coins": Altman's Brand in Europe 137
Lisa Dombrowski

Part III New Perspectives on Altman

9 Fantasies and Fangirls: Gender and Sexuality in Robert Altman's *Come Back to the 5 & Dime, Jimmy Dean, Jimmy Dean* 159
Sarah E. S. Sinwell

10 Countering Robert Altman's Sexual Outlaws: Visibility, Representation, and Questionable Social Progress 172
Justin Wyatt

11 The Affection of Death 190
Robert P. Kolker

Part IV Collaborator Interviews

12 Allan F. Nicholls 197
13 Alan Rudolph 202
14 Ira Deutchman 209
15 Matthew Seig 218
16 Wren Arthur 225
17 Joshua Astrachan 229
18 Anne Rapp 236
19 Andrew Dunn 243
20 Mitchell Zuckoff 252

Index 259

Figures

Int.1	Robert Altman on the set of *Cookie's Fortune*	4
Int.2	Paul Thomas Anderson, the stand-by director, with Robert Altman on the set of *A Prairie Home Companion*	8
I.1	Robert Altman on the set of *Short Cuts*	12
1.1	The Popeye-Oxblood Oxheart boxing match in the *Thimble Theatre* comic strip by E. C. Segar	18
1.2	Robin Williams, Linda Hunt, Peter Bray, and Paul Dooley during the Popeye-Oxblood Oxheart boxing match in *Popeye*	18
2.1	Robert Altman and Michael Murphy on the set of *Tanner '88*	34
2.2	Michael Murphy as Jack Tanner on his campaign bus with staff and reporters in *Tanner '88*	39
3.1	Kathryn Reed Altman and Lyle Lovett on the set of *Cookie's Fortune*	51
3.2	A map of the walk through the town of Holly Springs, Mississippi, made by Charles S. Dutton as Willis Richland in the opening scenes of *Cookie's Fortune*	58
4.1	Actors Tim Roth and Paul Rhys, cinematographer Jean Lépine, and Robert Altman on the set of *Vincent & Theo*	68
4.2	Robert Altman and Jennifer Jason Leigh as Blondie on the set of *Kansas City*	75
5.1	A list of characters and casting for *Hands on a Hard Body* featuring notes written by screenwriter Anne Rapp	91
II.1	Storyboard of the storm sequence in *Dr. T & the Women*	98
6.1	Robin Williams, Shelley Duvall, and Robert Altman on the set of *Popeye*	102
6.2	Songwriter Harry Nilsson and Shelley Duvall during the recording of the soundtrack for *Popeye*	109

7.1	Writer and actor Sam Shepard with Robert Altman on the set of *Fool for Love*	124
7.2	Tim Robbins and Robert Altman take a break from promoting *The Player* following its debut at the Cannes Film Festival	130
8.1	Robert Altman directs a scene in Moscow's Red Square for *Prêt-à-Porter*	143
8.2	Producer and actor Bob Balaban and Robert Altman confer on the set of *Gosford Park*	149
III.1	Robert Altman on the set of *Dr. T & the Women*	158
9.1	Cher and Robert Altman pose on the set of *Come Back to the 5 & Dime, Jimmy Dean, Jimmy Dean*	161
9.2	Karen Black and Cher in *Come Back to the 5 & Dime, Jimmy Dean, Jimmy Dean*	167
10.1	Helen (Bert Remsen) is interrogated by a fake vice squad in *California Split*	175
10.2	In *Streamers*, the flirtation between Richie (Michael Wright) and Carlyle (Mitchell Lichtenstein) destabilizes the power dynamic in the barracks	179
11.1	John C. Reilly, Woody Harrelson, Kevin Kline, and Robert Altman on the set of *A Prairie Home Companion*	191
IV.1	Stephen Rea in *Prêt-à-Porter* as drawn by fashion illustrator Gladys Perint Palmer	196
12.1	Allan F. Nicholls and Robert Altman	197
13.1	Alan Rudolph and Robert Altman on a yacht at the Cannes Film Festival	202
14.1	Ira Deutchman	209
15.1	Matthew Seig	218
16.1	Producers Wren Arthur and David Levy on the set of *A Prairie Home Companion*	225
17.1	Joshua Astrachan at the Berlin Film Festival press conference following the premiere of *A Prairie Home Companion*	229
18.1	Anne Rapp on the set of *Cookie's Fortune*	236
19.1	Andrew Dunn on the set of *Gosford Park*	243
20.1	Mitchell Zuckoff	252

Notes on Contributors

Tim J. Anderson is an associate professor and director of the Institute for the Humanities at Old Dominion University. He has published numerous book chapters, journal articles, and two monographs. His latest research project focuses on recordings, musicians, listeners, and the public sphere. Anderson's website is www.timjanderson.com

Lisa Dombrowski is a professor of Film Studies and a professor of East Asian Studies at Wesleyan University. She is the author of *The Films of Samuel Fuller: If You Die, I'll Kill You!*, the editor of *Kazan Revisited*, and has contributed essays to *Film Quarterly, Film History, Film Comment, The New York Times*, and the Criterion Collection, among others.

Philip Hallman is the Film Studies Field Librarian for the University of Michigan Library, the head of the Donald Hall Collection Library, and the curator of the Screen Arts Mavericks & Makers Collection which holds the archival papers of filmmakers Orson Welles, Robert Altman, John Sayles, Alan Rudolph, Nancy Savoca, Jonathan Demme, and specialty distributors Robert Shaye and Ira Deutchman.

Robert P. Kolker is professor emeritus at the University of Maryland and has taught cinema studies for over fifty years. He is the author of *A Cinema of Loneliness; The Altering Eye; The Extraordinary Image: Orson Welles, Alfred Hitchcock, Stanley Kubrick and the Reimagining of Cinema; Film, Form, and Culture; The Cultures of American Film; Eyes Wide Shut: Stanley Kubrick and the Making of His Final Film*, co-authored with Nathan Abrams; and editor of *2001: A Space Odyssey: New Essays* and *The Oxford Handbook of Film and Media Studies*. He is currently working on a biography of Stanley Kubrick with Nathan Abrams.

Nathan Koob is a visiting lecturer in the English Department and Film and Media Studies Program at the University of Pittsburgh. He received his PhD from the University of Michigan in 2015. His work examines the production process, authorship, and texts through their spatial and industrial contexts.

Mark Minett, associate professor of Film and Media Studies and English at the University of South Carolina, is the author of *Robert Altman and the Elaboration of Hollywood Storytelling*. His research focuses on developing close, contextualized accounts of approaches to storytelling within and across historical periods, industries, and media forms.

Richard R. Ness, professor of film studies at Western Illinois University, is the author of *Alan Rudolph: Romance and a Crazed World*, *Encyclopedia of Journalists on Film*, and *From Headline Hunter to Superman: A Journalism Filmography*. His articles have appeared in *Cinema Journal*, the *Hitchcock Annual*, *IJPC Journal*, *Miranda—Revue pluridisciplinaire du monde Anglophone*, the *Cahiers du Cinéma* collection *Print the Legend*, and anthologies on Robert Altman, Alfred Hitchcock, Michael Moore, and The Soundtrack Album.

Sarah E. S. Sinwell is an associate professor in the Department of Film and Media Arts at the University of Utah. She has published essays on Kickstarter, *Green Porno*, and Gamechanger Films in *A Companion to American Indie Film*, *Women's Studies Quarterly*, and *Indie Reframed: Women Filmmakers and Contemporary American Cinema*. Her recently published book *Indie Cinema Online* (2020) redefines independent cinema in an era of media convergence.

Chuck Tryon is a professor of English at Fayetteville State University. He is the author of three books, including *Political TV* and *On-Demand Culture: Digital Delivery and the Future of Movies*. He has also published essays for *Screen*, *Media Industries*, and *Popular Communication*.

Yannis Tzioumakis is a reader in film and media industries at the University of Liverpool. He is the author of five books, most recently of *Acting Indie: Industry, Aesthetics, and Performance* (co-authored with Cynthia Baron), and co-editor of six collections of essays, most recently of *United Artists*. He also co-edits the Routledge Hollywood Centenary and the Cinema and Youth Cultures book series.

Justin Wyatt is an associate professor of communication studies, journalism, and film/media at the University of Rhode Island. He is also the associate director of the Harrington School of Communication and Media at URI. Wyatt is the author of *High Concept: Movies & Marketing in Hollywood* and *The Virgin Suicides: Reverie, Sorrow and Young Love* and the co-editor of *Contemporary American Independent Film: From the Margins to the Mainstream*.

Acknowledgments

The inspiration for this project originated in the Robert Altman Papers collected at the Special Collections Research Center, University of Michigan Library. We are grateful for the support of Martha O'Hara Conway, the director of the Special Collections Research Center, and of Kathleen Dow, the Center's retired archivist and curator. Thank you also to the staff of the University of Michigan Library Special Collections Reading Room, past and present, and in particular to Kate Hutchens, who wrangled hundreds of archival boxes for our perusal.

Our primary partner in this project was Philip Hallman, the intrepid Film Studies Field Librarian and Curator of the Screen Arts Mavericks & Makers Collection, which houses Altman's papers. Phil first brought us together on a panel during the "Tastemaker International: Ira Deutchman and the Art & Business of Independent Cinema" symposium, which was sponsored by the University of Michigan Library and the Department of Film, Television and Media. Thereafter, Phil not only facilitated our research trips to Ann Arbor, but also provided invaluable advice and suggestions, assisted with the identification and acquisition of the illustrations, and contributed an essay to the anthology. He has been a great friend to us both, and we literally could not have completed the book without him.

We greatly appreciate the generosity of Wren Arthur, Joshua Astrachan, Ira Deutchman, Andrew Dunn, Allan F. Nicholls, Anne Rapp, Alan Rudolph, Matthew Seig, and Mitchell Zuckoff, who shared their experiences of working with Robert Altman.

Thanks also to Robert Singer, Gary Rhodes, and Frances Smith, the editors of ReFocus: The American Directors Series, for their enthusiastic support, close reading of the manuscript, and editorial suggestions. Gillian Leslie, Richard Strachan, and Eddie Clark of Edinburgh University Press expertly shepherded the project from start to finish.

Lisa's research work was supported by project grants from Wesleyan University. She received vital organizational, research, and translation assistance from Ben Yap, Kira Newmark, Hannah Cooper, and Ken Wu. Thank you to Ethan de Seife, a longtime friend and Altman fan, for putting us in touch with Allan F. Nicholls. Much love to Chuck, Carol, and Mike, with whom I watched my first Robert Altman films, and to Brett, with whom I watch them still.

Justin would like to thank Dean Jen Riley and Associate Deans Nedra Reynolds and Adam Roth at the University of Rhode Island for their support of this project. In addition, Robert Clark provided excellent research assistance for the book. Justin has also benefited from talking about the later Altman films with many colleagues and friends including Pete Richardson, Marybeth Reilly McGreen, Joanne Yamaguchi, Leslie LeMond, David Elperin, and Sharon Hodapp.

Finally, this book was completed in the midst of the COVID-19 pandemic with all of its attendant challenges, and we are grateful to our collaborators for their commitment to the project.

Introduction: Autumnal Altman—Rethinking his Last Quarter Century

Lisa Dombrowski and Justin Wyatt

Robin Wood, writing in 1986 about an essay he authored ten years earlier, makes the claim that Robert Altman's auteurism remains static: "I see no reason whatsoever to retract or substantially modify its argument: the account of Altman I offered ten years ago has received nothing but repeated confirmation from his subsequent work."¹ Wood proceeds to match films from Altman's first years of moviemaking with his films post-1975. Wood's stance is worth noting since it illuminates the attention given to Altman's films after his first major hit, *M*A*S*H* (1970).

If we consider the ten years post-*M*A*S*H*, Altman's films seem bracketed in two five-year periods. From *M*A*S*H* to *Nashville* (1975), most of Altman's films were critically acclaimed, but not significant in terms of box office. Interestingly, the support of the mainstream distributors buoyed Altman during these years regardless; Altman's films were distributed by MGM, Warner Bros., United Artists, Columbia, and Paramount in this period. Despite the lack of a hit after *M*A*S*H*, Altman was able to benefit from the Hollywood Renaissance period of the early 1970s in which aesthetic (and social) experimentation by selected auteurs was indulged by the major Hollywood studios. Even within the Hollywood Renaissance, Altman was somewhat of an outlier: a veteran television director, Altman was a generation older than the film school prodigies Martin Scorsese, Francis Coppola, Brian DePalma, and George Lucas. The anarchic tone and content of *M*A*S*H* nevertheless placed Altman in the same category as these other iconoclasts. For Altman, this period of filmmaking allowed for his innovations in storytelling and cinematic style. The freedom was quite short lived. In the second half of the 1970s, Altman's career was dominated by his deal with studio production chief Alan Ladd Jr. at Twentieth Century Fox. Altman made five films for Fox (*3 Women*, 1977; *A Wedding*, 1978; *Quintet*, 1979; *A Perfect Couple*, 1979; and *HealtH*, 1980).

Unlike his slate in the first half of the 1970s, these films generated neither critical nor public interest. *3 Women* elicited the most favorable reviews and it has become a *succès d'estime*.

Segmenting Altman's films of the 1970s into these two halves illustrates how his acclaimed period of innovation and artistic expression ran from *M*A*S*H* to *Nashville*. With the possible exception of *Brewster McCloud* (1970), which at least has a cult following, any of the remaining films from the early '70s could be used to demonstrate Altman's unique voice and vision. Invoking the second half of the decade makes the exercise more confused. To use Wood's pairing system, it would be difficult to join the genre revisionism of *McCabe & Mrs. Miller* (1971) with *Quintet* or the social/political critique of *Nashville* with the same in *HealtH*. How useful is it to connect the American social landscape of *Nashville*'s twenty-four characters with *A Wedding*'s forty-eight characters? During his tenure at Fox, Altman's support was linked to Ladd's presence. Once Ladd exited the studio, the new regime, lacking confidence in Altman's films given the performance of the first three (*A Wedding*, *3 Women*, *Quintet*), offered little support for *A Perfect Couple* and none at all for *HealtH*. Apart from the Fox films, Altman's only other project during this time, *Buffalo Bill and the Indians, or Sitting Bull's History Lesson* (1976), failed both commercially and critically.

In just one decade, Altman was able to realize the battery of critical and public acclaim as well as dismissal that would be repeated for much of the next quarter-century as he continued to direct and produce films. Just by considering the two halves of the 1970s, it is clear that canonical understandings of Altman's auteurism rest largely on the films bracketed by *M*A*S*H* and *Nashville*. The second half of the 1970s, with financial backing petering out, mixed reaction to the films, and sometimes limited release patterns, presents a picture that would be repeated for the remainder of Altman's career. Rather than vouch for the 1970–5 time frame, we want to suggest that the later period of Altman's career, especially from 1980 on, reveals a more complete picture of his auteurism and his innovations, both aesthetically and in business practice. Altman's turbulent second half of the 1970s is the omen for the rest of his professional career, which is marked by the regular alteration of critical and commercial successes and failures. In fact, the consistency of the 1970–5 period should be seen as exceptional, not illustrative of Altman's key strengths, weaknesses and areas of growth as an artist. A more nuanced understanding of Altman's authorship requires assessing the underexplored second half of his career.

WHY FOCUS ON ALTMAN'S LAST QUARTER CENTURY?

From 1980 through to his death in 2006, Altman continued to work, albeit under much different circumstances than in his initial 1970s period. During the 1980s, an era of exile from Hollywood following the disappointment of *Popeye* (1980),

Altman persevered through cable productions and projects adapting plays to film (*Come Back to the 5 & Dime, Jimmy Dean, Jimmy Dean*, 1982; *Streamers*, 1983; *Secret Honor*, 1984; *Fool for Love*, 1985; *Beyond Therapy*, 1987). Altman would also venture into opera, legitimate theater, and commercials as a way to express his creativity. Frustrated by the sense that Hollywood no longer embraced the kinds of projects he was interested in, Altman decamped to Paris in 1984 and sought opportunities for productions in Europe. Only after critics embraced *Vincent & Theo* in 1990 did Altman find his star on the rise in his native country again. In this period, there are arguably only three critically and commercially acclaimed projects: *The Player* in 1992, *Short Cuts* in 1993, and *Gosford Park* in 2001. Subsequent to *Short Cuts*, every peak in Altman's filmmaking is followed by a valley. Nevertheless, many projects in the final three decades warrant revisiting—from 1980s theatrical adaptations to the Southern-themed *The Gingerbread Man* (1998), *Cookie's Fortune* (1999), and *Dr. T & the Women* (2000); the ambitious social landscapes of *Prêt-à-Porter* (1994), *The Company* (2003), and *A Prairie Home Companion* (2006); and the self-reflexive political satire of the *Tanner* series (*Tanner '88*, 1988 and *Tanner on Tanner*, 2004).

This anthology considers post-1970s Altman as a way to rethink and reconceive his authorship. Rather than place aside the extensive work on Altman to date, the project attempts to offer texture and depth to previous ways of thinking about Altman's creativity and contribution to American cinema. In particular, essays expand our understanding of the development of Altman's personal aesthetic; his adaptation of existing source material; the representation of sex, gender, and identity in his films; his relation to the changing landscape of American independent cinema; his work with collaborators; and his unfinished projects. The goal of the book is not to minimize the impact of Altman's 1970s work, but to think about how the under-analyzed post-1979 films can be explored alone, together, and in relation to earlier work in an effort to craft a more compelling portrait of Altman's evolution as an artist.

The conversation around the significance of Altman's work has reignited since his passing in 2006, with new works on single films (e.g., Robert Self's *Robert Altman's McCabe & Mrs. Miller: Reframing the American West*); career overviews (e.g., Robert Niemi's *The Cinema of Robert Altman: Hollywood Maverick*); focused inquiries (e.g., Gayle Sherwood Magee's *Robert Altman's Soundtracks: Film, Music, and Sound from M*A*S*H to A Prairie Home Companion*); and collections of essays (e.g., Rick Armstrong's *Robert Altman: Critical Essays*; Adrian Danks's *A Companion to Robert Altman*). Altman's widow, Kathryn Reed Altman, co-authored with Giulia D'Agnolo Vallan a heavily illustrated book on Altman's career. While not academic in nature, the book provides much useful production and background information film by film, told from an insider perspective. Similarly, Mitchell Zuckoff's oral biography of Altman, published in 2009, presents an unvarnished view of Altman's career from collaborators, competitors, fans, and detractors. Ron Mann's 2014

Figure Int.1 Robert Altman on the set of *Cookie's Fortune*. Photo by Joyce Rudolph. Courtesy of Special Collections Research Center, University of Michigan Library.

feature-length documentary, simply titled *Altman*, takes a similar approach, especially with the input of Kathryn Reed Altman.

Yet there is much about Robert Altman still to be debated and explored, especially in relation to the less frequently addressed films of his late period. Facilitating this effort are the papers in Altman's archive, opened at the University of Michigan in 2013. With nearly 700 boxes, the collection covers the full range of Altman's career, although the later films have a remarkably comprehensive array of materials on their production, marketing, distribution, and reception that provide new avenues for research. With access to these secondary and primary materials, a consideration of Altman's last three decades and their relationship to the director's celebrated work of the early 1970s is a useful and needed addition to Altman scholarship.

Our anthology is composed of both scholarly chapters and original interviews with key Altman collaborators during this later period.[2] While these two strands allow us to cover the background and analysis of more films, the juxtaposition of the interviews with the academic chapters fosters an exchange between the two areas. This is partly by design: we developed interview questions for the practitioners that engaged with the content areas of the scholarly work. So, for instance, as Nathan Koob discerns the value to her husband's filmmaking of Kathryn Reed Altman's social events during production, we see this echoed and

INTRODUCTION 5

reinforced through several of the interviews. Our hope is that the hypotheses, theories, and insights on the academic side become part of a conversation alongside the collaborators' remembrances. We feel this intersection is a useful way to gather a more comprehensive appreciation of Altman's artistry.

THREE THEMES

Throughout the book, three unifying themes emerge: the nature of Altman's creative process; how the larger industrial framework shaped Altman's output in this period; and new perspectives on key films. Of course, the borders between these three areas are fluid and also worthy of consideration.

Moving far away from a narrow definition of auteurism as the single vision of a creative individual, several essays complicate, in a most useful manner, accounts of Altman as author. In his close analysis of Altman's *Popeye*, Mark Minett examines how collaborators, adaptation, and innovation all played key roles in the creation of this unusual musical. Minett places his case study in the larger framework of transmedial cultural production, highlighting the strategies utilized by screenwriter Jules Feiffer and subsequently Altman to embrace, abandon, or alter previous iterations of the Popeye character as seen in comic strips and cartoons. Chuck Tryon's chapter on the *Tanner* series, created by Altman and comic artist Garry Trudeau, similarly tackles how the co-creators integrated their artistic vision—namely, a fake presidential campaign—with preexisting material—a real presidential race. Matching improvisational acting with observational camerawork, Altman's "campaign" wreaks havoc with the conventions of both satire and documentary, blurring the lines between what is constructed and what is authentic and training viewers to question the creation of political media. Nathan Koob's unique chapter explores Altman's place-based production practices through carefully documented interviews and archival research. Koob isolates the director's spouse as a production worker whose labor has largely been disregarded by scholars yet served key creative and social functions, particularly on location. Richard Ness considers the relationship between Altman's authorship and that of his frequent collaborator and protégé, Alan Rudolph. Ness traces the two directors' intersecting interests while emphasizing their distinct approaches to narrative and style. Finally, the curator of the Robert Altman Papers at the Special Collections Research Center, University of Michigan Library, Philip Hallman, looks at unproduced or abandoned projects by the director through close examination of documents from the Altman archive. Weaving a portrait of how seemingly insignificant documents can reveal insight into the creative process, Hallman's chapter presents a novel way to examine and to value unrealized works in a director's career. The five essays together shine a light on the multiple ways that a conventional approach to auteurism fails to fully account for the circumstances and structures behind Altman's films. If we are analyzing Altman's authorship, the essays remind us that we need to rethink the basic tenets of auteurism as well, and to provide more nuanced portraits of collaboration and the creative process.

A more complete picture of Altman's auteurism also requires a consideration of how shifts in the domestic and foreign marketplace impacted the production, distribution, and reception of his films. Looking at *Popeye* from a commercial perspective, Tim Anderson traces how the film, while imagined as a blockbuster musical by Robert Evans and the distributors, actually falls squarely outside that category. Composer Harry Nilsson and Altman crafted a more experimental, auteur-driven musical, boldly challenging contemporary commercial expectations and genre norms. Both Yannis Tzioumakis and Lisa Dombrowski present new ways to consider how Altman navigated the evolving independent film marketplace in his final quarter century. Tzioumakis challenges attempts within independent film discourses to link the Hollywood Renaissance of the 1960s and 1970s with the indie cinema boom of the 1990s—a claim Altman's own career might conceivably illustrate. Instead, he analyzes how and why popular and trade presses were actually quite slow to discuss Altman as an independent filmmaker, despite his many years working in the specialty sector. Finally, Dombrowski considers the strength of Altman's brand as an anti-Hollywood filmmaker in Europe. Utilizing case studies of *Vincent & Theo*, *Prêt-à-Porter*, and *Gosford Park*, Dombrowski's chapter demonstrates how European markets offset the sometimes mixed reaction to Altman's films in North America and helped to ensure his continuing productivity. All three chapters suggest that an understanding of Altman's position in the marketplace is, indeed, fundamental to the construction of his authorship.

Often the history of Altman's films is shadowed by the critical response, the box office revenue, or both. These factors can make a *Gosford Park* or *The Player* appear to be the only high points in Altman's late career. What about those films, though, that, from the perspective of time, actually seem to be more interesting, more complex, or more confounding than they were originally given credit for? Several essays in the collection call for such a reexamination, making us aware of how we can be enslaved to canonical choices in a director's oeuvre. Both Sarah Sinwell and Justin Wyatt reconsider gender and sexuality in *Come Back to the 5 & Dime, Jimmy Dean, Jimmy Dean*. Sinwell makes a convincing case for the role of fandom in complicating the film's sexual politics and representations. Suddenly a film which, on the surface, seems to paint very clear distinctions between male and female becomes a much more complex take on sexuality. Wyatt, on the other hand, investigates how several of Altman's 1980s theatrical adaptations present roles for queerness and LGBTQ+ identities that are more regressive in nature. Despite the ostensible exploration of sexuality in these films, Wyatt argues that Altman's conservatism toward sex is one of the defining traits of his authorship. Other essays provide a reconsideration based on other premises. Robert Kolker, a preeminent Altman scholar, offers an analysis of *A Prairie Home Companion* as a summary film. His chapter illustrates how death is the most significant framework blurring fiction and non-fiction throughout the film. These chapters enrich our understanding of underrated and overlooked projects in Altman's body of work, revealing unexpected insights and connections to his more canonical films.

The interviews with Altman's collaborators complement the scholarly chapters to develop further the book's central themes. Mitchell Zuckoff, Altman's oral biographer, discusses the process of interviewing Altman and creating his book, shedding light on the director's attitude toward his own work and the integral role his wife, Kathryn Reed Altman, played in facilitating his legacy. Longtime Altman associate Allan F. Nicholls and cinematographer Andrew Dunn offer additional insights into the director's creative process and penchant for experimentation, particularly in regards to his soundtracks and use of a moving camera. Other interviews provide detailed, behind-the-scenes accounts of less widely recognized Altman projects. Screenwriter Anne Rapp describes the differences in the nature of her collaboration with Altman on *Cookie's Fortune* versus *Dr. T & the Women*. Producer Matthew Seig reveals the challenges faced by Altman and his team on *Kansas City* (1996) and the two *Tanner* series. Altman's underexplored role as a producer is highlighted by director Alan Rudolph in his revealing production histories of *Mrs. Parker and the Vicious Circle* (1994) and *Breakfast of Champions* (1999). Altman's career as a producer-director and position in the marketplace is further explored in three interviews. Wren Arthur, who worked her way up from Altman's personal assistant to producer, details the daily routines at Sandcastle 5, Altman's production company, and Altman's integral participation as chief salesman in the marketing of his films. Joshua Astrachan, who also rose through the ranks under Altman to become a producer, shares strategies utilized by the director to finance and sell his films while still maintaining his autonomy. Ira Deutchman, a prominent figure in the American independent cinema landscape who developed, marketed, and/or distributed six Altman-related projects in the 1980s and 1990s, provides an insider view of how the director's films operated in the marketplace and the nature of Altman's brand. Read alongside the scholarly chapters, the collaborator interviews fill in gaps, answer questions, raise theories, and advance the conversation regarding how we conceptualize Altman's authorship and legacy.

THE ALTMAN LEGACY

By integrating scholarly and industry voices and elevating the value of Altman's final quarter century, a more nuanced understanding of his legacy as a collaborator, businessperson, and artist comes to the fore. Those contributors

Figure Int.2 Paul Thomas Anderson, the stand-by director, with Robert Altman on the set of *A Prairie Home Companion*. Photo by Melinda Sue Gordon. Courtesy of Special Collections Research Center, University of Michigan Library.

who explore Altman's creative process consistently highlight his approach to collaboration as one of his most striking legacies.

While much has previously been written on Altman's openness to improvisation and generosity with actors on set, his embrace of collaboration was much more expansive. Repeat cast and crew members helped to define the nature of what was "Altmanesque," including actors Michael Murphy, Lily Tomlin, and Lyle Lovett; assistant director and music supervisor Allan F. Nicholls; cinematographer Pierre Mignot; production designer Stephen Altman; and editor Geraldine Peroni—an idea explored in Ron Mann's documentary on Altman. Altman regularly worked with novice screenwriters and elevated his production assistants to producer status, providing opportunities for entry and advancement in the field. During his later years when his health required a stand-by director, Paul Thomas Anderson shadowed Altman on the set of *A Prairie Home Companion*. And through it all, Kathryn Reed Altman provided the social glue to hold everything together. While Altman was clearly the decision-maker in charge of his productions, his interest in incorporating the ideas of others played a determining role in his production practices and provided a model of collaboration for all who worked with him.

Alongside his highly successful approach to collaboration, a consideration of Altman in relation to the independent film marketplace highlights that his career as a producer is marked by a high degree of adaptability. Following the loss of studio support in the wake of *Popeye*, Altman's drive to maintain his creative engagement led him to lower budgeted projects in a range of media where he wore a multitude of hats—much as many of the "hyphenates," or above the line talent cut loose from the studios, did in the 1950s. Similar to his industry forebears, Altman hung out a shingle as an independent producer and focused on development, utilizing the value of his brand to find supportive partners both in the United States and abroad. With the assistance of a core group of behind-the-scenes collaborators and anchored by his wife, Kathryn, Altman adopted an approach to production management that emphasized the necessity of continuous project development and demonstrated a willingness to seize the opportunities available to him, no matter how seemingly far from his primary wheelhouse. The result was an astonishing period of productivity in the final decades of his life—twenty-seven films and television projects completed in twenty-six years—an accomplishment unmatched by any other American filmmaker of his generation and a model of how to maintain a career as an independent content creator.

Finally, a critical reevaluation of projects from this period reveals the variety in form, quality, and content of his artistic legacy. In his last quarter century, Altman's impulse to work where and when he could saw him directing films, television episodes and movies, theater, opera, and commercials, and the distinct forms of each media shaped his aesthetic choices, further complicating definitions of his authorship that rest primarily on his 1970–5 output. Altman directed intimate chamber dramas and expansive sociological portraits, on stage and on-screen, on film and digital formats, adhering closely to source material and deviating dramatically. His interest in experimentation, comfort with risk, and confidence in his abilities enabled him to adjust his aesthetic approaches to his resources and subject matter—and work around his at times failing health. As is the case for any artist with a large body of work, Altman produced his share of not only critical hits but also misses. Yet the consistency of Altman's ups and downs is one of the defining elements of his entire career, more so than his critical triumphs of the early 1970s. Altman's collaborators propose a range of theories to explain the unevenness of his work—Deutchman points to the significant role played by the quality of his scripts, while Astrachan focuses on how success enabled caution to be thrown to the wind. What is remarkable is how Altman never let his failures define him—and in fact, refused to acknowledge his critical and commercial disappointments as failures at all. The essays and interviews in this volume support his perspective, illuminating how even the years he spent "in the wilderness" in the 1980s contribute valuable insights into his authorship. Contributors equally draw attention to subtle shifts in Altman's worldview as expressed in the films of his mature period. While satire and an interest in the absurdity of individual foibles continue to permeate his work, the mellowing his collaborators witnessed in Altman as he aged also makes its way into his films, revealing moments that illustrate painful and poignant truths regarding the human condition. Would an equivalent scene to the one in *Gosford Park* when a maid explains the redeeming value of love to a downhearted aristocrat consoling himself in a pantry by eating spoonfuls of jam have sat comfortably in Altman's early '70s films? We don't think so. Rather than defining Altman's auteurism in terms of the formal and critical consistency of his output in 1970–5, we argue that valuing his range and analyzing how his work changed over time are necessary corrections to the auteurist project.

This collection thus counters Wood's claim that Altman's authorship remains static, as the contributions in the anthology highlight dynamism. The genre experimentation, multiple protagonist plots, overlapping soundtracks, moving camera and zooms, and acerbic takes on American life that mark Altman's canonical early '70s films have been justly celebrated, yet his legacy is even more rich and robust. The shift in Altman's career from studio to independent filmmaking following *Popeye* initiated a distinctly new period that prompted change and growth, sparking new forms of experimentation in the projects he made as well as in how he made them. Some contain elements that clearly point back to his canonical works; others form clean breaks. Yet Altman's development during this period as a collaborator, businessperson, and artist is undeniable. By exploring Altman's creative process, industrial framework, and key projects during his last quarter century, we develop a more complete picture of the significance of his legacy as one of American cinema's most distinguished innovators.

NOTES

1. Robin Wood, *Hollywood From Vietnam to Reagan* (New York: Columbia University Press, 1986), p. 43.
2. Interviews with Altman collaborators were conducted in writing, over the phone, or on Zoom by Lisa Dombrowski and Justin Wyatt during 2019–20, then edited for length.

PART I

The Creative Process

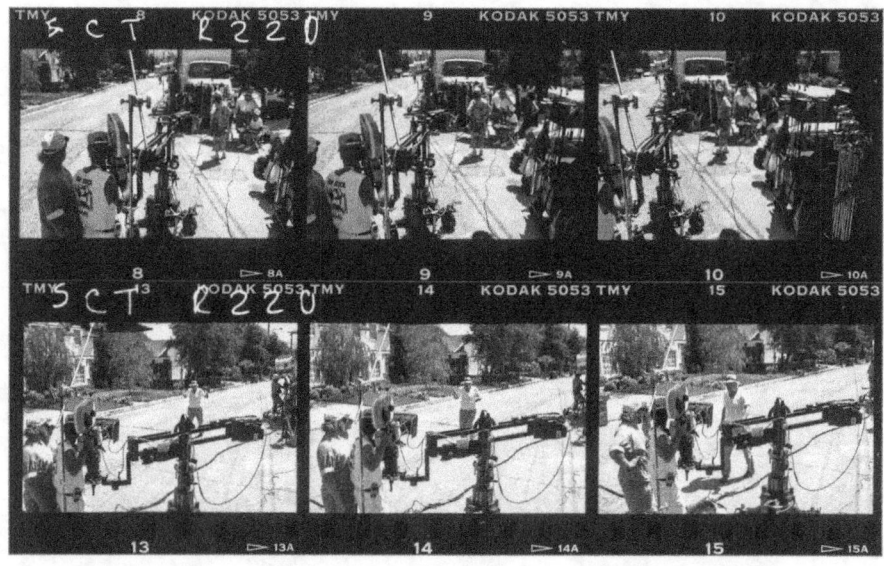

Figure I.1 Robert Altman on the set of *Short Cuts*. Photo by Joyce Rudolph. Courtesy of Special Collections Research Center, University of Michigan Library.

CHAPTER 1

I Yam What I Yam What I Yam: Altman and the Transpositional Poetics of *Popeye*

Mark Minett

Popeye introduced Hollywood Renaissance auteur Robert Altman to the New Hollywood blockbuster. His participation in the project came as a surprise to most industry-watchers, and not since *The Long Goodbye* (1973) had Altman joined a project so late in its development, with producer Robert Evans, screenwriter Jules Feiffer, and star Robin Williams already attached. Together with composer and songwriter Harry Nilsson, this filmmaking ensemble aspired to craft a blockbuster musical out of characters introduced in E. C. Segar's comic strips but probably most familiar to audiences from animated iterations stretching back to the Fleischer shorts of the 1930s. While Feiffer articulated a vision of the film rooted in hybridizing Segar with the Hollywood musical, once Altman began to exercise creative control the film was opened up to elaboration upon this core concept by more thoroughly integrating Popeye's transmedial history and Altman's own preferences. According to many accounts, the PG-rated *Popeye* ended up a critical, commercial, and professional disaster that drove Altman away from Hollywood for a decade. While *Popeye*'s reception and impact are more contradictory than these claims allow, the film's transpositional poetics—the story of Altman's adaptation of script to film—reveals an apparently out-of-place filmmaker engaging in largely characteristic problem-solving practices.

The road to *Popeye* began with Robert Evans attending the 1977 opening of the Broadway musical adaptation of *Little Orphan Annie*. His response was straightforward: "I want it. . . . The spirit it evoked was infectious, euphoric, for everyone from eight to eighty."¹ However, according to publicist Bridget Terry's promotional book *The Popeye Story*, when bidding for the film rights "soared to $10 million . . . Evans dropped out." Shortly thereafter, the Paramount-based Evans was reminded that Paramount "owned the music to

'I'm Popeye the Sailor Man'" and earned "$75,000 a year just on the song," and he was inspired anew. Popeye "was one of the most familiar characters of pop culture . . . an American institution. Nothing could have a more 'affirmative feeling' than 'Popeye the Sailor Man,' whose motto was 'I yam what I yam, and that's all that I yam.'" Paramount executives quickly purchased the rights from King Features Syndicate "to produce a real-life musical film based on the cartoon character."[2]

At the same time Evans was enjoying *Annie*, Alexander and Ilya Salkind were producing 1978's breakout hit *Superman* (Richard Donner, 1978). *Popeye* would eventually be released in December of 1980—the same month as De Laurentiis's *Flash Gordon* (Mike Hodges, 1980) and just months before the release of *Superman II* (Richard Lester, 1980). All four of these properties featured characters who had been part of the popular culture firmament since the Great Depression and initially attained popularity in comics form. Recognition of a burgeoning "comics" cycle, then, framed the release of *Popeye*, with reviews and articles contemplating how it could be that the film industry and film audiences now found themselves captivated by, or captive to, adaptations of these four-color phenomena. A *Wall Street Journal* headline proclaimed "Hollywood Strips Ideas to Comic Level," and offered explanations ranging from audience-comforting zeitgeist—"With economic times being so grim, we're trying to pack all the fun and escapism we can into our movies"—to the economic logic of the properties' "presold" status—"Securities analysts like the trend."[3]

This and many similar articles written around the same time rightly recognize an emergent trend. They also, though, tend to ignore the fairly expansive transmedial histories of these purportedly "comics" properties. This is not simply ignorant essentializing. It is partly the yield of deliberate strategies that sought to provide audiences, journalists, and, importantly, filmmakers with a focused hook. For *Popeye*, this strategy emerged when Evans offered the job of scripting *Popeye* to cartoonist, playwright, and screenwriter Jules Feiffer. "Feiffer," writes Terry,

> told Evans if he was talking about the Popeye of animated cartoons, then he wasn't interested. But if Evans was talking about the original comic strips by E. C. Segar, he would love to try it. Evans told Feiffer he would do whichever Popeye the writer wanted to do.[4]

WHAT AM I? FEIFFER'S CONSOLIDATION OF POPEYE'S ORIGIN AND E. C. SEGAR

Feiffer's contributions to *Popeye* can be understood as an attempted enshrinement, through rhetoric, research, and scripting strategies, of Segar's Popeye, as opposed to Fleischer's, as the sole basis for adaptation into a Hollywood musical, thereby narrowing the scope of what "Popeye" might mean for the film that Altman would be tasked to direct. *Popeye*'s publicity materials, following Feiffer, barely discuss the Fleischer cartoons and subsequent iterations—mentioning them almost exclusively to establish the character's continued popularity. Though the finished film begins with a distressed recreation of the opening of a Fleischer cartoon, its Popeye declares he is "in the wrong movie."[5] This hierarchizing re-formulation of a multiply iterated character is characteristic of cross-media franchising. Clare Parody argues that in many transmedia works,

> a core text or set of texts emerges, settling into dominance and canonicity through a conjunction of promotional strategies, paratextual maneuvers, and distribution circumstances . . . Other instalments then fall into hierarchies of importance, structured in terms of medium, authorship, and the level of investment required both to be aware of and find them.[6]

Feiffer's emphasis on Segar both relied upon and extended this process of canonization.

Feiffer sought to establish Segar as what Parody terms a franchise auteur figure, "invoked and constructed by both creators and audiences as part of negotiating the boundaries of the transmedia archive"—the body of texts, paratexts, and products related to a character.[7] Feiffer already possessed a fairly obscure 1971 Nostalgia Press collection of three storylines from 1936,[8] and according to Patrick McGilligan he "began [his research] by rereading *Popeye: The First Fifty Years* by Bud Sagendorf," which positions Segar explicitly as originator and implicitly as sanctioning auteur, whose work must be known, acknowledged, and respected by subsequent creators and audiences.[9] Feiffer, according to Terry, would also go on to view "about 100,000 feet of Segar strips preserved on microfilm."[10]

Re-hierarchizing Popeye meant that animated iterations were characterized as problems to overcome rather than possible sources of creative inspiration. An article in *Prevue* channels Feiffer's worry that his work would be hampered by the fact that "too many variations had evolved—and been accepted—by at least five generations of Popeye fans." The differences between the multiple animated iterations of Popeye over the years, declares Feiffer, is "subtle"—other than "a creeping vulgarization in all of them." His solution was to "pretend that Popeye had *never* happened before. Evolve the characters as originals . . . so they can develop their *own* life force." Feiffer sought to "write [*Popeye*] as if I were Segar . . . to write with his hand, his humor, his special kind of civility."[11] Essentially, Feiffer wished to re-originate Popeye by attempting to channel his originator.

The three pre-production drafts of *Popeye*'s screenplay held by the University of Michigan's Altman archive show Feiffer providing Popeye with this new origin story while also taking up several key strategies—narrative and thematic—that draw from Segar as well as the Hollywood musical. Rather than re-originating Popeye's narrative from the ground up, Feiffer employed adaptational strategies that would subsequently become commonplace in transplanting long-running comic book superheroes into feature films—the use of resonant tropes and concision. Concision proved a particularly useful strategy for reshaping Segar's stories to the norms of Hollywood narrative design as well as the conventions of the classical Hollywood musical.

Peter Coogan has argued that most successful adaptations of comic book superhero characters, of which Popeye is often viewed as a key progenitor, make use of "certain tropes—familiar and repeated moments, iconic images and actions, figures of speech, patterns of characterization—that . . . embody or symbolize some aspect of the character, and have gained this resonance through repeated use."[12] Popeye's "I yam what I yam" motto, the hook on which Evans and Feiffer hung *Popeye*'s thematic message, is one example, as is Popeye's climactic downing of a can of spinach—though this draws more from Fleischer than Segar. Segar bestowed upon many of his featured characters catchphrases, such as Wimpy's "I will gladly pay you Tuesday for a hamburger today," that are repeated in Feiffer's drafts. Indeed, Wimpy's common declaration to those seeking to find and/or punish him for his conniving—that he is not Wimpy but instead "one of the Jones boys"—is used as a motif across multiple drafts of Feiffer's scripts, culminating in Wimpy repeating it to himself as he kidnaps Swee'pea for Bluto, thereby providing psychic distance from his reprehensible actions.[13]

Feiffer used his Sweethaven-bound Popeye "origin story" as a forum in which to develop one variation of concision, which encompasses both the consolidation of multiple characters into a single character and the "folding together" of events and story situations from across a long-running character's history, often to create the kind of causal and thematic unity demanded by Hollywood storytelling.[14] In Segar's Depression-era strips, Popeye's home base was an unnamed and fairly nondescript American seaside town from which he would often set sail for adventure.[15] Feiffer chose instead to consolidate home and destination into the island village of Sweethaven, and his description of the milieu resonates with Segar's Depression-era setting.

As Gayle Sherwood Magee points out, Sweethaven also provides a setting that engages with the "fairy tale" tradition of the classical Hollywood musical, often set in mythic locales in which order must be restored through romantic coupling. The fairy tale sub-genre, according to Rick Altman, "stresses the musical's tendency towards transcendence of the real"—obviously apt for *Popeye*.[16] Feiffer's scripts, though, are probably best understood as synthesizing the fairy tale musical with the folk musical tradition "set in the America of yesteryear, from small town to frontier." Moreover, "the folk musical's integration of two disparate individuals into a single couple heralds the entire group's communion with each other."[17] Feiffer's drafts introduce Popeye as an outsider to Sweethaven, and he replaces the de facto ruler, Bluto, both in the heart of "first lady" Olive Oyl, and as Sweethaven's leader. In Feiffer's first draft, the featured cast members, adrift at sea, take turns singing "I am what I am," celebrating their victory over Bluto in what Feiffer describes as "a cat's cradle of Busby Berkeley-like configurations." "Everybody got their own I yams," declares Popeye. "I have give birt' to a epydemic [sic]."[18] Feiffer's second draft adds two "PULL BACK"s to this ending. The first is to Sweethaven's harbor, "jammed with CHEERING TOWNSPEOPLE" also singing "I am what I am," and the second is to a "STRATOSPHERIC VIEW of town, dock, sea" and the entire cast.[19] Feiffer envisioned a film, then, in which the entire village celebrates Popeye's victory and embraces his mantra, claiming a communal identity that is, ironically, integrated around individualism.

Sweethaven serves as venue for further concision of characters and storylines plucked from a decade's worth of story material and reformulated into a relatively coherent Hollywood narrative. The details of "Popeye's Search for Poppa," reprinted in the 1971 Nostalgia Press collection, inspires one of the film's plotlines. There, Popeye's father, like Feiffer's "Commodore," employs an octopus to keep unwanted visitors at bay, though Segar's octopus is simply "Charlie," while Feiffer's is the alliterative "Slimy Sam."[20] In both film and strip, Popeye's father first denies his parentage and then yells at his son to eat his spinach. In the comic strip, where Popeye had been consuming and promoting the virtues of spinach for years, he happily obliges: "Are YOU tellin' ME?" In the film, on the other hand, where Popeye has yet to become "Popeye," he repeatedly rejects spinach. In three successive drafts of the screenplay, discovering his father puts Popeye in a state of "bonkus of the konkus"—psychological trauma that serves as the subject of a 1933 storyline.[21] In the midst of his babbling, Popeye achieves clarity only long enough to shout, "I hates spinach!"[22]

As the partial basis of its second key plotline, Feiffer's drafts take up another adventure reprinted in the Nostalgia Press volume, "Popeye and the Jeep," in which Popeye receives a magical pet—a vaguely dog-like "Jeep" who secretly "has a fourth dimensional brain and the ability to tell the future."[23] Wimpy discovers the Jeep's secret and uses him to bet on horse races, but Popeye refuses to participate (in spite of Olive joining in), declaring that "I ain't goner set no bad example for me chil'ren friends by bettin' on race horshes. . . . I yam disgustipated!!"[24] Feiffer consolidates the Jeep with Popeye's foundling, Swee'pea, who receives the Jeep's prognosticating prowess. The revised storyline now motivates the scripted narrative's conventional "darkest moment" and climax. Popeye's principles isolate him from his romantic interest and prospective family. A greedy Bluto then preys upon this isolation, paying Wimpy to kidnap the child and present him to the Commodore—a kidnapping that prompts Popeye's climactic encounters with the Commodore and then Bluto.

Figure 1.1 The Popeye-Oxblood Oxheart boxing match in the *Thimble Theatre* comic strip by E. C. Segar, *E. C. Segar's Popeye*, vol. 3: "Let's You and Him Fight!" (Seattle, WA: Fantagraphics, 2008): 131.

Figure 1.2 (From left) Robin Williams, Linda Hunt, Peter Bray, and Paul Dooley during the Popeye-Oxblood Oxheart boxing match in *Popeye*.

Feiffer also revises and employs the subject of four consecutive Segar Sunday pages—Popeye's boxing battle with Oxblood Oxheart and his pugnacious mother, for which Wimpy serves as the referee.[25]

This bout is then integrated with the Swee'pea plotline, providing a venue for the revelation of Swee'pea's fortune-telling powers and Popeye's emergence as a hero.

Feiffer's script drafts, then, made particularly heavy use of concision as a means with which to channel Segar and re-originate Popeye. The attendant setting aside of Popeye's animated iterations and the reduction of these iterations to shades of vulgarity is, though, perhaps not just a reflection of Feiffer's predilections but also of the rhetorical situation. Though the Fleischer theatrical cartoons were aimed at all ages, they subsequently circulated on television, where they were recontextualized as children's entertainment.[26] For Evans and Paramount, repositioning the film as blockbuster required a broader audience. Whether this necessitated excising the particularly fondly remembered Fleischer shorts, though, is a more open question. In any event, as Feiffer saw it, the major risk to his coherent vision of a wholly Segar-based adaptation was posed by the hand-off of primary creative responsibilities to Robert Altman, who would oversee the script's transposition to finished film. Feiffer later recalled that there was a "price you pay for working with Altman . . . if there's not constant vigilance to make sure that the script is being followed."[27] In the context of *Popeye*, the price was that, "the further [Altman] got into the movie, the more it moved away from Segar and toward Max Fleischer."[28]

This critique is more explicit than Feiffer was willing to be at the time of *Popeye*'s release, and Altman's own public pronouncements toed the Segar-oriented company line. Moreover, Evans publicly, if implausibly, claimed that Altman was under his control. Whereas "Altman's typical movie deals called for him to write, produce, and direct," Evans had "hired him only to direct, and . . . to shoot the script as it was written." Ironically, Evans would later compose a letter on Altman's behalf which concluded that Altman's work did, in fact, include many of the duties of a producer.[29] Other articles and publicity pieces were more delicate, framing the filmmaking process as collaboration, though one in which Feiffer was initially very worried, "because [Altman's] reputation with writers was legendary. Basically, he writes his own scripts, using other people's material as a starting point." However, says Feiffer, when he "talked to him about Segar, after he read the books, he knew instantly what I meant, and he tuned the entire company to it."[30] An examination of the historical record and the final film, though, reveals that as Altman assumed more and more decision-making control over *Popeye*, beginning in pre-production and extending through shooting in Malta and post-production at his Lion's Gate studios, he was neither wholly "under control" nor fully "on board" with Feiffer's circumscription of the project to Segar.

EVERYTHING IS FOOD—ALTMAN'S EXPANSIVE TRANSPOSITIONAL APPETITE

I have argued elsewhere that, at least in the context of his early 1970s films, accounts of Altman's scriptual infidelity are overstated and we should reject formative claims like Aljean Harmetz's that "by the time one of his films is finished there's nothing left of the original script except a couple of soup bones of plot and a few expletives."[31] Instead, Altman typically retained the bulk of his scripts' narrative structures, employing them as support for elaborative transpositional practices that expanded the functional yield of his films. These practices included the multiplication of and increased emphasis on typically backgrounded characters and the targeted use of pre-approved improvisation by trusted actors. Both were frequently integrated with Altman's practice of complicating his scripts' indicated soundscapes, typically through overlapping dialogue and punctuative, ironizing sound effects and music. Altman also tended to excise what he deemed to be overly redundant, direct, or on-the-nose dramatic and thematic scripted elements, again frequently in favor of indirect ironization.[32] On *Popeye*, these practices reshaped Feiffer's scripted vision, and they were synthesized with a more expansive notion of how to integrate the character's transmedial history as well as a shabbier conception of the Hollywood musical.

Altman's predilection for multiplying and emphasizing background characters is clearly evident in his revisions to Feiffer's work. To be fair, in the script's first and second drafts, Feiffer has already packed Sweethaven with townspeople, but they largely constitute an undifferentiated chorus. Handwritten notes on the back of page six of the second draft, "6 Cowards, 6 Bullies, Olive's Girlfriends (Steinettes)," indicate Altman was pushing Feiffer to incorporate even more—three "sailors" in a second draft scene in Roughhouse's Café became six "toughs" in the third draft, dated one month prior to the start of production in Malta.[33]

These middlegrounded characters became the focus of a good deal of Feiffer's worries, Bridget Terry's publicity, and the film's reception. Terry's publicity materials report that creative difficulties developed prior to the move to Malta because "Altman, it seemed to Feiffer, had been spending too much time on casting the townspeople and not enough on the logistics of the . . . main story."[34] Interestingly, Feiffer's objections here were not about a lack of fidelity to Segar's visual conception of the characters. For the most part, the film's casting and performance concepts, its sets, and its costume, hair, and make-up were highly indebted to Segar, or to an idea of Segar-era comic strips. A great deal of money was spent developing workable "bulgy arms" for Popeye that reproduced his look in the comics and animation, and each of the primary characters was costumed in accordance with their iconic appearance.[35] Moreover, Terry's publicity materials offered extensive reporting on the steps taken to dress all of the characters in ways that recalled comic strips, including "decid[ing] that all the men would wear stripes and the women would wear polka dots . . . because when the artist sits down to draw those things, they are the easiest things to draw."[36] The shoes, which may receive more close-ups in the film than the actors, were crafted to replicate Segar's "bigfoot" approach to physiology, common in what Pascal Lefèvre calls the "cartoon mode" of newspaper comic strip drawing (as opposed to the "naturalistic mode" of Alex Raymond's *Flash Gordon*).[37]

Feiffer was concerned with the distraction to ensuring the coherence of his comic strip-inspired vision that was posed by the extensive time spent casting and rehearsing middlegrounded characters. Even so, Altman seems to have been motivated not just by his usual preferences but also by his own take on Popeye's comic strip origins. According to Terry, "casting was divided into two categories: The Townspeople and the Principal Players."[38] For the townspeople, cast largely from a parade of "circus performers, commedia dell'arte troupes . . . improvisational actors, street performers, ex-athletes, dancers," and some "classically trained actors," Altman employed a "silhouetting" approach during the three weeks of preparation and rehearsal on Malta prior to the start of shooting.[39] Altman, reports Terry, "wanted all the Sweethaven characters to have a resemblance to other characters in the comic strips, either specifically or where you could say, 'Oh, he could've been a comic strip character.'"[40] "The town of Sweethaven," said Altman, "would just have one of everything . . . Everybody would be a symbol. A silhouette on the horizon."[41]

Given that this plethora of middlegrounded comic strip characters included Chizzleflint, a conniver from the Segar days, and an upgraded Ham Gravy, a pre-Popeye *Thimble Theatre* protagonist, Feiffer's displeasure is, perhaps, surprising. It is possible, though, that he objected to the arguably reductive conflation of "comic strip" with Segar. For Feiffer, Segar would primarily be expressed in Popeye's narrative and thematic trajectory through the world, and in that world's general moral tone, rather than through what Drew Morton has called "stylistic remediation"—"the representation of formal or stylistic characteristics commonly attributed to one medium within another."[42] However, a strong emphasis of Altman's transpositional work—and conceptual flexibility—in developing and visualizing Feiffer's scripted material is the integration of his own preferences with Feiffer's scripted elements and this kind of stylistic remediation. Feiffer, meanwhile, was on high alert for anything that might distract from expressing Segar's unique "humor, his special kind of civility," where, significantly, "almost anything can take place . . . any kind of violence, nastiness, rottenness, man acting upon man, or woman acting in just as violent ways as the men, and somehow it was OK."[43]

On this count, Feiffer should not have been too worried, since Altman's oeuvre displays an analogous, though arguably more vulgar than civil, expressive attitude toward human failures. However, it is also true that Altman preferred indirect ironization rather than explicit expression as the avenue for thematic work. Feiffer's pre-production drafts end with the residents of Sweethaven explicitly won over by Popeye's morality, cheerfully singing "I am what I am." In the film, though, these newly middlegrounded characters are last seen, and heard, offering a series of individualized apologies, excuses, and encouragements to Popeye as he walks through town to confront the Commodore. No judgment of their cowardice is offered or incited by the film. Their attitudes are amusing rather than abhorrent.

Critics, perhaps prompted by the press kits they received, noticed the outsized presence of these characters, although their assessments of this aspect of Altman's transpositional contribution varied. While connecting this strategy to Altman's established practice, some also found a basis for their presence in the cross-media influence of comics—though they pointed not to Segar's civility but the vulgarities of *MAD* magazine. David Chute's review, essentially confirming Feiffer's anxieties, notes that "as vivid as [Popeye and Olive Oyl] are, the unmistakable figures in the foreground seem constantly in danger of being engulfed by the mob of walk-on wackos that swarms across the screen, like the bug-infested background hordes in an early issue of *Mad* [sic]."[44] Chute refers here to *MAD*'s strategy of lacing panels with what artist Will Elder called "chicken fat," after "the part of the soup that is bad for you, yet gives the soup its delicious flavor."[45] Indeed, *Popeye*'s editor, Tony Lombardo, told *Prevue* that multiple camera shooting was employed on *Popeye* "because there was so much going on, so many bits like the backgrounds in *Mad Magazine* [sic] stories."[46] This "chicken fat" approach also arguably extended to *Popeye*'s set design. Sweethaven was "overbuilt" in that its homes and shops were, according to Terry's publicity materials, not facades but more or less completed structures. It was also, though, as would become standard in franchise filmmaking, "overdesigned"—packed with an abundance of "fine details"—signs, labels, home décor, and so on that furnished a plethora of gags available but impossible to digest in one viewing.[47]

It is unclear whether this "chicken fat" approach to middlegrounding characters and overdesigning sets, the contours of which are reflected in the August 1980 shooting script, capture Feiffer's revisions in response to Altman's elaborative demands or contributions developed by Altman's troupe in rehearsals.[48] Either is plausible, and it is significant, and largely consistent with Altman's transpositional preferences, that these elaborations do not seem to have been the result of on-set improvisation. Instead, Altman characteristically employed only targeted on-set improvisation by favored performers. In an unpublished interview, Altman claims that, "in this picture, there really is no improvisation, except for Robin [Williams]."[49]

Altman's and Feiffer's attitudes towards Williams's side-of-the-mouth improvisation is a point of tension in accounts of *Popeye*'s production, a fact that is particularly interesting given that Williams's performance remediates the vocal performance of Jack Mercer as Popeye in the Fleischer cartoons. Indeed, this provides the basis of a rare instance of *Popeye*'s publicity materials admitting Fleischer into the canon, with Terry claiming that Williams prepared by "watch[ing] about fifty hours' worth of animated cartoons."[50] According to Leslie Cabarga, Fleischer's cartoons are unusual in that they contain what was, for the time, "a lot of dialogue," much of it "mumbled through closed lips by the characters . . . due to [the use of only loosely scripted] post-syncing." Mercer "delighted in improvising on the script as they rehearsed and ad-libbed like crazy during the recordings."[51] Michael Barrier claims that Mercer saved his mumblings for ad-libbed lines while synced mouth movements were retained for narratively important dialogue—parameters that correspond quite well with Altman's standing transpositional preference for elaborating around scripted narrative centers.[52]

In *Popeye*, Williams manages to integrate these Fleischer-inspired improvisations with narrative and generic mandates, synthesizing Mercer's strategy with Popeye's musical numbers. Mercer's voice operated in two registers, a gravelly voice for "regular" dialogue and a high-pitched voice for asides[53]—a distinction absent from Feiffer's first draft screenplay, though the second draft distinguishes between "mutters" and "falsetto."[54] *Prevue* reported that Williams's "dual-voiced bit seemed to provide a safety valve for the comedian/actor's energy," but the two voices also proved useful for Williams's musical performance. The gentler "aside" voice, a private voice in which Popeye speaks to himself and, perhaps, the audience, was the default for the character's numbers, where he sings his inner feelings. In the thematically central number, "I Yam What I Yam," set in a floating mechanical racetrack/betting parlor/bordello, Popeye and the Oyls confront Wimpy over having used Swee'pea's fortune-telling powers to gamble. However, once the Oyls realize how much money they might win, they take Swee'pea back to the "track," leaving the flummoxed Popeye alone to ask himself, in song, "What am I?" As he comes to his answer—"I yam what I yam"—Williams employs the gentler voice and is subsequently ignored by the crowd of gambling townspeople while seeking out Swee'pea. Only as the song reaches its climax, when Popeye finally shouts the song's titular lyric and then proclaims, "I'm Popeye the sailor man!" does Williams shift into the public, gravelly voice, causing everyone to finally take notice.

Williams's cartoon-influenced muttering, in combination with Altman's preference for production sound, complicated post-production, where Andy Dougan reports that "Williams had to re-dub his dialogue twice to get the right effect."[55] As the film moved through post-production at Lion's Gate, Altman's elaborative instincts led his team to do more than simply polish the targeted improvisations he had sanctioned during the film's shooting; he also worked to complicate the film's sound design by incorporating Fleischer-inspired "cartoon" elements. These elements, particularly prominent during sequences of violent action, include the variety of effects emitted by Popeye's pipe, the wobbly saw and barrel drum sounds accompanying Castor's pummeling by

Oxheart, ratcheting sounds as Ham Gravy gets squished and expanded during the engagement party sequence, and birds chirping after the strung-up Commodore lands in a heap after being cut down.

While these effects are broadly associated with animation sound, they belong most firmly to what Paul Taberham describes as the "zip-crash" mode dominant in the 1940s and 1950s. In that mode, popularized by Warner Bros. cartoons, sound is "highly mannered and ostentatious," and "plays an active part in the humor of the films." Furthermore, "voices are highly stylized," and music "is fragmented, shifting in tempo and genre, and frequently quotes brief excerpts of other compositions for comic effect."[56] As discussed above, the Fleischer cartoons certainly incorporate highly stylized voices, and *Popeye* employs surges, quoting "I'm Popeye the Sailor Man" when Popeye displays flourishes of superheroism. This musical motif, though, is not particularly humorous, and it is more coherent than fragmentary—tracking with what Williams and Altman conceived of as the character's journey from reality to cartoon iconicity.[57]

It seems that Altman's sound team operated from a consolidated notion of cartoon sound rather than one that differentiated between particular modes, let alone the particulars of the Fleischer shorts. Those shorts were largely produced during the 1930s, a period dominated by the "syncretic" mode, in which "the scoring of music and animation of movement were closely integrated."[58] Sound effects were "subsumed into the rhythm of the film," and were more musical than in the zip-crash mode.[59] Furthermore, plotlines in syncretic cartoons tended towards simplicity, "privileging play of movement over detailed stories." In the syncretic mode, music "prescribes how long characters walk, how many steps they take, and the speed at which they move."[60] Though the syncretic mode is most associated with Mickey Mouse cartoons and the term "Mickey Mousing," its practices are broadly characteristic of the Fleischer cartoons. For instance, Cabarga writes, "In the early Popeye cartoons, the characters never stood still," a practice extended to what head animator Myron Haldman describes as a "moving hold . . . timed to the musical beat."[61]

The syncretic mode's reversal of the standard Hollywood image-over-sound hierarchy, with sound determining rather than following movement, resembles Rick Altman's account of the approach taken by classical Hollywood musical numbers.[62] It is worth considering how these complementary practices may have been integrated and then elaborated upon by Robert Altman's transpositional preferences, and how they were re-shaped by his expressed desire to make an "un-musical" musical in *Popeye*.[63] Altman wanted to avoid the highly choreographed dance numbers typical of Hollywood musicals (on display in John Huston's subsequent adaptation of *Annie*, 1982).[64] This was partially accomplished by foregrounding the shenanigans of middlegrounded characters during the numbers, which a horrified Feiffer complained consisted of "madcap stunt improvisation" that "turned my movie into a circus act" and buried "[Nilsson's] songs amid dopey bits of business."[65]

Arguably, though, Nilsson's songs were tailor-made for Altman's simplified, sometimes shambling approach to the classical Hollywood musical practices with which Feiffer so badly wanted to meld Segar. Nilsson did complain that "songs written expressly for one character were being given by Altman to another"—or to others, as was the case with the "Food, Food, Food" number designated for Wimpy and Geezil in Feiffer's third draft but eventually performed, bit by bit, by half the middlegrounded townspeople.[66] Nilsson described his songs, though, as "walking music": "music that walks along with Popeye throughout the film."[67] This suggests a collaborative and rather non-hierarchical approach to music and image that departed from both non-musical and musical norms. It may be a stretch to cite Altman's employment of Nilsson's walking music as an intentional relaxation of either the syncretic mode or the classical Hollywood musical's standard practices, but it does seem to chime with Altman's general practice of "shabbying up" his films—retaining iconic generic aspects but removing their polish so as to achieve a greater sense of realism and to broaden their functional potential.

Nilsson, whose celebrated voice had become grizzled by the late 1970s, arguably embodied a similar kind of shabbiness, but his connection to *Popeye*'s narrative and thematic material ran deeper than his physical decline. Moreover, it did so in ways that served Altman's transpositional openness to the influence of animation and his preference for indirect ironization. Publicity focused discussion of Nilsson's selection for *Popeye* on his successful romantic compositions and his previous interpretations of romantic standards.[68] Given *Popeye*'s romantic musical framework—the Popeye and Olive relationship that Feiffer viewed as at the heart of his Segar-channeling script—this makes some sense. Less discussed, though, was Nilsson's history of writing songs for animation (*The Point*, Fred Wolf, 1971) and the poignant appropriateness of Nilsson in the context of the father/son relationship between Popeye and the Commodore, who abandoned Popeye as a two-year-old. Nilsson's own father walked out on him, and the Nilsson songbook is replete with anxious and ironic songs that reference and rework this tragedy. For instance, his 1967 album, *Pandemonium Shadow Show*, features the musically upbeat "1941," with the lyrics, "in 1941 a happy father had a son, and by 1944 the father walks right out the door." The child grows up, but the cycle recurs when "in 1961 the happy father had his son and by 1964 the father walks right out the door." The similarly jaunty "Daddy's Song" on 1968's *Aerial Ballet* begins with a tribute to the love between mother and father and father and son but then takes a turn when "the daddy went away." The boy's mother, sings Nilsson, "did explain, trying to take away the pain, but he just couldn't understand that his father was not a man and it all was just a game." Knowledge of this background certainly makes "Kids"—Nilsson's song for *Popeye*'s child-abandoning Commodore, which expresses the character's disdain for children—more darkly than playfully ironic. The push/pull nature of the Popeye and Olive duet, "Sail with Me, Stay with Me," is similarly complicated by familiarity with Nilsson. While we might be skeptical that audiences would necessarily bring this intertextual perspective to *Popeye*, the lyrics to *Popeye*'s songs arguably in and of themselves contain the kernels of these ironies.

This indirect dynamic seems complementary to the direct thematization present in Feiffer's scripts, where Popeye's domestication through his adoption of Swee'pea and his courtship with Olive is presented as conflicting with his infantilizing obsession with recovering his father. In the third draft script, Popeye enters the Commodore's cabin in search of his adopted son and "spots Swee'pea in Bluto's arms." When Popeye sees the Commodore, though, he "can not take his eyes off him. He forgets all else." While Popeye "stands transfixed before his father," developing his case of "bonkus of the konkus," Bluto sneaks up on Popeye, shoves his head through a porthole, and escapes with the baby. It is Olive who, following the syntax of the classical Hollywood musical, must merge these opposing values by convincing the Commodore to feed Popeye the restorative spinach.[69] Popeye, rejuvenated and heading out to confront Bluto, is then tossed another can of spinach by the Commodore, while "Olive stands nearby looking on in anticipation." Feiffer writes that Popeye "flips the can about in his hand, looks at Olive, looks at his father. A crackling exchange of stares." His divergent familial desires reconciled, Popeye declares, "I loves spinach" and "plunges into the sea."[70]

During the production process, the "bonkus of the konkus" material was removed, and in the film Bluto, holding Swee'pea, now escapes from the Commodore's cabin without Popeye noticing their presence. Likewise, the film excises the scripted culmination of the conflict between romantic coupling and childish longing to reclaim an absent father. Instead, as in so many Fleischer cartoons, Olive is kidnapped, and an atypically unwilling Popeye is forced by an unsuspecting Bluto to, very typically, eat his spinach and battle it out. The potent thematics of Feiffer's script, and the classical Hollywood musical, are replaced by slapstick action. While *Popeye*'s ending is devoid of the emotional ambiguity common to his previous films, Altman's transpositional revisions are consistent with his longstanding practice of liberally cutting any on-the-nose thematic material. Even so, as in Feiffer's previous scripts, Altman retains the premise that the Commodore's treasure chest is filled with mementos from Popeye's childhood. Altman has not altogether avoided what the Commodore, in Feiffer's script, refers to disparagingly as "sanktament," although he positions it as a joke rather than a message.[71]

CONCLUSION

Where Feiffer scripted a narratively and thematically coordinated denouement for *Popeye* indebted to, and quasi-metaphysically written by, Segar, Altman vulgarizes or, at least, popularizes Feiffer's dream. The Feiffer-scripted "Busby Berkeley-like" musical number discussed earlier where everyone joins in singing "I Yam What I Yam" in a moment of musical and thematic unity is replaced by Williams's improvised and quasi-professional dance atop the water, initially suggested only jokingly by Williams, to "I'm Popeye the Sailor Man"—the anthem of the Fleischer cartoons.[72] While Feiffer's scripts have more individuals declaring their individuality, it is arguably Altman's production that displays a broader set of "Yams."

This diversity should come as no surprise to those familiar with Altman, even if his decision to helm *Popeye* was surprising. Just as Altman's earlier career required the careful navigation of scripted narrative structure and thematic intent with his own authorial predilections and the sanctioned contributions of his collaborators, so too does *Popeye* display Altman's skill at recognizing and reconciling the potential contributions of multiple voices. *Popeye*, then, afforded Altman an opportunity to exercise the transpositional talents and preferences on clear display in his more celebrated early 1970s oeuvre, elaborating around and shabbying up Feiffer's purer vision of Segar wed to the Hollywood musical. Altman anchored his production in Feiffer's scripted contributions but took a more inclusive and less precious view of how Popeye's transmedial heritage might complement Altman's own unconventional and unpolished perspective. This elaborative approach may have confused audiences and critics expecting another New Hollywood family film blockbuster, but the details of *Popeye*'s reconception and the contours of the finished film, disastrous or not, display the recognizable signature of Hollywood Renaissance-era Altman.

ACKNOWLEDGMENT

Research for this chapter was funded in part by the University of South Carolina's Provost's Humanities Grant.

NOTES

1. Robert Evans, *The Kid Stays in the Picture* (New York: Hyperion, 1994), p. 293.
2. Bridget Terry, *The Popeye Story* (New York: Dell, 1980), pp. 4–5. Much of Terry's book also appears in the film's press kits, Robert Altman Papers, Special Collections Research Center, University of Michigan Library.

3. Earl C. Gottschalk, Jr., "Hollywood strips ideas to comic level," *Wall Street Journal*, 14 May 1980, B1.
4. Terry, *The Popeye Story*, p. 6.
5. See, for instance, Terry, *The Popeye Story*, p. 5.
6. Clare Parody, "A Theory of the Transmedia Franchise Character," unpublished PhD dissertation, University of Liverpool, 2011, p. 86.
7. Ibid. p. 66.
8. Steranko, "Film feature by Steranko," *Prevue*, Nov–Dec 1980, p. 14.
9. Patrick McGilligan, *Robert Altman: Jumping off the Cliff* (New York: St. Martin's Press, 1989), p. 493. Since Sagendorf's book was not released until 1979, it seems more likely that Feiffer was given access to the proofs than that he re-read it. Bud Sagendorf, *Popeye: The First Fifty Years* (New York: King Features Syndicate and Workman Publishing, 1979).
10. Terry, *The Popeye Story*, p. 8.
11. Steranko, "Film feature," p. 15.
12. Peter Coogan, *Superhero: The Secret Origin of a Genre* (Austin, TX: MonkeyBrain Books, 2006), pp. 6–7.
13. Jules Feiffer, "Popeye," Script—3rd Draft, 1 December 1979, pp. 86–7, Robert Altman Papers, Special Collections Research Center, University of Michigan Library.
14. Coogan, *Superhero*, p. 10.
15. For a map, see Sagendorf, *Popeye*, pp. 24–5.
16. Gayle Sherwood Magee, *Robert Altman's Soundtracks: Film, Music, and Sound from M*A*S*H to A Prairie Home Companion* (New York: Oxford University Press, 2014), p. 139.
17. Rick Altman, "The musical," in Geoffrey Nowell-Smith (ed.), *The Oxford History of World Cinema* (Oxford and New York: Oxford University Press, 1996), pp. 300–1.
18. Jules Feiffer, "Popeye," Script—1st Draft, p. 156, Robert Altman Papers, University of Michigan.
19. Jules Feiffer, "Popeye," Script—2nd Draft, p. 130, Robert Altman Papers, University of Michigan.
20. E. C. Segar, *E. C. Segar's Popeye*, vol. 5: "Wha's a Jeep?" (Seattle, WA: Fantagraphics, 2011), p. 73; Feiffer, "Popeye" Script—1st Draft, p. 124.
21. E. C. Segar, *E. C. Segar's Popeye*, vol. 3: "Let's You and Him Fight!" (Seattle, WA: Fantagraphics, 2008), pp. 86–91.
22. Feiffer, "Popeye," Script—3rd Draft, p. 120.
23. Segar, vol. 5, p. 47.
24. Ibid. pp. 53–4.
25. Segar, vol. 3, pp. 129–32.
26. David McGowan, *Animated Personalities: Cartoon Characters and Stardom in American Theatrical Shorts* (Austin: University of Texas Press, 2019), p. 209.
27. Mitchell Zuckoff, *Robert Altman: The Oral Biography* (New York: Alfred A. Knopf, 2009), p. 351.
28. Ibid. p. 357.
29. Robert Evans to Joseph J. Cohen, 3 December 1981, Robert Altman Papers, Special Collections Research Center, University of Michigan Library.
30. Steranko, "Film feature," p. 16.
31. Aljean Harmetz, "The 15th man who was asked to direct *M*A*S*H* (and did) makes a peculiar western," *New York Times Magazine*, 20 June 1971, p. 47.
32. Mark Minett, *Robert Altman and the Elaboration of Hollywood Storytelling* (New York: Oxford University Press, 2020).
33. Feiffer, "Popeye," Script—2nd Draft, p. 23; Feiffer, "Popeye," Script—3rd Draft, p. 26.

34. Terry, *The Popeye Story*, p. 84.
35. Ibid. pp. 154–66.
36. Ibid. p. 81.
37. Pascal Lefèvre, "Newspaper strips," in Frank Bramlett, Roy T Cook, and Aaron Meskin (eds), *The Routledge Companion to Comics* (New York: Routledge, 2017), p. 19.
38. Terry, *The Popeye Story*, p. 35.
39. Ibid. p. 37.
40. Ibid. pp. 105–6.
41. Ibid. p. 43.
42. Drew Morton, *Panel to the Screen: Style, American Film, and Comic Books During the Blockbuster Era* (Jackson: University Press of Mississippi, 2017), p. 8.
43. Steranko, "Film feature," p. 15.
44. David Chute, "Anchors awry: 'Popeye' takes a dive," *Boston Phoenix*, 14 December 1980, p. 16.
45. Bill Schelly, *Harvey Kurtzman: The Man Who Created MAD and Revolutionized Humor in America* (Seattle, WA: Fantagraphics, 2015), p. 261.
46. Steranko, "Film feature," p. 18.
47. Terry, *The Popeye Story*, pp. 64–82. On "overdesign" see Kristin Thompson, *The Frodo Franchise: The Lord of the Rings and Modern Hollywood* (Berkeley: University of California Press, 2007), p. 75.
48. Jules Feiffer, "Popeye," Shooting Script, 11 August 1980, Robert Altman Papers, Special Collections Research Center, University of Michigan Library.
49. Patrick McGilligan, "Altman Sidebar," p. 1, December 1980, Robert Altman Papers, Special Collections Research Center, University of Michigan Library.
50. Terry, *The Popeye Story*, p. 17.
51. Leslie Cabarga, *The Fleischer Story* (New York: Nostalgia Press, 1976), p. 64.
52. Michael Barrier, "King of the Mardi Gras Commentary," *Popeye the Sailor Volume One*, DVD (Burbank, CA: Warner Home Video, 2007).
53. "Sailor's Hornpipes: The Voices of Popeye," *Popeye the Sailor Volume One*, DVD, (Burbank, CA: Warner Home Video, 2007).
54. Feiffer, "Popeye," Script—2nd Draft, p. 2.
55. Andy Dougan, *Robin Williams: A Biography* (New York: Thunder's Mouth Press, 1998), p. 79.
56. Paul Taberham, "A general aesthetics of American animation sound design," *Animation: An Interdisciplinary Journal* 13, no. 2 (2018): 136–7.
57. Terry, *The Popeye Story*, pp. 143–5.
58. Taberham, "A general aesthetics," p. 132.
59. Ibid. p. 135.
60. Ibid. p. 133.
61. Cabarga, *The Fleischer Story*, p. 65.
62. Altman, "The musical," p. 299.
63. McGilligan, *Robert Altman*, p. 509.
64. Terry, *The Popeye Story*, pp. 22, 34.
65. Jules Feiffer, *Backing into Forward* (New York: Doubleday, 2010), pp. 410–11.
66. Feiffer, "Popeye," Script—3rd Draft, p. 54.
67. McGilligan, *Robert Altman*, p. 510.
68. Terry, *The Popeye Story*, p. 26.
69. Altman, "The musical," p. 299; Feiffer, "Popeye," Script—3rd Draft, pp. 103, 118.
70. Feiffer, "Popeye," Script—3rd Draft, pp. 123–4.
71. Ibid. pp. 140–1.
72. Zuckoff, *Robert Altman*, p. 358.

CHAPTER 2

For Real: *Tanner '88*, *Tanner on Tanner*, and the Political Spectacle in the Post-Network Era

Chuck Tryon

During an early scene in Robert Altman's HBO series, *Tanner '88*, fictional presidential candidate Jack Tanner is spotted carrying his own luggage while leaving the airport as he travels from one campaign stop to another. The image of Tanner lugging his own suitcase is captured by a news camera and is woven into a story for a local newscast, prompting one of Tanner's aides to lecture him, stating that the image conveys the idea that Jack "can't or won't delegate. It says 'Jimmy Carter.' People may want you to be for real, Jack, but they don't want you to be like him." Jack's gaffe had nothing to do with his innate qualities or political views. Instead, his error was directly linked to his inability to grasp the importance of creating and maintaining a polished image as a candidate. For Stella Bruzzi, Tanner's ineptitude parodies a long-term failure of Democrats to grasp "the importance of slick image-making."[1] However, while Altman and series co-creator Garry Trudeau certainly were not shy about mocking Democratic foibles when it came to political messaging, the Tanner saga should be understood primarily as a primer on how to watch political television. By calling attention to the ways in which candidate images are constructed, *Tanner '88* helped to diagnose the harmful effects of political media on our democracy. Sixteen years later, well into the era of cable news and internet-enabled political campaigning, Altman and Trudeau updated their critique of political media with *Tanner on Tanner*, a mockumentary that updates the storylines of all of the original series' major characters. In both cases, Altman directs his critical gaze towards the role of political media in failing consumers and citizens when it comes to enabling authentic dialogue around vital political issues.

CONSTRUCTING THE REAL

Tanner '88 was an unlikely collaboration between Altman and *Doonesbury* cartoonist Garry Trudeau, after HBO executive Bridget Potter suggested to Trudeau that he make a political television series. *Tanner '88* was a mockumentary that followed the efforts of Jack Tanner (played by Michael Murphy), a fictional former Congressman from Michigan who was seeking the Democratic nomination to run for President of the United States in the 1988 election. The series challenged televisual norms in that it was shot in a naturalistic, improvisational style designed to challenge traditional televisual depictions of the political spectacle. In fact, as Heather-Osborne Thompson pointed out, *Tanner '88* was shot on video, a format that is more typically associated with immediacy and liveness.[2] As a result, the camera positions us as observers taking an active role in evaluating the behavior of the social actors depicted in the film. Although Tanner is a fictional candidate, *Tanner '88* depicts his campaign as real. Tanner—and Altman's crew—followed the candidates across the country as they participated in all of the rituals associated with presidential campaigns including canvassing, fundraising, and TV interviews, with Tanner often stopping to interact with actual candidates and news reporters on the streets of New Hampshire. In addition, both *Tanner '88* and *Tanner on Tanner* featured a number of cameos, not just by the candidates themselves but also by professional political staffers and commentators, such as Chris Matthews, who was then the chief of staff for House Speaker Tip O'Neill, and Linda Ellerbee, then a network news anchor, while the later series included cameos by filmmakers ranging from Martin Scorsese to Robert Redford and politicians including Al Gore and Howard Dean. These cameos helped to illustrate the ways in which campaign narratives are constructed. By focusing on these backstage elements, Altman and Trudeau were able, as Joanne Morreale argues, to "indict the American political process, as well as political candidates who are literally the product of media representations."[3] Altman also edited Tanner into a real Democratic debate between party frontrunners, Rev. Jesse Jackson and Governor Michael Dukakis, using television monitors and careful editing and staging to make it appear as if Tanner was on stage with his Democratic rivals. Even Tanner's campaign slogan, "For Real," is a sly reference to the show's focus on questions of authenticity. In turn, Altman and Trudeau use these references to the political process to create what Horace Newcomb and Paul Hirsch refer to as a "cultural forum," in which audiences are presented with a range of ideas and ideologies ingrained within American political culture. In the case of *Tanner '88*, Jack's signature issues are civil rights and drug legalization, although through the course of his campaign, he eventually becomes more concerned about poverty and crime. However, Jack is also confronted with the limitations of a political media system, in which ideas become obscured by the obsessive focus on the personality traits of individual candidates.[4] Thus, the show is able to both engage with current political issues—the "War on Drugs," poverty, and unemployment—and to show how the political media works against dealing with those issues in a thoughtful way.

Throughout the film, Tanner is positioned as an outsider, someone who struggles with remaining true to his principles while also concerned about how he can craft a successful, well-polished political message. As Craig Hight has argued, Jack seems to be trying to reconcile his liberal political agenda with the increasingly demand to craft a "charismatic media profile" that will attract voters.[5] Similarly, Altman and Trudeau revisited the role of political media in 2004 in their follow-up series, *Tanner on Tanner*, which depicts Tanner's daughter, now herself a filmmaker, attempting to cash in on her father's celebrity by making a retrospective documentary about his failed presidential run, self indulgently called "My Candidate," while commissioning one of her students to make a documentary *about* her, creating a situation in which literally *everyone* has a camera and aspires to become a documentary filmmaker. In both cases, Altman and Trudeau use the tropes of mockumentary to engage with the broader questions of authenticity when it comes to representing presidential politics.

Tanner '88 unsettled the artificial separation between politics and entertainment that had historically dominated broadcast television. As Jeffrey P. Jones has argued, broadcast networks had maintained a division between news and entertainment divisions throughout the network era. But by the time that Tanner was made, many politicians were beginning to recognize the potential appeal of speaking to voters through entertainment television. In fact, conservative televangelist Pat Robertson and Republican Senator Bob Dole are clearly happy to play along with Tanner just to get a few extra seconds of screen time. Still, prior to the 1992 election, for Jones, "politics was found primarily in newscasts, Sunday morning talk shows, and documentaries," often on the grounds that these genres helped network affiliates to justify their claims of providing programming that served the public interest.[6] As Jones argues, this boundary became less sustainable as cable television offered increased competition for TV viewers. Although Jones has argued that the first "sustained blurring between the generic lines of political news and entertainment programming" takes place during the 1992 election, *Tanner '88* had already begun to erode these boundaries, both through its hybrid mockumentary format and through its radically democratic approach to storytelling, in which citizens increasingly became participants in both the electoral process and in the creation of narratives about it.[7] Similarly, as Geoffrey Baym has argued, the transition into the multichannel era also expanded what was considered to count as political, especially as cable news channels began to provide a twenty-four-hour news cycle that needed to be filled.[8]

Tanner '88 defied televisual conventions in other ways, as well. Unlike most other TV series of its era, episodes of *Tanner '88* were not broadcast at a set time or even day of the week. Instead they followed the campaign timeline rather than the regimented weekly schedule typically associated with broadcast television. As a result, the show could respond more or less immediately to campaign events as they happened. Although Altman and Trudeau hoped to create new episodes of *Tanner '88* up to the November general presidential election, HBO decided not to renew the series after the 1988 Convention. Amazingly enough, Tanner's campaign became so convincingly real that it was frequently framed as "real" in the wider non-fictional news media. In fact, during the Democratic Convention in Atlanta, *Good Morning America* host Charlie Gibson interviewed Michael Murphy in character as Tanner without revealing that Tanner was a fictional character.[9] *Tanner '88* and *Tanner on Tanner* used the tropes of the mockumentary as they sought to interrogate the concept of authenticity as it informs political narratives. These tropes serve a pedagogical function, guiding the viewer to see how political TV fails to provide citizens with the tools they need to effectively evaluate candidates for office or to inform the public about vital social issues.

BECOMING REAL

The critique of political media representations is evident from the opening shot of *Tanner '88*. The camera zooms back revealing that we are in the control room of WMUR, a New Hampshire TV station. A producer sits in front of a bank of monitors, with the audio track eventually settling on the voice of Jack Heath, the host of *New Hampshire's Close-Up*, a local public affairs show. While maintaining this audio track, Altman's restless camera pans across to another monitor where a second camera has focused on Jack Tanner, staring uncomfortably as he waits to be interviewed.

The interview emulates countless other candidate interviews: Heath invites Jack to introduce himself to the live TV audience, presumably undecided New Hampshire primary voters. Jack's answers are bland and seem pre-packaged, failing to offer any specific policy views that would compel voters to support him, although Jack's appearance on television is itself a victory for the campaign, as we see later when we hear several of Jack's staffers calling donors and voters on the strength of that TV appearance claiming that Jack is "coming on strong" as a candidate.

By placing emphasis on the political staffers who direct Tanner's campaign, we are positioned as viewers to watch how political professionals create and consume political narratives. Watching other people consume television can often serve a larger pedagogical role, heightening our awareness of how TV narratives

Figure 2.1 Robert Altman (center) and Michael Murphy (below) on the set of *Tanner '88*. Photo by Cliff Lipson. Courtesy of Special Collections Research Center, University of Michigan Library.

are constructed for maximum persuasive effect. As Jonathan Gray has argued, television programs that depict characters watching TV can be used to make people aware of the "manipulations" associated with TV style.[10] Deke's video, with its extreme distortions and flashy imagery, perfectly encapsulates political storytelling in the network TV era, and tutors the *Tanner '88* audience in strategies for consuming political images more cautiously and critically. In addition to satirizing candidate interviews, the pilot episode further engages with these questions about authenticity by cross-cutting between a scene in which Jack's staffers watch a biographical campaign video produced by Jack's videographer, Deke, and a simultaneous scene, in which Jack visits the home of a New Hampshire farmer as part of a campaign stunt meant to attract some local television "earned media" coverage. The campaign video is an important genre for political candidates, allowing them to introduce (or for incumbents, reintroduce) themselves to the American public by establishing a narrative about the candidate. Ronald Reagan's 1984 video helped to reinforce the idea that Reagan had ushered in a kind of American utopia, one that did not, of course, truly exist.

Deke's video functions as a parody of this type of campaign video. It opens with a shot of Tanner, in front of his modest Michigan home, shoveling snow. Off-screen, we hear a phone ring, and we watch Tanner through his window as he retreats into his home to answer it. Jack picks up the phone, metaphorically and literally, answering the call to run for president. Subsequent scenes include World War II footage that Deke admits he lifted from Bob Dole's campaign film and scenes from a college basketball game depicting basketball games that featured Wilt Chamberlain, despite the fact that Tanner never played basketball with (or against) him. Both scenes greatly exaggerate Tanner's biography for the sake of creating a more powerful narrative, one that cynically attempts to link him to politically attractive (and traditionally masculine) tropes such as military heroism and athletic prowess. Ultimately, the campaign film culminates with a pastiche of stock historical images of Martin Luther King, Jr. and John F. Kennedy, visually linking Tanner to the Civil Rights movements of the 1960s, using stereotypical images to tell Tanner's story. Notably, as we watch Deke's video, Tanner's staffers are also watching—and commenting—pointing out the ways in which the video distorts Tanner's biography, essentially fact-checking the film in real time. In this sense, *Tanner '88* is teaching us how to watch politics. The staffers' remarks—sarcastic, critical—instill in us a degree of skepticism towards these kinds of narratives. Later in the episode, Tanner's staffers host a test screening for a New Hampshire focus group, providing the group with electronic dialers that allow them to express positive or negative sentiment in real time as the video plays. During this test screening, the participants are dismissive of the video's most overt emotional appeals, especially its discussion of Tanner's daughter, Alex, who is a survivor of Hodgkin's disease. In a powerful scene that analyzes how audiences watch political television, a political science professor hired by the campaign explains that voters don't like candidates who use their family to pander to their emotions. Thus, the one scene in the video that is perhaps the most authentic depiction of Jack's biography turns out to be the least appealing to the focus group.

In addition to mocking campaign videos, the pilot episode also mocks the campaign ritual of candidates canvassing door-to-door to talk to voters. Although canvassing itself is an important and valuable political activity, these activities can fall into conventional formats, especially when cameras are present with the hope of capturing an authentic interaction with a potential voter. While Tanner's staff works with the focus group, Jack and his daughter make stops at town halls and shopping malls where they cross paths with several of the actual candidates who were campaigning in New Hampshire at the time. Notably he chats with televangelist Pat Robertson, who was running an insurgent campaign against Vice President George H. W. Bush. After the quick handshake, Taggerty, the fictional reporter who has been following Tanner, asks Robertson a question about whether or not he is willing to use "Christian hardball" to win the Republican primary, which Robertson dutifully answers as if Taggerty is an actual reporter. Later, Jack and Alex approach GOP Senator Bob Dole, with Dole gleefully bragging that "we have the Bushes on the run." In interviews,

Altman has stated that the Robertson cameo was a pivotal moment in the production of *Tanner '88*, when he became convinced that the show was capturing "something real" about the American political process.[11]

Ultimately, the pilot episode resolves these questions by showing what appears to be a candid, unscripted interaction between Jack and his staff, as they sit in a hotel room. Reflecting on the failure of Deke's campaign video to connect with the New Hampshire voters, Jack launches into a spontaneous monologue about the artificiality of modern politics. The monologue, framed around an anecdote in which Alex had asked several of Tanner's Democratic colleagues to name their favorite Beatle, allows Jack to launch into a discussion about which candidates could claim to be the most authentic heir of the politics of the 1960s. The scene's apparent naturalism and authenticity is augmented by how it is shot. As Jack begins to speak, the camera pans over to Deke who is surreptitiously filming Jack from beneath a glass table with a handheld video camera sitting in his lap. Once the camera cuts to the POV of Deke's camera, we see Jack obscured through the glass, with campaign posters and fliers reflected in the glass, while drinking glasses and the table legs themselves obscure our view of the candidate. As Dana Stevens has noted, the framing of this scene is what makes it so powerful: "Like the voter, the viewer is trapped by a frustratingly limited perspective, straining to see the 'real' Jack Tanner through a glass darkly."[12] Throughout the sequence, Jack weaves a narrative of American history marked by dissent and the capacity for self-reinvention before finally answering that the "correct" answer to the Beatle question is John. As Osborne-Thompson points out, Jack's speech functions as an indictment of slick politicians with pre-packaged slogans, especially given the ways that it appears to be unscripted and spontaneous.[13] However, Jack's expressions of authenticity are almost immediately undercut when, at the conclusion of Jack's speech, the camera pans to T. J., who immediately recognizes how it could be used and asks Deke if he got the video. The episode ends with a grainy shot of a Tanner campaign poster with his original slogan being torn away and replaced with his new slogan: "For Real." Jack's moment of authenticity has already been contained, repackaged as something that could be sold to voters. As a result, Jack becomes a product, and even Tanner's most authentic moments—his discussion of his daughter's illness, his heartfelt explanation for why he ran for president—are all woven into a campaign narrative, one that prevents meaningful engagement with real political issues.

PERFORMING THE REAL

Subsequent episodes expand this satire of the ways in which political media undermines the democratic process, producing candidates who are fake or inauthentic. During episode six, "Child's Play," one of Jack's staffers convinces him to consult with Dorothy Sarnoff, a widely known public speech coach and self-help guru, who teaches Tanner her techniques of making eye contact with the audience ("eye clicking") and contracting your abdomen ("The Sarnoff Squeeze") while speaking. Tanner ultimately adopts these methods, practicing his stump speech in front of his staffers who cheer wildly when Tanner is able to perform according to Sarnoff's standards, but this appearance of self-assurance is undercut when Tanner repeats the line "I am somebody," first with self-confidence, but then with a flicker of self-doubt, the episode's concluding freeze frame preserving him in this moment of uncertainty. Once again, the techniques used to package political candidates obscure what makes them authentic, attractive candidates in the first place.

The critique of political spectacle becomes even more explicit in the following episode, "The Great Escape," which focuses on Tanner's participation in a Democratic debate. Like other political rituals, debates often play a major role in shaping campaign narratives. They allow political staffers to construct candidate narratives and, more crucially, allow the political press to amplify the staffers' attempts to "spin" debate performances. While debates appear to allow access to spontaneous expressions by the candidates, they are in fact, carefully crafted media events. In fact, John P. Koch has argued that "presidential debates are not really debates at all, but canned mini-speeches at what amounts to a joint press conference."[14]

One of the problems with US political debates is that they have their roots in entertainment television. As Michael Socolow has persuasively argued, televised political debates grew out of efforts by network executives to restore TV's reputation after the quiz show scandals of the 1950s. The goal was to fulfill broadcast television's public interest imperatives even while maintaining television that would entertain TV's mass audience. Therefore, for Socolow, it is no mistake that so many debate stages resemble those of quiz shows.[15] As a result, debates have become designed to entertain rather than enlighten, with candidates expressing well-rehearsed soundbites rather than engaging in serious conversation. In response, debates are often framed by the discourses of "spin," created by campaign staffers who craft narratives about how their candidate performed. *Tanner '88* powerfully captures these limitations regarding political debates, through both the debate itself and through the efforts of T. J. and other staffers in shaping how the press interprets the debate. In fact, during the debate, the camera positions us in the spin room where staffers watch the debate and respond to reporters' questions, often in real time. Shots of Jackson, Dukakis, and Tanner appear on monitors, often partially obscured by the bodies of campaign staff milling around the room, allowing Altman to seamlessly edit between candidates who appeared in the debate and Tanner, who was edited in afterwards. Like other moments in the series, these scenes serve a pedagogical function, modeling a form of media literacy. We watch the debate at the same time the campaign staff and the political journalists do, learning *how* they watch and how they work to frame our interpretations of what happens on the debate stage.

We see this process play out as Tanner engages in debate preparation following his efforts to master the Sarnoff methods, including an attempt to memorize a canned attack line against Rev. Jesse Jackson, in which Tanner comes out in support of drug legalization. During the scene, which we see via a backstage monitor, Tanner even appears to interrupt Jackson in an effort to seem more forceful. The scene allows Altman to ground the show in the current political moment—Jackson and Dukakis's comments on the War on Drugs had grabbed headlines several weeks earlier—and to allow the show to function as what Newcomb and Hirsch refer to as a "cultural forum" around the issue of policing and drug legalization. In the debate segment, Altman quotes Jackson's answer to a question on the drug trade, in which Jackson calls for expanding border patrols to prevent illegal drugs from being carried across the border. Tanner retorts by comparing the War on Drugs to Vietnam, then fresh in the minds of American voters, and implying that the fighting the drug trade is "unwinnable." He adds that drug laws had led to the imprisonment of 25 million Americans before concluding his response by emphatically endorsing legalization. Reactions in the spin room portray Tanner's response as scandalous. Staffers for the other two candidates immediately pounce, attacking Tanner's position as well outside the political norms. However, by simply introducing the idea of drug legalization, Altman was able to push back against the ideology that the US needed to escalate the drug war. In turn, he was able to depict the ways in which media narratives focused less on the actual policies that Tanner was endorsing than on the conflict between the two candidates.

RETURN OF THE REAL

This critique of the political spectacle, and the related attempts to use Tanner's political campaign as a cultural forum for addressing relevant political issues, culminates in the show's eighth episode, "The Girlfriend Factor," in which Tanner returns to his home state of Michigan to make some campaign appearances. "The Girlfriend Factor" puts two visions of the future in contrast. The episode opens with a typical campaign appearance at a technology fair, where we see images of robots doing work that had previously been done by human workers while Prince Vince, a Detroit-based performer, raps about the shift to automation as a way to cut down on labor costs ("a manmade thing is taking over all the jobs that humans once used just to survive"). The rap lyrics counteract the utopian images of robots performing menial tasks, often in ways that are meant to humanize them and to make them appear non-threatening, such as a robot that greets Jack in what appears to be a friendly voice. The robot

Figure 2.2 Michael Murphy as Jack Tanner (right) on his campaign bus with staff and reporters in *Tanner '88*. Photo by Dean D. Dixon. Courtesy of Special Collections Research Center, University of Michigan Library.

immediately turns to mocking Jack, telling him he "looks taller on TV" and then hounding him about his position on drug legalization, a callback to the show's previous episode when Jack had forcefully taken that stance.

This scene frames a campaign stop in an inner-city neighborhood in Detroit, where a group of community activists from a group called SOSAD (Save our Sons and Daughters), is holding a rally to call attention to the effects of poverty, joblessness, and violence on their neighborhood. SOSAD was (and is) an actual activist group based in Detroit, and members of that organization and the broader community are given the opportunity to speak, one of the few times in the series that non-politicians portray themselves. As Tanner approaches the rally—in the back of his protected vehicle—we hear a reprise of Prince Vince rapping about issues facing the community while sirens blare in the background. Notably, Detroit police refused to escort Altman and his crew into the Cass Corridor neighborhood where the scene was filmed, but Altman chose to film there anyway.[16] A tracking shot from the perspective of Jack's car shows abandoned and destroyed buildings, many of them gutted by fire, followed by a shot of police investigating a crime scene, a stark contrast with the robotics fair and the downtown skyscrapers associated with Detroit's commercial center. We then hear Errol Henderson, one of the leaders of SOSAD, reading a poem mourning the death of his daughter who was killed by random gunfire. Following Henderson, Clementine Barfield, one of SOSAD's founders, speaks from the podium when Tanner arrives and tells Tanner simply, "We want some changes," echoing the lyrics from the Prince Vince song played earlier in the episode. Rather than seeking to provide stock answers to Barfield's questions, however, Jack opts to listen, at one point encouraging the community "take advantage of the cameras and tell the public what's going on." At this point, Tanner sits with actual members of the Cass Corridor community and invites people to speak about their concerns. According to interviews with Barfield and Henderson, Michael Murphy, who played Tanner, reportedly sat with members of SOSAD for hours, sincerely listening to them in much the same way that an actual political candidate might (or should). As Frank Caso points out, this scene provides an interpretive challenge for audiences. It is one of the few scenes in *Tanner '88* where Altman did not use celebrity cameos to distinguish the fictional from the real.[17] As a result, Altman provided a relatively unknown activist group with a national platform through which they could make their voices heard.

Once again, the episode functions as a type of cultural forum, compelling viewers to weigh carefully how drug policy affected the lives of ordinary citizens. The conversation with the SOSAD activists forces Jack to rethink one of his pet campaign positions, a promise to legalize all drugs. Faced with the impact of crack and other drugs on this inner-city Detroit neighborhood, Jack is confronted with the realization that his proposed policies might not benefit the people they were intended to help. Notably, Clementine Barfield and Errol Henderson both reported that members of SOSAD had initially been reluctant to appear on a satirical political comedy because they worried that the show would not adequately capture the gravity of their work in Detroit.[18] However, because of the participation of the activists, the audience for *Tanner '88* was offered just a brief glimpse of the conditions that political campaigns should address and to see the ways in which the political media was completely incapable of depicting.

Significantly, the episode concludes with Tanner discovering the dead body of a small child in the vacant lot where his car is parked. The episode ends in a freeze frame that captures Tanner's anguish at being confronted with the reality of gun violence, while the lines "brutally died" from another Prince Vince rap song plays on a seemingly endless loop. In fact, Errol Henderson recalled that when the episode was screened in the activist communities in Detroit, audience members gasped audibly when they viewed that scene, calling it a "gut punch" that helped to illustrate the conditions in Detroit at the time. Thus, even while Tanner is a fictional candidate, his campaign amplified voices that are rarely seen on television, turning members of the Detroit community into co-contributors in telling a real story about the impact of poverty and gun violence in their neighborhood.

BEYOND THE REAL

Altman and Trudeau ultimately used the Democratic Convention to provide closure to Tanner's campaign, but in 2004, they were given the opportunity to revisit the Tanner story, when the Sundance Channel rebroadcast the show—for the first time since the late 1980s—and to produce new segments, which were referred to as "Fireside Chats," in which some of the characters from the original series reflected on the significance of the Tanner campaign. These framing materials or paratexts helped to orient viewers as they sought to engage with the Tanner story.[19] The Fireside Chats help to frame the way in which most contemporary viewers encounter the storyworld. In addition to Sundance's rebroadcast, *Tanner '88* is also shown on Amazon Prime with the Fireside Chats, essentially making them the default way of consuming the show for contemporary viewers. As a result, they become what Jonathan Gray has called "entryway paratexts," texts that exist outside of the original program that provide viewers with frames for interpreting the original show.[20] For example, during the Fireside Chat preceding the pilot episode, Tanner in his office at Michigan State University, tells us that the 1988 election was when "the curtain on our private lives got pulled back," referring both to Gary Hart's aborted presidential campaign and to the ways in which Tanner's personal life would be scrutinized. In other cases, Jack, Alex, and T. J. engage in spin, as they seek to reshape the historical record. Before episode two, for instance, T. J. brags about the ways in which she was able to take an unscripted speech by Tanner and turn it into a set of advertisements they used to "bury" Democratic rival Al Gore. T. J.'s comments fill in historical details that were not included in the original narrative while also showing that T. J. is still engaging in self-promotion. By comparison, Tanner reflects on the ways in which the political media made a truly authentic presidential campaign doomed to failure. He remarks, for example, that a late-campaign makeover was "pure desperation" and notes that his most idealistic political commitments—including his opposition to Apartheid—were a "liability." While these Fireside Chats have received little attention, they explicitly function to display the limits of political TV coverage.

The Sundance channel followed the Fireside Chats up with a four-episode series, *Tanner on Tanner*. In many ways, *Tanner on Tanner* better fits contemporary definitions of the mockumentary. The story focuses on the efforts of Jack's daughter, Alex, now an aspiring filmmaker, as she works to make a documentary about her father's campaign. Meanwhile, Alex has commissioned one of her students to make a documentary about her as she works to complete her film, setting up a larger engagement with the politics of do-it-yourself (DIY) filmmaking. Like *Tanner '88*, however, *Tanner on Tanner* was fixated on the tropes associated with representing politics. In particular, one of the main running plots in the series pivots on questions about how political narratives are constructed. Alex's documentary invites Jack to reflect on his own political failure, but also ends up inadvertently creating a conflict for her father when she records video of him criticizing the Democratic nominee John Kerry for initially supporting the war in Iraq just after Kerry had announced that Tanner was being considered for a position in his Cabinet. Because Jack's comments would reflect poorly on Kerry, Alex is pressured to destroy the tape, which she believes would undermine the core message of her documentary. As a result, *Tanner on Tanner*, like its predecessor, addresses the issue of authenticity as it intersects with the Washington electoral institutions and their attempts to fabricate carefully crafted political images designed to sell candidates to a wider public.

Like *Tanner '88*, the follow-up series utilizes a mockumentary format and a loose, unscripted style, in which actors were invited to improvise lines. *Tanner on Tanner* also contains a number of cameos, including Hollywood stars Martin Scorsese and Steve Buscemi, and politicians and political advisors, including Al Franken (then a radio host of the liberal Air America network), John Podesta, and Ronald Reagan, Jr., as well as Vice President Al Gore and Vermont Governor Howard Dean, who had himself run an insurgent, grassroots political campaign. The series depicts Tanner's daughter, Alex, now an aspiring filmmaker, as she works to produce a documentary about her experiences on the campaign trail, "My Candidate." Meanwhile, Alex has self-indulgently commissioned one of her students to make a documentary about her filmmaking process. In fact, many of the series' cameos explicitly illustrate the ways in which politics functions through personal contacts and networks rather than through genuine merit. At one point, Alex asks Scorsese to review a copy of her film, and later, Podesta, then the president and CEO of the progressive think tank, Center for American Progress, tells Alex that he is interested in investing in documentary.

Although *Tanner on Tanner* is structured around the 2004 Democratic National Convention in Boston, it functions primarily as a satire of the emerging practice of DIY filmmaking. In fact, during promotional interviews, Altman remarked that "anybody with $1,500 and a computer can make a film, and they all do. They go out there with no thread, no passion, no idea, no anything."[21] In particular, *Tanner on Tanner* parodies a recent cycle of political campaign films produced by the children of prominent politicians, including *Journeys with George* (2002), by Alexandra Pelosi, the daughter of Democratic Speaker of the House, Nancy Pelosi. The film also mocked political documentaries such as Michael Moore's *Fahrenheit 9/11* (2004), which improbably became a centerpiece of the 2004 election. This focus reflects also Altman's growing concern about the rise of reality television. In fact, as Altman himself put it, "everyone has a fucking camera these days. We don't live our own lives."[22] While *Tanner '88* retains at least some optimism that an idealistic candidate could break through, *Tanner on Tanner* seems to have even less faith in the political process. Instead, we are confronted with the possibility that these forms of personal expression begin to supplant the real work of activism as people make—or consume—documentaries that serve to reinforce their pre-existing beliefs.[23]

Like *Tanner '88*, *Tanner on Tanner* opens with a mediated gaze. The first episode begins with a shot of Alex, seen through the lens of her inexpensive video camera speaking directly to her audience in a visual style that evokes the conventions of reality TV confessionals from shows such as MTV's *The Real World* (Jonathan Murray, Mary-Ellis Bunim, 1992–). Throughout the series, the narratives of DIY filmmaking are satirized. Alex admits to being thousands of dollars in credit card debt and acknowledges that her parents make her car payments and "loan" her money for rent but consistently shows a limited grasp on the story she wants to tell about her father. When Discover offers her a $10,000 line of credit, she immediately uses that to finance her film, emulating countless other aspiring filmmakers hoping to create the next great low-budget masterpiece. Later in the opening episode, we see Alex as she screens "My Candidate" at the Rough Cut Film Festival, an independent film festival in New York. Robert Redford, the founder of the Sundance Film Festival and a champion of independent cinema, in attendance. The film is poorly received by the audience, and even Redford calls out Alex's film as self-indulgent and lacking in substance, setting the stage for Alex to shift her energy toward covering her father's participation in the Democratic Convention.

Throughout the convention, Alex attempts to exploit her father's connections to get material for a documentary that will break through the clutter of media images. At one point, her father contacts T. J., now a Kerry campaign staffer, who subtly declines Alex's request for an interview with the nominee. Later, while still at the convention, Alex catches her father in a candid moment after a racquetball match where he complains that he doesn't see "any daylight" between Kerry and Bush on Iraq. The unguarded comments evoke Jack's impromptu "Beatles" speech in *Tanner '88*, showing Jack at his most passionate and authentic. However, Jack's comments immediately become inconvenient for him when he learns that he is being considered for a Cabinet position, leaving Alex pressured to destroy the tape—which has become the core of her documentary—or damage her father's political prospects. Once again, Jack's authentic political stance—in this case, opposition to the war in Iraq—is subverted by the need to maintain party discipline and not appear overly critical of Kerry, who had initially voted for the war.

The ambivalence about personal documentary is further reflected in a scene in which both Alex and real documentary filmmaker, Alexandra Kerry, daughter of presidential candidate John Kerry, compete to interview the child of another famous politician, Ronald Reagan, Jr., while Reagan himself is trailed by cameras from his own MSNBC show. Kerry and Alex eventually agree to interview Reagan, Jr., at the same time, with Kerry asking substantive policy questions while Alex asks Reagan to discuss what it is like to be the child of a famous politician. The scene becomes a profound, if satirical, commentary on the constant mediation that was becoming an increasingly commonplace aspect of our everyday lives.

CONCLUSION

Ultimately, both *Tanner '88* and *Tanner on Tanner* use the tropes of the mockumentary to parody the conventions of other media forms. While *Tanner '88* focused its attention on political television in the waning moments of the network era, *Tanner on Tanner* directed its satirical lens toward the emerging trend of DIY filmmakers. In both cases, Altman and Trudeau are mocking the conventions of non-fictional media in order to remind viewers of their role in constructing political narratives. *Tanner '88* offers a rich, textured critique of political media genres ranging from campaign biography films to local news interviews and political debates. As Morreale has argued, *Tanner '88*'s "visual style gives the impression of spontaneity, unpredictability, and unplanned observation" even while using those techniques to call into question "the idea of authentic representation" itself.[24] In fact, the character of Jack Tanner becomes completely defined by the media representations that engulf him. From the beginning, we see him through the lens of a TV camera, the local news anchor defining his candidacy even while Tanner waits impassively. In turn, Tanner's interactions with actual candidates serve as a reminder that their campaign personas are equally inauthentic. However, *Tanner '88* also adeptly uses the mockumentary form to amplify messages that might otherwise go ignored in the political news media. Tanner's visit to the Cass Corridor neighborhood in Detroit—including his interactions with the SOSAD activists—helped to provide that group with a national platform through which the issues of poverty, gun violence, and the crack epidemic could be addressed.

By comparison, *Tanner on Tanner* trains its lens on the falsely empowering narratives associated with the emergence of DIY filmmaking practices in the early 2000s, thanks in part to the widespread availability to inexpensive digital cameras, editing software, and distribution tools. In this sense, much like *Tanner '88*, *Tanner on Tanner* is concerned with the question of authenticity. In this case, Altman satirizes the vague platitudes of personal documentary as part of a broader critique of the artificiality of political media at the very moment when online media are starting to emerge as a major force, questions that still haunt us in our current moment in which cable news fails to serve the public interest. More than anything, Altman and Trudeau deployed the frame of authenticity to promote a cultural forum around vital social and political issues and to introduce political stances that often went ignored in the commercial news media. *Tanner '88* helped to invigorate discussions of the War on Drugs, poverty, and apartheid, while *Tanner on Tanner* offered an explicit critique of the Gulf War. In this sense, the Tanner story provides us with a powerful reminder of the role of entertainment television in challenging audiences to ask important political questions and to rethink the ways in which the news media depicts the American political system.

NOTES

1. Stella Bruzzi, *New Documentary: A Critical Introduction* (New York: Routledge, 2000), p. 142.
2. Heather Osborne-Thompson, "Tracing the 'fake' candidate in American television comedy," in Jonathan Gray, Jeffrey P. Jones, and Ethan Thompson (eds), *Satire TV: Politics and Comedy in the Post-Network Era* (New York: New York University Press, 2009), p. 73.
3. Joanne Morreale, "*Tanner '88*," in Gary R. Edgerton and Jeffrey P. Jones (eds), *The Essential HBO Reader* (Lexington: University Press of Kentucky, 2008), p. 107.
4. Horace M. Newcomb and Paul M. Hirsch, "Television as a cultural forum: implications for research," *Quarterly Review of Film Studies* 8, no. 3 (1983): 50–1.
5. Craig Hight, *Television Mockumentary: Reflexivity, Satire and a Call to Play* (Manchester: Manchester University Press, 2010), p. 148.
6. Jeffrey P. Jones, *Entertaining Politics: Satiric Television and Political Engagement*, 2nd edn (Lanham, MD: Rowman & Littlefield, 2010), p. 6.
7. Ibid. pp. 6–7.
8. Geoffrey Baym, *From Cronkite to Colbert: The Evolution of Broadcast News* (Oxford: Oxford University Press, 2009), pp. 12–13.
9. Zach St. Louis, "How a fake candidate blended fact and fiction on the campaign trail, 30 years ago," NPR, 7 May 2019. Available at <https://wamu.org/story/19/05/07/how-a-fake-candidate-blended-fact-and-fiction-on-the-campaign-trail-30-years-ago/> [audio] (last accessed 4 April 2021).
10. Jonathan Gray, *Watching with The Simpsons: Television, Parody, and Intertextuality* (New York: Routledge, 2006), pp. 7–8.
11. Robert Altman, *Altman on Altman*, ed. David Thompson (New York: Faber and Faber, 1989).
12. Dana Stevens, "Primary Colors," *Slate*, 1 February 2004. Available at <https://slate.com/culture/2004/02/altman-s-tanner-88-exposes-the-fiction-of-democracy.html>.
13. Osborne-Thompson, "Tracing the 'fake' candidate", pp. 74–5.
14. John P. Koch, "Presidential 'debates' aren't debates at all—they're joint press conferences," *The Conversation*, 12 September 2019. Available at <https://theconversation.com/presidential-debates-arent-debates-at-all-theyre-joint-press-conferences-125202> (last accessed 4 May 2021).
15. Michael Socolow, "Think presidential debates are dull? Thank 1950s TV game shows," *The Conversation*, 17 December 2019. Available at <https://theconversation.com/think-presidential-debates-are-dull-thank-1950s-tv-game-shows-128764> (last accessed 4 May 2021).

16. Robert Lloyd, "They believed in Jack Tanner," *Los Angeles Times*, 8 February 2004. Available at <https://www.latimes.com/archives/la-xpm-2004-feb-08-ca-lloyd8-story.html> (last accessed 4 May 2021).
17. Frank Caso, *Robert Altman, In the American Grain* (London: Reaktion Books, 2015).
18. Personal interviews with Clementine Barfield and Errol Henderson. Barfield, in particular, credited actor Michael Murphy for making a sincere effort to engage with the Detroit residents who participated in the screening.
19. Michael Sragow, "Robert Altman's double-feature smile," *Baltimore Sun*, 1 February 2004. Available at <https://www.baltimoresun.com/news/bs-xpm-2004-02-01-0402020384-story.html>.
20. Jonathan Gray, *Show Sold Separately: Promos, Spoilers, and Other Media Paratexts* (New York: New York University Press, 2010), p. 23.
21. Hill Staff, "Tanner's back, 16 years older," *The Hill*, 7 October 2004. Available at <https://thehill.com/capital-living/23877-tanners-back-16-years-older> (last accessed 4 May 2021).
22. Michael Agger, "Candidate," *The New Yorker*, 25 July 2004. Available at <https://www.newyorker.com/magazine/2004/08/02/candidate-10> (last accessed 4 May 2021).
23. Joy Press, "My fake candidate," *Village Voice*, 21 September 2004. Available at <https://www.villagevoice.com/2004/09/21/my-fake-candidate/> (last accessed 4 May 2021).
24. Morreale, "*Tanner '88*," p. 114.

CHAPTER 3

Home-makers: Examining the Altmans' Place-based Production Practices in *Cookie's Fortune*

Nathan Koob

When asked the meaning of the term, "Altmanesque," frequent Robert Altman cast member Lily Tomlin poignantly replied, "Creating a family."[1] While Altman is well-known for his distinctive directorial style that Robert Self has termed a "subliminal reality," a sense of family, or home, might seem negligible when thinking about his production strategies. Yet accounts from those who experienced Altman film productions reveal that a home-style sense of family is actually the central theme which defines everything else.[2] Altman shoots had a structure of home beginning with the fact that there were two familial figures organizing the production environments: Kathryn Reed Altman and her husband Robert Altman. More closely examining the role of Reed Altman in Altman films reveals that her work during productions often appeared as a form of homemaking—planning parties, social events, managing personalities—but in reality comprised the thoughtful construction of a social environment integral to the Altman creative environment. Through visits to production sites, archival materials, and personal interviews with cast, crew, and local figures involved in the Altmans' production process, the case of *Cookie's Fortune* makes it clear that to better understand the intricacies behind the Altman auteurial figure we must examine how they are framed by this specific, constructed social atmosphere. As an auteur, Robert Altman's name functions as a label which stands in for his distinctive directorial style and gives a sense of artistic authorship over his oeuvre. However, this auteur label does not on its own reveal the more intricate, unique, and impactful contributions of notable workers whose own personal styles and actions aid the formation of a recognizable "Robert Altman" film. More closely examining the contributions of Kathryn Reed Altman reveals that we have much more to learn about the type of labor the auteur label tends to subsume.

WORK AS HOME: RETHINKING AUTEURS

Though it might seem paradoxical, the best way to begin to understand how Kathryn Reed Altman foundationally contributed to Robert Altman's production environment is to acknowledge that Robert Altman is recognized as an auteur. Auteur study does have its benefits, but is more fruitful as the study of the production process—while also acknowledging the star power and cultural importance of the auteur label—as opposed to a fixation on a singular figure that subsumes the production process and assumes sole credit for the work of so many. As evidenced in interviews which follow the name of Altman, those who worked on an Altman film stood for more than just the man or his films, standing instead more strikingly for the production environments both Reed Altman and Altman created.

Thinking about Altman films in this way requires some re-packaging of the term "auteur" and examining how it functions. Despite the tendency of Andrew Sarris's auteur theory to limit media analysis to the specific orbit of a director, Francois Truffaut's coining of the term much more closely resembles recognition of the auteur as a type of author *functioning* as opposed to a hierarchical way to read a film.[3] In his original essay, "A Certain Tendency of the French Cinema," Truffaut splits the concept of cinematic author into two categories: the auteur, which corresponds more to a medium-specific artist, and the *metteur-en-scène*, which is the more serviceable scenarist. Timothy Corrigan has gone on to show, as the auteur label gained more popular appeal, the connotations and functions of the auteur have changed significantly in both industry practice and popular culture.[4] Recognizing Robert Altman as an auteur, then, includes artistic, commercial, and celebrity recognition, though the effects of the auteur label reach further than just his artistic products.

The auteur label functions apart from the text as much as it is tied to texts. In "What Is an Author?" Michel Foucault establishes that even after its poststructuralist "death" the concept of author continues to function, creating different types of relationships amongst texts dependent on context:

> Discourse that possesses an author's name . . . its status and its manner of reception are regulated by the culture in which it circulates . . . [T]he function of an author is to characterize the existence, circulation, and operation of certain discourses within a society.[5]

He characterizes the author-function as both historically and culturally variable, complexly constructed, and connected to institutions—thus presenting the author as a shifting discursive construction. If understood as variable within different contexts, what it means to be an author can change significantly in relationship to space/place and time. Therefore, the author-function clearly has implications beyond the text itself such as in its relationship to real environments.[6] The reason we must account for the work of Kathryn Reed Altman in a study of Robert Altman is due to how her defining of the production environments proved to have a significant impact on cast, crew, production communities, and the films themselves. In the case of Altman films, it was not Robert Altman alone who centrally defined these production relationships. His auteur status was created and sustained through the team of Robert Altman, who primarily managed the artistic making of the films depicting a social reality, and Kathryn Reed Altman, who created, maintained, and managed the actual social reality of production that informed each film's dynamic.

To understand Altman as an auteur, studies of his production practices most often focus on his distinct narrative and formal choices, including overlapping dialogue; large, seemingly chaotic sequences; free-moving camera effects; multi-track recording; direction to actors; philosophies behind narration; and use of the zoom lens.[7] These formal elements, combined with his consistent choice to film on location, are key to his overall style geared toward capturing his version of a more natural reality. The most frequently cited example of Altman's reality involves his use of overlapping dialogue—presenting conversations closer to "how they actually happen." Even basic conversation, for Altman, does not involve one clear message, but a series of contradictory and overlapping ones. His son and frequent camera operator Robert Reed Altman concisely describes the Altman-style:

> On *The Long Goodbye* the camera never stopped moving—dollying, zooming—he wanted the action to be caught as if by accident. He hated things being mastered, two-shot, "hit your mark," "say your line." He wanted the feeling to be natural and more relaxed—observational.[8]

Altman's formal style is built around his desire, as an observer, to just let life happen, though the aspects of life he most often displays is very telling. Most Altman films center around party scenes. A film like *Gosford Park* is built almost entirely out of party/dinner scenes, for instance, whereas *Nashville* is constructed around many scenes where disparate characters are forced to engage socially, such as in the famous car accident pileup near the opening of the film or the en masse arrival at the airport. Famous for using a multitude of diverse characters in most of his films, Altman continually uses scenes where characters are brought together to interact in social groups. This social art also relies, however, on a social reality throughout the production that focuses not only on the performers but also on the crew and local communities.

Altman's productions stand out as films made on location and films which really work to represent an everyday sense of those locations. Altman films continually highlight the complexities of filming locations—making it seem as though he produces films *with* communities instead of just *in* communities. The films often portray local neighborhood hangouts, dialect, slang, and local myths, which give a greater sense of an "insider" perspective than found in most films. In thinking about these issues in relationship to his work on *Nashville*, assistant director Alan Rudolph describes an implicit sense of fidelity to locations.

> One thing we never did with Bob . . . was come in and say [to them], "We're here, you're going to change for us!" It was always about adapting to what was really there. Always about how can we find what we're after without insulting what they're here for. That's not an articulation you verbalize, that's a feeling the community has for you . . . it's about trying to find your reality in their reality . . . Bob was [about], "How can this specific, random story we're trying to tell. How would it have happened in this real setting?"[9]

Rudolph positions Altman's productions as something other than the standard Hollywood team, who he implicitly likens to invaders who come in, take what they want, represent without regard to the place, and unceremoniously leave. In one aspect, the filming philosophy Rudolph outlines provides an artistic narrative to Altman's productions—that he had a desire to naturalize his process. In another, Rudolph also distinctly places himself, the crew, and even the local community as co-enactors of Altman's artistic desires, making the filmmaking a much more socially engaged process instead of a primarily individual one.

Altman, then, does work to inject a sense of home-feeling into his films. Whether an outsider or insider to that place, Altman aims to evoke a sense of daily life or local life from the material—thus his artistic career involves a recurring drive to create a sense of home. Upon gaining success in Hollywood, Robert Altman left his hometown of Kansas City and never looked back. Altman did not go on to adopt a new place as home, but instead began creating a concept of home which could travel with him. Altman wanted each shoot to be a place of social living instead of a standard film production work space. In Mitchell Zuckoff's oral biography of Altman he cites a number of stories which point directly to Altman's irremovable linkage of work and home. In discussing the book project, Zuckoff explains the difficulty of trying to separate Altman's work from his life:

> It soon became clear that the lines between his life and his work weren't just blurry, they were almost non-existent. After he returned from flying bombers in WWII, planning and making movies defined nearly everything he did. The films he eventually made weren't overtly autobiographical—not even *Kansas City* . . . he didn't need to make movies about himself because the entire process of filmmaking *was* his adult life.[10]

Figure 3.1 Kathryn Reed Altman and Lyle Lovett on the set of *Cookie's Fortune*. Photo by Joyce Rudolph. Courtesy of Special Collections Research Center, University of Michigan Library.

Kathryn Reed Altman described their life in terms of always moving on to the next production. Once they finished one film, they would head "home"—which acted more as a way-stop between productions—to begin planning the next one and create a new home at that shooting location." In Zuckoff's book in particular, it becomes clear that Altman's amalgamation of the normally much more separate spheres of work and life led to significant disruptions in standard hierarchies of family and job. Altman set up a dynamic which established the feeling and structure of a home life, created by Kathryn Reed Altman, in order to most efficiently, comfortably, and affordably make the kinds of films he wanted to make.

HOME AS WORK: RETHINKING PRODUCTION PRACTICES

For cast and crew, Altman's name does not just act as a moniker for a set of formal stylistic choices, but even more so for a set of place-based production practices. Altman productions created active social groupings to enhance a communal sense of working among locals. Through the largely uncredited work of Kathryn Reed Altman, the productions became synonymous with a transitory idea of home for Altman, his family, and the crew and cast working on the film.

This unique style of working and living inflected the Altman name with associations of family and comfort to an unusual extent, especially when compared to standard industry productions. Kathryn Reed Altman expertly balanced the more gendered labor of homemaking for their children and also the production-oriented labor of maintaining the "family" atmosphere so crucial to Robert Altman's artistic products.

When referring to the productions, I consider the Altmans a team because the production strategies were built so that Kathryn Reed Altman would provide a social environment for those working on the film while Robert Altman would artistically create social environments for the screen. These two processes aided each other. Even more than providing an easygoing spirit, Altman's work/life strategies had very practical elements, and the social aspects Reed Altman engineered were central. Producer Matthew Seig theorized:

> Why Robert Altman always did [location shooting], and there is a real logic to that, was that he gets the cast and crew away from their daily life and focused on the project and creates that family atmosphere that Altman's really known for. That was a part of the process of making the film . . . location shooting does have this huge social advantage: get people to concentrate, may even get them to hang out with each other as a social unit.[12]

As Seig points out, Altman's strategies revolve around the concept of daily life—not just getting them away from their typical daily lives, but also constructing new ones. Everyday experiences become structured by the Altmans through removing cast and crew from their known environments and embedding them into the new place-based environments in a welcoming way. Discovering new environments together causes the production team to bond and further encourages them to socially interact with local communities, encouraging good will toward the production.

To really understand Altman production environments and this "family" component, the relationship the Altmans forge to place is crucial. I use the term "place" here from cultural geography as distinct from "space." The latter is defined as "the simultaneous coexistence of social interrelations at all geographical scales."[13] (For example, the level of space could involve the complexity of spatial relationships surrounding a Target store more generally—your expectations upon arriving at a non-specific location—but would not adequately define a place, say, the Target on Victory Drive in Savannah, GA.) A "place," more specifically, "is formed out of the particular set of social relations which interact at a particular location."[14] Places are both multiple and contradictory, making it all the more difficult to grasp the ways in which they are understood and used by locals. The connection between home and place is strong—most people have a distinct sense of how they define their home. The Altmans' first priority at a new location involved Kathryn Reed Altman finding a defining "home" base for the Altman family to live in and to establish the social hub of the production for that place.[15] While fundamental to the ways in which audiences experience and appreciate Altman's cinema, studying Altman's technical feats has over-written the unique place-based production strategies, most noted by those who worked with him.

Creating the "feeling" the community has for the production, as mentioned by Alan Rudolph, was a battle fought on two fronts: the Altman production team and the Reed Altman social coordination team. When I asked documentarian and cousin John Altman about Reed Altman's role in productions he said, "I don't think there's any line item credit that's big enough to encompass what she did."[16] John Altman's quote perfectly encapsulates the feelings and testimonials provided by other crew members and local figures associated with Altman productions. It was difficult for them to separate what they regarded as the most effective qualities of Robert Altman's productions from Kathryn Reed Altman's central influence. Former Kansas City Film Commissioner Patti Broyles Harper stated, "She's an executive producer. If you try to think of the many roles that she fills every day . . . I would say that there's no one position."[17] When I asked Reed Altman a similar question, she referred to herself as a kind of "social coordinator"—"It's just social stuff. Dinners and kind of open houses. Actors would come to town and I would make them comfortable, we'd entertain them"—a label that others have described as both technically accurate and woefully incomplete.[18] If, as I claim, the most effective qualities of Altman's filmmaking are defined by his social production practices, then Kathryn Reed Altman's role in creating the social, family atmosphere was also consequently a central role in the productions as well.

The centerpiece of this overall social environment has to be the famous and frequent parties. Once the location was chosen for the shoot, Reed Altman would find a place for the Altman home, which she would continually manage throughout the shoot. It acted as the central hub for the production, and every week she hosted a large party with all of the cast and crew invited.[19] Throughout each week guest lists of various other parties, outings, or meals would change depending on what needed to be accomplished at what time, but from all accounts it was fairly common to have a party at least once a week (outside of dailies and meals) where everyone on the film was invited.[20] Reed Altman mentioned that these had a dual purpose for Robert Altman. First and foremost, both of them were very social people and enjoyed interactions through parties—it was their preferred way to live.[21] Secondly, Robert Altman apparently liked production questions to be asked in a party atmosphere where everyone was around:

> We'd make sure we made a big barbeque there and then Bob would invite everyone to come out and he'd be behind the barbeque cooking the stuff . . . he felt that way everybody got to talk to him enough rather than him having to go person-to-person and still make it social and still

get their point, get their questions asked. That was a little theory he had and it seemed to work well.[22]

Alan Rudolph similarly revealed that Altman made cast and crew approach him in a party setting because it reflected his desire to work creatively in a more active atmosphere where ideas had to go out to a group, rather than in isolated conversations.[23] Altman preferred creative questions be placed in a social environment—retaining the key Altman themes of complexity and observation. Interviews about the social environments surrounding Altman films continually reveal that pragmatic production strategies evolved out of making social preferences a central part of the Altman location environment—using basic elements of the couple's preferred home life for practical strategic effects when getting the films made.

Beyond weekend parties, Kathryn Reed Altman was busy arranging almost nightly dinners for smaller groups of cast, crew, or local figures. Often at the last minute, she would find large restaurant reservations, organize caterers, cook, and plan large parties. Robert Reed Altman states,

> She's always been like the queen mother in charge. She always made sure everything was running smoothly, that Bob was happy, that he could throw his parties and his gatherings with people . . . It was a continuous job for her, all the parties, all the entertaining, all the things to remember. She'd help Bob remember all the stuff on the social front, which was really the base to everything . . . Every time we'd move from one house to another to go on location she'd find the right house, she'd get all that stuff together, make sure it was good for entertaining, that it had what we needed. She kept this whole family together. Because like we said earlier, Bob was always just making the movies. She really had to run everything. She's like the grease between all the metal gears that kept everything running smooth and perfect.[24]

Here he not only praises Kathryn Reed Altman for her work but also describes her work as a necessity. A very common thread among conversations about her is the idea that none of it could have existed without her. Despite Robert Altman's preference for a social environment, all agree that its real creator was Kathryn Reed Altman. On the one hand, she created and maintained the atmosphere which he found to be most creative for him to work in. On the other, she was in charge of the very aspects that made Robert Altman's films most defining for those who worked on "his" productions.

The Altmans' culture of social interaction both explicitly and implicitly also involved local communities. City officials, location property owners, and other locals involved in the productions were often included in these festivities in strategic ways. As John Altman put it, "The right people were always fêted, or given access at the right time."²⁵ Altman offered dinners with known celebrities, including himself, in order to get local powers on his side by inviting municipal leaders or local business owners to dinners and making them feel included. Beyond simply inviting locals, however, the Altmans also made sure to integrate their social environments with local communities. Dinners, parties, and production needs all took advantage of local businesses, restaurants, and caterers. Taking the time to experience the environment showed a level of interest in each location as well as respect for the existing local character.

On top of the frequent dinners Kathryn Reed Altman managed, she also was in charge of frequent gatherings involving the cast and crew. Biographies and studies of Altman have consistently focused on his strategy for dailies, often kept hidden from cast and crew in other industry shoots, yet on Altman films everyone was expected to attend. Alan Rudolph remembers,

> Bob wants everybody to come to dailies for the collective energy, the collective thrill. But it's more than that. He wanted a democratic sense where everybody was rooting for everybody else, where you didn't bring your ego to dailies . . . There was this camaraderie, this spirit, so that nobody felt more important than anybody else.²⁶

Rudolph's statement encapsulates the idea that Altman worked to make a creative atmosphere where everyone felt equally inspired to succeed. Stephen Altman similarly remembers, "Everybody had to go to dailies, no matter what you did, who you were, you had to read the script, you had to know what the movie was about and dailies always turned into a big party. It was him."²⁷ While the experience of dailies fit Robert Altman's sensibility, the welcoming, easy-going, family-like "party" environment of dailies was more specifically constructed by Kathryn Reed Altman.

Beginning this discussion through the term "family" and suggesting that Kathryn Reed Altman, as wife and mother, has her credit for her labor largely subordinated under the name of her husband Robert Altman is certainly not a new concept, but the connection between gendered credit for labor and below-the-line credit under an auteur is striking. Given that the Altmans' production and personal relationships extend back to the early 1960s, the homemaking, supportive, and social labor provided by women for their husbands was standardly overlooked in favor of perceiving the husband's bread-winning as the structural basis of the family. Annette Kuhn explains that within the structure of the family, women's labor becomes isolated to use value, which has no visible return, whereas men's labor has exchange value, which results in visible profit and thus dominates. Kuhn explains,

> Women's labour becomes increasingly confined to the production of use values for consumption in the family, women's work is increasingly done

in the service of family members. This becomes institutionalised in the social relations of marriage to the extent that husbands are in a position of owning or controlling the labour power of their wives, a situation which may be legitimated in the written or unwritten terms of marriage contracts.[28]

In the case of the Altmans, the subordination of the marriage contract actually further reifies the subordination of the auteur label, or belief in the director position, when a person's name serves to stand in for an entire cinematic style or set of films. Here, the separation of value becomes all the more important as the family sphere extends into the business sphere—making Reed Altman a direct partner in the business/exchange value side. However, because her work remains relegated to aspects identifiable as homemaking and family support, such as party planning and social coordination, her work also remains invisible under the Robert Altman husband/auteur name.

Any family, home, or life requires supportive labor in order for it to function. In other words, homemaking and supportive work is a necessary part of the labor process. Paul Smith writes,

> Labour power is, then, seen as the result of a production process in which the depleted wage labourer and his means of subsistence enter as means of production to be transformed by domestic labour into the replenished labourer and his labour power.[29]

Therefore, if taking homemaking, use value labor as part of a production process that replenishes the laborer and allows for further exchange value labor to take place, it is clear that such work is fundamental. To put it another way, supportive work is about constructing an environment that allows exchange value work to continue forward under the best circumstances possible. In reality the two cannot be separated. Kathryn Reed Altman, however, did much more than provide such a supportive environment for her husband/family, she also worked to provide a sense of familial support to the entire production wherever they were located.

HOME-MAKING: RE-THINKING *COOKIE'S FORTUNE*

The case of Holly Springs, MS, and *Cookie's Fortune* illustrates how the Altmans' production strategies function in a real community. Holly Springs is relatively rare in that despite its small size (population 7,500) it maintains an active downtown square reminiscent of bustling small-town life complete with local stores, government buildings, churches, museums, eateries, and even a soda fountain—making it particularly attractive as a production site. Though not the first production in Holly Springs, the social climate of *Cookie's Fortune* and attention it gave to the town as a place has given the film a distinct and lasting position in the community. When other large productions have breezed through town, the result on locals seems to be vague memories and relative indifference. When asked about *Cookie's Fortune*, however, everybody has a set of tales to tell which seem to result largely from the social attention paid to the town. As local Holly Springs resident Lucy Carpenter stated, "He just blended in with us. We just felt like we were part of them."[30] Local Mark Millar further defined the *Cookie's Fortune* production against *Heart of Dixie* (Martin Davidson, 1989), another major production that had been in Holly Springs: "The *Heart of Dixie* crew wasn't friendly. There was no interaction with the community. *Heart of Dixie* didn't hold a premiere in Holly Springs. The Altman crew mingled. It was a community-wide thing."[31] Carpenter, Millar, and other locals retain a distinct air of respect for Altman and his production, as opposed to the indifference shown to other productions which have come through the area—the latter treated much more like tourists. It is in part these lasting stories that make *Cookie's Fortune* such an attractive option to highlight the social aspects of Altman's production practices.

Talking with locals reveals the felt place-based attention the Altmans' productions gave to location at the level of both text and production. When asked about *Cookie's Fortune*'s accuracy, locals agree that to some extent the film does represent the town and they are proud of that. As part of Altman's later career, the film focuses on the trials and tribulations of a small Mississippi town after local matriarch Jewel Mae "Cookie" Orcutt (Patricia Neal) dies. The film focuses heavily on the concept of small-town life, moving at an overall slower pace, and with smaller group interactions than is typically found in an Altman film, but arguably very reflective of the general social atmosphere of Holly Springs. Mayor Kelvin Buck gave a good outline of the most popular local response to the film: "the characters have a resemblance to people here. The plot could easily be seen played out in real life in Holly Springs."[32]

Local Mark Millar's experiences with the film point to how the production's use of local resources can add feelings of authenticity through forged connections with the town. Millar's family owned a number of clothing stores in the area which the production ended up using for wardrobe and material, and Millar's wife began catering for dailies and other parties, working closely with Kathryn Reed Altman.[33] Residents all saw some form of their daily lives represented on-screen both thematically and materially, whether in specific content elements, such as the depiction of race relations, the frequency with which characters just "stop by" to say hello, or the general "feel" of the film—taking a slower pace as more representative of small town life. Locals also recognized differences where the "outsider" status of the production is more

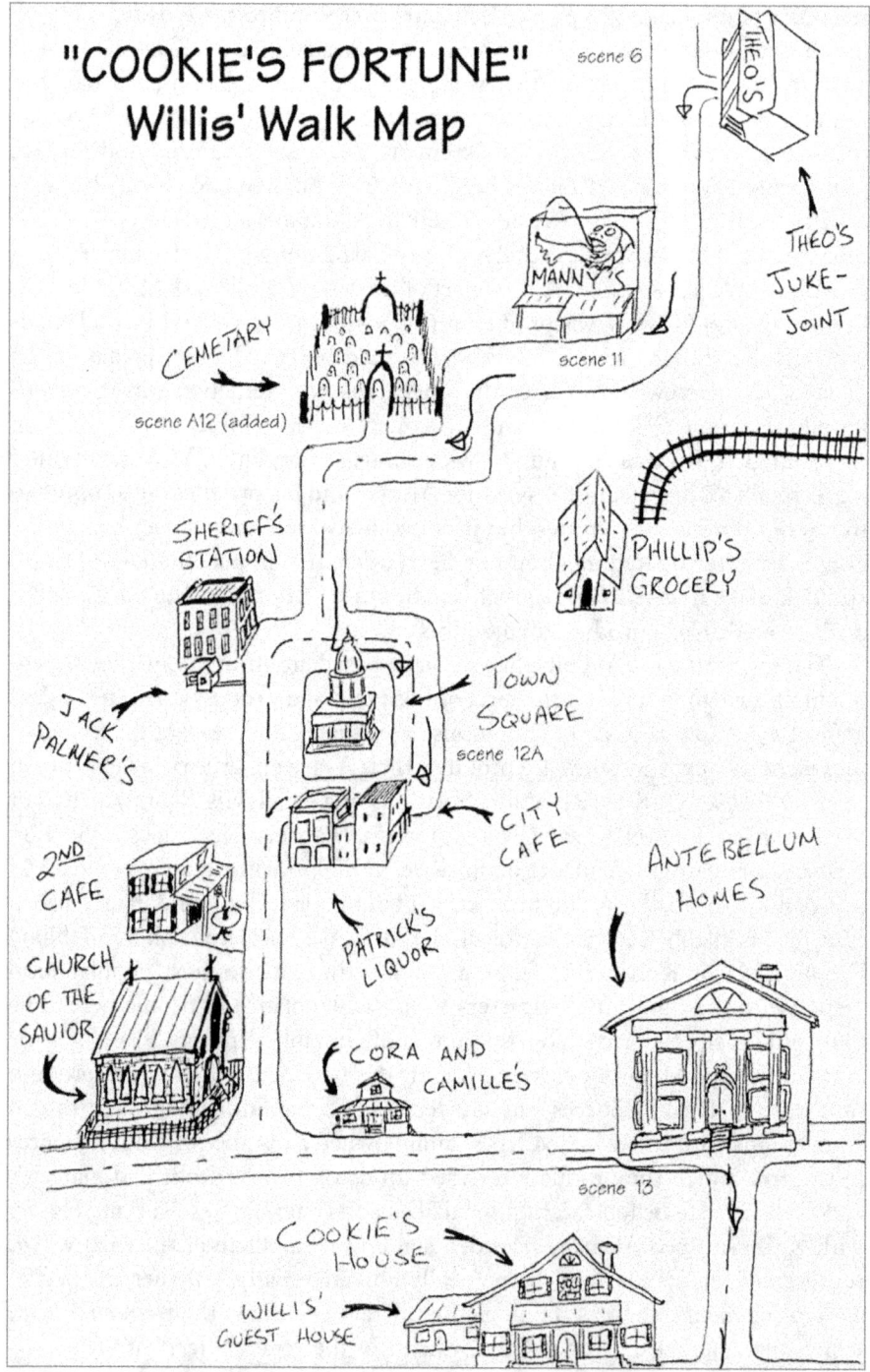

Figure 3.2 A map of the walk through the town of Holly Springs, Mississippi made by Charles S. Dutton as Willis Richland in the opening scenes of *Cookie's Fortune*. Courtesy of Special Collections Research Center, University of Michigan Library.

apparent, such as in scenes where characters make catfish enchiladas—a dish unknown to locals.[34] However, given the retained good will toward the film in the community, locals emphasize positive elements while the negative elements tend to be trivial at best. The *Cookie's Fortune* shoot also provides a clear example of how the Altmans worked in, as well as with, communities—their strategies for connecting with the community were reflective of strategies used to connect the cast and crew to both place and project. Stephen Altman, son and production designer, revealed that Altman took crew accommodations out of the usual hierarchies present in the industry, making the crew feel much more present and important than on standard shoots.

> On *Cookie's Fortune* we were all basically in three motels that were lining the highway, everybody. You know if only the third string grips and people were there then other people are in the second tier, like [for the shoot I'm on] right now where everybody's tiered . . . People get a little weird. With Bob it was like everybody would be in the same boat, he would usually have a big house to have parties at and he would all the time and invite everybody over. It was a pleasant familial feeling working on films with him, everybody was included.[35]

On Altman location shoots, the crew stayed in the same hotel, in the same kind of room, received the same per diem and ate with the cast and personnel, all of which was non-standard in the industry. Producer Matthew Seig recalls hearing from a first-time Altman crew member that he had never before worked on a set where the director and cast ate with the crew.

> He acknowledged that he had never before sat at a table at lunch or dinner with an actor or a producer. That in the work he does it was just the sort of below-the-line crew eating together. This was the first time he'd experienced the director sitting with the crew. It just was a totally different thing. That always happened, I was even shocked to hear that because it's so taken for granted on an Altman shoot that we're all together . . . And that was Bob and Kathryn, they made that happen.[36]

Because of a more inclusive atmosphere during the production, much of the cast and crew felt outside the typical hierarchies regardless of where their names would inevitably appear in the end credits. As an auteur director, Altman's name began to stand in for such practices and made people much more willing to work with him for a reduced pay rate in order to share in the unique environment.

Cookie's Fortune in particular shows Altman's production strategies at work in using local community resources in the form of the production as well. In the staging of *Salomé*, Altman hired a local theater troupe to mount a production of the scenes shown in the final film, allowing the director of the theater troupe control over the theatrical staging as it appears in the final film. Therefore, Altman worked to include a section of the film with a directorial style not his own, embedding both difference and local perspective directly into the larger tapestry. As just a short example from the *Cookie's Fortune* production, it serves to once again show that Altman's productions do not attempt to take over the place as a setting for the narrative. Instead, Altman's productions observe the meeting of different perspectives in order to tell stories. His portrayal of the contradictory nature of place occurs precisely in the lauded formal elements of his films, such as party scenes and overlapping conversations which often highlight characters' conflict in their desires to assert their own perspectives.

The way the *Cookie's Fortune* production blended with the local community in Holly Springs is quite astonishing and rarely seen. It was never accused of being a time when life continued on normally, but the stories surrounding the production are many, and built solidly around a sense of community felt both by the actors and by the locals. The following story from the local paper *The South Reporter* remains a personal favorite which connects these ideas:

> A customer from Red Banks came in the drug store and asked Bob [Lomenick] how everybody liked having the Hollywood stars around. "What's that Chris O'Donnell look like. He's a little short boy, isn't he?" the Red Banks customer asked. "Well somebody saw this guy jogging in Red Banks the other day. We were meetin' down at the BP and decided it must be one of those actors. Nobody jogs around Red Banks. We just don't do that."[37]

The differences between the local world and the production world are stark here; the simple act of jogging stands in as an identifier from another world. The local curiosity of this other world also stands out, but so does a sense of neighborly interest. The story is not intrusive, as stories of Hollywood in neighborhoods often are, and suggests that Hollywood stars felt comfortable enough to engage in everyday routines without a lot of fanfare. I maintain that this level of community between such different worlds is held together by the bonds created through Kathryn Reed Altman's work on the production. Her work clearly had the effect of putting everyone at ease and these effects looped outward even into the local community who had few if any direct ties to the production.

HOME-MADE: CONCLUSION

Kathryn Reed Altman, as an uncredited worker, exemplifies the tendency of collaborators to create an environment conducive to the creativity of a labeled auteur, yet not be considered a creative laborer in their own right. The work she did at the start of the Altmans' career/life together would most likely have fallen under the label of housewife, though her active involvement in these productions also extends well beyond the traditionally regarded limits of that role. In her book *Feeding the Family*, Marjorie L. DeVault refers to the practices surrounding the label of "housework" as "caring work." DeVault specifies that such work is critical in both daily life and exchange value work, yet has traditionally gone largely unnoticed and unheralded:

> Caring work in all its complexity, as activity deeply compelling for those who do it and critically important for group life. Though necessary for maintaining the social world as we have known it, caring has been mostly unpaid work, traditionally undertaken by women, activity whose value is not fully acknowledged even by those who do it.[38]

The term "caring work" gives both a sense of the nature of the labor—supporting/caring for the family/laborer—as well as suggests the overlooked nature of such work by choosing a word with a connotation often antithetical to the accumulation of wealth. Even though Kathryn Reed Altman's work unquestioningly exceeds the standard definition of "housewife" or "caring work," we also cannot ignore these traditional gendered labels, as their connotations and social expectations likely contribute heavily to how her work has been treated and remembered. While Reed Altman's work has not gone completely unacknowledged when taking into account those she worked with, it has certainly not been fully acknowledged when looking at Robert Altman's more public legacy.

DeVault's characterization of housework as central to forming and sustaining group life is also key here because Reed Altman maintained multiple family spheres. She did not simply make a home for her family, but performed those functions while also making sure that familial feeling was a part of the production experience for all those involved. Creating a home environment for the production involved planning event spaces, cooking for large groups of people, and hiring caterers—making her an integral piece of the production schedule. To clarify, by saying she was an integral piece of the production I mean that she was essential, but her work was often expected to fit into the existing schedule. When talking about the *Cookie's Fortune* shoot she told me,

> God I can't tell you how many dinners we had at our house. I was always trying to find somebody within the area that could take a last minute 12 for dinner. I found these two housewives who had a little business on the side doing parties and things. If I gave enough notice they could pull together and I'd help because I knew the whole house.[39]

Those involved in Altman productions credit her with further managing tempers/arguments during filming and performing community outreach. Her ability to manage her labor under the impression of an easy-going, inclusive family-oriented production environment is perhaps the greatest feat of them all.

As an artistic voice, it is certainly still valid to consider an Altman film as a film made by Robert Altman, but what I have shown here reveals that the label "an Altman film" subsumes very distinct production practices that extend well beyond that one figure. In recognizing these practices and largely silent partners our understanding of an Altman film and how it functions becomes much greater. What became clear through personal interviews was that to those who worked on or with Altman films, the most memorable and defining qualities were of the experience of making the film, not necessarily the movie that resulted. It was striking how many interviewees, unprompted, used the term "family" to describe the atmosphere of an Altman set, such as when Matthew Seig said,

> When people talk about the Altman experience or way of doing things, it's the Altman family. Family is often a mom and a dad. Kathryn handled that whole social part of it, made everyone feel welcome, have parties and dinners . . . That was just part of the process.[40]

The welcoming feeling extended even to the people of Holly Springs, who saw *Cookie's Fortune* as a stand-out experience compared to other big productions in the area due to their inclusion as a community. Despite the strong connection between family and work her labor possessed, no one I talked to defined Kathryn Reed Altman as a housewife. They all recognized that the broad-spanning home environment was central to Robert Altman's branded method, and it was a method which she was a full partner in creating. Robert Altman is established as an auteur filmmaker, but his distinctive style of filmmaking required the carefully maintained social atmosphere which Reed Altman monitored, controlled, and maintained. While Altman was making creative, formal choices in filmmaking, the environment for him to most effectively realize these choices was planned, structured, and maintained by Kathryn Reed Altman. Robert Altman made the homes that we all saw on-screen, though Kathryn Reed Altman made the homes that informed those artistic representations.

NOTES

1. Ron Mann (dir.), *Altman* (Epix, 2014), Netflix.
2. Robert Self, *Robert Altman's Subliminal Reality* (Minneapolis, MN: University of Minnesota Press, 2002).

3. Andrew Sarris, *The American Cinema: Directors and Directions, 1929–1968* (New York: Dutton, 1968); François Truffaut, "A certain tendency of the French cinema," in *Auteurs and Authorship*, ed. Keith Barry Grant (Malden, MA: Blackwell, 2008), pp. 9–18.
4. Timothy Corrigan, "The commerce of auteurism," in Virginia Wright Wexman (ed.), *Film and Authorship* (New Brunswick, New York and London: Rutgers University Press, 2003).
5. Michel Foucault, "What is an author?" in *Language, Counter-Memory, Practice*, ed. Donald F. Bouchard, trans. Donald F. Bouchard and Sherry Simon (Ithaca, NY: Cornell University Press, 1977), pp. 123–4.
6. Daniel Herbert and Timothy Corrigan have both also argued for the extra-textual possibilities of Foucault's author-function: Daniel Herbert, "Real monster/fake auteur: Humor, Hollywood, and Herzog in *Incident at Loch Ness*," *Quarterly Review of Film and Video* 26, no. 5 (2009): 353–64; Timothy Corrigan, "Producing Herzog: From a body of images," in Timothy Corrigan (ed.), *The Films of Werner Herzog: Between Mirage and History* (New York: Methuen, 1986), pp. 3–22.
7. See Self (in *Robert Altman's Subliminal Reality*), who studies Altman's films' more art cinema mode of address.
8. Mann (dir.), *Altman*.
9. Alan Rudolph (filmmaker), personal interview with the author, Seattle, WA, 21 March 2014.
10. Mitchell Zuckoff, *Robert Altman: The Oral Biography* (New York: Knopf, 2009), pp. xi–xii.
11. Kathryn Reed Altman (social coordinator), personal interview with the author, New York City, NY, 29 July 2013.
12. Matthew Seig (producer), personal interview with the author, New York City, NY, 1 August 2013.
13. Doreen Massey, *Space, Place, Gender* (Cambridge: Polity, 1994), p. 168.
14. Ibid.
15. Reed Altman, personal interview, 29 July 2013.
16. John Altman (filmmaker), personal interview with the author, Kansas City, MO, 13 October 2013.
17. Patti Broyles Harper (former Kansas City Film Commissioner), personal interview with the author, Lawrence, KS, 13 October 2013.
18. More accurately, I suggested the label "social coordinator" and she agreed with it. Reed Altman, personal interview, 29 July 2013.
19. Ibid.
20. Ibid.
21. "Bob really loved people. It's the old story, when people would say to me, 'Oh it's Bob's birthday, what can I possibly give him?' I'd say, 'give him a party' and that was the happiest thing; he liked it." Ibid.
22. This particular story was about *Nashville*. Ibid.
23. Rudolph, personal interview, 21 March 2014.
24. Zuckoff, *Robert Altman*, p. 263.
25. John Altman, personal interview, 13 October 2013.
26. Zuckoff, *Robert Altman*, p. 216.
27. Stephen Altman (production designer). Phone interview with the author, 13 August 2013.
28. Annette Kuhn, "Structures of patriarchy and capital in the family," in Annette Kuhn and AnnMarie Wolpe (eds), *Feminism and Materialism* (New York: Routledge, 2013), p. 55.
29. Paul Smith, "Domestic labour and Marx's theory of value," in Annette Kuhn and AnnMarie Wolpe, *Feminism and Materialism* (New York: Routledge, 2013), p. 202.
30. Lucy Carpenter (Circuit Court Clerk Marshall County), personal interview with the author, Holly Springs, MS, 25 February 2014.

31. Mark Millar, personal interview with the author, Holly Springs, MS, 25 February 2014.
32. Kelvin Buck (Mayor, Holly Springs, MS), personal interview with the author, Holly Springs, MS, 24 February 2014.
33. The role of local caterers mentioned in: Millar, personal interview, 25 February 2014; Reed Altman, personal interview, 29 July 2013; Linda Jones, "'Caterers to the stars!' Maia and Diane Cook!" *The South Reporter*, 16 July 1998, p. B1.
34. Marie Moore (Holly Springs Film Commissioner), personal interview with the author, Holly Springs, MS, 24 February 2014. This actually came up unprompted in several interviews as the main thing locals did not connect to in the film.
35. Stephen Altman, phone interview, 13 August 2013.
36. Matthew Seig, personal interview, 1 August 2013.
37. Walter Webb, "If you're jogging in Red Banks, you must be a movie star," *The South Reporter*, 4 June 1998, A4.
38. Marjorie L. DeVault, *Feeding the Family* (Chicago and London: University of Chicago Press, 1991), p. 3.
39. Reed Altman, personal interview, 29 July 2013.
40. Matthew Seig, personal interview, 1 August 2013.

CHAPTER 4

A Perfect Couple: The Altman–Rudolph Connection

Richard R. Ness

It was inevitable that when Robert Altman made his first foray into producing the work of another director with Alan Rudolph's *Welcome to L.A.* (1976), critics would make comparisons to his own films, particularly since it was the producer rather than the film's novice director who earned name-above-the-title credit in the publicity material, as well as being the first name to appear on the opening credits. Stanley Kaufmann dismissed the film as "imitation Altman,"[1] while Altman champion Pauline Kael claimed the similarities to *Nashville* were "mortifyingly close to plagiarism" and called Rudolph's effort "an Altman film with all the juice squeezed out,"[2] though critics generally were vague about what they regarded as the similarities between Rudolph's work and that of his mentor, focusing mainly on the multi-character ensemble storyline and the casting of several actors who had appeared in recent Altman films. In addition to acknowledging the multi-character structure and use of members of Altman's stock company in *Welcome to L.A.*, Dan Sallitt, in an unpublished monograph on Rudolph written in 1985, notes,

> Other resemblances between the two filmmakers' styles run a little deeper: the use of the slow zoom as a dramatic device; the frequent play with off-screen dialogue; and, most obviously, the aural density that comes from feeding several microphones into a multitrack sound system.

But, Sallitt adds, "These shared technical interests shouldn't conceal the utter dissimilarity between Altman's artistic temperament and Rudolph's."[3]

While Altman's brief period as a producer for other directors proved largely unsatisfying, his partnership with Rudolph in that capacity extended through four more films over two and a half decades.[4] Despite their close association, which continued throughout Altman's life, Rudolph has often asserted that he and his mentor have different approaches and visions. Interviewed for *Film Comment* at the time *Welcome to L.A.* was released, Rudolph declared,

> There's a certain amount of flattery in being called Bob Altman's protégé, but there's a certain amount of hype in that too. I was me before I met him . . . I believe in his vision, and I also have a different vision of my own.[5]

In his essay "Altman After Hours" for Kathryn Reed Altman and Giulia D'Agnolo Vallan's retrospective text, Rudolph wrote, "One thing was evident from the start. Though proudly, mightily influenced by Robert Altman, my signature was definitely not his. Nor could it be. Nor was it trying. Which was the point."[6] Rather than Rudolph simply being an Altman imitator or following in his mentor's footsteps, a comparison of the work of the two directors reveals that their relationship proved mutually beneficial and how each was able to deal with similar subject matter in his distinctive style.

In general, Altman's approach could be regarded as externalized and observational, while Rudolph's is internalized and introspective. Whereas Altman often set his films in established microcosms (an Army surgical hospital, a mining town in the Pacific Northwest, the country music capital, or a British manor house) and then explored the types of characters who would be found in these locations, Rudolph develops his characters and then creates a universe for them to inhabit. One need only compare Rudolph's sterile, anonymous depiction of the title location in *Welcome to L.A.*, which seems to be inhabited by only a handful of people, with the vibrant if superficial movie capital in Altman's *The Player*, where even the so-called extras are recognizable faces. While many of Altman's films take place in identifiable locations, as indicated in the titles of *Nashville* and *Kansas City*, and make use of recognizable landmarks, such as the Parthenon in the former film, even when Rudolph is shooting in familiar environments he transforms these spaces into his own unique universe (as Peter Rainer notes in his review of *Trouble in Mind* [1985], Rudolph uses the Seattle Space Needle as though it were specially designed for the film).[7]

Even the technical devices Rudolph learned from his work with Altman are, as Sallitt notes, employed for different purposes. For Altman, the visual and aural elements contribute to a realist aesthetic, while Rudolph uses these same techniques to create a stylized, hypnotic, dreamlike atmosphere. Both directors show a preference for a constantly moving camera and slow inward zooms, but Altman incorporates these devices to voyeuristically spy on the people who inhabit his microcosms, often watching them from outside through windows or doors, while Rudolph's more introspective camera seeks to get close to his characters, seemingly in an effort to psychoanalyze them.

Even though both directors earned a reputation for allowing actors to explore and develop their characters, Altman was known for encouraging improvisation on his sets whereas Rudolph, who usually writes as well as directs his films, favors greater fidelity to his scripts.

Although Rudolph initially was regarded as an imitator of Altman, as his directorial career developed his work, rather than merely echoing aspects of Altman's films, actually often anticipated them. This is evident in such thematic concepts as the concern over the interaction of art and commerce in *The Moderns* (1988), which was addressed by Altman two years later in *Vincent & Theo*; the polarized political climate explored in *Return Engagement* (1983) that foreshadows Altman's *Secret Honor* and the *Tanner '88* television series; and the employment of tropes of the noir and thriller genres in *Remember My Name*, *Trouble in Mind*, *Love at Large* (1990), *Mortal Thoughts* (1991), and *Trixie* (2000) that preceded *Kansas City*, *The Gingerbread Man*, and *Gosford Park*.[8] Yet even when dealing with common subject matter, each director approached it in different ways. A more detailed examination of the three issues identified above reveals how each director was able to employ these shared interests to express a personal vision.

ART AND COMMERCE

The ways in which the two filmmakers both converge and diverge becomes evident in comparing *The Moderns*[9] and Altman's *Vincent & Theo*.[10] Though both films deal with the issue of the effect of commerce on art and artists, the focus of each reflects its director's sensibilities. In *Vincent & Theo* Altman takes a largely reverent approach to his subject, providing a portrait of Vincent van Gogh as an undeniably brilliant if troubled artist who, like many of Altman's characters, is driven by a need to create but whose work went unappreciated in his time by all but his sympathetic sibling. While exploring van Gogh's human frailties, Altman respects his status as an artist and reserves his contempt for the art dealers and collectors who failed to recognize his talents. By contrast, in *The Moderns* Rudolph shatters the myths of the revered historical figures who inhabit the Paris of the 1920s (even demythologizing the city itself by shooting the film in Montreal and making use of stylized sets), depicting Ernest Hemingway (who to the American tourists is interchangeable with F. Scott Fitzgerald) as a somewhat uncertain scribe who has difficulty getting his plots and epigrams right, while Gertrude Stein is portrayed as an autocrat dispensing judgments from her salon sanctuary and authoritatively dismissing the thirty-three-year-old protagonist Nick Hart with finality because "American artists are 26 this year." Rather than focusing on the characters audiences would expect a film set in 1920s Paris to be about, Rudolph instead

Figure 4.1 (From left) Actors Tim Roth and Paul Rhys, cinematographer Jean Lépine, and Robert Altman on the set of *Vincent & Theo*. Courtesy of Special Collections Research Center, University of Michigan Library.

deals with those who are on the periphery of, but also profit from, this inner circle, including art forger Hart, the critic Oiseau, collectors Nathalie de Ville and Bertram Stone, and art dealer Libby Valentin. Yet, like Altman, Rudolph has respect for the artistic process, and his real targets are those who exploit or fail to recognize genuine talent, epitomized by the critic in the Museum of Modern Art at the end of the film who pontificates on the unique virtues of Hart's forgeries, believing them to be the real works.[11] Rudolph has indicated that the real myth of Paris in the 1920s was that the actual breakthroughs in what came to be regarded as modern art had occurred a few decades earlier but the 1920s were when these works became popular with Americans and the money started coming in.

The commercialization of art is a theme that Altman would address more explicitly in the opening of *Vincent & Theo*, which shows van Gogh's "Vase with Fifteen Sunflowers" being auctioned at Christie's in 1987 and as the voice-over bidding continues, eventually getting up to more than 22 million dollars, Altman flashes back to the impoverished and emaciated Vincent in his meager room. Lines such as Theo's uncle commenting, when visiting him at the gallery where he works, "It doesn't matter if the art is good as long as it sells," or Theo's description of his roommate, "He's studying the art of business and I'm studying the business of art," could easily have come out of Rudolph's film, and both filmmakers express contempt for those who place financial over artistic accomplishments. Rich entrepreneur Stone in Rudolph's film, who regards art as something to be possessed more than appreciated and declares, "This is art because I paid hard cash for it," has his counterpart in the doctor in *Vincent & Theo*, who claims to own several paintings by all of the major artists but instead of putting them on display keeps them in a vault.

The distinction between Altman's realist and Rudolph's formalist aesthetics is evident in the visual design of each film. While Altman's cinematographer Jean Lépine makes use of hues that evoke van Gogh's work, the production design provides a believable evocation of the period, whereas Rudolph's film presents a stylized Paris, particularly in a scene in which Hart and Natalie drive through the city while through the oval window behind them are seen not the expected street scenes but images from abstract paintings, and in Stone's suicide as he falls backwards into the Seine next to a blatantly artificial and scaled down replica of the Eiffel Tower. In keeping with his subject matter, Altman makes use throughout *Vincent & Theo* of mirror shots and frames within frames, as well as his familiar device of viewing his characters from the outside, as evidenced in the scene in which Vincent first meets Paul Gauguin, which Altman shoots through the window of a studio, with a woman at one point holding up an empty frame in front of Vincent's face. Rudolph makes use of a more open, less formal compositional style, though he also occasionally employs the frame within a frame approach, as in a shot of Hart in bed in his studio surrounded by both his forgeries and the original works he has copied.[12]

A key scene in both productions involves the destruction of works of art, though the motives of the perpetrators are different. In *Vincent & Theo*, Altman's swinging camera captures van Gogh's compulsive madness as the painter suddenly and violently destroys one of his canvases while standing in a windswept field of bright yellow sunflowers, seemingly because he is unable to get it to come out right. In the most audacious scene in *The Moderns*, Stone mutilates and burns a Matisse, a Modigliani, and a Cezanne, believing they are the forgeries painted by Hart and therefore have no monetary value (not knowing that he has inadvertently obtained the originals Natalie gave Hart to copy). Both scenes are in essence acts of madness, but for Altman the focus is on the artist and the obsessive drive of the creative process itself, while for Rudolph the real madness belongs to those who see art only in terms of its monetary value.

In his analysis of this moment in *The Moderns* in the *Senses of Cinema* online journal, Steven Rybin observes that it is the kind of scene that might appear in an Altman film, but also calls it "among the most deeply resonant in Rudolph's career, particularly in the way it asks us to think through the relative originality of Rudolph's filmmaking." In articulating the distinction in the approaches of the two directors, Rybin notes:

> Rudolph's approach transcends mere imitation of a master . . . Rudolph begins with details rather than whole pictures: as the camera tracks backward . . . different characters are progressively introduced without the sequence ever settling into a shot that gathers all of the psychological and spatial interest into one image. The result is an accumulation of details that, despite the film's ostensible depiction of a society, never coalesces into the collective picture that is often the point of departure or occasional resting point in Altman's films.[13]

Though both *Vincent & Theo* and *The Moderns* are presented as period pieces, it is not difficult to see these films as statements on the way creative people are treated by those with a financial interest in their work. As Vincent observes in defense of artists,

> There's no one there to help you. The families are all terrified. The politicians, they don't give a shit. The art dealers are simply out for what they can get. The only people who care about artists, the only people who really care about art are the artists themselves.

This may be the most direct comment in any Altman film on the director's attitude toward his own work. One can also sense both filmmakers' frustration with the studio system in Theo's declaration, "It's so aggravating working for people who only care about money." The final satiric comment in *The Moderns* is that Hart is planning to accompany Oiseau to Hollywood where the critic contends all the real art is now being produced. This conclusion not only sets up the critique of commercialism in art addressed in *Vincent & Theo* two years later, but also the milieu of Altman's next film, *The Player*, which takes place in a Hollywood where everyone is more concerned with making deals than with making art.[14] It is fitting that Rudolph himself appears in *The Player*'s famous opening tracking shot as one of the writers making a pitch to producer Griffin Mill and also appropriate that the pitch is for a "political thriller," acknowledging both a subject and a genre with which the two filmmakers will be concerned in the 1980s and '90s.

POLITICAL MYTHS

Although political elements figure in a number of Altman's earlier films, most prominently Hal Philip Walker's platform and entourage in *Nashville* and the competing candidates for president of the national wellness organization in

HealtH, these were generally presented more as satirical than serious political statements. The 1980s saw a shift in this approach, with two of Altman's most successful projects of the period, his film adaptation of Donald Freed and Arnold M. Stone's one-man monologue *Secret Honor* (subtitled "A Political Myth") and the HBO television series *Tanner '88*, addressing the American political climate directly, while combining aspects of fact and fiction and incorporating existing political figures. It seems not coincidental that both of these productions were preceded by Rudolph's vastly underrated documentary *Return Engagement* about the debates between self-professed cheerleader for the youth movement Timothy Leary and button-down representative of the Nixonian conservative era G. Gordon Liddy, which remains Rudolph's only venture into non-fiction production.

While the documentary format of *Return Engagement* would seem closer to the realist aesthetic of Altman's films than the more stylized approach of most of Rudolph's work, it is not as much of an anomaly as it might appear on the surface. The personas of Liddy and Leary have a kind of heightened reality, particularly in their onstage debates, that make them appropriate subjects for the director and allow him to address issues already evident in his script for *Buffalo Bill and the Indians*, the notion of politics as a form of show business (ideology packaged as entertainment) and the disparity between the public and private images of political figures. Offstage, through his surrogate interviewer Carole Hemingway, Rudolph keeps veering away from the political to the personal, enabling him to explore his fascination with the nature of romantic relationships, particularly in the scenes in which the wives of the two debaters are prominently featured. Ultimately, Leary and Liddy emerge as another of the director's dysfunctional duos, an idea summed up by a journalist near the end of the film who describes them as acting like an old married couple. Though, as in *The Moderns, Mrs. Parker and the Vicious Circle*, and the script for *Buffalo Bill*, Rudolph seeks to deconstruct the mythic nature of his central characters, he has designed the film to create the appearance of a careful balancing act, seemingly not taking sides (though one senses at times that he would like to) and allowing each of the debaters equal time to present his position (indicative of Rudolph's neutral approach is a scene in which Liddy's wife is clearly shown to have a black eye but the director does not dwell or comment on it, allowing viewers to draw their own conclusions about how it happened).

As with Rudolph's solo venture into the documentary format, the deliberately minimalist, artificial nature of filming a one-person stage production appears at odds with Altman's usual broader expansive ensemble work. But Freed and Stone's Nixon provides a fitting addition to Altman's gallery of flawed protagonists (McCabe, Philip Marlowe, Buffalo Bill, Griffin Mill) who are incapable of recognizing their weaknesses. Reinforcing a claim Altman makes in the commentary track on the DVD of *Kansas City* that he avoids asserting his own personality into the political aspects of his films,[15] Altman maintains an observational position toward his subject, voyeuristically watching in fascination as the former president makes his case. The surveillance monitors in Nixon's study take on the function of windows and mirrors in other Altman films, although he manages to work in one direct window shot when he focuses on Nixon's reflection as the former commander-in-chief is recreating his acceptance speech for his party's presidential nomination. Though Altman sets a satirical tone at the outset of *Secret Honor*, with Nixon fumbling in his efforts to get a tape recorder to work, as the film goes on a more nuanced perception of the former president emerges, a concept established in the opening claim that it was made "in an attempt to understand." Nixon elicits moments of empathy as he laments his efforts to earn the admiration of his mother, and by the end he has almost made a convincing argument that he needed to publicly disgrace his office with the Watergate crimes in order to prevent the powerful Bohemian Grove cabal from using him to escalate the war in Vietnam. One can even sense that Altman, who ended up making the film with graduate students at the University of Michigan when other attempts at funding fell through, feels a certain affinity with the former president in the last shot, as Nixon's final defiant cry of "Fuck 'em" is reproduced multiple times on the monitors. Discussing Altman's attitude toward the disgraced former president, Philip Baker Hall observed,

> Bob had a complicated perspective on Nixon. In certain ways I think he admired Nixon. I think he admired Nixon's cleverness, his ingenuity, his ability to dance around the truth and to play with the facts. In other ways, he thought he was a menace, a dangerous person to the Republic.[16]

Return Engagement and *Secret Honor* both emphasize the concept of politics as performance. Liddy and Leary literally have a stage on which to present their act and an audience to play to, with Liddy maintaining the stoic manner of a member of a debate team and Leary adopting the style of a stand-up comedian, while Nixon makes his case to the unseen "American jury," and shots of him on the surveillance camera monitors reinforce the distinction between the private Nixon we are seeing and the public image he fostered in the media as one of the first politicians of the television age (as well as reminding viewers of the obsession with surveillance that proved to be the former president's downfall). Altman further emphasizes the performance aspect by portraying Nixon as a Shakespearean figure who compares himself to Hamlet, and, like Buffalo Bill, indulges in a drunken rant alone in his study, railing against those he feels used or betrayed him (the Reed Altman and Vallan text describing him as "a tragicomic Hamlet,"[17] though he seems more akin to his namesake Richard III and Altman in interviews equated him with Willy Loman in Arthur Miller's *Death of a Salesman*).

Liddy and Leary have honed their act to the point where the debate scenes appear as much like carefully crafted performances as Philip Baker Hall's Nixon, and as they play to their supporters they seem to be reinforcing Rudolph's declaration in the *Buffalo Bill* script that "Truth is whatever gets the most applause." But the real truth that emerges occurs in the moments when Rudolph is able to catch these performers off guard, as when Liddy's usually silent wife suddenly takes the initiative to express her views on women's liberation, or when Leary is confronted during a Q and A session by a blind audience member who claims his condition was the result of being shot in the face by assailants tripping on acid.

While each film represents its director's personal preoccupations, what emerges in both is a sense of an increasingly divided political climate. *Return Engagement* is particularly prescient in its depiction of the polarized nature of the American political scene and perhaps is even more relevant in the age of Trump than in the Reagan era in which it was made. The shots of Liddy's supporters outside the auditorium holding their hands over burning candles, in homage to their hero's claim that he could do this without letting the pain bother him, serve as forerunners of the followers that now gather in red MAGA hats at Trump rallies. If the one-man format of *Secret Honor* does not allow for as direct a comment on political polarization as the Liddy–Leary positions in *Return Engagement*, the concept is suggested through Nixon's constant (and inadequate) comparisons of himself and his family to the Kennedys. Altman would address the divisive political climate more directly in the *Tanner '88* series, which again echoed *Return Engagement* in its seemingly spontaneous documentary style and depiction of the media circus that forms around, and is often manufactured by, political figures. While Leary and Liddy may have oversimplified and packaged their polarized political postures into commodities that can be sold as entertainment, Rudolph suggests that the positions themselves are worth debating by ending the film with a scene showing students to whom each of them had spoken earlier continuing to argue about the concepts they presented. Nearly forty years after Rudolph's and Altman's films were released, the divisions created by the extreme political positions they present seem even more evident in American society.

FILM NOIR AND THE TRADITIONS OF GENRE

Despite both Altman and Rudolph often being described as maverick or independent filmmakers (terms which themselves are as much about marketing as about actual practice) and their attacks in interviews on the conglomerate-controlled state of the modern movie industry, most evident on-screen in *The Player*, they share an appreciation and even reverence for the films of

Hollywood's past and an interest in playing with familiar genre patterns and tropes. Rudolph comes by this naturally, having grown up in Hollywood as the son of Oscar Rudolph, an actor and later director whose career began in the silent era, while Altman served a brief stint in the industry in the waning days of the studio system, which included appearing as an extra in *The Secret Life of Walter Mitty* (Norman Z. McLeod, 1947) and contributing the story for the noir drama *Bodyguard* (Richard Fleischer, 1948).

Nearly all of Altman's films include intertextual references to classic films, whether overt (such as the ruby red slippers found on the body of Margaret Hamilton in *Brewster McCloud*, the recreation of the Sophia Loren–Marcello Mastroianni striptease from *Yesterday, Today, and Tomorrow* [Vittorio De Sica, 1963] in *Prêt-à-Porter*, and the references to Charlie Chan films and Ivor Novello's work in *Gosford Park*) or suggested (the final shootout in *McCabe & Mrs. Miller* that recalls the climax of *High Noon* [Fred Zinnemann, 1952] but in a notably different setting). Altman employs these referential gestures as indicators of the pervasiveness of the cinema in our lives (a concept most obviously addressed in *The Player*) and the viewer's shared awareness of our collective cinematic past. Rudolph only occasionally makes use of direct intertextual references (such as the one-sheets for classic noir films that are a major element of the *mise-en-scène* of Pearl's apartment in *Choose Me* [1984] and anticipate the posters that adorn the studio offices in *The Player*, or the opening scene of Mike watching Alfred Hitchcock's *Notorious* [1946] in a theater in *Made in Heaven* [1987]), preferring instead to recapture the general ambiance rather than the specific details of classic films.[18] But his admiration for past Hollywood productions and genres is evident in the manner in which he often evokes memories of other films without specifically acknowledging them, including the echoes of *Strangers on a Train* (Hitchcock, 1951) in the murder at a carnival in *Mortal Thoughts*, the shot of Doc's second wife tossing him out along with his golf clubs in *Songwriter* (1985) that recreates Tracy's eviction of Dexter in *The Philadelphia Story* (George Cukor, 1940), the final shot of Eve and Mickey on the bus in *Choose Me* that recalls not only a major motif in *It Happened One Night* (Frank Capra, 1934) but the ambiguous ending of *The Graduate* (Mike Nichols, 1967), and even the parallels to *Blade Runner* (Ridley Scott, 1982) in the concluding scene of *Trouble in Mind*. As Roger Ebert notes in his review of the latter film, it is "a movie that takes place within our memories of the movies," and that "the characters and the mysteries and especially the doomed romances are all generated by old films."[19]

Over the course of his career Altman worked in nearly every kind of genre while demonstrating an ability to adapt the conventions of these formulas to his own personal vision, such as staging the final showdown in *McCabe & Mrs. Miller* during a snowstorm, providing a laconic treatment of Philip Marlowe in *The Long Goodbye*, or refashioning a traditional Agatha Christie type murder mystery in *Gosford Park* into an examination of the class system that becomes at least as important as the solution to the crime.[20] Rudolph has taken this tendency a step further by mixing elements of genre formulas, often in unexpected ways. In *Made in Heaven*, for example, within the framework of the kind of afterlife romances popular in the 1940s Rudolph provides a lengthy interlude involving the recording of an album (allowing the director to continue his fascination with musicians and the process of musical creation that was an aspect of his work as early as his debut film *Premonition* [1972] and is a prominent feature of *Welcome to L.A.*, *Roadie* [1980], and *Songwriter*). In several of his films, including *Choose Me*, *Trouble in Mind*, *Love at Large*, and *Trixie*, his characters feel like they should be in a romantic comedy but have somehow wandered into the dangerous urban landscape of a noir film. As Ebert observes in his review of *Trixie*, "Rudolph's characters exist at an angle from the reel world; when he works in a genre, he likes to avoid the genre's conventions, which sort of defeats its own purpose. With most genre movies we know what's going to happen next but don't care. With Rudolph, we care what's going to happen next but don't know."[21]

A comparison of *Trouble in Mind* and *Kansas City* is particularly illustrative of the way each director both appropriates and subverts genre conventions, as well as their differences in approach with regard to aspects of setting, characterization, and visual style. Both films are essentially crime stories that draw

Figure 4.2 Robert Altman and Jennifer Jason Leigh as Blondie on the set of *Kansas City*. Courtesy of Special Collections Research Center, University of Michigan Library.

on the archetypes and tropes of film noir and take place in urban landscapes beset by corruption, but Rudolph's Rain City, though clearly shot in Seattle, seems to exist in no definable period, combining a vaguely futuristic atmosphere with cars and costumes that appear to come from past eras, while Altman's *Kansas City* remains firmly rooted in the title location of his childhood, offering a loving recreation of the period and particularly the jazz clubs the director frequented in his youth. Structurally, both films set up a traditional noir plot, but then incorporate other elements that vie for attention. *Trouble in Mind* begins with the release of ex-cop John "Hawk" Hawkins from prison after serving time for killing a gangster to protect his former lover Wanda. The crime aspects of the story compete with Rudolph's usual romantic concerns, as Hawk tries to rekindle his relationship with Wanda while also becoming involved with the innocent Georgia, whose husband Coop is being drawn into the criminal underworld. *Kansas City* also establishes a noir plot involving the kidnapping of a politician's wife by would-be femme fatale Blondie, whose lover Johnny is being held in a jazz club run by Seldom Seen after committing a robbery in blackface. The setting of the Hey Hey Club provides Altman's justification for periodically cutting away from the crime plot to the jazz performances, particularly the recreations of the cutting contests between musicians.[22] In many ways *Kansas City* can be seen as a variation on *Trouble in Mind*, with both films involving two contrasting couples, one of which consists of a woman married to an unreliable husband with criminal tendencies, as well as a gangster who seems to hold the real power in the city, and with Altman substituting jazz performances for the romantic moments in Rudolph's film. Each film ends with the expected burst of violence, but in neither case is this presented in the manner of traditional noir movies.

Rudolph establishes his characters as archetypes, as indicated in the names of the two male leads, cop Hawk, who as the ending songs tells us, wants his "freedom to fly," and family man-turned-crook Coop, who initially feels trapped by his dead-end job, his marriage, and his dire financial situation. The two female characters also are presented as familiar contrasting types, tough dark-haired Wanda and innocent blonde Georgia. Yet, as the film goes on, Hawk's and Wanda's vulnerabilities begin to show in their interactions with Georgia (the one character who undergoes the least change and retains her innocent outlook), while a running gag has Coop altering his appearance in increasingly outlandish ways until he looks more like a member of a glitter rock band than a small-time hood. Altman also sets up a familiar noir archetype, the femme fatale, but then reveals that seemingly ruthless kidnapper Blondie O'Hara actually has modeled her tough gal persona on characters she has seen in the movies. In another example of Altman making use of movie references, Blondie is particularly enamored of Jean Harlow, whose look she tries to emulate, and at one point she and her kidnap victim Carolyn Stilton hide out in a theater showing Harlow's *Hold Your Man* (Sam Wood, 1933). The willingness of each director to defy genre conventions is most evident in the casting of the main gangster role in each film. For Rain City's Hilly Blue Rudolph cast 300-pound transvestite Divine (in one of his few appearances in male garb) as a kind of effeminate Sydney Greenstreet, while in *Kansas City* Seldom Seen is played by Harry Belafonte in an atypical negative characterization that the singer-actor initially told Altman he did not think he could play.

Visually, Rudolph captures a noir look for his film from the opening shot of Hawk being released from a shadow-infused prison and an unseen door opening to light his face, but manages to combine this with the dreamlike neon palette that has become his trademark, causing Peter Rainer to comment that "no one has ever reworked the genre the way Rudolph has . . . He's taken the genre's inherent visual elegance and brought it into the realm of abstract art. He's given film noir a modernist, out-of-the-mainstream flavoring."[23] In keeping with the differences in the two directors' styles, Altman provides a less stylized look for *Kansas City*, opting for a nostalgic ambience, though he acknowledged the film's noir tradition in his observation on the DVD commentary that he used muted Technicolor to create a kind of black and white look.[24]

Both films climax with scenes of violence, though, as noted earlier, in neither does this play out in the manner of traditional noir or gangster films. At the end of Altman's film the two female leads reverse roles. A badly wounded Johnny returns to his devoted Blondie (who has finally lived up to her name and realized her Harlow fantasy by dying her hair platinum blonde, equating her with the innocent Georgia in Rudolph's film), but as she breaks down while trying to hold in his guts and stop the bleeding Carolyn suddenly takes on the role of femme fatale and shoots Blondie in the head (though Altman refers to this on the commentary track as a mercy killing), then coolly walks out into the breaking dawn to reunite with her waiting husband, while Altman cuts to the Hey Hey Club, where Seldom Seen is counting his money as the jam session continues into the morning hours. Rudolph's conclusion is more extreme, reducing the usual climactic shootout to absurdist farce, as Hawk's shooting of Hilly during a party at the gangster's mansion sets off a chaotic gun battle in which all the guests seem to be packing heat but none of them know how to use these weapons and began firing wildly and randomly at each other, while Coop walks calmly through the melee unscathed. Whereas Altman presents violence realistically as an inevitable aspect of human existence, Rudolph employs it as further evidence in support of his absurdist worldview.

CONCLUSION: THE REALIST AND THE ROMANTIC

In their choice of subject matter and similar interests in art, politics, and the traditions of classic Hollywood, Robert Altman and Alan Rudolph can be seen as two sides of the same coin (even to the inversion of their initials), but as the above comparisons indicate, even when their films have similarities in subject matter, structure, and characterization, each director employs these elements for different purposes. If Altman occasionally allows the inhabitants of his films transcendent moments of romantic expression while working within a realist framework, Rudolph remains a romantic whose characters at times have to confront the limitations of reality. Although it may be an oversimplification to equate their differing approaches with the debates that have existed since the beginning of cinema about realist vs. formalist aesthetics, the techniques that Altman developed in his early films, such as his use of multi-channel soundtracks, were intended to make films seem more like real life, whereas Rudolph's introduction of stylized elements and willingness to defy cinematic conventions and expectations (as in the moment when Dr. Nancy Love suddenly appears behind Eve while they are having a phone conversation, even though it has been established that Nancy is on the air at her radio station) are designed to make real life seem more like the artificial reality of the movies.

If an analysis of Rudolph's films in relation to Altman's indicates what Rudolph learned during his apprenticeship with his mentor, they also demonstrate his own emerging sensibility. As Ignatiy Vishnevetsky, in an article for the *AV Club* website states,

> In his own work, Rudolph took the basics of Altman's heightened realism—the ensemble casts, the overlapping sound design, the zooms—and used them to create alternate realities of atmosphere, glister, and visual rhyme that owed more to the roundelays of Max Ophüls and the glow of classic Hollywood,[25]

while Ebert noted, following the release of *Choose Me* and *Trouble in Mind*, that Rudolph was "creating a visual world as distinctive as Fellini's and as cheerful as Edward Hopper's."[26] Even in *Mrs. Parker and the Vicious Circle*, which with its large-scale ensemble and widescreen composition would seem to be the most Altmanesque of the Rudolph films Altman produced, Rudolph's reduction of this broad canvas to his favorite device of the romantic triangle and his deflating of the myth of the Algonquin Round Table are indicative of his own vision.[27] While the impact of Altman on cinema and later filmmakers has been widely acknowledged, aspects of Rudolph's work are also evident in a number of films of the last few decades, particularly his approach to the use of music, his heightened romanticism and incorporation of deliberately artificial stylized effects, and his willingness to defy expected cinematic conventions.[28] As Rybin notes, "While Altman is frequently mentioned as an important influence on Paul Thomas Anderson, the more earnestly romantic shades of Anderson's sensibility are straight from Rudolph."[29] If it is safe to say that Altman, in his roles as producer, mentor, and friend, was tremendously beneficial in encouraging and fostering Rudolph's directorial career, it is also evident in comparing the work of the two directors that Altman's later films demonstrated the benefits of their relationship. Although Altman in his autumnal period continued to paint in broad strokes on large canvases, while Rudolph concentrated on intimate detail in his work, each of them contributed to the vision of the other, and it is likely that their films would have been significantly different without this association.

NOTES

1. Stanley Kauffmann, *Before My Eyes: Film Criticism and Comment* (New York: Da Capo Press, 1980), p. 286.
2. Pauline Kael, *When the Lights Go Down* (New York: Holt, Rinehart and Winston, 1980), p. 284.
3. Dan Sallitt, "Thanks for the use of the hall," 19 August 2016. Available at <http://sallitt.blogspot.com/2016/08/alan-rudolph-1985.html> (last accessed 12 June 2020).
4. Altman's difficulties as producer for Robert Benton's *The Late Show* (1977) and Robert M. Young's *Rich Kids* (1979) are described in Robert Altman, *Altman on Altman*, ed. David Thompson (London: Faber and Faber, 2005), p. 99. Despite the problems with *The Late Show*, which underwent extensive re-editing after a disastrous initial screening, and the arguments between director and producer, Benton credits Altman with teaching him how to be a director and states, "I owe him more of a debt than any other filmmaker I can think of. If the movie is good, it's because of him" (quoted in Mitchell Zuckoff, *Robert Altman: The Oral Biography*, New York: Alfred A. Knopf, 2009, p. 317).
5. "Disneyland by night," *Film Comment*, January–February 1977, p. 13.
6. Alan Rudolph, "Altman after hours," in Kathryn Reed Altman and Giulia D'Agnolo Vallan (eds), *Altman* (New York: Abrams, 2014), p. 137.
7. Peter Rainer, *Rainer on Film* (Solana Beach, CA: Santa Monica Press, 2013), p. 57.
8. In addition to their mutual interest in certain subject matter, the films of the two directors often demonstrate narrative and structural similarities. Even the shaggy, freewheeling comic atmosphere of Rudolph's *Roadie* anticipates Altman's *O. C. and Stiggs* (1985), with the heroine's obsessive pursuit of Alice Cooper in the earlier film echoed in the determination of the title heroes of Altman's film to attend a King Sunny Ade concert. And while Altman's swan song, *A Prairie Home Companion*, invites obvious comparisons to *Nashville*, it also has parallels to Rudolph's *Songwriter*, not only in its use of country-folk performers but in its depiction of the crippling corporate control of the entertainment business.
9. Although released in 1988, *The Moderns* is a film that Rudolph had been attempting to make for more than a decade, and following the death of co-writer Jon Bradshaw he felt compelled to complete it.
10. For purposes of this essay I am considering both Altman's original four-part television production and the pared down theatrical release.
11. It is worth noting here that both filmmakers were experienced painters.
12. Interestingly, in both Rudolph's film and in Altman's theatrical cut of *Vincent & Theo* these scenes occur at about the fifty-five-minute mark.
13. Steven Rybin, "Rudolph, Alan: great directors," *Senses of Cinema*, August 2016. Available at <https://www.sensesofcinema.com/2016/great-directors/alan-rudolph> (last accessed 8 September 2020).

14. It is likely that the conflict between art and commerce would have been explored further by Altman if he had been able to complete his proposed film *Paint*, which centered on the contemporary art scene.
15. Robert Altman, "Commentary," *Kansas City*, DVD, directed by Robert Altman (Burbank: New Line Home Entertainment, 2005).
16. Mitchell Zuckoff, *Robert Altman: The Oral Biography* (New York: Alfred A. Knopf, 2009), pp. 386–7.
17. Altman and Vallan, *Altman*, p. 176.
18. In this regard Rudolph has similarities to, and indeed may have influenced, Wong Kar-Wai, who began his directing career a few years after the release of *Choose Me* and *Trouble in Mind*.
19. Roger Ebert, *Roger Ebert's Movie Home Companion*, 1990 edition (Kansas City: Andrews and McMeel, 1989), p. 784.
20. For a detailed examination of Altman's treatment of genre in his early films see Norman Kagan, *American Skeptic: Robert Altman's Genre-Commentary Films* (Ann Arbor: Pierian Press, 1982).
21. Roger Ebert, "Trixie," *Chicago Sun-Times*, 14 July 2000.
22. Although in these scenes Altman wanted to recreate the atmosphere of the clubs he frequented in his youth, the increasing emphasis on music in his later films again suggests the influence of Rudolph, and Altman even employed Rudolph's most frequent musical collaborator, jazz musician and composer Mark Isham, on the scores for *Short Cuts* and *The Gingerbread Man*.
23. Rainer, *Rainer on Film*, p. 57.
24. Altman, "Commentary," *Kansas City*, DVD.
25. Ignatiy Vishnevetsky, "The rainy, smoky, lovesick world of Alan Rudolph, the last of the romantics," film.avclub.com, 27 April 2018. Available at <https://film.avclub.com/the-rainy-smoky-lovesick-world-of-alan-rudolph-the-l-1825590203> (last accessed 29 March 2020).
26. Ebert, *Roger Ebert's Movie Home Companion*, p. 784.
27. This is one of only two films Rudolph shot in a 2.35:1 aspect ratio, the other being *Investigating Sex* (2001).
28. See, for example, Peter F. Parshall, *Altman and After* (Lanham, MD: Scarecrow Press, 2012).
29. Rybin, "Rudolph, Alan: great directors," *Senses of Cinema*.

CHAPTER 5

Unmade Altman: What the Archive Tells Us

Philip Hallman

Nestled among the nearly 700 boxes that comprise the massive Robert Altman Papers, part of the Screen Arts Mavericks & Makers Collection at the Special Collections Research Center, University of Michigan Library, is the subsection known as "Unfinished or Suspended Projects (1960–2000s)". Here are boxes filled with documents that help push the boundaries of film industry studies while broadening the methods of auteurism to include unmade work and to acknowledge the contributions of producers, screenwriters, and actors in the production process. An examination of Robert Altman's approximately eighty unfinished projects is especially helpful in understanding his authorship, as his production method typically featured several overlapping projects and multiple collaborators, presented in alternating non-linear sequence with movement between and among them. Just as he is comfortable juggling multiple narratives within his films, Altman is equally comfortable juggling multiple potential projects. David Levy, a longtime associate and friend of Altman and producer on several projects including *Gosford Park*, confirmed this to me during numerous conversations. "Bob would often say his approach to work is like making pommes frites," Levy said. "Whichever French fry rose to the top first is the one we made next."[1]

As the curator for the University of Michigan's Screen Arts Mavericks & Makers Collection, I have never received reference inquiries about Altman's unproduced projects in nearly a decade's work. But it makes sense, doesn't it? Why would people ask about movies that were never made? These are, after all, movies with unfamiliar storylines starring actors who committed to them but never actually performed any scenes for them. People want to discuss what they can see. What questions and concerns come up for a project whose production history lies within the confines of an archival box? How can an exploration of unproduced projects—a frequently unrecognized tier in a filmmaker's career—add to our understanding of their authorship and production practices?

Unfinished works are not dismissed in other art forms. In music, for instance, they are performed regularly; in the art world, they are displayed in exhibitions; in the literary world, they are sought out for publication; in architecture, blueprints for unrealized buildings are exalted. In the film world, however, unfinished works have been more or less entirely ignored, except by biographers, who often use them to reach different kinds of conclusions than I propose here.[2] Filmmaking is a marathon and not a sprint, thus it is the nature of the industry to create work that doesn't make it to the finish line. To me, it seems shortsighted to disregard work that never went into the final phase of production—shooting before the camera—particularly since evidence of other stages of production development are available and viewable in archives. Unfinished projects allow us to see starts and stops in the artist's thinking and see at first hand how they contend with the creative process; to fill time gaps between finished projects; to understand the mechanisms of the industry; to comprehend how the artist dealt with rejection or, to some degree, failure; and ultimately to recognize the work that was completed even if an audience never viewed it.

Since 2013, my colleague Matthew Solomon and I have co-taught a research seminar in which both undergraduate and graduate students learn methods of primary-source archival research through a semester-long "deep dive" into the Maverick collections resulting in a student-curated physical and/or online exhibition. We have taken the approach that the archive drives the scholarship and not the other way around. Too often scholars come to an archive with the intention of verifying an idea they think is genuine. While their insight into the artist's creative process may indeed be valid, it does not mean that it is "provable" by finding a document within the collection that supports their thesis. Instead of the plow before the ox approach scholars sometimes take, we insist that the students find documents within the archives first, from among the thousands of letters, memos, script drafts, revisions and notes, photographs, personal objects like diary entries, membership cards, and daily planners and then explore the meaning behind them before privileging a prescribed thesis. We want them to show us something we don't already know. Since they are newcomers to the archival research process, this approach leads them to work at a more micro level. It forces them to rely on their own insights and observations. It is a classic example of less truly being more. But ultimately it empowers them to create original ideas they can claim as their own rather than try to do what is commonly associated with higher learning in the humanities: support or refute the published work of past and present scholars.

This essay will examine three of the projects Altman considered making during the last chapter of his career, a period when he had an overabundance of choices: *Mata Hari* (n.p., developed 1990–5, 2000–4); *Paint* (a.k.a. *Ultraviolet*, n.p., developed 1998–2004), and *Hands on a Hard Body* (n.p., developed 2004–6). My approach is to replicate the method Solomon and I have used in our archival research methods seminar. Our methodology follows the advice of organizational psychologist and professor Scott Sonenshein, author of *Stretch: Unlock the Power of Less—And Achieve More than You Ever Imagined*, who urges managers and laymen alike to "stop worrying about what you don't have and start engaging with what you do have in more useful ways."[3]

My goal is to demonstrate how an analysis of specific single documents that might otherwise be ignored or dismissed can yield rich insights about unfinished projects. If explored, the details of a seemingly unimportant letter or a note tucked into a file folder can take us in new directions. As Robert Altman typically communicated his filmmaking intentions verbally, a close examination of archival documents and the contributions of his collaborators can provide key clues regarding his creative process. In the *Mata Hari* files, a series of letters reveals how Altman developed a unique approach to the historical source material. Research memos in the *Paint* files highlight the work done by Altman's collaborators to ensure authenticity and provide space for improvisation. A daily planner and a Post-it note suggest the strategies adopted during the development of *Hands on a Hard Body* to ensure that Altman could complete the shoot despite his ill health. Exploring these unmade films draws attention to Altman's process of filmmaking and provides a more nuanced sense of the collaborative and contingent nature of filmmaking.

MATA HARI: INTERPRETING THE SOURCE MATERIAL

What determined when Altman developed specific projects? Altman collaborator David Levy pointed to the three Cs: cash, cast, and calendar.[4] In order to move out of development and into production, all three Cs needed to be aligned, which was not easy to accomplish without the support of a studio. Throughout his career, as for most independent directors, the three Cs often failed to line up.

In the early 1990s, Altman tried to mount the story of Mata Hari, the exotic Dutch dancer who entranced European audiences while supposedly serving as a double agent for the Germans against the French during WWI, as a feature film. The April 1992 release of *The Player* put Altman in a position of prominence he had not known in more than a decade. It was an outright hit that performed well at the box office and with critics. The success of *The Player* gave Altman an opportunity to get *Mata Hari* made, but the infamous "calendar" that Levy cited interfered. The film was to have been financed by a recently revived RKO and was to have starred chanteuse Ute Lemper, but ultimately fell through. A decade later, Altman developed the film in conjunction with

HBO as a made-for-TV movie vehicle for Cate Blanchett but the calendar again interrupted forward progress. In both incarnations, one of the major challenges involved distinguishing Altman's interpretation of the story from prior film versions.

Unlike previous film versions of the Mata Hara story (1931, 1964, and 1985),[5] which centered on Mata Hari's erotic powers to seduce and manipulate men while promulgating the false idea that she passed important military secrets to the enemy, Altman sought to present her more as a dupe used by incompetent military officials to camouflage their own ineptitude. This approach was consistent with films like *M*A*S*H* and *Buffalo Bill and the Indians, or Sitting Bull's History Lesson*, in which Altman aimed to expose American institutions and myths through satire. What stands out from the finished script of the first incarnation of *Mata Hari* and various conversations with contributors are three key points that line up with other examples of Altman's work. First is Altman's interest in skewering the mythology of a recognized historical character. Second is Altman's fascination with characters who are defined by self-deception, a quality certainly attributable to Mari Hari, whose self-delusions made her think she was more important to military leaders than she was. Third is Altman's exploration of the hypocrisy of government bureaucracies. In this case, French officials used Mata Hari to distract from the war's disastrously high death count while treating her as an expendable scapegoat to cover their bumbling. Ultimately, Altman hoped to overturn what we think we know about Mata Hari in order to reveal something even more damning.

Altman selected the 1986 book *Mata Hari: The True Story* by Russell Warren Howe as the source material for the film. Howe was a methodical writer and authored some twenty books in his lifetime. His biography offers a fairly straightforward account of the woman born in 1876 as Margaretha Geertruida Zelle and known as Greta, although he emphasizes the special access he had to previously sealed documents. In contrast to other published accounts of the life of Mata Hari, Howe concludes from this privileged information that "the German military attaché in Madrid sent telegrams to Berlin designed to compromise Mata Hari in codes he knew . . . had [been] broken."[6] The French, who decoded the telegrams, knew that she was little more than a paid courtesan for military officials and had no information of value and sacrificed her in order to cover their incompetence and losing war effort.[7]

In a 4 November 1991 letter to Altman, David Brown, who was a producer on *The Player* and was known, according to his producing partner Richard D. Zanuck, for having "a great story sense,"[8] wrote: "I have studied Russell Howe's book *Mata Hari* carefully, and while the subject still intrigues me, I have one major concern. Her life story is fascinating but is the myth of Mata Hari more entertaining than the reality?"[9] He added: "From this book, by no means the only source, she is more of a bungler than a true spy and more a victim of low morale in wartime France, than a menace."[10] He concluded: "Would Greta Garbo, had she known in 1931 what Howe conveys to us today, have wanted to celebrate the truth about Mata Hari?"[11] Altman ultimately decided against Brown's assessment and chose to emphasize the mythology surrounding Mata Hari's supposed intrepidness. In a typical Altman move, he flipped the conventional wisdom and made her mythology the main subject of the film, thus offering a cinematic subversive take on female empowerment and male authority.

This understanding of Altman's intentions is further validated by two additional letters in the archive, one by Howe and another by David Williamson, a writer recommended for the project by David Levy. Regarded as one of Australia's premier playwrights, Williamson is equally known as a hardworking screenwriter and a legendary fixture of the 1970s and 1980s Australian New Wave film movement. He had the ability and skill to do both intimate drama and highly plotted historical narratives that mix romance and political intrigue. His script for *Gallipoli* (Peter Weir, 1981) no doubt influenced Levy's recommendation as it rendered the futility of war and loss of innocence needed for the Mata Hari project.

During February of 1993, Altman met separately with both Howe and David Williamson. Howe's 3 February follow-up letter expresses his thanks for "a delightful and inspiring evening," while indicating one thing they discussed over dinner:

> Here is the sequence I mentioned from my book of weapons diplomacy [*Weapons: The International Game of Arms, Money, and Diplomacy*, 1980] dealing with Zaharoff, "leveraged warfare," and how WWI was kept going for the greater financial good of people like him.[12]

Included within what might appear at first glance to be an inconsequential thank-you note is the first mention of the name *Zaharoff*, which appears in several other archival documents.

The same name appears in a congratulatory fax Williamson sent to Altman on 24 February 1993 after Altman received an Academy Award nomination as Best Director for *The Player*. Williamson offered gratitude for their meeting and thanks for having received material on Basil Zaharoff, a wealthy Greek industrialist known for his corrupt business practices.[13] Zaharoff was also an infamous arms dealer who notoriously sold weapons, including Hiram Maxim's automatic machine gun, to European nations and the US throughout the first third of the twentieth century. This small detail in Williamson's letter indicates that Zaharoff's life was partly serving as inspiration for his draft outline of the script and suggests the direction that Altman and the writer had agreed on for the project. A 25 April 1993 follow-up letter from Howe to

Altman suggests that he subsequently encouraged Williamson to read Donald McCormick's biography of Zaharoff, "which," Howe wrote, "includes a narrative of how Zaharoff and other arms dealers fended off the possibility of an early peace in World War One."[14] While Zaharoff himself never appears as a character nor is referenced in the various drafts of the script, his historical embodiment of war profiteering permeates the tone of the film and underpins its orientation.

What fascinates me about this sequence of letters is that they demonstrate a direct connection to the inspiration for a specific artistic choice—a rarity in the Altman archive. Relatively few letters *from* Altman are found in the archive, leaving his part in the creative process mostly invisible for posterity. Altman chose to communicate his intentions verbally, either publicly through print and television interviews, or privately over the telephone, during meals or other in-person meetings, or professionally while on the set. The latter left few traces, obliging researchers to reconstruct the trajectory of his creative decisions indirectly through letters like these and various drafts of the script. A careful comparison of Williamson's two drafts clearly shows a progression, with the first version being a more traditional approach to the story of Mata Hari and the second draft dramatizing the true causes of her downfall: the French officials' greed and immorality.

Williamson has said as much:

> Our final meeting was in Paris where I got to watch him shoot some of *Prêt-à-Porter*. I told him that there was new evidence that Mata Hari preferred her own sex and had one particularly strong relationship which colored her life. He was ecstatic. "Go for it," he urged. "Don't restrain yourself. Don't pull back."[15]

With Altman's encouragement, Williamson included this new information in the revised second draft found in the archive. Through Greta's association and romance with the character Henrietta, Williamson expands and deepens Greta's character by extending into her past and details her exploitation at the hands of men throughout her life through flashbacks. The second draft expands the character of Marie, a nun assigned to perform suicide watch in the days prior to her execution. Previously introduced late in the third act in the first draft, she now is a major character whose piety acts as a feminist foil to explain Greta's sexual promiscuity. These added characteristics, driven by Altman's casual creative cheerleading, deepen our understanding of Mata Hari more than any previous film version and the development of the script showcases Altman's collaborative style.[16]

Sadly both versions of the film failed to move into the shooting phase, in large part due to the third of David Levy's three Cs: calendar. The archive, however, offers a more complete understanding of the various complexities both projects faced in no small part due to the changing industry trends at this period when funding sources shifted from big to small screens.

PAINT: RESEARCHING THE SUBJECT

Another project in development during Altman's late period was *Paint*, a thriller set in the competitive and backstabbing contemporary art scene in downtown New York. A press release sent out in May 2003 announced that the project, then called *Ultraviolet*, was a 16 million-dollar film to be financed by Capitol Films, financiers of Altman's previous two efforts. Salma Hayek, in her first role since her Oscar nomination for *Frida* (Julie Taymor, 2002), and James Franco, appearing at the time in *The Company*, Altman's latest film, would star.

Paint had the potential to utilize the art world as *Tanner '88* had politics or *Prêt-à-Porter* had fashion, namely to allow Altman to explore a world outside of his own and combine actors with real-life artists to poke fun at the superficialities of contemporary painting circles, tease out the human foibles of the characters, and expose the frailties of humanity using irreverence and satire. Central to its success, however, would be Altman's ability to authentically integrate the fictional story with the real art world.

Paint's origin lay in a treatment written by longtime Altman associates Matthew Seig and Wren Arthur in 1997 called *New York Arts and Entertainment*. In their television series pitch, they indicated "this series offers behind the scenes access to the theater world like you've never seen before."[7] Similar to earlier Altman works, the fictional and the real worlds interact and co-exist in the project.

After expressing great interest, Altman pivoted unexpectedly to embrace another pitch he heard around the same time that also used the device of fictional characters interacting with real life people. Jeffrey Lewis, Emmy-award winning writer on the influential 1980s drama *Hill Street Blues* (Steven Bochco, Michael Kozoll, 1981–7), crafted the first version of a *Paint* teleplay entitled *Proust*, named for a bar popular with artists. The show promised to be "*Twin Peaks* in the art world."[8] The pilot centered on an art heist from a major New York museum. After Fox passed on the idea, it expanded into a feature film with a shared story credit by Lewis and Altman and underwent several additional rewrites and plot changes before becoming *Paint*. The success of cable television at this time had removed the stigma of working in television Altman faced in the 1980s and he welcomed the opportunity to move from one medium to another if that ensured getting a project funded and eventually made.

Altman's interest in the art world did not arrive out of the blue. He had an affinity for painting and tinkered with the medium as a young man. In addition to holding 700 boxes of papers, the Altman Collection also features numerous sketches and drawings by him as well as a self-portrait painted in oil. Scholars, critics, and Altman himself often compared his work as a filmmaker to the work of an artist. Scholar Robert Self wrote that Altman's visual choices "reveal the eye of a painter rather than the voice of a narrator."[19] And Altman has said: "I look at film as closer to a painting or a piece of music; it's an impression . . . an impression of character and total atmosphere."[20] Additionally, Altman had already focused intensely on the life of an artist in *Vincent & Theo*, about the relationship between Vincent van Gogh and his brother Theo.

For *Paint* to work, Altman and his production team determined that authenticity was key to success. Altman said to Charlie Rose during a television interview that he couldn't show the satire of a situation unless he was at the core of it, meaning he had to know the world he was portraying inside and out. Although Altman is often considered a champion improviser while on set, the archive reveals that a great deal of critical preparation and research allowed him to feel comfortable to improvise freely. It is that preparedness that gets into the muscle memory that allows the great jazz musicians to riff and Altman was no different. The art scene was a world in close proximity to his own. A 3 March 1998 memo from Wren Arthur documents that after raiding his rolodex, she encouraged Altman to begin contacting some of his most renowned New York-based artist friends to pick their brains on the project including Helen Frankenthaler, George Segal, Jim Dine, Yuri Kuper, and Julian Schnabel.[21]

The archive also reveals the scope of the research required and other significant contributions from Altman's collaborators. Producers David Levy and Joshua Astrachan and art director Steven Altman, along with many others, scoured Manhattan to create a complete and accurate picture of the art scene, both physically and conceptually. An entire archival box is filled with brochures, flyers, documents, and photos of gallery after gallery, a large amount given that the film had not even gone into actual production. Location spaces were measured, both interior and exterior, to determine viability. At this point, the production team considered making the Dia Chelsea gallery the sole location for the majority of the shoot, even for locations other than the gallery scene. (One specific reason was that as Altman's health fluctuated during this time, it was necessary to pare down locations and travel time between setups.)

One noteworthy memo to Lewis attributed to Altman is actually a summary of voluminous script notes written by Matthew Seig and Joshua Astrachan regarding Lewis' original pilot. It indicates that even the vision of an auteur like Altman is the culmination at times of his or her collaborators. Among the issues raised by Seig and Astrachan are a litany of concerns that Lewis had failed to accurately render the art world. For instance, Seig wrote:

> The script's attitude toward artists is that Morton is supposedly a stockbroker turned major artist. It feeds into the "my three-year-old can paint

better than that" stereotype. Many wealthy artists today certainly do know a great deal about the stock market, have aspirations that are more commercial than creative, and in many ways behave more like businessmen than how we think "artists" are supposed to behave. I don't think a stockbroker being accepted as an artist at Morton's level is an honest characterization and it demeans the community.[22]

Astrachan added: "This is not to say there is no room in this show to satirize the pretentious and self-serving behavior of New York's art scene. But if all the luminaries are humbugs, we lose too much."[23] Seig also took umbrage with the script's depiction of the Museum of Modern Art (MoMA):

There is no parking garage at MoMA. There is no "executive entrance" to the building. Curatorial staff and directors enter through the main front door. I worked there once. I feel pretty foolish for even mentioning such minor details, but if details don't matter then why not make up a name for the museum instead of calling it MoMA?[24]

Memos passed back and forth between the production team reveal a determination to get it correct. One set of memos from David Levy shows him raising a series of questions he wanted to ask experts concerning artist-related activities such as gallery openings and afterparties. "Afterparties: where [and] what are they like," the document begins. "Jeff's reads so dated and familiar. It was originally Moomba and it reads like something second hand, dated and overly-known (again from other films/tv too). There must be a better idea." What does one serve at a gallery opening was another question they raised. In the same memo, he asked: "The opening: would there ever be crudités? I doubt it." Behavior was also questioned: "How does the artist behave at their opening? Instead of the cynical posturing that Preston now exhibits?"[25]

In addition to the great artists of their generation available to them at the touch of their fingertips thanks to Altman's rolodex, the *Paint* production team surrounded themselves with leading critics, curators, and thinkers like Maurice Tuchman, Steven Watson, and Ted Volpe to further connect with the art world in order to get it right. A telling document in the archive written by Tony Oursler, another of these added expert voices, provides a pithy understanding of the day-to-day work of a typical artist and seems to address the objections Seig leveled at the first draft. Oursler, one of the first multimedia and installation artists to be widely exhibited in leading national museums and galleries, acted as a film consultant and inspiration of sorts for Samantha, Salma Hayek's character. His memo features twenty-nine bullet points that detail succinctly the work of an artist and served as a treatise for how to create an accurate depiction of an artist's character. Among the practical tasks conducted by an artist according to Oursler:

> Work day jobs; lecture about themselves; teach; do editions/prints; make shows; travel to do installations; store work; do studio visits/ see other artists' stuff; get mailing lists together—part of the endless business of self- and cross-promotion (it's a pathetic cottage industry); document their own shows (photograph their work or videotape their installations); hire assistants whom they hate, love, fuck.[26]

Included as well is an equally long list of items that fall into the category of less practical daily tasks and reveal qualities that we might consider more along the lines of character:

> Admire a cast of others, living and dead; live on the shoulders of giants; get pissed that dealers don't go to auctions to protect their work; hate openings/love openings; wonder if collectors will collect them; have real estate issues; have fallings-out with dealers.[27]

It is these intangibles documented in his collaborators' memos that sparked Altman's creative mind. If one were to reduce the strategy on *Paint* to a formula, it might read something like: research, accuracy, and expertise lead to authenticity. This document from Oursler confirms Altman's trust in expertise, a belief in preparation, and an openness to the spontaneity that drives credible work. Altman has repeatedly indicated in the press that his job is done once the casting of actors is completed. All that's left for him to do, once on the set, is guide them. Others have frequently said that his approach is collegial and improvisational. Yet memos such as these show a more nuanced relationship to his work and approach to directing. These small details tucked inside unseen documents challenge our notion of what we think "Altmanesque" is and reveal that it is more complex than we may have initially thought.

HANDS ON A HARD BODY: CHOREOGRAPHING PRODUCTION

Hands on a Hard Body was days away from moving into the final phase of preproduction when Altman died. Unlike *Paint* which necessitated rigorous preplanning and research, *Hands* was intended to be the polar opposite. Altman described it as "this is going to be fast and furious."[28] In part, the limited nature of the plot required a direct visual approach but in actuality, his failing health would not allow for any other option. The story had been captured previously in a 1997 documentary by S. R. Bindler. Altman didn't want to replicate the documentary scene for scene nor did he want to make a mockumentary. Stephen Harrigan, his final scriptwriter of three (Beth Henley and Anne Rapp being the first two) wrote to him: "I think our movie should have no irony. The tone should be straight-ahead drama (or comedy when it naturally arises) with no winking at the audience."[29] Altman hoped to tell his version of a classic

CHARACTER LIST – HANDS ON A HARD BODY
APRIL 6, 2005 (revised 4/12/06)

1. Car dealership owner: Chet Ramsmeyer (Tommy Lee Jones) (Ted Danson)
2. Television reporter: Sherman Stork (Ted Danson) (William H. Macy) Clooney
3. Contest coordinator: Ruth Ann Port (Mary Steenbergen)
4. Television anchor and Sherman's nemesis: Betty Birdsong (Julianne Moore) (Julia Roberts)

AROUND THE TRUCK

RIGHT FRONT FENDER:
5. Suzanne – woman with two kids whose car broke down and she is stranded (Diane Lane)
6. Harold – man with one arm, right-wing military (Chris Rock)
7. Vivian - upper class woman whose children entered her in the contest (Diane Lane)

LEFT FRONT FENDER:
8. Monica – woman whose husband works off shore on an oil rig (Hillary Swank)
9. Jason – irresponsible kid, can't stick to anything, bonds with Suzanne (actor not cast)
10. Buddy – young kid who always wants to have sex on his breaks (actor not cast)

RIGHT BACK FENDER:
11. Robbie – customer service guy who abuses his fiance (Jake Gyllenhaal)
12. Ben – personal trainer who is gay and wins truck, has a heart attack (The Rock, Dwayne Johnson)
13. Marla – young girl trying to go back to nursing school (Kirsten Dunst?)

LEFT BACK FENDER:
14. Wayne – quiet mysterious guy living with his cousin who eventually gets arrested (Steve Buscemi)
15. Rhonda – girl who works in a pet store, enters a lot of contests (Laura Dern)
16. Consuela – girl who only speaks Spanish, religious woman (Salma Hayek)
17. Clint – grade school teacher, bonds with Rhonda (Woody Harrelson)

THE PIT:
18. Tracey – Robbie's fiance who he eventually abuses (Christina Ricci)
19. Jonathan – Ben's gay partner – also a personal trainer (Thomas Haden Church)
20. Percy Boudreaux – Wayne Thibodeaux's cousin (actor not cast)
   Harold Jr. – Harold's teen son (actor n

OTHER:
21. Larry – Monica's husband, who works off shore and comes back McConaughey)
22. Frank – TV tech, works with Sherman Stork (actor not cast)

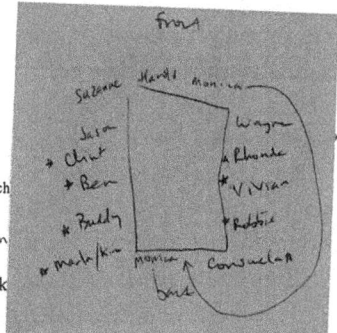

Figure 5.1 A list of characters and casting for *Hands on a Hard Body* featuring notes written by screenwriter Anne Rapp. Courtesy of Special Collections Research Center, University of Michigan Library.

American situation involving consumerism, exploitation, and greed and not control it but allow the event itself to tell its own story.

Laugh out loud funny, the script was perfectly calibrated for Altman's unique perspective and had "Altman movie" written all over it: intersecting plotlines featuring dozens of disparate characters, controlled chaos, a three-ring circus environment, a team of jaded television journalists capturing it all for the cameras hoping to film the potential carnage, and a cynical view of media's insistence on making fifteen-minute celebrities in between commercial breaks. Inspired by an actual annual competition held in Longview, Texas, the endurance contest features twenty-four contestants, drawn from a lottery, who are required to keep one hand on a brand-new Nissan truck at all times. Like the dance marathons of the depression era, hour after hour the contestants must overcome their exhaustion in order to keep their sanity in check. Grueling and cruel, it's *Survivor* set in a parking lot with a group of working-class Texans.

Dozens of top actors wanted the opportunity to work with him, even in some cases for small, almost cameo-sized roles, and Altman and casting director Pam Dixon had an easy time filling the various slots. Verbal agreements were in tow from Academy Award winners Meryl Streep, Tommy Lee Jones, Hillary Swank, Billy Bob Thornton, and Mary Steenburgen (who was also in a producing partnership role with her husband Ted Danson); discussions were underway with Julianne Moore, Reese Witherspoon, Salma Hayek, John C. Reilly, and James Franco and some popular draws such as Dwayne "The Rock" Johnson and Ryan Gosling. Comic actors including Lily Tomlin, Chris Rock, and Jack Black were also in negotiations and ensured that their off-the-cuff abilities would enable Altman to successfully use a semi-improvisational approach.[30]

Included in the archive is an eye-opening document that shows the reality of what the director faced health-wise. For the past decade, Altman had underplayed his deteriorating physical condition. Rumors of a work stoppage during the shooting of *Kansas City* leaked out and the possibility of a heart transplant had circulated in the industry press, but he denied them all. Altman was unable, however, to deny the need for a backup director to assist him on the set of *A Prairie Home Companion* (longtime Altman admirer Paul Thomas Anderson) and everyone knew time was against him.

The daily planner from the week of 31 January 2005 confirms this. On Monday, the week began with an 11:30 a.m. meeting with Steenburgen, Danson, and Keith Addis, Danson's longtime producing partner, to discuss the project. Altman then needed to follow up on calls received on the previous Friday from Garrison Keillor concerning *A Prairie Home Companion*, combining two characters into one, and the Dangerous Woman character; respond to Elliott Gould's greeting; talk with Pam Dixon about Diane Lane's expressed interest in being cast in *A Prairie Home Companion*; look at a project veteran ICM agent Toni Howard sent over; respond to the latest draft of *The Widow Claire* by

Horton Foote, another project in the pipeline; speak with Robert Newman about *Variety* squashing a story on *A Prairie Home Companion*; and answer his agent and friend Sam Cohn's call. In the upcoming week were scheduled soirees with director Sidney Lumet and a public appearance at a screening at Soho House of *3 Women* hosted by Julianne Moore. In between the high-profile work were appointments to see doctor after doctor for a colonoscopy appointment, kidney procedure, renal ultrasound, renogram, kidney sonogram, EGD stomach test, blood test, blood work, MRI, and CT scan.[31] The daily planner makes crystal clear the nearly obsessive drive and desire Altman had to work and be active and, simultaneously, his parallel need to tend to his failing body. It also is a subtle illustration of how his compromised health dictated the terms regarding how he would approach the style of *Hands on a Hard Body*.

Documents in the archive suggest *Hands on a Hard Body* might have been a fascinating combination of two approaches he took in making films. One involved a large ensemble in the style of *Nashville* or *Gosford Park* and painted in broad strokes, making bold proclamations regarding cultural targets. The other, found in his small-scale adaptations of plays such as *Secret Honor, Come Back to the 5 & Dime, Jimmy Dean, Jimmy Dean*, and *Streamers*, demonstrated a more inward focus and intimate working style. Altman's filmmaking team creatively sought out ways to represent cinematically the originally staged source material through clever and controlled explorations of time, space, and place. Working with smaller casts and a single location, they nevertheless created a definite world as much as the expansive vistas of *Nashville* but did so in a boutique store approach rather than a department-store-like method.

Much as with Altman's 1980s theatrical adaptations, *Hands on a Hard Body* is limited to a single location and features a cast of characters who primarily do not move throughout the film. Buried within character interviews and personality profiles Anne Rapp developed to help her write the script, I found a post-it note she appears to have drawn depicting the location where she envisioned each character would stand throughout the film.[32] A rectangle shape in the middle of the post-it represents the truck with front and back written at the top and bottom of the note to indicate placement within the frame. Surrounding the shape are the names of fourteen characters with stars next to some of them. Monica, a character initially deemed to be located near the front of the vehicle has a line moving her to the back of the vehicle although there is no indication why. The post-it is affixed to a written description of who each character is and who might play them and functions in a way as a cheat-sheet to keep track of who is playing who in the large cast.

It's one of these telling details that can get lost to history because she was not the final writer on the project and the ephemeral and disposable nature of the information does not scream *important*. And yet it visualizes the problem of the movie in a single image. It's not even clear if Altman actually saw it.

My sense is that whether or not he saw it, it was discussed and it triggered in Altman a sense of how to frame the movie cinematically, i.e. how the blocking of the truck would be shot within the film frame. How do I not make it claustrophobic despite the limitations, he no doubt asked himself. "I think I know how to do it like a documentary," he told biographer Mitchell Zuckoff.[33] "What I want to do is set up the event and turn on the switch and let the event happen and film it with several cameras."[34]

Altman told Zuckoff two weeks before his death that he envisioned *Hands on a Hard Body* as his swan song: "I'm getting to the point where I'm seeing it as sort of my last thing. I don't foresee anything beyond that. So now I'm getting to the position where I want it to be really special," he told Zuckoff.[35] Indications are that it would have been.

CONCLUSION

These short discussions of the unmade Altman projects are based on specific documents that tell me the direction the project was going, but the fascinating thing about archives is that they allow for multiple interpretations and emphases based on what documents one encounters and how one interprets them. The archive reveals unexpected historical and creative turns in the filmmaking process. What's inspiring is that they can function as both foundational examination for the seasoned scholar and simultaneously serve as a springboard for the untrained newcomer to Altman's storied career, or any artist for that matter. The methodology that Solomon and I have employed for nearly a decade works because it's based on looking, on observation, and on further investigation that lead to making new connections that are not based on being told what to think. Small discoveries may lead to small claims, but they also help build larger skills like critical thinking and the ability to sift through clutter and start to see and make one's own connections. Ultimately it is about learning what the creative process is, what it entails, and how approaching a new topic or idea with an open mind allows us to be willing to see new perspectives. The documents allow us to be mired in the minutiae of a single project or step back and see the vista of the career in its entirety. A perspective that feels slightly Altmanesque.

Robert Altman's entire career was built around a model of multiple projects waiting to move into the next phase of production. Screenwriter Anne Rapp compared him to a farmer: "a good farmer and a good artist just keep turning out work. Bob made a movie every year. Every time he had one ready to go, all he was doing was talking about the next one."[36] For Altman, breathing was working and as long as he was breathing he was working. "I like to work. It's the only time I'm really happy," he told interviewer Charlie Rose.[37] But regrettably, Altman's appetite to work far exceeded his capacity. It's no wonder that in addition to the nearly forty feature films he made, he would have nearly twice that many projects left unmade. Despite how prolific he was, a variety of circumstances and happenstances and the unanticipated appearance of the third C, calendar, prevented him from completing all the work he hoped to do during this late stage resurgence. What's fortunate for those of us interested in studying the trajectory of his circuitous career path, and in particular the unmade projects, is that remnants remain and permit us to dig deeper into the trenches. We can have a front row seat and observe his approach to work which was more layered and stacked than horizontal and will continue to produce a valuable harvest for generations to come.

NOTES

1. David Levy (producer), interview with the author, 22 April 2020.
2. Matthew Harle, *Afterlives of Abandoned Work: Creative Debris in the Archive* (New York: Bloomsbury Academic, 2019), p. 3.
3. Scott Sonenshein (author), "Scott Sonenshein talks with Daniel H. Pink," 2017, Amazon. com. Available at <https://www.amazon.com/Stretch-Unlock-Power-Achieve-Imagined/dp/0062457225/ref=sr_1_1?crid=8LJ1K22RNA8O&dchild=1&keywords=stretch+sonenshein&qid=1601219745&sprefix=stretch+son%2Caps%2C164&sr=8-1> (last accessed 13 May 2021).
4. Levy, interview, 22 April 2020.
5. *Mata Hari* (George Fitzmaurice, 1931); *Mata Hari, Agent H21* (Jean-Louis Richard, 1964); *Mata Hari* (Curtis Harrington, 1985).
6. Christopher Andrew, "She blew a kiss to the firing squad," *The New York Times*, 8 June 1986, section 7, p. 13. Available at <https://www.nytimes.com/1986/06/08/books/she-blew-a-kiss-to-the-firing-squad.html>.
7. Russell Warren Howe, *Mata Hari: The True Story* (New York: Dodd, Mead & Company, 1986), p. 143.
8. Bruce Weber, "David Brown, film and stage producer, dies at 93," *The New York Times*, 2 February 2010. Available at <https://www.nytimes.com/2010/02/02/arts/02brown.html> (last accessed 13 May 2021).
9. David Brown to Robert Altman, 4 November 1991, *Mata Hari* Correspondence, Robert Altman Papers, Special Collections Research Center, University of Michigan Library.
10. Ibid.
11. Ibid.
12. Russell Warren Howe to Robert Altman, 3 February 1993, *Mata Hari* Correspondence, Robert Altman Papers, Special Collection Research Center, University of Michigan Library.
13. David Williamson to Robert Altman, 24 February 1993, *Mata Hari* Correspondence, Robert Altman Papers, Special Collections Research Center, University of Michigan Library.
14. Russell Warren Howe to Robert Altman, 25 April 1993, *Mata Hari* Correspondence, Robert Altman Papers, Special Collections Research Center, University of Michigan Library.
15. David Williamson, "Him, me and *Mata Hari*," *Sydney Morning Herald*, 23 November 2006. Available at <https://www.smh.com.au/entertainment/movies/him-me-and-mata-hari-20061123-gdow3j.html> (last accessed 13 May 2021).

16. *Mata Hari* Script by David Williamson, August 1994, Robert Altman Papers, Special Collections Research Center, University of Michigan Library.
17. Matthew Seig and Wren Arthur, *New York Arts and Entertainment* Treatment, 18 August 1997, *Paint/Ultraviolet* Treatments, Robert Altman Papers, Special Collections Research Center, University of Michigan Library.
18. Matthew Seig, Notes for *Proust*, 16 June 1998, *Paint/Ultraviolet* Script Notes, Robert Altman Papers, Special Collections Research Center, University of Michigan Library.
19. Robert T. Self, *Robert Altman's Subliminal Reality* (Minneapolis: University of Minnesota Press, 2002), p. 62.
20. Ibid. p. 62.
21. Wren Arthur, Fax to Robert Altman, 3 March 1998, *Paint/Ultraviolet* Legal Correspondence, Robert Altman Papers, Special Collections Research Center, University of Michigan Library.
22. Matthew Seig, Notes for *Proust*.
23. Joshua Astrachan, Fax to Robert Altman, 12 June 1998, *Paint/Ultraviolet* Script Notes, Robert Altman Papers, Special Collections Research Center, University of Michigan Library.
24. Matthew Seig, Notes for *Proust*.
25. David Levy, Script Notes (undated), *Paint/Ultraviolet* Script Notes, Robert Altman Papers, Special Collections Research Center, University of Michigan Library.
26. Tony Oursler, Statement (undated), *Paint/Ultraviolet* Script Notes, Robert Altman Papers, Special Collections Research Center, University of Michigan Library.
27. Tony Oursler, Statement (undated).
28. Hannah Tucker, Daniel Fierman, and Missy Schwartz, "Deal report," *Entertainment Weekly*, 9 June 2006, p. 23.
29. Stephen Harrigan, *Hands on a Hard Body* Notes on Henley Script, 15 August 2006, Robert Altman Papers, Special Collections Research Center, University of Michigan Library.
30. Tentative Character List, *Hands on a Hard Body*, 6 April 2005, Robert Altman Papers, Special Collections Research Center, University of Michigan Library.
31. *Hands on a Hard Body* Production Schedules Day to Day, Monday, 31 January 2005, Robert Altman Papers, Special Collections Research Center, University of Michigan Library.
32. Character List, *Hands on a Hard Body*, 6 April 2005 (revised 12 April 2006), Robert Altman Papers, Special Collections Research Center, University of Michigan Library.
33. Mitchell Zuckoff, *Robert Altman: The Oral Biography* (New York: Alfred A. Knopf, 2002), p. 503.
34. Ibid. p. 503.
35. Ibid. p. 503
36. Ibid. p. 466.
37. Robert Altman, interview by Charlie Rose, *Charlie Rose*, WNET, PBS, 5 January 1993. Available at <https://charlierose.com/videos/18415> (last accessed 13 May 2021).

PART II

Industrial Frameworks

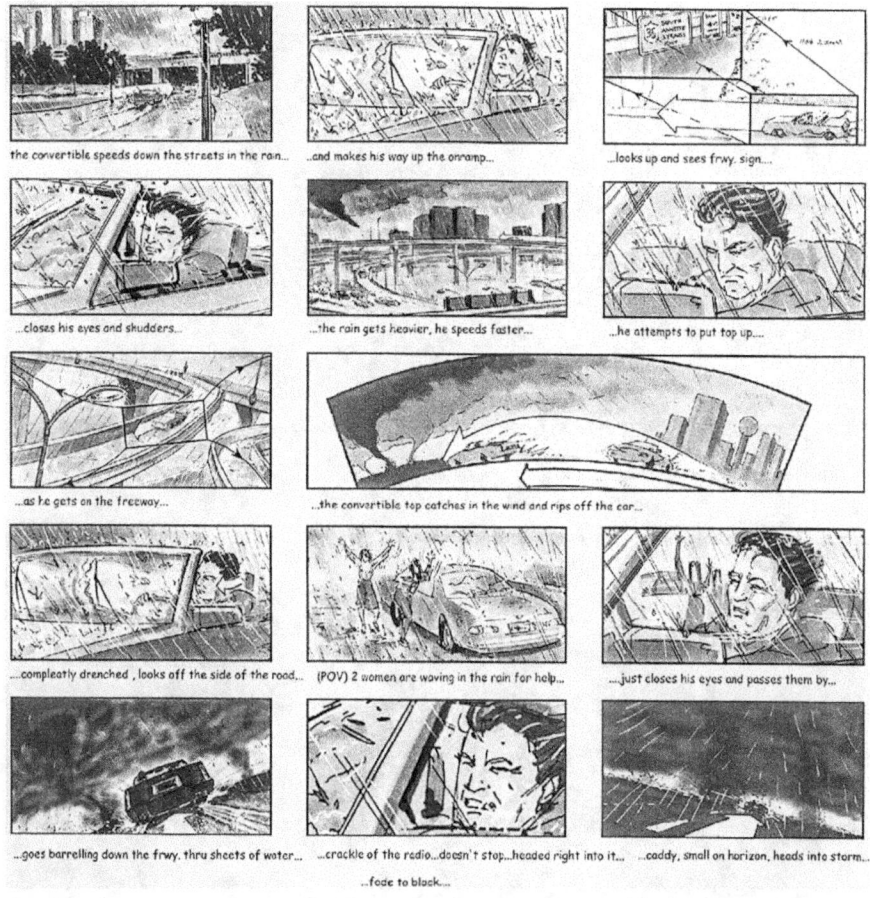

Figure II.1 Storyboard of the storm sequence in *Dr. T & the Women*. Courtesy of Special Collections Research Center, University of Michigan Library.

CHAPTER 6

Offbeat and Out of Sync: *Popeye* and the Failure of an Auteur-Driven Franchise

Tim J. Anderson

"Then *Popeye* happened"[1]

In the story of Robert Altman's career his 1980 musical *Popeye* exists as an economic misstep. Produced by Robert Evans, Altman's ambitious integrated musical cast then-TV star of *Mork and Mindy* (1978–82) Robin Williams as Popeye alongside Shelley Duvall as Olive Oyl, and recruited prominent songwriter and recording artist Harry Nilsson to write the songs and compose the music that would become the soundtrack. Accompanied with a "making of" book—the kind that accompanied so many other highly-anticipated films of the late 1970s and early 1980s—*The Popeye Story* offered an "inside look" at the project and noted that the film "has already been called 'the most anticipated film of the year.'"[2] The book conceded that "there really is no guarantee that the film will meet with huge critical or financial success," while claiming that "that the *Popeye* project will be regarded as one of the most unusual and ambitious creative collaborations in filmmaking."[3]

The phrase "unusual and ambitious" as it applies to this film would be an understatement. Writing eleven years after its release, Beverly Walker commented that,

> when finally unveiled, *Popeye* proved so original that neither the film media nor marketing mavens quite knew what to do with it. Though it looks like a cartoon, it is, of course, live-action; and though the characters don't *look* realistic, they feel that way.[4]

Over a decade later Walker considered *Popeye*, along with *McCabe & Mrs. Miller* and *3 Women*, as three of Altman's films that "seem just about perfect, each mesmerizing in its own way."[5] Few, if any, shared that assessment when the film was released. While Roger Ebert celebrated Altman's film and Nilsson's songs,[6] Vincent Canby writing in *The New York Times* called the film an "immensely appealing mess of a movie, often high-spirited and witty, occasionally pretentious and flat, sometimes robustly funny and frequently unintelligible."[7] *The Washington Post* was far more adamant: "there are sequences, so deadly or wrongheaded that you feel as if you're attending his professional funeral" and wrote that Harry Nilsson had "been allowed to impose a dirge-like song score, which weighs on the production like a terminal illness."[8] Despite the criticisms, *Popeye* turned a significant profit. Yet, therein lies the lesson: the profits were not enough and Altman's film quickly became reviled throughout Hollywood. Beverly Walker explains that *Popeye* generated "a brushfire of hostility toward Altman that caught wind throughout the industry." As Walker explains, "Altman was, in essence, blackballed as only the movie business can do it: no one returned his phone calls. In 1982 he sold his production company, Lion's Gate, and left the West Coast."[9] Indeed, *Popeye*'s failure was quite literally the stuff of obituaries. Upon Altman's passing in 2006, *The New York Times* wrote of *Popeye* that the film was a " crushing blow" and "though it eventually achieved modest commercial success, the movie was considered a dud because it made less money than had been expected."[10]

The chapter does not necessarily address a textual failure. Substantially profitable films as unique as *Popeye* are rare and often celebrated. Instead, this paper investigates a question of reputation: why, despite turning its $20 million budget into $60 million in receipts, did *Popeye* gain a reputation as a career killer? This chapter argues that the reason for this is that the film's existence is something of an auteur-blockbuster musical where the project's failings as a blockbuster find significant expression in the soundtrack. In short, as a soundtrack, Nilsson's songs and arrangements simply did not fit into a then-emergent understanding of blockbusters where musically oriented cinema positioned their musical assets both as textual elements and for-profit, cross-promotional investments.[11] For the remainder of this chapter I draw on trade and periodical literature that places both the film and the soundtrack in a dialogue of the expectations that *Popeye* held as a post-studio system musical blockbuster with franchisable ambitions. Throughout, I secure *Popeye*'s place within this specific historical moment of the late 1970s and early 1980s when Hollywood and the American music industry both transitioned into and experimented to find a set of blockbuster-oriented cinema practices where the soundtrack is understood as not only important merchandise but as a key to a franchise's overall success. Finally, the chapter ends with an analysis of *Popeye* as an ambivalent musical property whose use of Nilsson's compositions and lyrics connects to a unique vision of the film musical whose aesthetic success simply could not find a fit with the commercial demands of a successful franchise.

BLOCKBUSTER AMBITIONS

There is no doubt that Altman understood he was producing a "blockbuster musical." However, it is not clear if he or anyone else fully understood what the soundtrack would require to help the film achieve this status. For our purposes, it is convenient to place *Popeye* alongside Robert Evans's other music-oriented production of the same year, *Urban Cowboy* (James Bridges, 1980). Like *Popeye*, *Urban Cowboy* presented a star in John Travolta, who, in this case, was clearly associated with the music-oriented films of *Grease* (Randal Kleiser, 1978) and *Saturday Night Fever* (1977). All three of Travolta's music-oriented films were, like *Popeye*, distributed by Paramount and all three claimed soundtracks that were viewed as substantial to these media properties' successes. All three were accompanied by multimillion-selling double albums that reinvigorated the apparently stalled careers of the musicians on them. At the same time, these films and their soundtracks were playing an exceptional part in accelerating the rise of specific music genres. After *Saturday Night Fever*, the seemingly then disregarded Bee Gees saw a three-year peak in North America and disco was elevated to a position as a dominant music genre. While *Grease* heightened the popularity of the United States then-ongoing interest in 1950s nostalgia, Travolta's star in *Urban Cowboy* helped increase both the popularity of country music and the then-fading career of Mickey Gilley. Placed in this perspective, *Popeye*'s soundtrack and its conception fits into a model of connecting a television star with a pop star and a specific musical genre. Casting Robin Williams as the film's lead echoed Travolta, who was also a television star at the time of his casting in *Saturday Night Fever*. Working with Harry Nilsson, a star that had faded significantly from his 1971 commercial peak with the release of *Nilsson Schmilsson*, the soundtrack would engage the genre of the film musical. Nilsson's versatility as a songwriter would be leveraged for the film musical. Indeed, Nilsson's compositions had found success on *The Monkees* television series (1966–8), the *Midnight Cowboy* soundtrack film with the hit "Everybody's Talkin'" (1969), and even composed an entire the soundtrack of songs for the 1971 animated music-oriented film *The Point* (Fred Wolf, 1971), whose script he co-wrote. Yet unlike *Saturday Night Fever, Urban Cowboy*, or *Grease, Popeye* would be distinguished by two key factors. First and most importantly, *Popeye* engaged a property with fifty plus years of pre-existing popularity. This was particularly attractive to several investors who imagined creating a significant franchise from characters that had mass distribution since 1929 when they were first established as the *Thimble Theatre*. Secondly, *Popeye* would be directed by an established auteur in Altman whose style could be marketed as a defining touch.

Nevertheless, *Popeye* simply failed to impress. In retrospect the reason is clear: while the film was profitable the project did not meet its expectations as a franchise. When Beverly Walker notes in 1991 that Altman's *Popeye* met

Figure 6.1 Robin Williams, Shelley Duvall, and Robert Altman on the set of *Popeye*. Courtesy of Special Collections Research Center, University of Michigan Library.

with "very, very, bad timing" her words are hardly an understatement.¹² The model for the high-concept blockbuster—a model that Evans had made significant contributions to forming—was still being established and *Popeye* would be caught up in this moment of uncertain formation as a failed experiment. Compared to the previously mentioned comparison properties it is easy to see why. The reported $3.5 million budget of *Saturday Night Fever* returned $237 million, while *Grease*'s $6 million claimed close to $400 million. Even *Urban Cowboy*'s $10.5 million investment cleared $50 million at the box office. Indeed, both *Saturday Night Fever* and *Grease*'s success would invite investments and sequels, while *Cowboy* would be considered for an adaptation for television. None of this was in the offing for *Popeye*. As Justin Wyatt notes, the perception of *Popeye*'s failure derives "from the strong commercial orientation of the initial project." The project's "presold nature" "illustrates one of the many traits of the blockbuster which had become more and more significant as a market force through the 1970s."¹³ Drawing from Douglas Gomery and Robert Allen, Wyatt argues that cinema and its attendant products are invariably "shaped by the changing marketplace in which it is produced and consumed."¹⁴ Fourteen years after *Popeye*'s release, Wyatt explains what constitutes high concept films,

> High concept films are differentiated with the marketplace through an emphasis on style and through an integration with their marketing.

These two factors are not mutually exclusive. The tie between marketing and high concept is centered on a concept which is marketable (i.e., that contains an exploitable premise of pre-sold properties, such as stars).... Advertising is key to the commercial success of these films through representing the marketable concepts of the films, but, more basically, advertising as a medium of expression is fundamental to the very construction of the high concept films. Indeed, the style of the films reflects, in many respects, the graphic design and print layouts associated with contemporary consumer goods advertising.[15]

To take this one step further: the style of the high concept film is the style of the franchise and it extends to every aspect of a franchise's licensing and promotion.

In the case of the soundtrack, its development is not simply as a consumer good, but rather as a source of promotion. Take, for example, Wyatt's understanding that the integrated musical of *Grease* is not simply an expression of the musical genre, but a prime example of high concept blockbuster filmmaking. Comparing *Grease* to 1979's critically touted musical *All That Jazz* (Bob Fosse), *Grease* is "high concept" production while *All That Jazz* is "low concept" because of the assemblage of their assets. High concept films are defined by production with inherent marketing opportunities in mind. High concept films are often reduced to one-line pitches, while low concept films are produced without the consideration of significant marketing opportunities or storylines that cannot be simply reduced to one-sentence explanations. As Wyatt explains, in the case of *Grease*,

> assets were driven first and foremost through *Grease*'s star power: John Travolta, directly after his rise to stardom in *Saturday Night Fever*; pop star Olivia Newton-John; and, to attract the older audience, a host of media stars evoking the film's period of the '50s, including Frankie Avalon, Ed "Kookie" Byrnes, Eve Arden, and Sid Caesar. Of these media icons, Travolta was the most significant ... With *Grease* released only six months after *Fever*'s debut, the association with *Saturday Night Fever* was fresh.[16]

The inclusion of pop music stars such as Olivia Newton-John was accompanied by a few other music stars. Frankie Avalon and Ed "Kookie" Byrnes both released numerous records in the late 1950s and early 1960s. Frankie Valli's inclusion would reference his fame with the musical act, the Four Seasons. In the case of the longstanding fifties revival act Sha Na Na, the group had begun starring in their own syndicated variety television program one year earlier (1977). The result was an original soundtrack album littered with pre-sold assets that could be pitched to a variety of radio programmers. Indeed, the *Grease* soundtrack was a key element for cross-promotional opportunities.

In the case of *Popeye*, its Nilsson-composed soundtrack followed a similar tack. However, Nilsson existed only as a composer and providing none of his vocal talents. Importantly enough, no one apart from Ray Walston, who appeared on the film soundtrack of *South Pacific* (Joshua Logan, 1958) and the original cast record of *Damn Yankees* (George Abbott, Stanley Donen, 1958), could boast any significant pop music releases, let alone hit records.[17] Still, the soundtrack offers little stylistic or performative purchase for radio other than providing programmers the chance to play Nilsson's latest compositions *sans* Nilsson himself. Even the low concept film of *All That Jazz* included the George Benson rendition of the Mann, Weill, Leiber, and Stoller hit, "On Broadway." Bringing with him a history of well-selling jazz records, the single had appeared on Benson's 1978 release *Weekend in L.A.* and had been a top-ten hit in both soul and pop charts. The question for *Popeye* remains: if a "low concept" film such as *All That Jazz* could find a way to place a popular record, recording artist, and song on its soundtrack that could possibly promote the film on an occasional radio playlist, then one may ask why would a producer as successful as Evans not understand the problems that the *Popeye* soundtrack contained for possible radio programmers who may have taken a chance on a record with a Nilsson vocal but had no interest in any Shelley Duvall cut?

MAKING A "HIGH CONCEPT BLOCKBUSTER" AS THE MODEL IS BEING MADE

Part of the answer to this question lies in understanding the nature of how formulas and standards emerge as large-scale structural changes take place. The effects of a crumbling studio system in a post Paramount Decision environment are well known. This is also true of the emergence of a new Hollywood that rose in the late 1960s/early 1970s and morphed in the 1980s as more and more studios were conglomerated with other assets through multiple media mergers that sought a more global marketplace for their wares. Looking back, it is tempting to see these mergers, the moves to high concept filmmaking, and the adjustment to a more globalized market, as logical organizational responses to crises and growth. What is often less understood are the many failures that are key to any long-term structural change. In the case of moving from a vertically integrated studio system to establish a new Hollywood system dominated by high concept productions any number of experiments, many of which fail and are forgotten, much to our detriment, will and must take place in order to discover any new model of success.

THE FAILURE OF AN AUTEUR-DRIVEN FRANCHISE 105

Such a failure was the case of *Popeye* as it tried to become a high concept blockbuster. One of its more notable investors, Disney, understood the need to experiment with an emerging high-concept blockbuster format. In 1980 *The New York Times* reported that, "though [Disney] hit the $1 billion mark in total assets for the first time two years ago, it seems to be failing in the area where its expertise was once unassailable: making pictures people want to see."[18] The company that had once been synonymous with products that defined childhood no longer seemed to be able to create films that appeal to children or adults. While films such as *Close Encounters of the Third Kind* (Steven Spielberg, 1977) and *The Empire Strikes Back* (Irvin Kershner, 1980) continued to draw younger audiences and Disney expanded its investments in theme parks, Disney began searching for a "new success 'formula.'" Unfortunately, as *The New York Times* reported, "no one knows just what that formula should be."[19] *Popeye* would be one of two experiments in discovery as Disney would engage into a joint finance agreement—a first for Disney—with Paramount to produce and present both *Popeye* and *Dragonslayer* (Matthew Robbins, 1981).[20] This would mean the famously family friendly studio would be working with Robert Evans, a producer who had recently been convicted of cocaine possession.[21] Despite Evans's dodgy character, Disney believed that the risk of this association was offset by the fact that *Popeye*'s characters had long held a place within American popular culture as wholesome and unthreatening. Like Disney, both Paramount and King Features Entertainment, the Hearst holding and longtime syndicator of the Popeye comic strip, hoped the project would propel the franchise into blockbuster status with accompanying ancillary products. For example, *The New York Times* reported in late August 1980 that the paper goods producer, Mead Products, were introducing lines of paper products ready for back to school season. As the nation's largest producer of school supplies, Mead expressed that the company thought Popeye would quickly take over from the Star Wars franchise. Claiming to possess marketing surveys where an "independent marketing company found that children from kindergarten through ninth grade said they would rather own notebooks with Popeye's picture than any other," Mead's then-president claimed that this was due to a new conservatism where people were "turning back to basics all around the country and there is nothing more basic to American hero worship than Popeye." As such, Mead was investing in a "completely new line of wirebound books, pencils, portfolios and writing tablets in December to coincide with the release of Robert Altman's motion picture 'Popeye.'"[22] To be sure, Popeye had a long history of being in front of the eyes of children. King Features had not only syndicated the cartoon to newspapers for over five decades, but for two decades had also syndicated "Popeye and Friends" cartoons to US television stations as children's programming. When explaining why he was not worried about the release of another film based on King Features' property, *Flash*

Gordon (Mike Hodges, 1980), being released one week before *Popeye*, Paramount's then vice president of marketing, Laurence Mark, explained that Popeye was already differentiated enough in its pre-sold nature that audiences would be fine with two cartoon-based films as "'Popeye' is Coke, and 'Flash Gordon' is Pepsi." Mark furthered that, while *Popeye* did not "have the trendy advantage of being a science-fiction movie," because the film starred *Mork and Mindy*'s Robin Williams, Paramount would not have to introduce an unknown star and could "reserve its $1.5 million of television advertising for a saturation blitz the week before the movie opens."[23]

CHANGING THE RECORD: *POPEYE* AND THE MAKING OF A HIGH CONCEPT SOUNDTRACK

To understand the importance of the soundtrack at this moment in American film history is to view it as an object composed of knotted desires from various stakeholders. In this framework the soundtrack is not simply an ancillary product but a constellation of investments, one of which was an investment in marketing. Justin Wyatt's argument about high concept is primarily concerned with the film's visual style; however, he also notes that stylistically high concept's most important component may be the "relation of the image to the soundtrack." For Wyatt this stylistic marriage becomes more significant throughout the 1980s as the growth of cable, satellite, and cassette allow for more distribution opportunities wherein portions of high concept films "composed of extended montages which are, in effect, music video sequences" can find purchase as programming fare elsewhere.[24] Wyatt explains that "the commercial applications of music within film (e.g., music video, soundtrack) aid their separation from the rest of the film's elements."[25] While *Popeye* would be released almost nine months before the debut of MTV, the soundtrack had ambitions to find its songs in radio playlists and dancefloors.

"Popeye" in jukeboxes, on the radio, and on the dancefloor was nothing new. The "Popeye" character and name had already found itself in numerous songs and records. The Sammy Lerner song "I'm Popeye the Sailor Man" had a decidedly strong association with the character since its initial publication by Famous Music in 1933. Founded in 1928, Famous Music was the long-time music publisher for Paramount Pictures, and the company was well aware of the need to adjust music to the demands of a changing film industry. Marvin Cane, Famous Music's then-president, had a long history of working music to promote films. Three years before *Popeye*, Cane ruminated to *Billboard* in 1977 that while songs were long used to promote films, how it was done was changing. While contemplating how to use the theme song from Paramount's upcoming reboot of *King Kong* (John Guillermin, 1976) "Are You in There," Cane noted that the music industry was "as tough now as it has ever been" and that a lot was changing fast: "songs that had a three-month stay on the charts are going up and down in six weeks. Everybody is going bananas."[26] With *Popeye*, Famous Music could test these changing waters once again and in a manner that exploited a uniquely presold property that they themselves had a history in selling.[27] As the American music trade magazine *Record World* explained:

> With the high recognition factor that naturally accompanies the name Popeye and its worldwide longevity as a popular comic strip, Cane envisions the film and soundtrack to reach record-breaking sales figures. "Popeye is as big in Hoboken as it is in Japan and this film is strictly a high-class musical with several songs that I am going to work my butt off on . . . People are going to be terribly curious about this movie and worldwide, this will probably give some of the recent big sellers a run for their money.[28]

In the words of Cane, nothing had "excited him more" than the *Popeye* musical. As Cane noted, "I feel, from what I've seen and heard of 'Popeye' that it has a quality and uniqueness that I've never seen in a motion picture."[29]

With Famous Music engaged, the publisher now looked to finalize a deal with a label. While it is not clear why Famous Music chose the label they did, it was clear that they wanted a label with significant distribution capacity, promotional acumen, and overseas rights.[30] In choosing Boardwalk, Famous Music chose a new label led by the former Casablanca label leader, Neil Bogart. While leading Casablanca, Bogart had helped develop significant record sales for acts such as Donna Summer, The Village People, and Kiss. In 1976 Casablanca had merged with Peter Guber's independent film company, Filmworks, Inc., and produced both the hit movies and soundtracks for *The Deep* (Peter Yates, 1977) and *Midnight Express* (Alan Parker, 1978) as Casablanca Record and Filmworks, Inc. Bogart and Guber's efforts at Casablanca had helped its artists win three Academy Awards, two for best scores with *Midnight Express* and *All That Jazz* and one best song for "Last Dance" from the *Thank God It's Friday* (Robert Klane, 1978) soundtrack.[31] In 1980 Bogart and Guber sold Casablanca and Filmworks to PolyGram and founded the Boardwalk Entertainment Company where Bogart would helm the record division. By August, Boardwalk had signed a distribution and pressing deal with CBS Records and in September announced it signed a long-term licensing deal with Bellaphon as the sole distributor of their records in Germany, England, Switzerland, Austria, Scotland, Ireland, and Wales.[32] In winning a bidding war for the *Popeye* soundtrack, *Record World* reported that Bogart was "'elated' about the acquisition" and that the deal would underscore "Boardwalk's identity as a cross-marketing force."[33] Boardwalk would not only provide product to be distributed by CBS, but would work with CBS's new "Video Enterprises Division developing audio/visual product." The deal included joint ventures on select projects, the first of which involved placing Kenny Loggins's Top Forty hit "I'm Alright" on CBS as the theme in the Jon Peters film production *Caddyshack* (Harold Ramis, 1980). Peters had worked with Casablanca, was a partner in Boardwalk, and had a history of working with Barbra Streisand on *A Star is Born* (Frank Pierson, 1976) and *The Main Event* (Howard Zieff, 1979).[34] The *Popeye* soundtrack would present a significant challenge to Bogart's company where the Christmastime release would be the first album for the new company, which hoped to heavily promote it as a "gift."[35]

Popeye's alliance of young film producers and record executives was not unusual. While the most valued function of the soundtrack would be to act as a source of promotion for its own sale and the film itself, in this emergent paradigm this meant creating popular music soundtracks that attracted young audiences. Hollywood's turn toward young audiences throughout the decade was so assertive that by 1978 *The New York Times* had dubbed the movement as the "youthenescence."[36] The reason was clear. Surveys in 1978 showed that the average filmgoer was twenty-two years old, thereby making younger film producers who understood popular music coveted assets. Traditional film producers, as one screenwriter put it, "[were] not the sort of men and women who ride to work playing Led Zeppelin tapes in their Mercedes."[37] By the late seventies the close collaboration between elements of the music industry and film producers had become an established norm. Bob Mercer, then worldwide head of music operations for EMI Films in London, considered that this trend of dual promotional campaigns by film and music companies was likely to continue as, "The film audience and music audience have similar age and demographic patterns."[38]

The crystallization of the youth-oriented blockbuster model began in 1978 as a slew of new musicals and music-oriented films that would be released in a post-*Saturday Night Fever* movement. These included adaptations of the Broadway musicals *The Wiz* (Sidney Lumet, 1978), *Hair* (Milos Forman, 1979), and *Grease*; a film based on the 1967 Beatles album *Sgt. Pepper's Lonely Hearts Club Band* (Michael Schultz, 1978); musical biopic *The Buddy Holly Story* (Steve Rash, 1978); a film set in a 1970s progressive radio station, *FM* (John A. Alonzo, 1978), one set in a disco (*Thank God It's Friday*), and two with stories of teenage rock fans (*Almost Summer* [Martin Davidson, 1978] and *I Wanna Hold Your Hand* [Robert Zemeckis, 1978]).[39] By 1980 the relationship between popular music labels and performers had begun to crystallize into something more than a trend. Discussing *Popeye* alongside *Flash Gordon* with Queen's score, and *Ragtime* (Milos Forman, 1981) with Randy Newman's score, Ed Ochs noted that, "halfway through 1980, it looks like the 'Year of the Soundtrack.' The high-water marks are everywhere."[40] While film companies would use the soundtrack to help find young audiences, for record companies it was clearly early on that a soundtrack was beneficial simply because the promotional budget for a Hollywood film dwarfs promotional budgets for records. In 1980, Bruce Bird of Casablanca records explained that from the standpoint of the record business, "You're getting the expectation of a film that might have a $4 million budget for advertising alone. A $4 million budget for a record company to spend on an album—you'd be out of business quick. But for a soundtrack they can do it."[41]

A CONSTELLATION OF INVESTORS MEETS AN AUTEUR BLOCKBUSTER

Up until now this paper has offered nothing that looks like *Popeye*, which is partially the point: before the film was created, it was a collection of interlocking investments in search of a franchise. Known for his large ensemble casts and a style notably dedicated to observation instead of a driving story, Altman's *Popeye* was expected to service this ensemble of expectations. Of course, while the project offered the chance to make Altman a significant commercial force, it also provided Nilsson a chance to resuscitate his own career and reputation.

Figure 6.2 Songwriter Harry Nilsson and Shelley Duvall during the recording of the soundtrack for *Popeye*. Courtesy of Special Collections Research Center, University of Michigan Library.

By 1979 Nilsson's image in the music industry had suffered from shrinking sales, a shot voice, and alcoholism. His longtime label, RCA, had let his contract expire. *Popeye* was a way to place himself back before American audiences and airwaves.[42] Working with notable studio talent including Ray Cooper, Klaus Voorman, Doug Dillard, and Van Dyke Parks, Nilsson's part in the project had generated some hope for rejuvenating his songwriting career through a prominent Hollywood blockbuster with a Christmastime release.

Nilsson's attempt at a musical score is both odd and ambitious. *Popeye*'s songbook and score are distinctly subdued. Writing in Nilsson's biography, Alyn Shipton claims that, "Altman's original idea had been that Nilsson would 'supply simplicity,' and that is what [Nilsson] was briefed to do."[43] The result was an unconventional score that plays with repetitive lyrics, acoustic instrumentations, and Van Dyke Parks's arrangements that produce a music that often stands out because of its excessive simplicity. Instead of providing show-stopping moments, the songs often interweave within Altman's use of overlapping sound and dialogue. At the same time, songs such as "I'm Mean," "He's Large," and "He Needs Me" trade in a lyrical minimalism composed for limited ranges to be all but recited in *sprechgesang*. The result is that the songs and their arrangements never achieve any moment of excessive pronouncement, nor is there a showstopping sequence. Instead, the songs and their recordings operate as confessions of character. Nilsson's style throughout *Popeye* aims for an intimacy that feels at odds with the both the Hollywood film musical of the studio era and the emergent music-oriented blockbuster films of the day. Take the cases of Bluto and Olive Oyl. Played by Paul L. Smith and sung by John Wallace, when Bluto sings his "I'm Mean" the character provides what Shipton calls a "patter song,"[44] repeatedly lacing almost spoken pronouncements of the titular lyric over a samba beat in a manner that announces that Bluto has little growth potential: he is and will remain mean. When Shelley Duvall sings/explains as Olive Oyl "I'm Large" and "He Needs Me," her naïve warble is employed to betray psychic states of reluctant engagement and adoration. As one 2017 critic noted about the soundtrack, the repetitive use of visual motifs and phrases of dialogue are echoed in the songs in a manner that "underline the characters' sense of limited horizons and options."[45] Finally, ensemble numbers like "Sweethaven (An Anthem)" and "Everything is Food" express an almost collective ennui rather than a sense of purposeful unity. The residents of Sweethaven in Altman and Nilsson's *Popeye* are neither celebratory nor mournful. In their anthem the citizens of Sweethaven cheer, but the cheers never achieve a level of enthusiasm just above half-hearted.

Sweethaven's tepid ambivalence, the result of Bluto's tyranny, is offset and threatened by the arrival of Popeye and Swee'Pea, both of whom bring energy and hope to the community. Yet Altman and Nilsson never allow the Sweethaven community to fully embrace these two characters' most affirmative characteristics. *Popeye* has the elements of a "happy ending" as Popeye comes to terms with his distaste of spinach, defeats Bluto, rescues Swee'Pea and Olive, and reunites with his father (Pappy). While the trio of Popeye, Olive and Swee'Pea constitute a new family as Popeye sings "Popeye the Sailor Man," it is unclear if the residents of Sweethaven will find better lives or even a life beyond Bluto. Yet even this aspect of relative musical minimalism is not fully embraced. Altman enlisted Tom Pearson to create a lush, more traditional orchestral score for the incidental music, thus overshadowing what Shipton notes are "the spare, simple songs [of Nilsson] that should have been the musical heart of the movie."[46]

Robert Altman's vacillation between following a genre's rules and open defiance of them should come as no surprise. For example, *Popeye*'s "emphasis on family groupings and the home" might best fit in the subgenre that Rick Altman calls in his book *The American Film Musical* a "folk musical."[47] Yet, Rick Altman notes that Robert Altman had previously deconstructed and critiqued the "folk musical" form in his movie with music *Nashville*.[48] Indeed, *Popeye*'s lack of conventional generic staples makes it never feel quite like a musical. Such is the state of *Popeye*, a musical that seems to reject some of the very formal tenets of the American film musical—i.e. excessive unity of the collective through choreographed demonstration, showstopping performances, binary coupling, etc.—in order to produce a musical that wants to embrace an excessive emphasis on the repetitive simplicities of its songs. Kelly Kessler rightfully places *Popeye* in a space between musicals of the post-studio era that "embraced the norms of an earlier era" (e.g. *Thoroughly Modern Millie* [George Roy Hill, 1967] and *Grease*) and those that rejected those norms (e.g. *Tommy* [Ken Russell, 1975] and *All That Jazz*). In this position, Kessler argues that Altman's musical is part of a number of musicals in the post-studio era that exhibit a tension between new and past values. For Kessler, a film like *Popeye* produces an ambivalence that vacillates between celebrating and rejecting the arcadian virtues of simple pleasures and community, family and form.[49] *Popeye* exists alongside other musicals between 1966 to 1983 that neither fully reject the ideological norms of the Hollywood musical nor completely embrace them. Rather, it, along with others, "exists in a state of tension" that "present a newer and less affirming vision of the movie musical."[50] Nilsson's soundtrack of acoustic arrangements and inexpert vocals places the residents of Sweethaven on the edge of the not-quite-modern world while securing a tense ambivalence between traditional folk values while amplifying their bindings.

When compared to other soundtracks of its day, *Popeye*'s reflective atavism distinguishes itself because of what it does not have. Unlike the above-mentioned Travolta films of *Grease* and *Saturday Night Fever* or its brethren *Xanadu* (Robert Greenwald, 1980) and *Can't Stop the Music* (Nancy Walker, 1980), *Popeye* does not offer one track that could find its way into discos or radio playlists. Other 1980 releases such as *Flash Gordon*, *Urban Cowboy*, and *The Blues Brothers* (John Landis, 1980) have soundtracks with investments in relatively contemporary radio-friendly genres of the day in rock, country, and rhythm and blues. Nilsson's score is not "folk" but its acoustic instrumentation mixed with Van Dyke Parks's orchestral arrangements all but declare little interest in creating hits for any contemporary radio format of the day. Upon its release the soundtrack was simultaneously contemporary and out of time, a perception that would mark the soundtrack as the eccentric acoustic accompanist to Altman's own "Brigadoon" in Sweethaven. Writing in *Record World*, Sophia Midas reported that Boardwalk was certain that while the album would appeal to everyone who grew up with Popeye, the album would "become a favorite among children."[51] Yet in its "Recommended LPs" column, *Billboard* almost immediately began to throw cold water on the project upon its release:

> What is expected to be one of Christmas' big film releases could translate into vinyl sales if it lives up to expectation. Yet despite lyrics by Harry Nilsson and music arranged and conducted by Van Dyke Parks, Robin Williams' Popeye and Shelly Duvall's Olive Oyl come across as two voices that at first seem like novelties but steadily grow weary. Best cuts: Pick your own.[52]

Looking back, it is unsurprising that neither of the two singles released, Robin Williams's rendition of Nilsson's penned "I Yam what I Yam" nor The Townspeople of Sweethaven's "Sweethaven (An Anthem)," could find significant purchase on radio playlists.

As musical soundtracks go, *Popeye* was by all accounts a commercial failure, with the album peaking at 115 on the *Billboard* charts and staying in the Top 200 for only ten weeks.[53] So severe was the failure in the face of these expectations that one can only imagine that it was a substantial contributing factor to Boardwalk's dramatic restructuring of its production and distribution agreement with CBS Records. On 1 May 1981, *Record World* reported that Boardwalk would both abandon the standard major practice of list pricing and, more importantly, move its distribution to independents, with Neil Bogart claiming that, "the CBS-Boardwalk deal was modified primarily because of differences in philosophy, particularly in the area of promotion."[54] To be sure, the movie that made money was a franchise failure best expressed by a soundtrack that disappointed the publisher, the label, and the studio. As for Nilsson, *Popeye* would be the last album of original songs he would release in the United States.

CODA: IT IS WHAT IT IS

So, what is *Popeye*? For one, it is a musical experiment where both director and composer feel dedicated to the creation of something of an auteur-blockbuster musical. Lesley Chow conveniently sums up Altman's film as one that "follows no recognizable model of narrative suspense or interest, and is happy to have most of its plot points as foregone conclusions." For Chow, "the marvel of this film is that it manages to reconcile actors as diverse as Walston, Williams, and Duvall."[55] She was not alone in underscoring the film's odd collection of talents. Robert Evans's selection of Altman and Nilsson positioned *Popeye* to become a coalition of what Robert Self calls, drawing from Jean-Louis Baudry, "producer-subjects." For *Popeye* this meant the musical "highlights the relations of production normally suppressed by the name of the director in traditional auteur studies." This particular constellation is unique:

> Robert Evans, of *Love Story* and the *Godfather* films, produced the film for Paramount and Walt Disney; Jules Feiffer, successful playwright and cartoonist, adapted the script from the E. C. Segar cartoon strip of the 1930s; Grammy-award winner Harry Nilsson wrote the music and lyrics; Ray Walston, Robin Williams, and Shelley Duvall starred; Giuseppe Rotunno, of Fellini's *Satyricon* and *City of Women* and Bob Fosse's *All That Jazz*, was director of photography; and Robert Altman directed—a strong mixture of accomplished, talented authors and strong, independent egos—all with different interpretations of the meaning they intended in the film.[56]

If anything, what this assemblage makes clear is that the talents of the personnel contributed to making a unique product, but did so at the expense of the franchise. It is not so much "*Popeye* the Musical," rather it is an "Altman/Nilsson/Williams *Popeye*." In short, it is a musical ambivalent about musicals that produced a soundtrack with almost no explicit interest in radio airplay or dancefloor potential.

In 2017 the *Popeye* soundtrack received a celebratory two-disk reissue that included music that had been left off the original album, substantial liner notes, and an extra disk of Nilsson's demos with Nilsson's vocals on each of the songs. Offering a positive review of the reissue, *Pitchfork* called the record a "mournful little under-appreciated classic," "a mangy patchwork, and like the film, it begs to be underestimated. Many of the songs play out like napkins with the titles written on them, the lyrics meant to be filled in later."[57] In essence, *Popeye*'s soundtrack is like the "the souls of Sweethaven, [souls who] are beaten down by the forces governing them, small-minded and bickering and fearful."[58] In this context, Nilsson's songs "feel written for characters that behave more like cawing penny-arcade machines than humans."[59] The soundtrack exhibited a "mind meld" between Altman and Nilsson that generated a musical for an ensemble dedicated to celebrating the odd and eccentric.[60] In 1981 Altman explained that he understood he was a director whose films "commercially . . . are not very successful, but I can always find a little pocket of cult people who seem to like them."[61] When he sold his studio,

Altman declared, "I feel my time has run out. Every studio wants '*Raiders of the Lost Ark.*' The movies I want to make are movies the studios don't want. What they want to make, I don't."[62] One thing was clear: as depressing as it was that the *Popeye* franchise flopped, Altman nevertheless declared, "I don't think I'd be very pleased if I had a film that went out like *Grease* and made $200 million and yet everybody I ran into said, 'That's the worst film I've ever seen.' I think that would depress me more."[63]

NOTES

1. Beverly Walker, "Altman '91," *Film Comment* 27, no. 1 (1991): 6.
2. Ibid. p. 2.
3. Ibid. p. 2.
4. Ibid. p. 6.
5. Ibid. p. 7.
6. Roger Ebert, "Reviews: Popeye," *RogerEbert.com*, 1980. Available at <https://www.rogerebert.com/reviews/popeye-1980> (last accessed 6 May 2020).
7. Vincent Canby, "Screen: A singing, dancing, Feifferish kind of '*Popey*e,'" *The New York Times*, 12 December 1980, C5.
8. Anon., "Alas, poor 'Popeye,'" *Washington Post*, 13 December 1980, D2.
9. Walker, "Altman '91," p. 6.
10. Rick Lyman, "Robert Altman, director with daring, dies at 81," *The New York Times*, 22 November 2006, A1. Available at <https://www.nytimes.com/2006/11/22/movies/robert-altman-director-with-daring-dies-at-81.html>.
11. This was not the first time Hollywood turned to popular music to boost their bottom line. A number of authors have addressed this, but the best place to begin this research is with Jeff Smith's excellent *The Sounds of Commerce*: Jeff Smith, *The Sounds of Commerce* (New York: Columbia University Press, 1998).
12. Walker, "Altman '91," p. 6.
13. Justin Wyatt, *High Concept: Movies and Marketing in Hollywood* (Austin, TX: University of Texas Press, 1994), p. 58.
14. Ibid. p. 18.
15. Ibid. p. 23.
16. Ibid. p. 1.
17. It should be noted that Ray Walston also released a record marketed toward children in 1964. Titled, *My Favorite Songs from Mary Poppins and Other Songs to Delight*, the record attempted to piggy back on Walston's then-hit television show, *My Favorite Martian* (1963–6).
18. Sally Ogle Davis, "Wishing upon a falling star at Disney," *The New York Times*, 16 November 1980, pp. 6, 144.
19. Ibid. p. 144.
20. Ibid. p. 144.
21. Ibid. p. 6.
22. Steve Lohr, "Advertising: Pondering account publicity," *The New York Times*, 22 August 1980, D13.
23. Aljean Harmetz, "At the movies: Cukor, at 81, is back behind the camera," *The New York Times*, 28 November 1980, C2.

24. Wyatt, *High Concept*, p. 17.
25. Ibid. pp. 36–7.
26. Roman Kozak, "A day in the life of Marvin Cane: Famous music president's life is tied to movies, gorillas & c'rights," *Billboard*, 15 January 1977, p. 27.
27. Not only had the Sammy Lerner song been recorded and released numerous times as a children's record, but "I Am What I Am" had found its way onto at least two disco records, once in 1977 by the American disco act Wing & A Prayer Fife & Drum Corp, and once again by a Japanese act, Spinach Power. However, this was hardly the first time that Popeye was associated with the dancefloor: 1962, a banner year for "Popeye dance records," produced "The Popeye Twist," by the British instrumental act The Tornados; a release by Chubby Checker titled "Popeye (The Hitchhiker)"; and in the same year The Mar-Keys, Stax Records' studio band, released an album titled, *Do the Pop-Eye*. The Mar-Keys LP is, in many ways, a record of instrumentals conceived around Popeye and his friends. Out of the twelve cuts, eight of them have Popeye oriented titles such as "Pop-Eye Stroll," "Wimp Burger," "Straight from the Can," "Sweet-P Crawl," and "Sailor Man Waltz."
28. Joseph Ianello, "'Famous' Cane bullish on 'Popeye Shogun,'" *Record World*, 2 August 1980, pp. 6, 50.
29. Ibid. pp. 6, 50.
30. Ibid. pp. 6, 50.
31. Richard Imamura, "Boardwalk pacts with CBS for pressing, shipping," *Cash Box*, 30 August 1980, p. 5.
32. Anon., "Alas, poor 'Popeye'"; Sam Sutherland, "CBS-Boardwalk distribution pact includes records and video projects," *Record World*, 30 August 1980, p. 61.
33. Sutherland, "CBS-Boardwalk distribution pact," p. 61.
34. Paul Grein, "Boardwalk & CBS agree on disk/tape/video contract," *Billboard*, 30 August 1980, p. 3.
35. Rick Forrest, "Label super-product campaigns target holiday giving," *Billboard*, 25 October 1980, RSG-4.
36. Janice Selinger, "'Saturday Night Fever' – Back Stage," *The New York Times*, 30 April 1978, NJ26. Available at <https://nyti.ms/1kPciKs>.
37. Hugh Fordin, "Film musicals—rock calls the tune," *The New York Times*, 12 March 1978, D15. Available at <https://nyti.ms/1H8IYTz>.
38. The connections between music and film had become so significant that in just 1980 *Billboard* could list the following musical tie ins: The Village People and The Ritchie Family on *Can't Stop the Music* (Casablanca); Neil Diamond in *The Jazz Singer* (Capitol); The Blues Brothers in *The Blues Brothers* (Atlantic); Paul Simon in *One Trick Pony* (Warner Bros.); Meat Loaf and Blondie in *Roadie* (Warner Bros.); Bette Midler returning in *Divine Madness*; Olivia Newton-John and Gene Kelly in *Xanadu* (MCA); Roger Daltrey in *McVicar*; Willie Nelson in *Honeysuckle Rose*; *Carney* with Robbie Robertson and Gary Busey of *The Buddy Holly Story*; Dolly Parton with *The Best Little Whorehouse in Texas* and *Nine to Five*. The column further noted that "films are in various stages of production focusing on four classic albums: Willie Nelson's 'Red Headed Stranger,' the Eagles' 'Desperado,' and Elton John's 'Goodbye Yellow Brick Road' and 'Captain Fantastic and the Brown Dirt Cowboy.'" Kenny Rogers' "Gideon" is being considered for a film or Broadway adaptation ... Films are also said to be in the works based on three hit singles: Johnny Paycheck's "Take This Job and Shove IT," Vicki Lawrence's "The Night the Lights Went Out In Georgia," and Michael Murphey's "Hard Country." Projects with strong country orientation such as *Bronco Billy* (Elektra), *Urban Cowboy* (Elektra), *Every Which Way but Loose II* (Elektra), *Second Hand Hearts* and *Smokey and the Bandit II* (MCA). See Paul Grein, "Large surge in record & film tie-ins," *Billboard*, 31 May 1980, p. 33.

39. Fordin, "Film musicals, " D15.
40. Ed Ochs, "Mining gold from the silver screen," *Billboard*, 2 August 1980, M-1.
41. Ochs, "Mining gold," M-3.
42. Before recording and releasing *Popeye*, Nilsson did release *Flash Harry*, his first LP in three years. It would be both the first and last for his new label, Mercury Records. *Flash Harry* would be distributed only and never receive a proper US release. See Val Falloon, "Record World International: England," *Record World*, 6 September 1980, p. 40.
43. Alyn Shipton, *Nilsson: The Life of a Singer-Songwriter* (New York, NY: Oxford University Press, 2013), p. 244.
44. Ibid. p. 245.
45. Jayson Greene, "Harry Nilsson, *Popeye*: Original motion picture soundtrack," Album Review, *Pitchfork*, 4 September 2017. Available at <https://pitchfork.com/reviews/albums/harry-nilsson-popeye-original-motion-picture-soundtrack/>.
46. Shipton, *Nilsson*, p. 245.
47. Rick Altman, *The American Film Musical* (Bloomington: Indiana University Press, 1987), p. 273.
48. Rick Altman describes *Nashville* as the first film "to fully exploit the folk musical's paradoxical folk art/mass art foundations, revealing every contradiction, every false assumption, every self-deception of the folk musical." Furthermore, "*Nashville* is not just a film with music which fails to be a musical for lack of joy or appropriate staging; it is a calculated and brilliant point-by-point deconstruction of the folk musical" (p. 324). See Rick Altman, *The American Film Musical*, p. 323.
49. Kelly Kessler, *Destabilizing the Hollywood Musical: Music, Masculinity, and Mayhem* (New York, NY: Palgrave Macmillan, 2010), p. 22.
50. Ibid. p. 22.
51. Sophia Midas, "Retail rap," *Record World*, 8 November 1980, p. 40.
52. "Billboard's recommended LPs," *Billboard*, 6 December 1980, p. 46.
53. Joel Whitburn, *Top Pop Albums: 1955–1996* (Menomonee Falls, WI: Record Research, Inc., 1996), p. 917.
54. Dave Schulps, "Boardwalk to indie distribs, will abandon list pricing," *Cash Box*, 30 May 1981, p. 7.
55. Lesley Chow, "Focus on Robert Altman: Three takes on *Popeye*," *Bright Lights Film Journal*, 19 April 2018. Available at <https://brightlightsfilm.com/focus-on-robert-altman-three-takes-on-popeye/#.XpS_k1NKh24>.
56. Robert Self, "Robert Altman and the theory of authorship," *Cinema Journal* 25, no. 1 (Fall 1985): 4. Available at <https://www.jstor.org/stable/1224836>.
57. Greene, "Harry Nilsson, *Popeye*,"pitchfork.com.
58. Ibid.
59. Ibid.
60. Ibid.
61. Dennis Altman, "Robert Altman: Building sand castles," *Cinema Papers* no. 33 (July–August 1981): 246.
62. Harmetz, "At the movies," A15.
63. Dennis Altman, "Robert Altman: Building sand castles," p. 246.

CHAPTER 7

"Here Comes the Hot-Stepper": Hollywood Renaissance, Indie Film and Robert Altman's Comeback in the 1990s

Yannis Tzioumakis

This chapter revisits Robert Altman's 1992 rather unexpected return to commercial success and critical adoration with *The Player* after a decade or so in "an oblique Eighties wilderness,"[1] a period during which the filmmaker made, arguably, culturally insignificant films, while also working in television. Starting from the position that most of Altman's film output at that time is located in the emerging but very lively American independent film scene, the chapter asks why Altman has not been examined as an independent filmmaker and part of that scene. This question is particularly pertinent given that during a period that extends from 1980 and the release of *Popeye* to 1992 and his "comeback" with *The Player* Altman was involved as a director in no fewer than fifteen projects, ranging from low-budget independent films released by key specialty film distributors to made-for-television films that were often adapted from plays by major American playwrights; from films made for television based on original screenplays to independent features released theatrically by distributors associated primarily with exploitation pictures; from participation in a "portmanteau" picture to producing a highly critically acclaimed political television show for a key cable broadcaster; and even one studio production, *O. C. and Stiggs*. Finally, immediately prior to *The Player*, Altman's last output was another relatively low-budget quality independent film, *Vincent & Theo*, which he produced at the same time as a four-part television series for the international television market.[2]

As will be noted in the main body of this chapter, it was the critical success of *Vincent & Theo* that precipitated Altman's return to "critical and public favor" before *The Player* signaled this return as a major comeback for a great artist.[3] However, what the above brief chronicle of Altman's work in the 1980s clearly suggests is that accounts that label this work "Eighties wilderness" or a time when Altman "lost his way"[4] may have been exaggerated. As is clear, Altman continued to work, often on more than one project at a time, and remained as prolific as he was in the 1970s, a period when he was also involved as a director in fifteen projects, fourteen feature films and an episode for TV series *Saturday Night Live* (1975–). It is just that in the 1980s he was not working for the Hollywood majors, while his involvement with filmed plays and television series seemed to be at odds with the kind of work that characterized his critically successful films of the 1970s, with one reviewer suggesting that he had become "a more polished craftsman than a virtuoso."[5] In this respect, it is important to question why "Robert Altman, independent filmmaker" did not appear on the critics' radar in the same way that, say, John Sayles, Jim Jarmusch, Wayne Wang, and other filmmakers associated with the independent film scene of the time did.

In a chapter that treads similar ground to the present work, Dimitrios Pavlounis makes a convincing argument about critical and promotional discourses surrounding Altman's work over-emphasizing the few films he made in the early 1970s in terms of possessing Altman's essence as an auteur filmmaker.[6] These discourses, driven by what Dana Polan terms "auteur desire," had bestowed so much critical investment on such films as *M*A*S*H*, *McCabe & Mrs. Miller*, and *Nashville* that, if other Altman films were not characterized by the stylistic and narrative qualities that marked these pictures, they were almost automatically received, if not as failures, as disappointments.[7] Pavlounis examines the contours of this argument by looking at questions of film authorship. He is interested in the extent to which such questions relate to the concept of the "comeback" as it is examined within a critical approach guided by the legacy of the Hollywood Renaissance of the late 1960s and early 1970s and the subsequent "New Hollywood" of the late 1970s and beyond that is associated with the rise of the blockbuster and high-concept filmmaking.[8]

This chapter, on the other hand, has a different objective. Driven by popular and (certain) academic accounts that see the Hollywood Renaissance of the 1960s and 1970s as having left its legacy on contemporary American independent cinema, it examines certain aspects of this argument by investigating how Robert Altman may be bridging these two fields and eras. As he represents one of the main figures of the Hollywood Renaissance and as all his three "comeback" films in the first half of the 1990s (*The Player*, *Short Cuts*, and *Prêt-à-Porter*) were produced and released within the indie film scene of the time, Altman is uniquely placed in the history of American cinema for such a project.

The ensuing analysis will demonstrate that the links between Hollywood Renaissance and American independent cinema are also exaggerated as they are often based on assumptions that are highly selective. Similarly, Altman's positioning within independent film discourses tends to be awkward. He is ignored almost completely as a "1980s independent," by contemporary critics, despite working consistently in the independent film sector of the time with such companies as Cinecom, United Artists Classics, and Cannon Films. On the other hand, Altman receives some recognition as a "1990s indie" but accounts of American independent cinema tend to praise him primarily as an influence on the young indie filmmakers of the 1990s than as an indie filmmaker himself. In examining how all these threads are intertwined, this chapter locates Altman as an "independent" and "indie" filmmaker within very particular industrial and institutional configurations that tend to have tenuous links with the Hollywood Renaissance. This is despite the fact that aspects of Altman's authorial signature as developed in the early 1970s can also be detected in his comeback films of the early 1990s.

THE HOLLYWOOD RENAISSANCE AND INDIE CINEMA: CLOSE RELATIVES OR DISTANT FRIENDS?

The Hollywood Renaissance (a term used often interchangeably with the "New Hollywood" and the "American New Wave") has often been perceived as close "in spirit," if not in material detail, with contemporary (post-1980) American independent cinema. Roughly extending from the late 1960s to the mid-1970s, the Hollywood Renaissance tends to represent "a wide range of formally and thematically challenging films made (and in many cases released with great success at the box office)" primarily by the major Hollywood studios.[9] Often seen as destabilizing the classical Hollywood paradigm by adopting "alien aesthetic norms" and providing progressive representations, these films represent a period of "consistent formal experimentation and institutional flux" in American cinema that has stood out in its history[10] and that continues to attract significant critical and cinephilic attention. On the other hand, a particular expression of American independent cinema, "organised around the quality, low-budget, theatrically distributed and exhibited feature length fiction film," emerged in the 1980s as an alternative to the Hollywood studio films, giving voice to minorities, examining social problems and uncovering "hidden histories," while also encouraging aesthetic experimentation.[11] Even though it quickly became institutionalized through the financial and institutional support of the Hollywood majors, and has continued to evolve as later labels such as "indie" and "indiewood" suggest, it maintained its status as a space where particular filmmakers could continue to experiment with form and provide representations that were absent from the films of the majors.

As is clear from these two very basic definitions, the possibilities of seeing the Hollywood Renaissance and contemporary American independent cinema as closely linked are evident. It is not surprising then that once American independent cinema studies started to emerge as a field there was substantial attention given to how the two may be connected. Popular criticism, in particular, did a lot to emphasize these links as linear and immediate, especially with reference to the more institutionalized indie cinema that would emerge in the late 1980s and early 1990s. Peter Biskind's *Down and Dirty Pictures* (2004), which examines the period between 1989 and 2002, is arguably the most representative of such efforts.[12] Biskind starts his book by calling it "a sequel, of sorts"[13] to his earlier, best-selling *Easy Riders, Raging Bulls* (1998), which provides an anecdotal and hugely entertaining account of the American film industry during the years of the Hollywood Renaissance.[14] He proceeds to call the independent filmmakers of the 1990s "a loose collection of spiritual and aesthetic heirs" to the New Hollywood,[15] basing his argument on Hollywood's gradual abandonment of the experimentation of the 1970s and its loss of interest in "how-we-live-now small films about real people."[16] This gap enabled the emergence of filmmakers who were initially completely outside the system and who, according to Biskind, had absorbed the Hollywood Renaissance filmmakers' "anti-Hollywood aesthetic,"[17] managing in the process to build "an identity and an audience" for independent film by the mid-1980s.[18]

Biskind makes further comparisons between the two eras, noting the introduction of a new generation of character actors that were comparable to the ones introduced in the 1970s as well as the less concrete idea that both eras were "pregnant with change."[19] However, where academic film histories would look at the 1990s as a period during which independent film and Hollywood would enjoy a symbiotic relationship, often epitomized by the acceptance of the much more hip and nondescript label "indie" as opposed to independent,[20] Biskind thinks of this as a "harsh" conclusion. Instead, he sees the 1990s as the period in which the seeds planted in the 1980s "grew and blossomed,"[21] with an outburst of filmmaking activity making the sector extremely visible and increasingly commercial. He does admit, however, that independent film also has differences from the Hollywood Renaissance but includes only one, the absence of flamboyance in contemporary independents' use of visual style (bar the films of Quentin Tarantino) compared to filmmakers like Martin Scorsese, Brian De Palma, and, of course, Altman.[22] This is a rather odd summation given the strong aesthetics in the films of other filmmakers of the time such as Todd Haynes, Gregg Araki, the Coen brothers, and Richard Linklater.

Biskind was hardly the only popular critic to compare indie film to the Hollywood Renaissance. Sharon Waxman's *Rebels on the Backlot* (2005) and James Mottram's *The Sundance Kids* (2006) made very similar claims,[23] with the latter going as far as pairing contemporary filmmakers with ones from the Hollywood Renaissance (with Paul Thomas Anderson in particular seen as evoking the spirit of Robert Altman in his films).[24] However, neither Biskind nor Waxman nor Mottram showed any interest in examining Altman's work in the 1980s and 1990s as part of the independent film scene of the time, opting instead to concentrate on the young, hip filmmakers who emerged at that time: Steven Soderbergh, Paul Thomas Anderson, Quentin Tarantino, Spike Jonze, and others.

Academic criticism, on the other hand, has been more cautious in making such links and, when it did so, has advanced its argument with qualification. Writing three years before Biskind, Jim Hillier starts the introduction to his *American Independent Cinema* volume with this point, suggesting that the "sense of renewal and experimentation in Hollywood filmmaking" that characterized the films of the Hollywood Renaissance "has much in common with the sense of renewal in later independent filmmaking."[25] He includes Altman as the key example of a filmmaker who represents this continuity having worked through the 1970s to the early 1990s but, following Justin Wyatt,[26] he is quick to suggest that Altman's 1990s independent films were the product of different "economic opportunities,"[27] something that will be discussed in more detail in the next two sections. More importantly, Hillier makes the point that links with the Hollywood Renaissance represent only American independent film's "most immediate context,"[28] given the presence of other forms of independent filmmaking (exploitation, avant-garde, documentary, pornography) that have been around, which have also influenced contemporary quality independent film in numerous ways.

Although other scholars such as John Berra have made more assertive claims about the ways in which the Hollywood Renaissance has shaped American independent cinema,[29] and Claire Perkins has produced a detailed and interesting study on how cynicism in Altman's 1970s films has influenced the films of Paul Thomas Anderson and Noah Baumbach,[30] Hillier's pointing to other "less immediate" contexts demonstrates the dangers of assuming such a linear relationship. Biskind himself raised the issue of the absence of counter-cultural values in the period covered by *Down and Dirty Pictures* and noted the disconnect between politics and culture in the 1990s compared to the 1970s. He even used the "benefit of hindsight" to ascertain that the indie cinema of the 1990s *was* a movement, "however ill-defined and *unlike the New Hollywood*" (emphasis added).[31] Waxman and Mottram, on the other hand, provide little evidence on the nature of the kinship of the filmmakers of the 1990s to the ones of the 1970s, while Perkins does not want to make broader claims about how the two eras connect, arguing that this link is a widely-held "assumption" that is founded in an "idealized philosophy of male auteurism" and therefore does not investigate its broader validity.[32] Finally, Berra's position has been critiqued exactly for not considering the other "less immediate" contexts that exerted influence on the quality independent cinema of the 1980s and 1990s.[33]

One could also offer other reasons as to why such comparisons are problematic, starting from the industrial landscape and its difference between the two eras. Hollywood histories have demonstrated in great detail how the Hollywood studios overextended during the late 1960s and went through a deep recession in the 1969–71 period, losing collectively $500 million and looking outside the tried and tested, including in the exploitation film sector, for product that could connect with an audience.[34] The theatrical audience itself had reached its nadir in terms of size in 1971, while one by one the studios were being taken over by conglomerates coming from outside the industry in order to stay afloat. Compare this to the late 1980s and early 1990s and a booming economy. Having recalibrated their business to focus on blockbuster and high-concept films, the studios had re-asserted their control of the market. The industry had stabilized and new conglomerates coming from the broader media and content delivery sectors were starting to buy the studios, not to keep them afloat but to extend the value of their product by focusing on the potential for synergies at a time when new technologies were making home entertainment an increasingly lucrative market.

It is exactly at this point that independent film also starts to become strongly linked to the Hollywood studios, which determined that (1) it represented an increasingly lucrative market for a relatively small investment and (2) films from that sector could supplement films made by the studios in being distributed around the world and in the home entertainment market. It is clear then that the independent cinema of the late 1980s and 1990s emerged during a time when the film industry was much more stable than in the era of the Hollywood Renaissance.

However, arguably the most significant reason why such a link is overstated and problematic is the fact that it ignores pretty much a whole decade of American independent cinema from the late 1970s to the late 1980s—a decade where independence was practiced overwhelmingly away from the studios and in a variety of forms and guises, some of which had few, if any, points of contact with the Hollywood Renaissance films of the 1970s. Whether referred to as "the seeds planted" in the 1980s by Biskind,[35] or "movies that [did not break] through to a wide audience," by Waxman,[36] the key issue with these accounts is that they tend to be (often very) selective in how they approach contemporary American independent cinema, including their use of the labels "independent" and "indie."

As the next section will argue, independent cinema and indie cinema can be (and have been) approached as concepts with different specificities, with the latter arguably more productively defined in relation to the former and its evolution though the 1980s than in relation to developments that took place twenty years prior.[37] Taking such definitions on board, the chapter will argue that the discourses that surrounded Altman's work away from the studios in the 1980s resisted labelling him an independent filmmaker, even though he made five pictures of such designation during that period. This is because

Altman's films were not always a great fit with the dominant form of independent filmmaking at that time. On the other hand, when the term "indie" cinema started to get traction (and visibility and marketability) in the early 1990s on account of certain characteristics that provided it with a strong brand identity, it was much easier for Altman to fit in it. By that time, any links of indie cinema to the Hollywood Renaissance were rather redundant, despite some of the accounts discussed in this section.

"HERE COMES THE COLD-STEPPER": INDEPENDENT ALTMAN

As I mentioned in the introduction to this chapter, following *Popeye* in 1980 and before the release of *The Player* in 1992, Robert Altman was credited as the director of fifteen works, thirteen of which were released in the 1980s. Putting aside five made-for-television films, the TV show *Tanner '88*, his contribution to the portmanteau film *Aria* (1987), and *O. C. and Stiggs* that was a major studio production, Altman directed five independently produced and theatrically released films in the decade. *Come Back to the 5 & Dime, Jimmy Dean, Jimmy Dean* and *Secret Honor* were released by key independent film distributor Cinecom; *Streamers* was released by United Artists Classics (the first specialty film division of a major studio in the 1980s); *Fool for Love* was financed and released by one of the key independent distributors of the 1980s, Cannon—operating in the genre and exploitation film part of the sector rather than the quality film one; and *Beyond Therapy*, released by leading exploitation film company New World Pictures, which nonetheless occasionally ventured into quality film territory as well releasing non-US arthouse films. Finally, his first film in the 1990s, *Vincent & Theo*, was also an independent film, financed and released by Hemdale, a well-established production company that branched out into distribution in 1986.

Such a substantial output of different types of films, from play adaptations in a limited setting (*Come Back to the 5 & Dime, Jimmy Dean, Jimmy Dean, Streamers*) to one-man shows (*Secret Honor*) to more expansive and higher-budget productions (*Fool for Love, Beyond Therapy, Vincent & Theo*), financed outside Hollywood and distributed by an assortment of companies associated with the independent film sector clearly telegraphs Altman as an independent filmmaker in the 1980s. And yet, Altman did not develop an identity as an independent filmmaker. As was noted, almost all accounts of his 1992 "comeback" frame his earlier work as "absence" from Hollywood or as "self-imposed exile" rather than as a filmmaker working regularly and consistently in the independent film sector, which during the 1980s had a clear identity as providing an alternative to the films of the Hollywood majors.

Figure 7.1 Writer and actor Sam Shepard with Robert Altman on the set of *Fool for Love*. Photo by Douglas K. Hall. Courtesy of Special Collections Research Center, University of Michigan Library.

Given that Altman has always had a reputation of being "anti-Hollywood," a filmmaker "who has banged heads with the Hollywood system harder and more often than any other filmmaker," as one career profile put it,[38] one wonders why popular and trade press discourses of the time did not make this connection. This is particularly strange as one of the first critical accounts of American independent cinema in the early 1980s highlights its oppositionality to Hollywood, with Annette Insdorf arguing that it was distinguished in terms of "casting, pace, cinematic style and social and moral vision. Countering big stars with fresh faces, big deals with intimate canvasses and big studios with regional authenticity, [independent] filmmakers treat[ed] inherently American concerns with a primarily European style."[39]

Taking this definition as a starting point, Altman's 1980s films were certainly characterized by several of these elements. With most of the films being adaptations of plays in limited settings, one can certainly see the intimate canvasses supported by a slow narrative pace that enables strong characterizations to register with audiences. Based on plays by masters of American drama such as David Rabe, Christopher Durang, and Sam Shepard, the films do not shy away from key social and moral dilemmas, that involve questions of race and sexuality (*Streamers*), gender and identity (*Come Back to the 5 & Dime, Jimmy Dean, Jimmy Dean*), and class and familial relationships (*Fool for Love*). Despite most of his films shot in studio facilities, films such as *Fool for Love* also allow for a strong regional authenticity, while the limited settings force Altman to eschew his "free floating camera" and opt instead for more steady compositions that showcase dialogue and drama and arguably confirm his transition to "polished craftsman." Indeed, it is only in the element of casting that Altman's films may diverge from Insdorf's definition as even during these so called years of "wilderness" Altman was often able to secure established actors (Sandy Dennis, Jeff Goldblum, Kim Basinger, Karen Black) or stars in other media (Cher, Sam Shepard) together with a host of "fresh faces" many of whom received some of their earliest credits in Altman's films (Matthew Modine, Philip Baker Hall, Kathy Bates, and others).

Yet, despite all these characteristics and the involvement of companies such as United Artists Classics, Cinecom, Cannon Films, and New World Pictures, which were strongly identified with the independent film sector of the 1980s, Altman's name stayed away from discourses of independence. A brief examination of the reviews of his five independent films in the *New York Times*, all of which were by Vincent Canby, demonstrates that not only did Altman not register as an independent filmmaker but that his films continued to be scrutinized in terms of how they deviate from his signature style and not being inventive (and good) enough as adaptations of plays.

For instance, in his review of *Streamers* and under the subtitle "Play *Streamers* Adapted by Altman," Canby compares the film to Altman's earlier play adaptation *Come Back to the 5 & Dime, Jimmy Dean, Jimmy Dean*, but rather than interpreting both films' stagy aesthetics as an example of independent cinema that goes against the codes of (classical) Hollywood realism, he complains of the "unfortunate effect of [Altman] calling attention to the highly literary quality of the script."[40] Equally, in his review of *Fool for Love*, tellingly titled "Shepard's 'Fool for Love," Canby wonders why Altman's and Shepard's "opening up" of the play does not make the film more "cinematic," and accuses Altman of destroying the film by "chopping" scenes with a lot of close ups, as he did in *Streamers* and *Come Back to the 5 & Dime, Jimmy Dean, Jimmy Dean*.[41] At no point do the reviews of these films and of *Beyond Therapy*[42] try to contextualize his work as an example of independent cinema or mention anything about the companies with which he had been collaborating. Only the review of *Secret Honor*, the one film of this group Canby reviewed positively, mentions independence. But even there, independence is equated with the film's location shooting in Michigan and the support it received by the University of Michigan and the Los Angeles Actors' Theater rather than as an example of a specific film sector that encourages experimentation and deals often with political issues.[43]

A potential answer to the reason why Altman's independence in the 1980s was not perceived as such can be provided by the evolution of "independent" to "indie" cinema in the late 1980s and early 1990s. As I have argued elsewhere, the 1980s independent film scene was dominated by the "low-budget, low-key quality film," which mostly dealt with mature themes that targeted primarily an adult, educated audience.[44] Characterized primarily by the elements noted above by Insdorf, key examples of such films included work by John Sayles (*Return of the Secaucus 7*, 1980), Wayne Wang (*Chan is Missing*, 1982), Jim Jarmusch (*Stranger than Paradise*, 1984), Spike Lee (*She's Gotta Have It*, 1986), Bette Gordon (*Variety*, 1983), and others. These kinds of films exerted hegemony in the sector, arguably to the detriment of films that may have also been financed and released outside the studios but may not fully fit this description. On the other hand, films such as *Dirty Dancing* (Emile Ardolino, 1987)—and other Vestron productions such as *Anna* (Yurek Bogayevicz, 1987) and *China Girl* (Abel Ferrara, 1987)—have also been ignored as examples of independent cinema, as have been quality films that were released by companies with an emphasis on exploitation, horror, and soft core such as New Line Cinema (*Buddies*, Arthur J. Bressan, Jr., 1985) and New World Pictures (*Suburbia*, Penelope Spheeris, 1984; and indeed Altman's *Beyond Therapy*).

However, since the late 1980s and especially following the critical and commercial success of *sex, lies, and videotape* (Steven Soderbergh, 1989), the independent film sector started to become increasingly popularized and commercialized, while filmmaking became much more diverse under the "indie" label. Still, a particular type of film once again exerted hegemony in the sector with its key characteristics now including: the use of stars, even if stardom in this case appealed to a niche demographic; strong but creative uses of genre; substantial emphasis on questions around marketing and targeted audience demographics; and an extremely strong investment in authorship as both a marketing hook and a point of entry for engaging with the work, which quickly led to the emergence of filmmakers such as Steven Soderbergh, Hal Hartley, Quentin Tarantino, and others as poster children of indie cinema.[45]

It is at this stage that Robert Altman suddenly starts "clicking" for critics as an *indie* (and not an independent) filmmaker. As Justin Wyatt argued, during the second half of the 1970s, Altman's work had few points of contact with the ways in which mainstream Hollywood cinema had been developing following the increasing success of market-driven blockbuster films. As he put it, "Altman's projects, usually lacking stars, an exploitable premise, and an obvious marketing approach, deviated significantly from this overall change in the industry."[46] I would like to argue that Altman's "deviation" was exacerbated during the 1980s when the blockbuster and high-concept trends intensified in the industry at large and when, indeed, Altman stopped working for the Hollywood majors altogether. However, despite making films that were characterized by many of the elements identified by Insdorf and adhering to the "low-budget, low-key quality film" approach that exerted hegemony in the sector, his output was not *coherent* enough to enable him to develop an identity as an independent filmmaker: his independent films were released by a mixture of quality and exploitation distributors; they included adaptations of well-crafted drama (*Come Back to the 5*

& Dime, Jimmy Dean, Jimmy Dean, Streamers, Fool for Love) and farce (*Beyond Therapy*), supplemented by a one-character film (*Secret Honor*); the majority featured minor stars but *Secret Honor* did not; any possibility of an oeuvre, a collective articulation of Altman's further development as an artist, was compromised not only by the lack of an aesthetically cohesive body of work but also by the fact that it was interspersed by work in other media as well as by a barely released studio film. Under these circumstances, it is not surprising that even his authorship was challenged as in Canby's review for *Fool for Love* that, as I mentioned above, highlighted Shepard rather than Altman as the film's creative force.

On the other hand, once independent cinema started evolving into indie cinema, with its increased emphasis on the use of stars, genre experiments, authorship, and marketing, Altman's films suddenly seemed to be much more in tune with these developments. And this starts with *Vincent & Theo* two years before his widely perceived comeback with *The Player*. With that film adhering to the generic framework of the biopic, casting up-and-coming British star Tim Roth in the role of Vincent van Gogh—two years before his star-making turn in *Reservoir Dogs* (Quentin Tarantino, 1992)—targeting a very particular arthouse demographic and containing nudity, it fell comfortably within the emerging US indie cinema of the time. At the same time, the strongly developing institutional infrastructure that supported indie cinema started building bridges with Altman, as we will see in the next section.

Although *Vincent & Theo* was not successful commercially, with a domestic theatrical box office gross of just $2.2 million,[47] it was reviewed very positively, with Anne Thompson highlighting in her review that "although the media would rather uncover a young upstart than rediscover an old master, the critics who will review [*Vincent & Theo*] and the positive world of mouth that will undoubtedly attend its November premiere opening should remind moviegoers of how important a filmmaker Altman is."[48] Thompson was right. Just a few weeks after the film's release in January 1991, *Variety* reported that Altman was in talks with key independent production company Hemdale to finance his passion project "LA Short Cuts," for the substantial budget of $12 million,[49] a film he had been developing since the 1980s. However, by March of the same year that project seemed to have been pushed aside when it was announced that Altman would direct "Avenue's *The Player*."[50]

"HERE COMES THE HOT-STEPPER": INDIE ALTMAN

The critical and industrial/institutional discourses surrounding *Vincent & Theo* suddenly gave Altman the identity he was missing in the previous decade. Despite the film's poor box office at a time when *sex, lies, and videotape* was redefining the commercial potential of American independent cinema,

Altman's proximity to indie cinema was becoming increasingly evident. Through sponsorship by organizations such as the Independent Feature Project/West (which organized a screening of *Vincent & Theo*) and the California Film Institute (which invited Altman to screen *Vincent & Theo* at its Mill Valley Film Festival as well as to hold a retrospective of his work),[51] through participation in other film festivals such as the Chicago Film Festival,[52] through support by key industry critics such as Anne Thompson, and through his involvement with companies associated with quality indie films, such as Hemdale and now Avenue, Robert Altman was emerging, if not as an indie filmmaker per se, as a filmmaker with a profile that could benefit from the expansive institutional apparatus that supported a constantly evolving independent cinema. His next three films would confirm fully his integration into the indie film scene, and this final section will demonstrate this through a detailed examination of the production and distribution history of *The Player*.

Like Hemdale, Avenue was a significant player in the burgeoning indie film sector. Having emerged in 1987 from the ruins of Island/Alive, an important independent film distributor of the early 1980s, and under the leadership of Cary Brokaw and Bingham Ray, Avenue made a splash in 1989 with the release of Gus van Sant's *Drugstore Cowboy*. Considered together with *sex, lies, and videotape* as one of the paradigmatic indie films of the late 1980s, *Drugstore Cowboy* telegraphed Avenue as a key player in the indie film scene. However, in 1990 Ray left the company to start October Films, which, in tandem with the commercial underperformance of a number of Avenue's films in 1990 and 1991, left the company at a precarious position in the distribution market.[53] In this respect, its involvement with *The Player* entailed only finance and production, and even this was in partnership with another independent production company, Spelling Entertainment.

The film's indie pedigree, however, goes much deeper than the finance and production companies involved in it. Although it started from more mainstream Hollywood sources, producer David Brown (once half of the Zanuck-Brown partnership that had produced Steven Spielberg's *Jaws* in 1975) optioning Michael Tolkin's titular novel in 1988,[54] it moved quickly to firm indie film ground. Failing initially to raise finance and put a package together, Brown became a partner in Island World, an independent production company the origins of which could also be traced to Island/Alive.[55] While in Island World, Brown started developing the project again by asking his manager and one of the executive producers of *sex, lies, and videotape*, Nick Wechsler, to be involved. It was Wechsler who brought in Brokaw and Avenue Pictures as they had worked together on *Drugstore Cowboy*. Given both films' recent critical and commercial success, Wechsler and Brokaw were successful in raising half of the film's $8 million budget.[56] Wechsler was also credited with securing the other half of the budget by convincing Spelling Entertainment to invest in the film.

Meanwhile Altman had relocated to California in 1990 after having spent time living in Europe and agreed to representation by one of the industry's key talent agencies. It was through the William Morris Agency that he received the script for *The Player*, while the agency was also responsible for recommending Altman as a potential director to the producers of the film.[57] Both Brokaw and Brown had collaborated with Altman in the 1970s but reportedly were not particularly warm to the idea of Altman as the film's director. However, a deal was struck, and production took place smoothly, with a rough cut of the film being ready as quickly as October 1991, seven months after the film's announcement in the trades.[58]

One of the interesting aspects of this account is that contrary to firmly held ideas about indie films originating in filmmakers' vision, *The Player* bucked the trend. Altman was hired after the property had been developed, with Sidney Lumet once attached as the director before disagreements with the producers and the size of his fee forced him to leave the production.[59] Indeed, the trade press had announced *The Player* for the first time in September 1990, before even *Vincent & Theo* had been released. By March 1991, when Altman was publicized as the film's director, *The Player* was ready to go into production, led by two very experienced producers.[60] On the other hand, despite his late arrival and reports that wanted Brokaw and Brown insisting that Altman respects the film's "structured story line" and "real plot" before he brings in "improvisation and other touches" associated with his style,[61] Altman was able to claim *The Player* as a strongly authored project, as an "Altmanesque" picture. Significantly, the "Altmanesque" style coincided fully with the dominant characteristics of the indie film of the early 1990s, turning Altman into an "indie filmmaker."

If indie cinema was about the use of stars, even if stardom was meaningful to a niche demographic, *The Player* achieved a double coup on that front. A cast of character actors, many of whom had already emerged as indie film stars with credits in key films of the era (Tim Robbins, Peter Gallagher, Richard E. Grant), or had been associated with the broader independent film sector (Dean Stockwell, Fred Ward), anchored the film. However, their presence was overshadowed by the cameo appearances of over fifty Hollywood stars who played themselves and who provided the film's narrative as it unfolds in the world of Hollywood studio filmmaking with a very strong sense of authenticity. Not surprisingly, the nature and extent of these cameo appearances attracted huge critical attention.

Indie films' creative use of generic frameworks could not have dovetailed more perfectly with a filmmaker like Altman who had built a large part of his auteur identity in the 1970s through experimentation with and deconstruction of genres such as the war film (*M*A*S*H*), the Western (*McCabe & Mrs. Miller*) and the detective film (*The Long Goodbye*). While this experimentation

Figure 7.2 Tim Robbins and Robert Altman take a break from promoting *The Player* following its debut at the Cannes Film Festival. Courtesy of Special Collections Research Center, University of Michigan Library.

had continued in his later films, critics remained unimpressed as sci-fi films such as *Quintet* and political parodies such as *HealtH* did not connect with audiences and failed commercially. *The Player*, however, gave Altman ample opportunities for genre play, with one reviewer suggesting that the film veered "from psychological thriller suspense to goofball comedy to icy satire. It's Patricia Highsmith meets Monty Python meets Nathanael West."[62] Altman's license for this level of experimentation was given by the strongly held view that *The Player* was critiquing Hollywood at a time when studio films were becoming increasingly homogenous and standardized, a side effect of a wave of conglomeration in the late 1980s and early 1990s that saw the studios being taken over by giant media and content delivery global corporations. With the quality of American movies "in free fall," as Jack Kroll put it in *Esquire*,[63] a film like *The Player* had to distinguish itself from the films it criticized, while at the same time emphasizing its credentials as an example of indie cinema.

As far as indie films go, *The Player* also appealed to clear demographics that could be targeted by its marketing campaign. *The Player*'s multi-layered approach, complete with major Hollywood stars playing themselves, made it much more than a Hollywood satire. Its adherence to a structured storyline—the executive's crime, his relationship with the victim's girlfriend, the police investigation—allowed the film to work as a psychological thriller which encouraged its distributor to hope that it would play well across the United States and not just in major cities on the two coasts that tend to be the major markets for more niche films without these commercial elements.[64] In these locations, *The Player* was expected to attract an upmarket, educated audience associated with arthouse film, while the novelty of the star cameos would also give the film an additional drawing power. And if these commercial elements were not enough, like other indie films of that year (*Reservoir Dogs, Bad Lieutenant* [Abel Ferrara, 1992]), *The Player* also utilized violence, sex, and nudity that undoubtedly enhanced its potential to become a crossover success.

With *The Player* utilizing strongly niche stardom, genre experiments, sex and violence, and being able to target different demographics, the last element it needed to complete its perfect indie film credentials was to package all the above under the auspices of a strong authorship. Not surprisingly, this became *The Player*'s major selling point and entry point to critical engagement with it. Altman's history as a major Hollywood auteur in the early 1970s and his long absence from the mainstream film industry had helped him cultivate an "outsider-insider status"[65] that enabled him to anchor the film's critical take on Hollywood in the strongest possible way. This was especially the case as stylistically and narratively the film did invoke many of the "quintessential" Altman trademarks that had made him a critics' favorite in the early 1970s: free-floating camera (including an eight minute long take as the opening shot of the film), overlapping sound, an ensemble cast (amplified by the frequent use of star cameos), acting improvisation (especially by the stars who reportedly were not given a script for their cameo roles) and indeed a whimsical sensibility that was corroborated by the filmmaker's love–hate relationship with Hollywood (another aspect in which the star appearances helped).[66] As a reviewer aptly put it, "the director's sensibility and history is a crucial part of the [film's] enterprise; just as it's difficult to picture anyone but Altman directing the film, it's easy to imagine much of its reflexive irony being lost to viewers unfamiliar with his past work."[67] In this respect, despite not having originated the film, Altman easily managed to overcome this issue, integrated himself into the indie film sector and became "the real star" in a film that knows "the difference between movies and what passes for them."[68]

To push this perfect indie film package in the marketplace, New Line Cinema's specialty film division Fine Line Features beat all other companies who bid for the film's distribution rights.[69] Led by Ira Deutchman, who had carved a very successful career in the independent film sector, first at United Artists Classics and then at Cinecom, Fine Line Features was a key contributor in the emergence of indie cinema in the 1990s. Deutchman's experience in the independent film sector and his relationship with the various creative agents of *The Player* helped him secure its North American distribution rights for $5.1 million (Spelling retained international rights as part of its co-finance deal).[70] Reports suggested that the producers were convinced by Deutchman's "aggressive" approach who thought that Altman's "insider's account was a strong marketing hook,"[71] especially as the film would be distributed by an indie film company that also enjoyed a symbiotic relationship with Hollywood.

Equally importantly, the producers deemed the studios as distributors that would not know how to market a film that, according to Deutchman, was "not necessarily a broad-audience movie (at face value) but one that could be built into (a successful wide release),"[72] and that would probably be lost among the releases of bigger films that tend to drain distribution resources.[73] Indeed, Fine Line was very careful with its marketing campaign, which was designed after the company itself considered the possibility of opening the film wide. Deciding that it would play better as "big art film, rather than a small commercial film,"[74] the campaign focused on the promotion of *The Player* to "an upscale audience," with publicity concentrated on print media, and on Altman and Tolkin involved in media engagement in the top twelve markets.[75]

Fine Line's approach proved extremely successful. Having spent $5.1 million to acquire the film and approximately $1.5 million to market it,[76] it saw *The Player* grossing close to $22 million, a runaway hit in the indie film circuit, and the company's highest grossing film to that point.[77] The film was also nominated for three Academy Awards, including one for Robert Altman's direction, which signaled in the strongest possible way the filmmaker's "comeback" to prominence. More importantly for the purposes of this chapter, *The Player* was also the recipient of the Independent Spirit Award for Best Feature, which confirmed fully both the film's status as an indie and Altman's recognition as an indie film auteur.

CONCLUSION: COMPLETING INDIE REINVENTION

Following the success of *The Player*, Altman remained firmly engulfed in the discourses of American indie cinema. Weeks into the release of the film, the trade press announced that Altman's long planned pet project *Short Cuts* was finally greenlighted as a co-production between New Line Cinema and Spelling Entertainment for $15 million, through a deal brokered again by the William Morris Agency.[78] Cary Brokaw would retain his involvement with the filmmaker by restructuring his deal with Avenue Pictures in order to take over producer duties,[79] while Spelling Entertainment executive Sol Jessel would make a similar arrangement with his own company to produce Altman's follow-up to *Short Cuts*, *Prêt-à-Porter* (with the deal for the latter also announced while *The Player* was still in release).[80] Both films would be handled theatrically by divisions of larger companies, with Fine Line distributing *Short Cuts* and Miramax, fresh from its takeover by Disney, releasing *Prêt-à-Porter*. Both films would also receive strong critical acclaim but would prove commercially disappointing, with *Short Cuts* grossing just $6 million at the domestic box office.[81]

Beyond these titles, the William Morris Agency enabled Altman to integrate himself even deeper into the indie film structures of the time by securing from a variety of "domestic and foreign money sources" an unprecedented "indie financing deal" for the filmmaker, "a completely independent structure that [would] give him the authority to greenlight and have the final cut on his movies." As part of this multipicture deal, "Altman would direct and, in some cases, just produce, helping aspiring filmmakers get their films and television projects off the ground."[82] Altman protégé and frequent collaborator Alan Rudolph's *Mrs. Parker and the Vicious Circle* became the first film to be released under this deal.

Even though this deal turned out to be short-lived as Altman switched from William Morris to International Creative Management in October 1995,[83] the filmmaker continued to work firmly in the indie film sector in the next decade, releasing films for an assortment of key distributors in the field: *Kansas City* for Fine Line, *Cookie's Fortune* for October Films, *Dr T. & the Women* for Artisan, *Gosford Park* for USA Films, *The Company* for Sony Pictures Classics, *A Prairie Home Companion* for Picturehouse, while he also made *Gingerbread Man* for the short-lived, mid-size distributor Polygram Films. With such a record, it is not surprising that trade and popular press discourses finally start to label Altman as an "indie filmmaker," with *Boxoffice* commenting on Altman's move to do *Short Cuts* with Fine Line as "continuing to go the indie route,"[84] and the *Hollywood Reporter* referring to Altman as one of the "indie filmmaker clients" of William Morris together with the *crème de la crème* of the 1990s indie film scene: Tarantino, Linklater, Soderbergh, Van Sant.[85] Even the more reticent popular press would capitulate and identify Altman and his films as indie, especially following the victory of *Short Cuts* at the 1993 Independent Spirit Awards,[86] while as he continued to work in the sector the title of "indie film icon" was bestowed on him by the *Los Angeles Times*.[87] The ultimate recognition arguably came in 2007, a year after his death, when the Independent Feature Project/West launched the Independent Spirit Robert Altman Award for ensemble cast, director and casting director of a film as part of the Independent Spirit Awards.

In the process and within this context of a constantly evolving independent cinema, Altman's past in the Hollywood Renaissance was not necessarily forgotten but was rather rendered irrelevant. And even though popular and academic film criticism in the field of American independent cinema would ignore his indie film output and continue to privilege the "Altman effect" on younger filmmakers,[88] this chapter has demonstrated that perhaps it is time for Altman's status as a Hollywood outsider to be qualified further to account for his role in US indie cinema.

NOTES

1. Tim Roby, "How Robert Altman blew up the rule book," *The Telegraph*, 31 March 2015. Available at <https://www.telegraph.co.uk/film/altman/robert-best-movies/>.
2. The combined budget for the film and the television series was $6 million. "Film Festival debuts in K.C.," *Daily Variety*, 8 March 1991.
3. Michael Wilmington, "The Altman of the '90s," *Los Angeles Times*, 11 November 1990, p. 22.
4. Robert Breskin, "Robert Altman: The *Rolling Stone* interview," *Rolling Stone*, 16 April 1992, p. 74.
5. Wilmington, "The Altman of the '90s," p. 26.
6. Dimitrios Pavlounis, "Staging the rebel's return: *The Player*, *Short Cuts*, and the precarious art of the comeback," in Adrian Danks (ed.), *A Companion to Robert Altman* (Cambridge: Wiley Blackwell, 2015), pp. 932, 938.
7. Pavlounis, "Staging the rebel's return," p. 934.
8. Pavlounis, "Staging the rebel's return," pp. 943–4.
9. Peter Krämer and Yannis Tzioumakis, "Introduction," in Peter Krämer and Yannis Tzioumakis (eds), *The Hollywood Renaissance: Revisiting American Cinema's Most Celebrated Era* (New York: Bloomsbury Academic, 2018), p. xiv.
10. Henry Jenkins, "Historical poetics," in Joanne Hollows and Mark Jancovich (eds), *Approaches to Popular Film* (Manchester: Manchester University Press, 1995), p. 114.
11. Yannis Tzioumakis, *American Independent Cinema*, 2nd edn (Edinburgh: Edinburgh University Press, 2017), pp. 257, 193.
12. Peter Biskind, *Down and Dirty Pictures: Miramax, Sundance, and the Rise of Independent Film* (London: Simon and Schuster, 2004).
13. Ibid. p. 1.
14. Peter Biskind, *Easy Riders, Raging Bulls: How the Sex 'n' Drugs 'n' Rock 'n' Roll Generation Saved Hollywood* (London: Bloomsbury, 1998).
15. Biskind, *Down and Dirty Pictures*, p. 1.
16. Ibid. p. 9.
17. Ibid. p. 19.
18. Ibid. p. 18.
19. Ibid. p. 22.
20. See, for instance, Tzioumakis, *American Independent Cinema*, pp. 224–56.
21. Biskind, *Down and Dirty Pictures*, p. 21.
22. Ibid. p. 23.
23. Sharon Waxman, *Rebels on the Backlot: 6 Maverick Directors and How they Conquered the Studio System* (New York: HarperCollins, 2005); James Mottram, *The Sundance Kids: How the Mavericks Took Over Hollywood* (London: Faber and Faber, 2006).
24. Mottram, *The Sundance Kids*, p. xxviii.
25. Jim Hillier, "Introduction," in Jim Hillier (ed.), *American Independent Cinema: A Sight and Sound Reader* (London: BFI, 2001), p. ix.
26. Justin Wyatt, "Economic constraints/economic opportunities: Robert Altman as auteur," *Velvet Light Trap* 38 (Fall 1996): 51.
27. Hillier, "Introduction," p. x.
28. Ibid. p. x.
29. John Berra, *Declarations of Independence: American Cinema and the Partiality of Independent Production* (London: Intellect, 2008), p. 30.

30. Claire Perkins, "Kicking and screaming: Altmanesque cynicism and energy in the work of Paul Thomas Anderson and Noah Baumbach," in Adrian Danks (ed.), *A Companion to Robert Altman* (Cambridge: John Wiley, 2015), pp. 1056–100.
31. Biskind, *Easy Riders, Raging Bulls*, p. 23.
32. Perkins, "Kicking and screaming," p. 1057.
33. Yannis Tzioumakis, "Academic discourses and American independent cinema: In search of a field of studies, Part 2: From the 1990s to date", *New Review of Film and Television Studies* 9, no. 3 (2011): 331.
34. See, for instance, David A. Cook, *Lost Illusions: American Cinema in the Shadow of Watergate and Vietnam 1970–1979* (Berkeley: University of California Press, 2002), pp. 9–14.
35. Biskind, *Down and Dirty Pictures*, p. 20.
36. Waxman, *Rebels on the Backlot*, p. x.
37. For a detailed discussion of a definition of indie cinema as the next step in the evolution of independent cinema in the 1980s see Yannis Tzioumakis, "'Independent,' 'Indie,' and 'Indiewood': Towards a periodisation of contemporary (post-1980) American independent cinema," in Geoff King, Claire Molloy, and Yannis Tzioumakis (eds), *American Independent Cinema: Indie, Indiewood and Beyond* (London: Routledge, 2012), pp. 33–6.
38. Jack Kroll, "Robert Altman gives something back," *Esquire* May (1992): 86.
39. Annette Insdorf, "Ordinary people, European style: How to spot an independent feature," *American Film* 6, no. 10 (September 1981): 58.
40. Vincent Canby, "Play 'Streamers' adapted by Altman," *New York Times*, 9 October 1983, p. 73.
41. Vincent Canby "Shepard's 'Fool for Love,'" *New York Times*, 6 December 1985, C12.
42. Vincent Canby "'Beyond Therapy': A match made in the ads," *New York Times*, 27 February 1987, C8.
43. Vincent Canby "Nixon tale, 'Secret Honor,'" *New York Times*, 7 June 1985, C8.
44. Tzioumakis, "'Independent,' 'Indie,' and 'Indiewood,'" p. 32.
45. Tzioumakis, "'Independent,' 'Indie,' and 'Indiewood,'" p. 35.
46. Wyatt, "Economic constraints/economic opportunities," p. 59.
47. Details of the film's box office and release schedule were obtained from its Internet Movie Database page: <https://www.imdb.com/title/tt0100873/>.
48. Anne Thompson, "Robert, Vincent and Theo: A perfect match," *LA Weekly*, 2 November 1990.
49. Jane Lieberman, "Altman, Hemdale in 'Cuts' talks," *Daily Variety*, 8 January 1991.
50. "Untitled," *Screen International*, 15 March 1991.
51. "Film shorts," *Hollywood Reporter*, 4 December 1990; Jim Harwood, "Four world premieres set at Mill Valley Film Fest," *Daily Variety*, 13 September 1990, p. 6.
52. "Rambling reporter," *Hollywood Reporter*, 19 October 1990.
53. Claudia Eller, "Avenue's road leads to bank," *Daily Variety*, 14 August 1992, pp. 1, 12.
54. Peter Bart, "Altman's revenge," *Variety*, 10 February 1992.
55. Don Groves, "David Brown taking new post," *Variety*, 24 September 1990, p. 21.
56. Jeanie Kasindorf, "Home movie," *New York*, 16 March 1992, p. 53.
57. Ibid. p. 53.
58. Ibid. p. 53.
59. Bernard Weinraub, "When Hollywood is a killer," *New York Times*, 5 April 1992.
60. Groves, "David Brown taking new post," p. 21.
61. Kasindorf, "Home movie," p. 53.
62. Terrence Rafferty, "The current cinema," *New Yorker*, 20 April 1992, pp. 81–2.
63. Kroll, "Robert Altman," p. 89.

64. Hilary De Vries, "My fourth comeback," *Los Angeles Times Magazine*, 26 April 1992, p. 32.
65. Peter Rainer, "Here's the deal: *The Player* takes Hollywood genre one step beyond," *Los Angeles Times*, 19 April 1992.
66. Wilmington, "The Altman of the '90s," p. 26.
67. Godfrey Cheshire, "Three women and a little murder", *NY Press*, 8 April 1992, p. 20.
68. Julie Salamon, "Film Hollywood skewered in a whodunnit," *Wall Street Journal*, 9 April 1992.
69. Weinraub, "When Hollywood is a killer."
70. John Evan Frook, "Fine line inks Player pact," *Daily Variety*, 14 February 1992.
71. Bernard Weinraub, "Hollywood captivated by an Altman film about how awful it is," *New York Times*, 18 February 1992.
72. Frook, "Fine line inks Player pact."
73. Kasindorf, "Home movie," p. 55.
74. Ira Deutchman, interview with Yannis Tzioumakis, 2 June 2011.
75. Frook, "Fine line inks Player pact."
76. Ira Deutchman, interview with Yannis Tzioumakis, 2 June 2011.
77. The film's domestic box office gross was taken from *The Numbers*. Available at <https://www.the-numbers.com/movie/Player-The#tab=summary>.
78. Robert Marich, "Altman, "Cuts" to Spelling, NL", *Hollywood Reporter*, 13 May 1992, pp. 1, 25.
79. Adam Dawtrey, "Spelling, FLF take 'Short Cuts,'" *Daily Variety*, 13 May 1992.
80. Colin Brown, "Jessel dons off-the-peg-Altman," *Screen International*, 22 May 1992.
81. The figure has been taken from *The Numbers*. Available at <https://www.the-numbers.com/movie/Short-Cuts#more>.
82. "Rudolph and Altman to reconnect," *Daily Variety*, 11 August 1992.
83. "Untitled," *Daily Variety*, 17 October 1995.
84. "Hollywood updates," *Boxoffice*, 1 September 1992, p. 6.
85. Kirk Honeykutt, "Elwes to head WMA indie unit," *Hollywood Reporter*, 6 March 1994, p. 41.
86. Jeannie Williams and Ann Oldenburgh, "Altman, clear-cut indie film winner," *USA Today*, 21 March 1994.
87. Irene Lacher, "A declaration especially for independents," *Los Angeles Times*, 2 April 1999. Available at <https://www.latimes.com/archives/la-xpm-1999-apr-02-cl-23388-story.html>.
88. See in particular Emmanuel Levy's influential *Cinema of Outsiders* (1999) in which the author is more interested in exploring the "Altman effect" on filmmakers such as Alan Rudolph, Tim Robbins, Paul Bartel, and Christopher Guest than Altman's films in the 1990s. Emanuel Levy, *Cinema of Outsiders* (New York: New York University Press, 1999), pp. 252–4.

CHAPTER 8

"I Fiddle on the Corner Where They Throw the Coins": Altman's Brand in Europe

Lisa Dombrowski

To investigate, as John Caughie encourages, "the way in which the author is constructed by and for commerce" is to consider the author as having a brand.[1] Mark Batey defines a brand as "a set of associations, perceptions, and expectations" resulting both from marketing efforts as well as a consumer's experiences with the branded object.[2] Batey suggests, "the nature of the brand-consumer relationship is defined by what the consumer looks for and expects from the brand."[3] In their study of film director brands, Camille Pluntz and Bernard Pras highlight that human brand identity is rooted both in "the professional attributes of the branded individual" and in "how those attributes resonate within a given social, cultural, and temporal context."[4] Thus, a film director can gain legitimacy when her brand embodies characteristics valued by constituencies—such as industry figures, critics, or audiences. At the same time, various constituencies may differ in how they value the range of attributes that constitute a director's brand, both in a given historical moment and over time.

Robert Altman's brand, like that of all above-the-line film workers, was shaped by both textual and extratextual factors, including recurring formal choices and themes in his films; marketing campaigns; interviews and profiles; and critical and commercial reception. While not fully in control of how his films were marketed and received, Altman nevertheless actively shaped the meaning of his brand by weighing in on advertising and trailers; promulgating a defined biographical legend to journalists; and soliciting the favor of critics. As David Sterritt notes in his analysis of the critical reception of Altman's films, "Altman was a crafty artist as well as an ingenious and audacious one."[5]

Altman's brand contained two reinforcing elements: an association with European art and attitudes, expressed both formally, through aesthetic and technological experimentation that critics and scholars aligned with European art cinema, and thematically, through his filmic critiques of American provincialism; as well as what Justin Wyatt describes as a "hostility toward the studio distribution apparatus," well-documented by journalists and promoted by Altman through a series of lawsuits and public spats with distributors over the handling of his films.[6] The anti-Hollywood element of Altman's brand particularly endeared him to European cinephiles eager to celebrate cinematic artistry and to push back against American cultural dominance.[7] As described in *Volkscrant*, a top Danish newspaper published out of Amsterdam, Altman was "the obstinate American who refuses to accept the conventions of the American film tradition, who has always found more recognition in Europe than in his own country."[8] Even when Altman's later output at times lacked the formal innovation or sociological insight attributed to the 1970–5 films that initially elevated his brand, his association with artistry over commerce and disdain for Hollywood continued to endear him to overseas industry figures, critics, and audiences. European consumers of Altman's brand thus proved crucial to the maintenance of his career in the 1980s when American studios lost interest in his work, and to his professional revitalization in the 1990s and 2000s when critical and commercial success in the United States was uneven.[9] Describing his embrace of European stories and financing later in his career, Altman explained, "I fiddle on the corner where they throw the coins."[10]

This chapter utilizes previously untapped archival materials, as well as trade and popular press accounts, to investigate how Altman's brand inspired European financing and shaped publicity, reception, and box office for his films. Three pictures Altman shot in Europe, *Vincent & Theo*, *Prêt-à-Porter*, and *Gosford Park*, provide particularly useful case studies, as their distinct approaches to European subject matter tested local support for Altman's brand. Both *Vincent & Theo* and *Prêt-à-Porter* generated negative reviews in the countries of their subjects, as local critics questioned Altman's ability to fully grasp the particularities of their cultures. Nevertheless, outside of the Netherlands, *Vincent & Theo* generated nearly universal critical acclaim and set the stage for Altman's Hollywood comeback in *The Player*, while the massive publicity generated by *Prêt-à-Porter* and European grosses three times higher than those in the US insured subsequent European financial support for Altman's filmmaking. In contrast to *Vincent & Theo* and *Prêt-à-Porter*, *Gosford Park* proved to be Altman's only European picture to be fully embraced by the country whose culture is the topic of the film and marked the critical and commercial pinnacle of Altman's last years. An analysis of these case studies highlights how Altman's brand as a maverick critical of Hollywood and its conventions fostered overseas critics and audiences, provided reliable financing and markets outside of North America, and added significant revenue to his films' balance sheets, thereby aiding his productivity to the very end of his career.

VINCENT & THEO: THE ROAD BACK TO HOLLYWOOD

Vincent & Theo, an exploration of the troubled yet loving relationship between the painter Vincent van Gogh and his brother Theo, arrived on the heels of Altman's little seen HBO political mockumentary *Tanner '88*, and the television movies *The Caine Mutiny Court-Martial* (1988) and *Basements* (1987). Altman's exalted reputation in Europe and decades-long experience directing television recommended him to Dutch producer Ludi Boeken, head of Belbo Films, who planned a four-hour miniseries to coincide with the centennial of van Gogh's death. Yet Altman initially had little interest in directing a conventional biopic for a reduced rate; he was already invested in helming a more lucrative and experimental project in Italy, a "fragmented, rather Fellini-esque comedy" about the life of the Italian opera composer Gioachino Rossini starring the actor Richard E. Grant.[11] *Vincent & Theo* only moved to the front of Altman's queue once he negotiated the ability to craft a theatrical feature out of footage from the miniseries and to create an impressionistic portrait of artistic frustration and failure.[12] The multinational financing and distribution arrangements for *Vincent & Theo* were a testament not simply to the appeal of a van Gogh project but also to the appeal of a van Gogh project as directed by Robert Altman. Enlisting Altman as director enabled Boeken to increase the budget, secure additional financing, and pre-sell television and film rights to Germany and Italy as well as all rights to Spain.[13] Altman's existing relationship with John Daly, chairman of the independent producer and distributor Hemdale—which released Altman's *Images* (1972) in the UK—facilitated Hemdale's acquisition of the theatrical rights to the film in the US and Canada. *Vincent & Theo* thus became Altman's first entirely European film, financed and produced by multiple European entities, shot in Holland and France with predominantly local crews, starring actors from the UK and the continent, and featuring Dutch subject matter. Yet it also posed a test for Altman's brand, as the director was most closely associated with sociological explorations of the cities, cultures, and myths of his native land. Would the appeal of his brand hold when he turned his lens on a legendary European artist? *Vincent & Theo*'s successful use of foreign money and pre-sales for financing, employment of existing relationships to secure distribution, and reliance on Altman's anti-Hollywood brand to generate publicity, shape reception, and stimulate European box office established an industrial template that was repeatedly activated or modified during the latter phase of his career.

Altman's brand proved central to the marketing campaign for the film version of *Vincent & Theo*, priming critical discourse that highlighted parallels between the filmmaker and his subject. The initial promotion of the television version featured recognizable van Gogh iconography and associations, suggesting a standard biopic with conventional pleasures—precisely the image Altman was trying to avoid. Instead, Joseph McBride's early review in *Variety* from a trade press screening in April of 1990 provided the key hooks for the European press rollout, positioning the film as Altman's "mainstream comeback" and a "provocative examination of the art-commerce clash that has bedeviled Altman's career."[14] Mike Kaplan, the former distribution president at Lion's Gate Films and Altman's long-time marketing guru, featured a quote from the review in a simple, text-only ad created to promote the film's screening at the Marché du Film, the industry component of the Cannes Film Festival where most distributors, programmers, and critics had their first opportunity to see the picture and where Altman took initial press meetings for the film:

> A masterpiece . . . The respect for the artist and his struggles that suffuses *Vincent & Theo* is an empathy that comes from the depth of the soul and one that shows the brilliantly original but often erratic director at the mature height of his powers.[15]

The same quote is featured in the UK theatrical ad campaign, along with a distant image of the artist and a blank canvas on an easel.[16] The campaign consciously avoided exploiting van Gogh's iconographic painting style, as suggested by Kaplan.[17] Instead, the ads highlighted not only one of the primary strategies utilized to sell the film—the return to feature filmmaking of a master of film art—but also provided critics and journalists with a significant talking point rooted in Altman's brand—namely, the similarity between the director and his subject, also a "brilliantly original but often erratic" artist haunted by the lack of recognition for his work.

The emphasis on Altman's authorship in European reviews of *Vincent & Theo* and popular press profiles of the filmmaker mirrored the focus of the marketing campaign, positioning the film not only as a comeback for a director on the outs in Hollywood but also as a commentary on the relationship between art and commerce. In *La Revue du cinéma*, Daniel Sauvaget found the film was "likely to restore the reputation of Robert Altman, who has disappointed some people with a few recent low-budget films."[18] German critics applauded Altman as an "American anti-Hollywood director" who successfully avoided the biopic's potential for melodrama and mere reportage to create "a large, radical, uncompromising work of art."[19] In Britain, *Vincent & Theo* unspooled in theaters at the same time as the re-release of Altman's *McCabe & Mrs. Miller*, while in France the film played concurrently to the re-release of *The Long Goodbye*, prompting journalists to consider the newest film in light of the director's "spectacular rise and fall in Hollywood."[20] In *The Guardian*, Derek Malcolm argued the film was personal: "Altman seems to be making the point that innovatory work in all fields, even his own, is rarely given the succor it deserves."[21] Yet in *Positif*, Jean-Loup Bourget expressed confusion regarding how the film's formal approach related to Altman's brand: "Does he sign here, in the manner of a King Vidor, a relatively academic work to later reconnect with independence and boldness?"[22]

Only in the Netherlands, where the film first premiered at the end of April 1990, did the reception of *Vincent & Theo* fall uniformly flat, as critics either viewed Altman as incapable of offering a nuanced portrait of a non-American subject or considered the film as too conventional for the director's brand. Some writers criticized Altman for not grounding the story in the known historical record. In *Het Parool*, Roel Naarding chides, "Altman goes through the china cabinet of European culture like an unwieldy elephant. A quiet American, full of good intentions and misjudgments," while in *Trouw*, Hans Kroon celebrates the film's performances but critiques the lack of attention to van Gogh's paintings and the Parisian art world: "Unfortunately, Altman treats them like an American who believes that Europe can be done in ten days: without obligation and superficially."[23] Drawing on stereotypes of Americans who are hopelessly ignorant of European culture, the reviews suggest Altman is out of his depth. Other Dutch critics focused less on Altman's nationality and the film's historical accuracy and more on its relationship to Altman's previous body of work. Henk van Gelder, writing in *NRC Handelsblad*, notes "the parallel between the misunderstood artist of a hundred years ago and the unruly filmmaker of this moment" but faults the film for its conventionality: "So far, [Altman] has often sought to break open and turn upside down the genres in which he has seemingly moved himself . . . Here he has conformed to the rules."[24] Van Gelder finds Altman's aesthetic approach in *Vincent & Theo* more conservative than that typically associated with his brand, recalling Bourget's review in *Positif*. The Dutch reviews suggest *Vincent & Theo* did not uniformly fulfill critical expectations, highlighting a challenge the director faced when tackling European subject matter. As an American director critiquing American provincialism, Altman was aligned with European sensibilities; as an American director exploring European subject matter, he ran the risk of appearing provincial *himself*.

Vincent & Theo swept through the major European markets well before its North American premiere at the Toronto Film Festival, generating waves of celebratory publicity and the first talk of an Altman masterpiece in more than a decade. By the time the film debuted in the US in early November 1990, the critical consensus outside of the Netherlands had already solidified: though *Vincent & Theo* was not as formally ambitious as Altman's greatest work and might appear, in its subject and genre, uncharacteristic, it nevertheless was deeply personal, a statement on the corrosive role of commerce in art made by a director who understood failure. The financial returns for *Vincent & Theo* certainly outstripped those experienced by the painter in his lifetime. Although definitive European grosses are unavailable, the picture played for more than three months on German screens and likely returned a profit for Telepool, its German and Italian distributor.[25] It opened impressively in London on two art house screens, netting a healthy per screen gross of $13,411 and providing the Everyman Cinema with its best opening weekend in twelve months.[26] And in the US, the film grossed $2.23 million in its thirteen-week release; ticket sales, together with video and Hemdale's output deal with HBO, likely generated enough to produce a profit for the distributor.[27] *Vincent & Theo* provided Altman with an unexpected means to transition back to feature film directing and to elevate his profile. On the one hand, its European subject matter and intimate scope expanded perceptions regarding his interests and capabilities, amplifying his brand as one of constant risk, experimentation, and renewal. On the other hand, the differences in form and content between *Vincent & Theo* and Altman's canonical early '70s films challenged perceptions of Altman's brand in some quarters, especially in the Netherlands. Nevertheless, Europe's critical and commercial embrace of *Vincent & Theo* helped to reignite interest in Altman's work in the US, leading to another for-hire job that would change the course of his late career: *The Player*.

PRÊT-À-PORTER: IN THE CENTER OF THE CIRCUS

Less than four years after wrapping production on *Vincent & Theo*, Robert Altman was back in France shooting his second film with distinctly European subject matter, *Prêt-à-Porter*, yet the circumstances could not have been more different. Now, instead of utilizing the project to work his way back into feature filmmaking and reinvigorate his brand, Altman was at the center of the show. A farcical look at the Parisian fashion world inspired by Altman's 1983 visit to the unveiling of a Sonia Rykiel collection in Paris with his wife, Kathryn Reed Altman, *Prêt-à-Porter* enabled Altman to work with Miramax, the hottest major independent in American cinema, his largest budget since *Popeye*, and an expansive ensemble of stars from film and fashion. As with *Vincent & Theo*, pre-sales of overseas distribution rights provided a key revenue stream for *Prêt-à-Porter*. Following the critical and commercial successes of *The Player* and *Short Cuts*, demand from regional distributors was so high that rights to Germany and Italy sold at the 1993 American Film Market nearly a year before production began; by the time filming ended, France and the UK were the only major territories still available—as Miramax was seeking extraordinarily high prices.[28] Miramax's president of marketing, Mark Gill, touted the value of overseas audiences to the film, noting before *Prêt-à-Porter*'s domestic debut that distribution rights to 80 percent of worldwide territories were already sold, thereby reducing the risk that less than stellar early reviews might decrease revenues.[29] The pre-release deals for *Prêt-à-Porter* found Altman at one of the highest peaks of his late career rollercoaster—and about to go down. In the fall of 1993, mere months before production began, Altman suffered a stroke.[30] The film lacked a fully developed script, Altman

Figure 8.1 Robert Altman directs a scene in Moscow's Red Square for *Prêt-à-Porter*. Photo by Etienne Georges. Courtesy of Special Collections Research Center, University of Michigan Library.

remained thin and fatigued, and controversy erupted on set almost as soon as shooting started. The subsequent American release was marred by tepid reviews and underwhelming box office. Yet the strength of Altman's brand in European markets provided a second chance for the film, allowing for reoriented promotional campaigns and producing voluminous publicity, some sympathetic reviews, and substantially larger box office receipts than in the US. European critics' and audiences' continuing eagerness to engage with Altman's work—even by debating its quality—encouraged overseas financing and production support for future projects and prevented the kind of career deflation that Altman experienced at the beginning of the 1980s after his last big budget disappointment.

The pre-release publicity for *Prêt-à-Porter* that began during production in Paris and continued through the film's American release generated waves of press and controversy for nearly a year before its European debut, ensuring high name recognition for the film, piquing curiosity, and shaping the narrative of its reception according to Altman's brand. Set during the week when the Autumn-Winter fashion collections are unveiled and shot in the midst of and adjacent to actual runway shows, *Prêt-à-Porter* brought together over a hundred stars of film and fashion—some playing characters, others playing themselves, all speaking their own languages—in a manner tailor-made for gossip columns and glossy photo spreads. Altman utilized his trips to European film festivals to seed pre-production publicity, first namedropping *Prêt-à-Porter* in 1992 to journalists at Cannes while promoting *The Player*, then appearing in the fashion press in September 1993 during a research visit to Paris after he won the Golden Lion at the Venice Film Festival for *Short Cuts*.[31] Although the Parisian fashion world was initially giddy with excitement at being the subject of its own *The Player*-esque exposé, with *Women's Wear Daily* describing the start of shooting in early March 1994 as "the moment Paris has been waiting for," production coverage drastically shifted the very next day.[32] The fashion trade paper reported Altman had "fallen from grace," with Karl Lagerfeld and Valentino banning his film crew from their fashion shows, editors asking to be seated outside of the camera's range, and attendees at a Christian Dior party recoiling from signing a release to appear in the film.[33] The apparent drama initiated a narrative of fashion industry backlash that stood in marked contrast to Hollywood's public embrace of the similarly "real life meets fiction" *The Player*, sparking a debate regarding exactly what prompted the erosion of support and if Altman was capable of delivering a knowing satire of fashion.[34] Once again, the shift in the director's lens away from American subject matter threatened to undercut his brand as a director with sensibilities more European than American. Behind-the-scenes production stories were picked up and amplified by over fifty European journalists with access to the set during shooting—who reported the fashion world tiffs both initially and when they ran their stories prior to the film's debut in their territories—and by cheeky on-set diaries written by actors Richard E. Grant and Tracey Ullman and screenwriter Barbara Schulgasser published in major glossy magazines prior to *Prêt-à-Porter*'s US debut.[35] Miramax generated additional publicity when it decided a month before the US premiere to change the film's title to the more American-friendly *Ready to Wear*. Then the MPAA deemed fashion photographer Patrick Demarchelier's nearly nude images of supermodel Helena Christensen in the American ads too revealing, providing Miramax with an opportunity to follow its standard marketing playbook and milk the controversy.[36] Both mishaps generated giggles in the European press, which tagged them as examples of Americans' lack of sophistication. *Prêt-à-Porter*'s pre-release publicity set the stage for European reception to be shaped not only by the film's attitude toward the fashion industry but also, as with *Vincent & Theo*, by critics' perceptions of Altman's brand and his understanding of European culture.[37]

The distribution of *Prêt-à-Porter* in Europe kicked off two months after its late December 1994 US release, allowing distributors in individual markets to adjust their ad campaigns in a manner designed variably to amplify or abandon Altman's brand. In France, the film's promotion heightened associations of the film with artistry and provocation, two elements closely linked to Altman's authorship. Denise Breton, the former head of European publicity for Twentieth Century Fox and Altman's long-time French publicist and European advisor, organized a four-day international press junket to support the premiere, timed to capitalize on Altman's attendance at the César Awards, where *Short Cuts* was nominated for Best Foreign Film. As if in a direct response to the US ad scandal, Gaumont's marketing campaign was, in the words of Miramax International's vice president of marketing, "as provocative as possible," featuring five fully naked models alongside a roll call of the film's stars and a carefully placed banner announcing Altman's name and the film's title.[38] The international arm of Miramax's parent company, Buena Vista International, distributed *Prêt-à-Porter* in the UK and adopted a distinctly different sales approach, pitching the film as an entertaining slice of pop culture for fifteen- to twenty-four-year-olds rather than highlighting Altman's brand or controversy. "We're not interested in people who went to see *The Player*," BVI's Robert Mitchell told *Screen International*. "Fashion, music, and the film industry are all the things that kids love, and this has all three."[39] BVI's publicists placed features in fashion magazines, organized sponsorship of the UK charity premiere by *Vogue*, and encouraged coverage in youth-leaning publications such as *Looks*, which touted the picture as "the ab fabbest film of the season" and highlighted the soundtrack, the US ad scandal, and the US premiere afterparty alongside stills from the film featuring supermodels and major stars.[40] Perhaps prompted by *Prêt-à-Porter*'s failure at the US box office, BVI's campaign suggests a lack of faith in the value of Altman's reputation to sell the film. In Germany, however, a delay in *Prêt-à-Porter*'s theatrical release due to a lawsuit by fashion designer Karl Lagerfeld bound the film more tightly to anti-authoritarian elements of Altman's brand.[41] Reigniting the gossip surrounding Lagerfeld's shunning of the film during production, the lawsuit requested a block on the distribution of *Prêt-à-Porter* due to defamation of character, as a line of dialogue in the film referred to the designer as a "thief."[42] The seemingly tit for tat nature of the lawsuit generated a final wave of scandal surrounding *Prêt-à-Porter* and its engagement with the world of fashion, priming critics and viewers to expect a more caustic take on the industry than what the film actually contains.

Prêt-à-Porter divided press across Europe, yet the film's massive pre-release publicity and European critics' intense interest in Altman's work ensured heated debates. The production notes supplied to critics provided fodder for two potential readings of the film: first, by stressing parallels with the more biting *M*A*S*H**, *Nashville*, and *The Player* as well as Altman's "extensive research" and "acute understanding of the fashion industry," the notes heightened expectations of a knowing satire; second, by situating *Prêt-à-Porter* as a farce with a "carefree, carnival spirit," the notes suggested the film was designed as entertainment.[43] Some who were against the film critiqued its lack of aesthetic and thematic sophistication, finding it a "smug, unfocused, facile swipe at the follies of the fashion world" (*Time Out*), "without surprise and lacking charm" (*Cahiers du Cinéma*), with "not an ounce of dramatic intention" (*Libération*), and "a huge disappointment—an artistic debacle" (*Evening Standard*).[44]

Others criticized its lack of authenticity—recalling Danish critiques of *Vincent & Theo*—with *Studio* describing it as "a disappointing caricature" and *Premiere* declaring it "too eagerly awaited . . . in *Prêt-à-Porter* Altman is like a tourist who cannot even reinvent the worn clichés attached to the world of fashion."[45] Both critical approaches highlighted expectations raised by Altman's brand—formal artistry and a knowing sociological critique—that the film seemingly failed to meet. Critics in favor of the film adopted overtly oppositional stances grounded in a celebration of Altman's authorial vision, including enthusiastic reviews in *Positif* that championed the picture as "a true auteur film" and "a rich and disillusioned work that once again blends, with the mastery of the great days, the whirlwinds of reality with the rituals of representation"; in *Next Fashion*, C. L. Walker celebrated the film as "*docufarce vérité*" that held up a mirror to the "uncontrived insanity" of contemporary life.[46] Only in Germany was the reception more consistently positive, as critics expressed little of the disappointment of their foreign peers who knocked *Prêt-à-Porter* for lacking profundity. German critics chose instead to taunt those—including Karl Lagerfeld and his "sensitive mind"—who would ever take the fashion world seriously.[47] *Einblick* argued, "those who expect a satirical reckoning with the fashion circus after *The Player* and *Nashville* are misguided. Altman can't get under the surface of this glittering world, because there's nothing underneath."[48] The review in *Kino* concurred: "where there is nothing, there can be nothing. Altman's view of this scene will be absurd enough for the attentive observer."[49] The willingness of critics to embrace the film's frivolity as either entertainment or a cultural critique largely determined their take on the film.

Although *Prêt-à-Porter* is commonly considered Altman's biggest bomb of the 1990s due to its sizeable budget paired with disappointing reception and box office in the US, the film played significantly more strongly in Europe, allowing the picture to merely dent the director's career resurgence rather than derail it. The film's massive pre-release publicity, series of public scandals, and wide-ranging reviews positioned it in Europe as the center of an ongoing debate regarding the value of Altman's authorship, arousing curiosity and encouraging strong turnout for opening weekends. In France, *Prêt-à-Porter* debuted at the top of the box office in its first weekend despite mixed reviews, drawing primarily young audiences and particularly strong attendance in Paris.[50] The film also opened well in London, generating the highest per screen average in the theatre-heavy West End, and landed fourth in the UK box office for the week.[51] In Germany, *Prêt-à-Porter* produced the country's highest per screen average during its opening weekend in a limited release, even as box office was beginning to drop in the rest of Europe due to mixed word of mouth; in another sign of Germany's unusual fondness for the film, a federal agency that evaluates the merit of films awarded *Prêt-à-Porter* the rare "especially valuable" designation and the film stayed in theaters for three and a half months.[52] Miramax seized on *Prêt-à-Porter*'s European box office success in a conscious attempt to change the narrative about the film, running a full-page ad in *Variety* congratulating Altman on the "spectacular international opening."⁵³ Harvey Weinstein amplified the message at the Big Picture Conference in early April 1995, claiming, "Because of their love of Robert Altman, [the film] opened number one in every [international] territory it's been in so far—Spain, Italy, Germany, England, Australia"—a typically Weinsteinian exaggeration.⁵⁴ In contrast to Miramax's standard "spray and pray" strategy, which called for films that lacked affirmative press coverage, awards, and box office to be quickly cut loose, Weinstein committed heavily to *Prêt-à-Porter* even after its initial domestic failure, not only recognizing the potential value of European markets but also eager to maintain a positive relationship with Altman given his cultural cachet.⁵⁵ In the end, *Prêt-à-Porter*'s foreign theatrical rentals were four times higher than domestic, while overseas broadcast and pay television receipts outstripped those in the US as well.⁵⁶ As with *Vincent & Theo*, *Prêt-à-Porter* challenged perceptions of Altman's brand—particularly his ability to successfully skewer another culture—yet the tornado of publicity generated by the film and the continuing eagerness of European audiences to debate the merits of his work ensured ongoing financial support for Altman's projects—including from CiBy 2000, one of France's most esteemed art house producers and the backer of his next picture, *Kansas City*.

GOSFORD PARK: A RETURN TO THE SUMMIT

Altman's third and final European production with local subject matter, *Gosford Park*, followed a career stretch marked by intermittent health scares, challenging shoots, and uneven response to his work. Few predicted it would become the greatest triumph of Altman's late career and the ultimate validation of the continuing strength of his authorship. The project originated in 1999 with his longtime friend, actor/writer/director/producer Bob Balaban, who pitched him the idea of an Agatha Christie-style country hour murder mystery set in the 1930s. Yet Altman had little interest in the lives of the British upper crust. Recalled Balaban,

> I convinced him, a bit, to look at it as a film that would show things from the view of upstairs, but with the dramatic weight being downstairs. As soon as he thought about it that way, it became more in his mind an Altman movie.⁵⁷

Balaban turned to actor and writer Julian Fellowes, with whom he had already been working on two film adaptations of classic literary works, to draft a script. Fellowes, conscious of Altman's thematic and formal preferences, crafted a sociological portrait of interwar Britain featuring thirty major characters and fifteen primary plotlines. The story's expansive number of characters, dated cultural customs, and seemingly out of fashion genre trappings complicated financing and increased the risk of production. Without the name recognition of its predominantly British cast and eventual UK financing agreement, the picture would never have gotten off the ground. The close attention paid to authenticity during scriptwriting and production and the alignment of the film's class critique with the ideological values of the European critical establishment enabled Altman to sidestep the charges of cultural ignorance lobbed by the Dutch at *Vincent & Theo* and by the French at *Prêt-à-Porter*. *Gosford Park*'s marriage of the European production model of *Vincent & Theo*— overseas financing, production locations, and casting, as well as a reliance on existing relationships to secure distribution—with a project that reaffirmed key thematic and aesthetic components of Altman's brand in an unexpectedly original way distinguished the film from Altman's other European pictures and set the stage for the greatest critical and commercial success of his late career.

Although Julian Fellowes's script, revised with Balaban and Altman, laid the foundation for *Gosford Park*'s eventual success, its distinct genre characteristics seemingly clashed with Altman's brand and initially served as impediments to acquiring funding and distribution. Balaban explained, "I think it frightened people, the investors, to see Robert Altman directing a movie that you're used to seeing from Merchant-Ivory because it had to be respectful and Bob is not respectful."[58] Balaban and Altman decided to finance screenplay and preproduction themselves, initiating casting in London in the summer of 2000.[59] Altman's reputation and charm secured commitments from top British actors, including Maggie Smith, Helen Mirren, Eileen Atkins, Alan Bates, and Derek Jacobi, despite a tiered pay scale that provided a fraction of their standard fees. Balaban attributed the actors' eagerness to participate in the project to Altman's exalted status outside of his home country: "In the US, he's not exactly chopped liver, but in England, he's caviar."[60] Altman announced the details of *Gosford Park* during press interviews for *Dr. T & the Women* at the Venice Film Festival in September, but still had not secured financing by the time he moved to London for preproduction at the start of winter.[61] By the end of the year the London-based sales company Capitol Films assumed the cost of the picture, then mitigated its exposure by securing a European bank loan, pre-sales of theatrical rights territory by territory, and lottery funding through the UK's Film Council, which provided $2.8 million from its new Premiere Fund—producing grumbles in some quarters that its first and largest investment went to an "uncommercial" American director.[62] Ironically, the UK theatrical rights were amongst the last to sell in the fall of 2001, as UK buyers considered the film "a bit boring" and unlikely to interest local audiences due to its association with the out-of-fashion country house murder mystery.[63] The strength of Altman's brand abroad assisted with the acquisition of European funding and distribution, yet lingering uncertainty regarding the director's appropriateness for the distinctly non-American subject matter posed a test for the film's reception.

Figure 8.2 Producer and actor Bob Balaban and Robert Altman confer on the set of *Gosford Park*. Photo by Mark Tillie. Courtesy of Special Collections Research Center, University of Michigan Library.

The pre-release publicity on *Gosford Park* in Britain directly engaged with Altman's brand as a cultural critic, yet ultimately proved much more supportive of him than the press in France during the shooting of *Prêt-à-Porter*. In on-set interviews with British journalists, Altman overtly acknowledged the potential for him to be once again taken to task for portraying non-American subject matter. "The big criticism that will come to me is: 'What are you doing making an English film about manners?'" he told Geoffrey Macnab in *The Guardian*. "I suppose if I was a Hungarian, it wouldn't be so bad, but the idea that an American is doing this will undoubtedly draw fire from the local press."[64] In the *Evening Standard*, Alexander Walker amplified the concern, describing Altman as "going where few Americans ever boldly go: into a place more rarefied than space, the English class system."[65] Another journalist described the English country house murder mystery as a risk not just for an American director, but for any director, as it was "a genre every sane person imagined had been banished to television two decades ago."[66] Yet despite the potential pitfalls, journalists on set visits uniformly highlighted Altman's joy in working with the British cast and crew, whose training and absence of ego he repeatedly praised (and, unlike on the sets of *Vincent & Theo* and *Prêt-à-Porter*, whose language he could speak). Articles on the film's production also noted how Altman's approach to shooting—in which everyone is miked and equally capable of being at the center of any shot—was reminiscent of the egalitarianism of a British repertory theater company, while the director's worldview also appeared simpatico: "the Brits like him; his sly, sardonic take on life and work and his willingness to speak his mind seems to chime with their own attitudes."[67] Despite the difference in nationality between the director and the subject, cast, and crew, the pre-release publicity initiated a narrative of Altman as the perfect fit to direct *Gosford Park*—an American director more at home working in Britain than in Hollywood.

Bolstered by publicity that reinforced Altman's brand as a director more European than American, the marketing campaign for *Gosford Park* focused on the film's quality and sophisticated style, highlighting the combination of a "top-line director," "solid-gold cast," and a "fresh spin on the genre."[68] These elements are graphically foregrounded in *Gosford Park*'s primary promotional image—utilized throughout Europe and the US—featuring the back of a man in white tie and tails, set against a bed of roses and stabbed in the shoulder by a pen supporting a scroll; the scroll announces the film's title, tagline ("Tea at four/Dinner at eight/Murder at midnight"), and cast list, bordered by Altman's credit at the bottom. The roses and white tie and tails evoke the luxury and rituals of the story's historical setting—also highlighted by "Tea at four/Dinner at eight"—while the pen in the back and the end of the tagline alert audiences to the film's genre twist, thereby aligning the film's seemingly un-Altmanesque subject with the reinvigoration of its genre—a defining aspect of Altman's brand. The picture's debut at the London Film Festival and showcase at the Berlin Film Festival, where Altman was awarded a Golden Bear for lifetime achievement, further associated *Gosford Park* with his legacy as a film artist, an assessment reinforced by subsequent reviews and awards.

Critics in the UK and Europe championed *Gosford Park* as an Altman masterpiece, highlighting its employment of the defining formal elements of his brand and declaring it as incisive and knowing a cultural critique as his canonical American satires *Nashville* and *The Player*. *Positif* continued to herald Altman's auteur status, declaring, "he once again delivers a major work, one of those polyphonic stories of which he knows the secret," while *The Independent* argued the film "showcases aspects of his talent—the relaxed, improvisatory movement, the expert directing of an ensemble, the incisive wit—we haven't seen in a long while."[69] Expanding on the pre-release publicity, critics also remarked on Altman's ability to authentically capture a slice of English life with a more critical eye than a native might muster. In the *Sunday Express*, Henry Fitzherbert opined, "This is such a naturalistic study of upper-class Englishmen in their habitat that you half expect David Attenborough to pop up and commentate," while in *Sight & Sound*, Geoffrey Macnab wrote, "This is a quintessentially British movie, but one which only an outsider with Altman's energy could have made."[70] French critics—many of whom were mercilessly critical of *Prêt-à-Porter*—also embraced *Gosford Park* for its historical accuracy and cultural critique. *Inrockuptibles* favorably compared the picture to "insipid, old-fashioned" Merchant-Ivory historical dramas, while *Télérama* described it as "a life-size anthropological experience, conducted with a truly astounding mastery," a point echoed by *Charlie Hebdo*: "it is the accumulation of facts and correct details, without demonizing or beatifying, that gives the film its power of denunciation."[71] Only Stephen Fry's bumbling police inspector struck a wrong tonal note for many, a complaint limited to British critics all too familiar with the actor's comedic work.[72] Enchanted by Altman's precision when tackling the rituals of English interwar culture and energized by the appearance of his signature formal strategies, European critics embraced *Gosford Park* with full-throated enthusiasm and unity previously unseen in his European productions. The critical success of *Gosford Park* culminated in a Golden Globe for Best Director, a BAFTA for Best British Film, and six Academy Award nominations and one win for Best Original Screenplay, making it Altman's most lauded picture since *Nashville*. *Gosford Park*'s Oscar nominations enabled Capitol Films to even sell distribution rights to territories that historically had little interest in an English drawing-room drama, including Germany, East Asia, Mexico, and South America, further expanding its global reach.[73]

The unusual combination of an Altmanesque social critique and a stylish English period drama proved more popular with audiences than distributors ever anticipated, generating the highest box office gross of Altman's career. After a platform release in the US that built to more than 700 screens, *Gosford Park* opened strongly in the UK and remained in the top ten for three months, generating nearly an $18 million gross—the largest by far in a territory outside of the US and a stinging rebuke to local distributors who had not foreseen an audience for the film.[74] In France, the picture broke attendance records for its initial nine a.m. screening in Paris and finished its first week at the top of the charts, netting nearly $4 million by the end of its run.[75] The unexpected critical and commercial success of *Gosford Park* revived British period drama and paved the way for Fellowes's television phenomenon *Downton Abbey* (2010–15). Yet few of the costume pictures or series released in *Gosford Park*'s wake offered the multifaceted and unsparing critique of class difference that Altman uniquely brought to the genre. Marked by a carefully crafted authenticity and married to Altman's signature narrative and stylistic traits, *Gosford Park* proved to remaining doubters that the "obstinate American" could apply his distinct approach to filmmaking as successfully overseas as at home.

CONCLUSION

Altman's reputation as an anti-Hollywood filmmaker with a keen eye for the absurdities of American culture had endeared him to European film industry professionals and audiences, who often considered his work, thematically and aesthetically, as more European than American. In the mid-1980s, his relocation to Paris in the wake of an increasingly challenging production environment in the US enabled him to accomplish his perennial, primary goal—to keep working—by activating the strength of his brand in Europe and the network of relationships he had developed among European financiers, distributors, film festival programmers, publicists, journalists, and critics since the 1970s. Yet Altman's turn from shooting American stories in Europe to directing transnational European productions rooted in distinctly local subject matter raised questions regarding his ability to maintain European support: would Altman's brand survive a reorientation of his critical lens away from the US and toward Europe, or would his decision to "fiddle on the corner where they throw the coins" spark an industry and audience backlash?

An analysis of the financing, publicity, marketing, reception, and box office of Altman's three European production between 1990 and 2001 reveals the centrality of consistent—though at times uneven—European support to Altman's late career productivity. *Vincent & Theo* provided a production template that was both adopted and varied for Altman's subsequent transnational European productions, including financing and shooting in Europe with local casts and crews, focusing on local subject matter, and the leveraging of personal relationships to secure distribution. As would also prove to be the case with *Prêt-à-Porter* and *Gosford Park*, Altman's brand shaped the discourse surrounding *Vincent & Theo* despite the cultural and historical specificity of the subject matter. In the face of resistant Dutch critics, the film demonstrated Altman's ability to tackle foreign subject matter while retaining the loyalty of overseas audiences, priming him for a return to American independent feature filmmaking with *The Player*. While the critical and commercial drubbing of *Prêt-à-Porter* in the US market had the potential to set Altman up for another *Popeye*-style career crater, in Europe the picture's massive publicity, recalibrated marketing campaigns, and ongoing critical debates enabled it to generate stronger reviews and box office overseas than domestically, thereby ensuring continued financial support for his filmmaking. *Prêt-à-Porter* confirmed the strength of Altman's brand in Europe, as critics and audiences did not look to the film's failure in the US as an indicator of a lack of quality, but rather displayed a willingness to engage with the film as the product of an auteur worthy of examination—even in the case of a lesser work. *Gosford Park* featured Altman tackling perhaps the most unexpected subject matter of his late career in a nevertheless quintessential manner, a combination that seduced critics and audiences around the globe. The picture saw Altman learning the lessons of his prior European productions, not only utilizing British financing, locations, craftspeople, and talent, but also focusing on historical and cultural authenticity and getting in front of potential criticism of him as an American interloper. The end result revitalized Altman's brand in the new century.

Together, these pictures make a strong case for the necessity of expanding how we define both Altman's authorship and his relationship to the film industry. Rather than conceiving of Altman as a singularly American director struggling against the vicissitudes of US studio and independent filmmaking, it is useful to consider Altman's transnational productions and how his work was received outside of the domestic market. European financiers, distributors, festival programmers, critics, and audiences consistently demonstrated a willingness to support Altman's work even when their American peers' faith in him wavered, suggesting the distinct cultural resonance of Altman's "more European than American" brand overseas. Even when aspects of individual Altman films failed to meet expectations, the value placed by European consumers on Altman's association with artistry over commerce maintained European loyalty. Investigating Altman's ability to speak powerfully to critics and audiences outside his own country and his recurring reliance on overseas financing and distribution enables a more nuanced understanding of his astonishing late career resurgence.

ACKNOWLEDGMENT

Thanks to Benjamin Yap, Kira Newmark, and Hannah Cooper for research and translation assistance.

NOTES

1. John Caughie, "Preface," in John Caughie (ed.), *Theories of Authorship: A Reader* (London: Routledge and Kegan Paul, 1981), p. 2.
2. Mark Batey, *Brand Meaning* (London: Routledge, 2012), p. 6.
3. Ibid. p. 8.
4. Camille Pluntz and Bernard Pras, "Exploring professional human brand identity through cultural and social capital: A typology of film director identities," *Journal of Marketing Management* 36, nos 9–10 (2020): 834.
5. David Sterritt, "Breaking the rules: Altman, innovation and the critics," in Adrian Danks (ed.), *A Companion to Robert Altman* (Oxford: John Wiley and Sons, Inc., 2015), p. 93.
6. Justin Wyatt, "Economic constraints/economic opportunities: Robert Altman as auteur," *The Velvet Light Trap* 38 (Fall 1996): 57. For scholars who associate the formal qualities of Altman's films with European art cinema, see Helene Keyssar, *Robert Altman's America* (New York: Oxford University Press, 1991), pp. 16–38; and Robert T. Self, *Robert Altman's Subliminal Reality* (Minneapolis: University of Minnesota Press, 2002), pp. 47–53.
7. David Thompson, interview with Denise Breton, *Projections* 13 (2004): 147, 150–1.
8. Peter van Bueren, "Altman's personal answer to van Gogh," *Volkscrant*, 26 April 1990, translated by publicist, Robert Altman Papers, Special Collections Research Center, University of Michigan Library.
9. Author interview with Matthew Seig (producer), 20 March 2020; author interview with Wren Arthur (producer), 9 June 2020; author interview with Joshua Astrachan (producer), 29 July 2020.

10. Hal Hinson, "Robert Altman, his way," *Washington Post*, 18 November 1990, K1.
11. Richard Combs, "The world is a bad painting: An interview with Robert Altman," *Monthly Film Bulletin*, 1 July 1990: 57, 678.
12. John C. Tibbetts, "After 35 years, still the 'action painter' of American cinema," *Literature/Film Quarterly* 20, no. 1 (1992): 39.
13. Jerome K. Walsh, deposition in Boeken, Belbo Films v. Altman; Memo from Jerome Walsh to Robert Altman, 3 July 1990; Statement of Accounts by Territory, 11 July 1991; all in Robert Altman Papers, Special Collections Research Center, University of Michigan Library.
14. Joseph McBride, Review of *Vincent and Theo*, *Variety*, 2 May 1990, p. 285.
15. Ad for *Vincent & Theo* Marché du Film screening, with letter from Mike Kaplan to Kathy Morgan, 9 May 1990, Robert Altman Papers, Special Collections Research Center, University of Michigan Library.
16. Full- and half-page print ads for screenings in London, Bath, Cambridge, and Birmingham, Robert Altman Papers, Special Collections Research Center, University of Michigan Library.
17. Mike Kaplan summary of meeting with Martin Rabinowitz and Gary Shapiro on 19 April 1990, combined with further thoughts stimulated by conversations with Robert Altman, Robert Altman Papers, Special Collections Research Center, University of Michigan Library.
18. Daniel Sauvaget, Review of *Vincent & Theo*, *La Revue du cinéma*, 1990, translation by Hannah Cooper, in Robert Altman Papers, Special Collections Research Center, University of Michigan Library.
19. Wilfried Wiegand, "Im Kampf mit der Legende," *Frankfurter Allgemeine*, 5 May 1990; see also Gunter Göckenjan, Review of *Vincent & Theo*, *Tageszeitung*, 5 May 1990; Birgit Warnhold, "Gegen den Rest der Welt," *Berliner Morgenpost*, 3 May 1990; translation by Hannah Cooper; all in Robert Altman Papers, Special Collections Research Center, University of Michigan Library.
20. "The director who loses direction: Robert Altman, Hollywood maverick," *The Independent*, 23 June 1990, p. 18.
21. Derek Malcolm, "Artists more flawed than their creations," *The Guardian*, 1 July 1990, p. 25.
22. Jean-Loup Bourget, "Le triomphe du docteur Gachet," *Positif*, June 1991, p. 58; translation by Hannah Cooper.
23. Roel Naarding, "Veel detailfouten in *Vincent and Theo*," *Het Parool*, 26 April 1990; Hans Kroon, "Eén ziel in twee lichamen," 26 April 1990; translation by Hannah Cooper; both in Robert Altman Papers, Special Collections Research Center, University of Michigan Library.
24. Henk van Gelder, "Slechte tanden, verf aan de vingers," *NRC Handelsblad*, 26 April 1990, translation by Hannah Cooper, Robert Altman Papers, Special Collections Research Center, University of Michigan Library.
25. Memo from Jerry Walsh to Robert Altman, 3 July 1990; Letter from Jerry Walsh to David Lowe, 31 July 1990; both in Robert Altman Papers, Special Collections Research Center, University of Michigan Library.
26. "Art house fans shrug off World Cup fever," *Screen International*, 3–6 July 1990, Robert Altman Papers, Special Collections Research Center, University of Michigan Library.
27. Memo from Jerry Walsh to Robert Altman, 3 July 1990, Robert Altman Papers, Special Collections Research Center, University of Michigan Library.
28. Louise Bateman and Ana Maria Bahiana, "Companies report brisk sales at AFM," *Screen International*, 12 March 1993, p. 5; Michael Williams, "Bac bites 'Bullets'; 'Pret' price Gauling," *Variety*, 12–18 September 1994, p. 14.
29. Greg Evans, "Marketing a la mode," *Variety*, 19 December–1 January 1994, p. 6.

30. Mitchell Zuckoff, *Robert Altman: The Oral Biography* (New York: Knopf, 2009), pp. 440–1.
31. "Fashion the victim," *Los Angeles Times*, 15 May 1992, p. 9; "Fashion's new 'Player,' " *Women's Wear Daily*, 21 September 1993, p. 4.
32. "Paris: lights, camera, action!" *Women's Wear Daily*, 7 March 1994, pp. 1, 5.
33. Godfrey Deeny, "Paris: the sequel," *Women's Wear Daily*, 8 March 1994, p. 8.
34. For an overview of the fashion world's issues with the film, see "Not ready for viewing," *New York Observer*, 14 November 1994, in Robert Altman Papers, Special Collections Research Center, University of Michigan Library; and Amy Spindler, "Altman embraces fashion; Does fashion embrace him?" *New York Times*, 18 December 1994, A10.
35. *Prêt-à-Porter* Marketing Outline, 11 November 1994, Robert Altman Papers, Special Collections Research Center, University of Michigan Library.
36. Justin Wyatt, "The formation of the 'major independent': Miramax, New Line, and the New Hollywood," in Steve Neale and Murray Smith (eds), *Contemporary Hollywood Cinema* (London: Routledge, 1998), p. 83.
37. For European reactions to *Prêt-à-Porter*'s American ads and title change, see Kevin Smith, "Helena film ad ruffles feathers in Hollywood," *London Evening Standard*, 20 December 1994; Jeff Dawson, "Front desk clips: LA lore," *Empire*, February 1995; and "Bum's the word," *Just Seventeen*, 22 February 1995, all in Robert Altman Papers, Special Collections Research Center, University of Michigan Library.
38. Memo from Christian Grass to Scott Bushnell, 13 February 1995, Robert Altman Papers, Special Collections Research Center, University of Michigan Library.
39. Mike Goodridge, "UK marketing: Handle with care," *Screen International*, 3 March 1995, p. 20.
40. "*Prêt-à-Porter*: The film of the decade," *Looks*, March 1995, Robert Altman Papers, Special Collections Research Center, University of Michigan Library.
41. Memo from Christian Grass to Scott Bushnell, 8 December 1994, Robert Altman Papers, Special Collections Research Center, University of Michigan Library.
42. David Molner, "Designer suit blocks pic bow," *Variety*, 20–5 March 1995, p. 5.
43. *Prêt-à-Porter* Production Notes, 1994, Robert Altman Papers, Special Collections Research Center, University of Michigan Library.
44. Geoff Andrew, *Time Out*, "Prêt-à-Porter," 1 March 1995; Excerpted and translated reviews in memo from Denise Breton to Christian Grass re: French Media Report and Reviews—*Prêt-à-Porter*, 4 March 1995; Alexander Walker, "Ready to wear? Ready to walk out," *London Evening Standard*, 14 December 1994; all in Robert Altman Papers, Special Collections Research Center, University of Michigan Library.
45. Excerpted and translated reviews in memo from Denise Breton to Christian Grass re: French Media Report and Reviews—*Prêt-à-Porter*, 4 March 1995, Robert Altman Papers, Special Collections Research Center, University of Michigan Library.
46. Christian Viviani, "*Prêt-à-Porter*: La Robe sans coutures," *Positif*, April 1995; Yann Tobin, "*Prêt-à-Porter* de Robert Altman: Made to measure," *Positif*, April 1995; C. L. Walker, "Altman goofs with fashion," *Next Fashion*, Spring 1995, p. 11; translations by Hannah Cooper, Robert Altman Papers, Special Collections Research Center, University of Michigan Library.
47. "Prêt-à-Porter," *Einblick*, April 1995, translation by Hannah Cooper, Robert Altman Papers, Special Collections Research Center, University of Michigan Library.
48. Ibid.
49. "Vanity Fair," *Kino*, April 1995, p. 11, translation by Hannah Cooper, Robert Altman Papers, Special Collections Research Center, University of Michigan Library.
50. Don Groves, "Upscale pix draw big Euro crowds," *Variety*, 13–19 March 1995, p. 12; "La mode est à la mode," *le Parisien*, 7 March 1995, translation by Hannah Cooper,

Robert Altman Papers, Special Collections Research Center, University of Michigan Library.
51. Groves, "Upscale pix draw big Euro crowds," p. 12.
52. "Modenschau," *VIDEO Woche*, 23 April 1995, translation by Hannah Cooper, Robert Altman Papers, Special Collections Research Center, University of Michigan Library; Molner, 5.
53. Transcript of CNN's *Showbiz Today*, 5 April 1995, Robert Altman Papers, Special Collections Research Center, University of Michigan Library.
54. *Prêt-à-Porter* ad, *Variety*, 13 March 1995, p. 13.
55. Alisa Perren, *Indie, Inc.: Miramax and the Transformation of Hollywood in the 1990s* (Austin: University of Texas Press, 2012), p. 102.
56. *Ready to Wear* Participation Statement, 31 December 1998, Robert Altman Papers, Special Collections Research Center, University of Michigan Library.
57. Robert Koehler, "Genre bender," *Variety*, 10–16 December 2001, A8.
58. Bob Balaban quoted in Mitchell Zuckoff, *Robert Altman: The Oral Biography* (New York: Knopf, 2009), p. 471.
59. Author interview with Joshua Astrachan (producer), 29 July 2020.
60. Tom King, "Hollywood journal," *Wall Street Journal*, 8 February 2002, W7.
61. "Altman to come to UK for next feature," *Screen International*, 15 September 2000, p. 21; Zuckoff, *Robert Altman*, pp. 473–4.
62. Adam Dawtrey, "Brits ignite 'Gosford' spark: 9 BAFTA noms," *Variety*, 18–24 February 2002, A4; Adam Dawtrey, "Film Council grapples with fiscal reality," *Variety*, 15–21 October 2001, A2.
63. "UK distribs reconsider after 'Gosford' success," *Variety*, 22–28 April 2002, p. 15.
64. Geoffrey Macnab, "What's an American director doing making an English film about manners?" *The Guardian*, 8 May 2001, p. 14.
65. Alexander Walker, "Altman goes Upstairs, Downstairs," *Evening Standard*, 9 May 2001, p. 30.
66. Charles Gant, "Altman's Shooting Party," *The Times*, 26 January 2002, Robert Altman Papers, Special Collections Research Center, University of Michigan Library.
67. Charles Gant, "Altman's Shooting Party"; David Gritten, "Gladly giving up a few pounds," *Los Angeles Times*, 9 March 2002, F1.
68. Noemi Rev, *Gosford Park* Positioning Document, 30 January 2001, Robert Altman Papers, Special Collections Research Center, University of Michigan Library.
69. Olivier de Bruyn, "*Gosford Park*: Sale temps pour ceux qui ont des secrets," *Positif*, 2002, translated by Hannah Cooper, in Robert Altman Papers, Special Collections Research Center, University of Michigan Library; Anthony Quinn, Review of *Gosford Park*, *The Independent*, 1 February 2002, p. 10.
70. Henry Fitzherbert, "A tremendously high-class romp," *Sunday Express*, 3 February 2002, p. 68; Geoffrey Macnab, Review of *Gosford Park*, *Sight & Sound*, February 2002, p. 46.
71. Serge Kaganski, "Meurte dans un jardin anglais," *Inrockuptibles*, 19 March 2002, p. 46; Aurélien Ferenczi, Review of *Gosford Park*, *Télérama*, 20 March 2002; Michel Boujut, "La Règle du jeu (bis)," *Charlie Hebdo*, 20 March 2002, translations by Hannah Cooper, all in Robert Altman Papers, Special Collections Research Center, University of Michigan Library.
72. Stephen Dalton, "It's no walk in the park," *The Times*, 21 January 2002.
73. Cathy Dunkley, "Oscar noms help sell Altman pic to Japan," *Variety*, 25–31 March 2002, p. 6.
74. "UK distribs reconsider," p. 15.
75. Memo from Denise Breton to Wren Arthur, 20 March 2002, re: Paris Opening; Alain Grasset, "'*Gosford Park*' fait le plein," *Le Parisien*, 31 March 2002; *Gosford Park* Cumulative Global Box Office Report, 27 May 2002; all in Robert Altman Papers, Special Collections Research Center, University of Michigan Library.

PART III

New Perspectives on Altman

Figure III.1 Robert Altman on the set of *Dr. T & the Women*. Photo by Zade Rosenthal. Courtesy of Special Collections Research Center, University of Michigan Library.

CHAPTER 9

Fantasies and Fangirls: Gender and Sexuality in Robert Altman's *Come Back to the 5 & Dime, Jimmy Dean, Jimmy Dean*

Sarah E. S. Sinwell

Within Robert Altman's oeuvre, *Come Back to the 5 & Dime, Jimmy Dean, Jimmy Dean* has received relatively limited critical or academic attention. As Justin Wyatt notes, Robert Altman's work was largely "admired by critics and largely ignored by the mainstream moviegoing public."[1] Though the film won the Best Film Award at the Chicago International Film Festival and a Golden Globe nomination for Best Actress in a Supporting Role for Cher's portrayal of Sissy, *Come Back to the 5 & Dime, Jimmy Dean, Jimmy Dean* was released by the independent distributor Cinecom Pictures rather than the larger studios so that it might play longer at art house venues. Adapted from a theatrical script from Ed Graczyk that Altman also directed for a Broadway production, *Come Back to the 5 & Dime, Jimmy Dean, Jimmy Dean* features six women in the small town of McCarthy in Texas who are reuniting for the twentieth anniversary of the Disciples of James Dean fan club from 1955. Taking place in 1975, the twentieth anniversary of James Dean's death, the film uses flashbacks to tell the stories of these women as they recall their fandom of James Dean and reveal their histories. Based on the play written in the Southern Gothic tradition of Tennessee Williams and William Inge and the first of Altman's stage-to-screen chamber pieces, it was filmed on one set (the 5 & Dime) and utilizes Altman's iconic mobile, fluid camera, problematizing the representation of identity and characters' points-of-view via its use of *mise-en-scène* and cinematography.

Altering "conventions of cinematic space and narrative structure,"[2] and focusing on culture and politics and the transformation of character, time, and place via Altman's "promiscuous camera," *Come Back to the 5 & Dime, Jimmy Dean, Jimmy Dean* builds upon this use of cinematography and *mise-en-scène* as a means of delving into the interiority and inner psychology of its characters. In the case of *Come Back to the 5 & Dime, Jimmy Dean, Jimmy Dean*, this critique of American culture and focus on the fragmentation of characters' subjectivities and interiorities extends to a critique of both femininity and masculinity that is structured around stars, memory, and history. Altman's use of physical and metaphorical windows and mirrors into the past enables a visual reimagining of cinematic time, as well as a reconstruction of the characters, their genders, and their sexualities. Thus, this essay will revisit not only the critical reception of *Come Back to the 5 & Dime, Jimmy Dean, Jimmy Dean*, but also interrogate the ways in which film scholars of Altman understood both the film and its representation of both gender and trans* identities.[3]

With particular focus on female fandom, this chapter will question the construction of female fans as passive consumers and reimagine how female fans can be constructed as participants in their own fandom. Exploring the ways in which the film uses cinematic and visual style and on-screen space to portray the characters' personal histories and memories, this chapter draws attention to how female (and gay male) fans have transformed in relation to the star persona of James Dean. In particular, the chapter draws upon the work of feminist, queer, and fan studies scholars as a means of analyzing how the fans of James Dean in *Come Back to the 5 & Dime, Jimmy Dean, Jimmy Dean* can be understood historically, culturally, and socially. Examining understandings of Dean's gender and sexuality, this chapter also investigates how these fans gain access to Dean as a fantasy and as a star text. Thus, this essay argues that the film both limits and opens up the representation of female fandom by drawing attention to both its ubiquity and contradictions.

RETHINKING GENDER AND FANDOM IN *COME BACK TO THE 5 & DIME, JIMMY DEAN, JIMMY DEAN*

Come Back to the 5 & Dime, Jimmy Dean, Jimmy Dean reimagines concepts of gender and sexuality in relation to its representation of James Dean fandom. By intertwining the characters' memories of the past with their retellings in the present, the film draws attention to the intersections between male, female, heterosexual, and trans* identities while also pushing the boundaries of both male and female fandom. These intersections occur not only through the characters and their recollections, but also through the transitory use of fractured glass and mirrors within the *mise-en-scène* of the 5 & Dime. Drawing attention to women's and trans stories is a reminder of the ways in which these stories are often omitted from history, particularly in relation to both female and gay male fandom.

Even from its opening moments, the film exhibits what Ashley Hinck calls in *Politics for the Love of Fandom* an emotional/affective tie to the object of

Figure 9.1 Cher and Robert Altman pose on the set of *Come Back to the 5 & Dime, Jimmy Dean, Jimmy Dean*. Courtesy of Special Collections Research Center, University of Michigan Library.

fandom.[4] As the film begins, the camera pans to images of James Dean on the walls of the Woolworth's 5 & Dime and informs us that the day is 30 September 1975, the twentieth reunion of the Disciples of James Dean. The screen is also filled with images of the American flag and streamers, as well as iconic images of a neon Jesus, rock and roll musicians, and the stars of *Photoplay* magazine. This focus on the objects of fandom also constructs the characters as the film draws attention to Americana such as rock and roll and movie stardom as a means of mapping out the characters' identities and memories.

The film begins in 1975 as the camera lingers over images of the owner of the 5 & Dime Juanita (Sudie Bond), as she swats flies and tidies up the store. The first guest to arrive at the reunion at the 5 & Dime is Sissy (Cher). As the other members of the fan club arrive, Mona (Sandy Dennis), Stella Mae (Kathy Bates), and Edna Louise (Marta Heflin) reminisce about their pasts in the fan club and their mutual love of James Dean. The film then transitions back to 1955 as Sissy, Mona, and Joe (Mark Patton) sing and dance to the McGuire sisters' song, "Sincerely." The film moves almost seamlessly from the present to the past via the use of glass and two-way mirrors, often superimposing images of the characters as it comments on the overlaps and contradictions between these women's past histories and their memories. As Robert Self notes, in this way, the women are depicted in "mirrored images and fractured relationships."[5]

This retelling of the past is significant for both women's and LGBTQ+ histories as these histories and stories of minorities and underrepresented groups are often unseen, hidden, omitted, or even lost. As Gilad Padva notes in *Queer Nostalgia in Cinema and Pop Culture*, "[R]einventing or retelling the past is a major part of the creation of gay, lesbian, bisexual, and transgender heritage with its own role models, icons, symbols, emblems, and glorified imageries."[6] The film moves back and forth in time but not space via mirrored memories of flashbacks and windows to the past, drawing upon the metaphor of mirroring the self in both the past and the present. The film's focus on the past insists upon the intersectionalities between male, female, heterosexual, and trans* identities while also drawing attention to the ways in which these subjectivities can be connected through fandom.

In her discussion of the film's use of the close-up, Helene Keyssar notes,

> But both by distributing close attention among the diverse faces of the women in *Jimmy Dean* and by capturing women's faces not as perfect objects of beauty but as subjects viewing each other, Altman avoids the fetishism associated with women that both critics and Altman himself have condemned in many movies.[7]

In fact, these women only look at each other. Rather than being fetishized (from the outside of the 5 & Dime, from society, or from the male point of view), the film instead enables these women to enact their own embodied realities and inner subjectivities by intertwining their memories of the past with their retellings in the present.

In a flashback to their fan club of 1955, the women of the 5 & Dime argue over who will reveal the news that Elizabeth Taylor and Rock Hudson will be coming just sixty-two miles away to film *Giant* (George Stevens, 1956) in Marfa, Texas. Stella Mae reveals that "The radio said it's all about giants or something" as the women get excited about the possibility that it might be "a monster movie like the creature from the black lagoon" rather than the epic story of a cattle rancher and his family. Like the photographs and statues of Dean that grace every inch of the 5 & Dime, Mona's insistence upon gathering broken pieces of the house from *Giant* (and her almost religious worship of these damaged objects) is also evidence of her need to have physical and tactile evidence of her encounter with James Dean. This focus on these physical objects throughout the store and as emblematic of the character's own pasts also constructs fandom as what John Fiske describes as a "constant struggle between fans and the industry, in which the industry attempts to incorporate the tastes of the fans, and the fans to 'excorporate' the products of the industry."[8]

James Dean's association with masculinity, homosexuality, juvenile delinquency, rebellion, and melodramatic fantasy is also part of his appeal. Through his portrayal of a troubled teenager in *Rebel without a Cause* (Nicholas Ray, 1955), a misunderstood loner in *East of Eden* (Elia Kazan, 1955), and a ranch hand in *Giant*, Dean became the iconic image of juvenile angst and rebellious imagination. However, unlike many stereotypes of female fans, the women of the Disciples of James Dean fan club are not represented as screaming, fainting, or passive consumers, rather, their fandom of James Dean enables them to create a community of inclusion and solidarity that acknowledges their stories and histories.

As Matt Hills notes in his work, fan cultures include both the cultural struggles over meaning and affect, as well as associated contradictions and negotiations.[9] These contradictions and negotiations are especially difficult to define when it comes to gendered expectations of fandom. Diana Anselmo-Sequeira writes on what she defines as the screen-struck girl, pointing out the lack of discussion of female fans since they were associated with affective, immature, passive, and unreliable film patrons and the necessity of acknowledging girl fans contributions to the establishment of the Hollywood star system.[10] As Suzanne Scott argues in *Fake Geek Girls*,

> it is precisely because of the convergence culture industry's gendered depathologization and affirmation of *certain* fans and *certain* fan practices that we must reinvest in and reimagine fan studies' commitment to studying female audiences and feminist modes of fannish resistance.[11]

Though the women's fandom revolves around James Dean's presence in the film (the last film he would star in before his sudden death in 1955), their lack of knowledge about *Giant* despite their constant references to *Photoplay* magazines and other stars is evidence of their exclusive fandom for James Dean. At the same time, the nervous thrills they seem to be exhibiting over the possibility that the film might be a monster movie also points to the ways in which monster movie fandom is not associated with female fans. However, the women's knowledge of their own fears and delights in seeing a film that does not fit the gendered expectations of the female fan is also included as essential to that fandom and enables an opening up of female fandom to include other possibilities beyond the romance, melodrama, or soap opera.[12]

In fact, Mona's love of James Dean extends far beyond love or sexual desire. She desires to have access to Dean's persona, both emotionally and sexually. She remarks that everyone is jealous of her: "Jealous because I was chosen to bring the son of James Dean into this world." As Sissy stated, "I thought he belonged to James Dean fans everywhere, conceived in Mona and dedicated to the population." While Mona replied, "He chose me from everybody else to bring his child into this world." Mona's desire to be chosen, not just as a woman but as a mother, is how she defines her own identity. Without this interaction with James Dean, her life and her child have very little meaning to her. At the same time, however, her insistence upon Dean's desire for her also reveals her own insecurities and the limited possibilities for a woman of very little means in a small town in Texas.

Robert Kolker writes of the characters of *Come Back to the 5 & Dime, Jimmy Dean, Jimmy Dean:* "these characters represent women not merely as victims of patriarchal demand but as crippled by it."[13] However, I would argue that these women are not crippled by patriarchy, but rather only limited by it. Subjected to the limitations associated with beauty, femininity, family, marriage, and the patriarchal home, even within these constraints, these women are attempting to live their best lives within the confines of their emotional, psychological, and material realities. However, though these women are subjected to the limits of patriarchy, rather than being seen as an escape from their everyday lives, their James Dean fandom is essential to their understandings of themselves, their identities, their community, and their futures.

At the same time, fandom in *Come Back to the 5 & Dime, Jimmy Dean, Jimmy Dean* is linked not only to understandings of gender, but also to sexuality. A symbol of sex, James Dean represented rebellion, not only in terms of his relationship to juvenile delinquency, but, also in terms of his appeal to both women and gay men. As an icon of resistance to the moral order as well as a representation of both alienation and disconnectedness, Dean appealed to his female fans and the characters of the film as a means of acknowledging and expressing the contradictions and challenges within their lived experiences.[14] Thus, through its representation of female and gay fandom, the film also constructs a more inclusive representation of trans* identities and sexualities that pushes the boundaries of most other trans* representations within media history.

DEFINING TRANS* IDENTITIES IN *COME BACK TO THE 5 & DIME, JIMMY DEAN, JIMMY DEAN*

Revisiting *Come Back to the 5 & Dime, Jimmy Dean, Jimmy Dean* almost forty years after its release and analyzing it through both feminist and queer lenses enables a reimagining of its representation of femininity, masculinity, and trans* identities. While the film may participate in the trope of the trans* character as object of derision and victim of violence, at the same time, it also portrays its trans* character as one who is both empathetic and multi-faceted. Thus, even though one might imagine the film would be limited in its representation of trans* identity because of its situatedness in the 1950s and 1970s, the film nevertheless conveys a message that encourages both tolerance and inclusion of the trans* community.

Though Sam Feder's 2020 documentary *Disclosure: Trans Lives on Screen* featured numerous references to the representation of trans* identities within film and television history—including such films as *The Crying Game* (Neil Jordan, 1992), *Boys Don't Cry* (Kimberly Peirce, 1999), *The Danish Girl* (Tom Hooper, 2015), and *Ace Ventura: Pet Detective* (Tom Shadyac, 1994)—*Come Back to the 5 & Dime, Jimmy Dean, Jimmy Dean* was nevertheless omitted from this history of trans* representation. This omission speaks not only to the relative obscurity of Altman's film, but also to the invisibility of this film in relation to trans* film history.

In addition, the representation of trans* identity in *Come Back to the 5 & Dime, Jimmy Dean, Jimmy Dean* is certainly limited by the vocabulary of 1980s America. The film never uses the word trans* to define the character of Joanne. But, rather, Joanne names herself both a "she" and a "freak." In fact, academics and critics such as Robert Self, Helene Keyssar, and Robert Kolker also neglect to use the term trans* in their analyses of the film. Yet, at the same time, unlike later films like *The Crying Game*, *Boys Don't Cry*, *The Danish Girl*, and *Ace Ventura: Pet Detective*, one could also argue that Joanne's portrayal of a trans* person who is neither a sissy nor solely a victim of violence or derision captures a moment in American film history in which trans* identity is seen as an object of both hatred *and* compassion.

As Halberstam points out in 2016, "Transgender is the new gay, the new orange, the new reality show, the newest classification of exclusion and pathology to be seamlessly transitioned into a marker of acceptance and tolerance."[15] In 1982, few film texts had discussed the presence of trans* lives within popular culture. By even attempting to relay a message of inclusion and tolerance, *Come Back to the 5 & Dime, Jimmy Dean, Jimmy Dean* may be understood as breaking the codes of trans* representation, not only for its time, but even within the context of more contemporary mediamaking.

Susan Stryker argues in her book *Transgender History* that transgender can be referred to as "people who move away from the gender they were assigned at birth, people who cross-over (*trans-*) the boundaries constructed by their culture to define and contain their gender."[16] Rather than representing trans*-ness via a physical or emotional transformation on-screen, we are introduced to Joe and Joanne as separate characters. This constructs trans* identity through both male and female embodiment and characterizes Joanne's trans* identity as linked to female performativity.

Only one man (Joe, played by Mark Patton) appears in the cast and he appears on-screen only in memory segments of the film.[17] At first, it is unclear exactly how Joe does not conform to gender norms beyond his choice of friends and song and dance choices (as the third member of the McGuire sisters). His visual presence via his clothing, hair, and bodily movements can be read as cis-male. But, when it is revealed later in the film that Joe is now Joanne, though many of the other characters are uncertain about how to understand this transition, Mona continues to refuse to treat Joe differently and her acceptance of this new identity has even more implications for the understanding of trans* lives in both 1950s and 1980s America.

When Mona expresses her nostalgia for their old James Dean fan club by wondering about what happened to their only male member Joe, Juanita reminds her, "He should have friends that are boys. Not you and Sissy. It's just shameful the three of you dressed him up as lookalikes." She continues saying, "He is a sick boy." Defending him, Mona responds by saying, "He's just different, that's all. It's not his fault. It's theirs." As Juanita states that "In the eyes of God, he does not belong," Mona replies by saying "Then God is wrong." This commentary on Joe's "difference" and his association with femininity is seen as "sick" by Juanita, who sees herself as a good upstanding Christian woman. On the other hand, Mona is accepting and inclusive of Joe's gender and sexual differences and reminds us of the social and societal implications of insisting upon upholding gender norms. In this way, Mona also insists that it is not Joe's fault that he is different, but rather it is society that refuses to accept this difference.

In *In a Queer Time and Place: Transgender Bodies, Subcultural Lives*, Halberstam proposes that "we might privilege friendship networks over extended families when assessing the structures of intimacy that sustain queer lives."[18] In this vein, Mona's support of Joe's difference and acknowledgment of his embodied and emotional realities can also be seen as progressive. Thus, opening up an understanding of the film that includes an analysis of Joanne's trans*-ness also enables a rethinking of the film's understandings of both femininity and sexuality.

Kate Stable comments on the representation of Karen Black as a trans* woman in her review of the DVD of *Come Back to the 5 & Dime, Jimmy Dean, Jimmy Dean* for *Sight & Sound*. Calling it "part women's picture, part memory-driven melodrama" and "a therapy piece."[19] "But in an era when transgender characters were routinely tragic (*Dog Day Afternoon*, Sidney Lumet, 1975) or monstrous (*Dressed to Kill*, Brian De Palma, 1980), Karen Black's elegant, straightshooting Joanne is a thoughtful revelation."[20] However, Karen Black's portrayal of the character of Joanne was rarely discussed in comparison with Dustin Hoffman's performance in Sydney Pollack's *Tootsie* from that same year. I would argue that it is precisely because Karen Black is portrayed as feminine, "elegant," and "straightshooting" that her performance did not receive the attention or accolades of Dustin Hoffman's performance.

When Joanne (who we later learn is formerly Joe and is played by Karen Black) finally arrives at the 5 & Dime, at first, the other women at the reunion can't quite figure out why she looks so familiar to them. Joanne asks Mona, "Are you the mother of his son? I saw one of your signs down the highway: See the son of James Dean. Visit Woolworth's 5 & Dime." Mona then tells Joanne that when her son Jimmy Dean was first born, nearly 3,000 people a week swarmed into town just to see the son of James Dean. They were the busiest and most prosperous 5 & Dime in all of Texas. They were even given a plaque. Thus, Mona's romantic and sexual encounter with James Dean not only makes the 5 & Dime a tourist attraction, but also authorizes the women's

Figure 9.2 Karen Black and Cher in *Come Back to the 5 & Dime, Jimmy Dean, Jimmy Dean*. Courtesy of Special Collections Research Center, University of Michigan Library.

fandom, implying that those who are the most devoted will reap the rewards and the attention.

As the film flashes back to the past, we see an image of young Joe's face. His face is bleeding since he has just been beaten up by Lester T., who kept calling him Joanne as he punched him in the face. As the film passes from Joe to Joanne's faces, it also layers these gendered identities. Keyssar describes Altman's "promiscuous camera" as one which "not only refuses to establish a star for this movie but also reminds us that part of what this movie is about is the destructive force of the worship of stars by many Americans."[21] She continues, saying, "By denying us the illusion of access to the 'interior' of characters, Altman's limited use of the close-up importantly draws our attention *away* from concern with those characters' past histories."[22] At the same time, however, the camera indicates not only the destruction of identity, but also the intertwining of identities, not only those of the past and present, male and female, but also those that are filled with compassion for each other. As Joe says, "Maybe they're right. Maybe I should have been born a girl all along," the film then cuts back to the present where Joanne is insisting upon upholding her own identity rather than dwelling upon the past. Juanita tells Joanne, "You are not a she. You are only pretending to be one just like you always did." While Joanne says, "I'm not Joe Sissy, I'm Joanne." As she puts on lipstick, she says, "Unlike apparently all of you, I have undergone a change." In this way, Joanne points out that change is not limited to the body, sex, or gender, but rather can be inclusive of politics, emotions, psychology, and interiority.

As the women learn from a special bulletin on the radio that twenty-four-year-old James Dean has died in a head-on collision, Joe says to Mona "Just cause he's dead, don't kill me off, too." As Mona insists that she slept with James Dean not Joe, that she wanted to be noticed, that she was chosen, Joe hugs her and says, "I chose you, I loved you" and we learn that Joe is Jimmy Dean's father. Joanne's desire not to be dead, to be acknowledged, to live also speaks to Lee Edelman's idea of the queer death drive and the limits of futurity.[23] As Edelman notes, the queer death drive is associated with the end of childhood since queerness is also associated with a loss of innocence.[24] This understanding of queerness is also intertwined with a resistance to compulsory heteronormativity. Thus, the symbolic death of Joe (and the denial of his fatherhood) can also be intertwined with the death of James Dean and the birth of Joanne necessitates that death.

The end of the film is also evidence of this movement toward death and decay. When Joe insists on making a pact that the fan club will meet again in twenty years, Mona walks away, Juanita and Joanne leave, and only Joe, Mona, and Sissy are left to perform the McGuire sisters' final number as the camera sweeps through the broken and empty 5 & Dime, lingering over the ripped-up streamers and broken mirrors and windows on the floor.

At the same time, as Michael DeAngelis notes in his analysis of gay fandom and crossover stardom, the ambiguity associated with James Dean's death is also particularly queer. In his analysis of James Dean's stardom and crossover appeal to both gay and straight audiences and fans, Michael DeAngelis writes that "his premature death paradoxically secures his ability to emerge perpetually, for decades to come, as a figure whose ambiguity and rebellion extend to the realm of sexuality."[25] Just as Dean's early death enabled his star persona to be enmeshed within American culture, so too does the death of Joe and birth of Joanne signify an insistence upon the remembering and rewriting of queer histories.

Robert Self writes of *Come Back to the 5 & Dime, Jimmy Dean, Jimmy Dean*, "The fictional, metaphoric and actual destruction of the male and the related construction of divergent, pathological, interdependent femininity comes to its most forceful expression in Jimmy Dean, where Joe's self-renunciative castrations gives birth to his feminine identity, Joanne."[26] In this way, Self argues that the film reveals "the construction of the self as an act of retreat from phallic authority."[27] However, I would argue that this psychoanalytic reading of the film limits its possibilities for understanding both femininity and trans* identities.[28] Through the reunion of the fan club and their mutual love of James Dean, as well as their compassion for each other, the women of *Come Back to* *the 5 & Dime, Jimmy Dean, Jimmy Dean* enable a space not for retreating from phallic authority, but for recreating their own identities both from within and outside of phallic authority.

Additionally, as noted in *Disclosure: Trans Lives on Screen*, it may also be argued that because Joanne/Karen Black was neither represented as a sissy, nor a tragic figure (unlike the trans* characters of *The Crying Game*, or *Boys Don't Cry*, or *The Danish Girl*), she has been given less attention as a trans* character within American film history. As Annamarie Jagose writes, "Queer is always an identity under construction, a site of permanent becoming."[29] The character of Joanne can be read through this lens of becoming. Rather than focusing on the limitations of gender representation, *Come Back to the 5 & Dime, Jimmy Dean, Jimmy Dean* opens up the possibilities for both identification and interpretation.

CONCLUSION

By analyzing *Come Back to the 5 & Dime, Jimmy Dean, Jimmy Dean* through the lenses of contemporary feminist and queer theories, as well as revisiting its understandings of both fan cultures and female and gay male fans, it is possible to reimagine the ways in which the film comments upon femininity and trans* identity. The film may tap into more traditional representations of femininity through the characters of Sissy and Juanita. Whereas the sexed-up Sissy represents the whore, Christian and God-fearing Juanita represents the virgin. However, the characters of Mona, Joe, and Joanne push the boundaries of representation of both gender and sexuality. Mona's exhibition of compassion for Joe and Joanne and her ability to see beyond stereotypes and homophobia creates a space for the inclusion of the trans* community even within a small town in Texas in the 1950s and 1970s. While Joanne's presence on-screen, her empowerment, and her insistence upon reminding us of her own lived realities enables an embodiment of trans* identity that also acknowledges its histories and materialities. While this film may have been overlooked within Altman's oeuvre as well as within trans* media histories, its representation of female and trans* fantasies and fandom enables the reconfiguring of those identities. For, as Alexis Lothian writes,

> To look queerly at fannish temporalities is to attend to moments in which they refuse narratives of development and progress by which particular moments in media and LGBT history are seen as passing into irrelevance; reconfigure norms of gender and sexuality; and use the affective technology of fannish love to build spaces that both reproduce and subvert dominant economies.[30]

NOTES

1. Justin Wyatt, "Economic constraints/economic opportunities: Robert Altman as auteur," *Velvet Light Trap* 38 (Fall 1996): 51.
2. Robert Kolker, *A Cinema of Loneliness: Penn, Stone, Kubrick, Scorsese, Spielberg, Altman* (Oxford: Oxford University Press, 2011), p. 360.
3. I use trans* with an asterisk here to mark Jack Halberstam's concept of trans* as a term that "puts pressure on all modes of gendered embodiment and refuses to choose between the identitarian and the contingent forms of trans identity." See Jack Halberstam, *Trans*: A Quick and Quirky Account of Gender Variability* (Berkeley: University of California Press, 2018), p. xiii and Jack Halberstam, "Trans* gender transitivity and new configurations of body, history, memory and kinship," *Parallax* 22, no. 3 (2016): 366–75.
4. Ashley Hinck, *Politics for the Love of Fandom: Fan-Based Citizenship in a Digital World* (Baton Rouge: Louisiana State University Press, 2019), p. 9.
5. Robert Self, "Robert Altman and the theory of authorship," *Cinema Journal* 25, no. 1 (Autumn 1985): 8.
6. Gilad Padva, *Queer Nostalgia in Cinema and Pop Culture* (New York: Palgrave Macmillan, 2014), p. 8.
7. Helene Keyssar, *Robert Altman's America* (New York and Oxford: Oxford University Press, 1991), p. 257.
8. John Fiske, "The cultural economy of fandom," in Lisa K. Lewis (ed.), *The Adoring Audience: Fan Culture and Popular Media* (New York and London: Routledge, 1992), p. 38.
9. Matt Hills, *Fan Cultures* (New York: Routledge, 2002), pp. xi–xiii.
10. Diana Anselmo-Sequeira, "Screen-struck: The invention of the movie girl fan," *Cinema Journal* 55, no. 1 (Fall 2015): 1–28.
11. Suzanne Scott, *Fake Geek Girls: Fandom, Gender, and the Convergence Culture Industry* (New York: New York University Press, 2019), p. 47.
12. See Janice Radway, *Reading the Romance: Women Patriarchy and Popular Literature* (Durham, NC: University of North Carolina Press, 1991), Barbara Klinger, *Melodrama and Meaning: History, Culture, and the Films of Douglas Sirk* (Bloomington: Indiana University Press, 1994), Henry Jenkins, *Textual Poachers: Television Fans and Participatory Culture* (New York and London: Routledge, 2012), Adrienne Trier-Bieniek (ed.), *Fan Girls and the Media* (Lanham, MD: Rowman and Littlefield, 2015), Suzanne Scott, *Fake Geek Girls: Fandom, Gender, and the Convergence Culture Industry* (New York: New York University Press, 2019), and Elana Levine, *Her Stories: Daytime Soap Opera and US Television History* (Durham, NC: Duke University Press, 2020).
13. Kolker, *A Cinema of Loneliness*, p. 413.
14. See Michael DeAngelis, *Gay Fandom and Crossover Stardom: James Dean, Mel Gibson, and Keanu Reeves* (Durham, NC: Duke University Press, 2001).
15. Jack Halberstam, "Trans* gender transitivity and new configurations of body, history, memory and kinship," *Parallax* 22, no. 3 (2016): 366–75.
16. Susan Stryker, *Transgender History* (Berkeley: Seal Press, 2008), p. 1.
17. Helene Keyssar describes *Come Back to the 5 & Dime, Jimmy Dean, Jimmy Dean* as "a dramatic world inhabited only by women, framed by a society dominated by men" in *Robert Altman's America*, p. 243.
18. Jack Halberstam, *In a Queer Time and Place: Transgender Bodies, Subcultural Lives* (New York: New York University Press, 2005).
19. Kate Stables, Review, *Come Back to the Five & Dime, Jimmy Dean, Jimmy Dean*, *Sight & Sound* 29, no. 11 (November 2019).
20. Stables, Review.

21. Keyssar, *Robert Altman's America*, p. 257.
22. Ibid. p. 29.
23. Lee Edelman, *No Future: Queer Theory and the Death Drive* (Durham, NC: Duke University Press, 2004).
24. Ibid. p. 19.
25. DeAngelis, *Gay Fandom*, p. 7.
26. Robert Self, *Robert Altman's Subliminal Reality* (Minneapolis: University of Minneapolis Press, 2002), p. xxvi. In 1985, Robert Self wrote of Joanne's characters in *Cinema Journal*, "The fictional, metaphorical, and actual destruction of the male and the related construction of the divergent, pathological, interdependent femininity comes to its most forceful expression in Jimmy Dean in the creation of Joanne by the self-renunciative castration of Joe"; quoted in Self, "Robert Altman and the theory of authorship," p. 8.
27. Self, *Robert Altman's Subliminal Reality*, p. xxvi.
28. Self's somewhat limited (and limiting) focus on the psychoanalytic understanding of masculinity, femininity, and castration can also be seen in this critique of the film. "Films like *Come Back to the 5 & Dime, Jimmy Dean, Jimmy Dean* display a pathological fear of castration in a society seen as emasculating, and project a drive toward castration in a culture where the masculine principle is psychologically and socially dehumanizing"; quoted in Self, "Robert Altman and the theory of authorship," p. 9.
29. Annamarie Jagose, *Queer Theory: An Introduction* (New York: New York University Press, 1996), p. 131.
30. Alexis Lothian, "Sex, Utopia, and the queer temporalities of fannish love," in Jonathan Gray, Cornell Sandvoss, and C. Lee Harrington (eds), *Fandom: Identities and Communities in a Mediated World* (New York: New York University Press, 2017), p. 239.

CHAPTER 10

Countering Robert Altman's Sexual Outlaws: Visibility, Representation, and Questionable Social Progress

Justin Wyatt

Lauded as one of the leading directors of the New Hollywood, Robert Altman is frequently cited for his innovations in sound, his creative use of actors and key aesthetic contributors, and for his ability to present a cross-section of American society. On this last aspect, Altman's films, featuring the large ensemble casts of *M*A*S*H*, *Nashville*, *A Wedding*, *Short Cuts* and many others, are often described as presenting a social critique.[1] Indeed, Altman's films are mined for their views on social institutions, especially the prejudices that exist within American society. These imbalances are most evident by social class, with Altman presenting clear divisions between his characters created by old vs. new found money, white collar vs. blue collar, and social manners vs. plain speaking. If Altman is keenly aware of social class and the distinctions between different social groups, his track record across the decades on other inequalities, especially those connected to gender and sexuality, is much more dubious. Of course, identifying a pattern of these representations means only that they appear in the Altman films, not necessarily that Altman purposely added them into the films to make a statement. Regardless of attribution though, their presence is worth isolating and examining in greater detail, especially because Altman's films often appear to paint a picture of the social landscape impacting their characters.

Throughout the 1970s, Altman's films are littered with negative representations of gay people and those who stray from the parameters of conventional heterosexuality. Altman's focus in many of these films is rethinking genre, but this reconsideration does not shine a light on sexual minorities. Those beyond the conventional sexual norms are either in the margins or absent altogether in Altman's American cinematic landscapes. Interestingly, this treatment changed considerably after Altman was ostracized from studio moviemaking post *Popeye* in 1980. Altman's theatrical adaptations in the 1980s address sexuality, sexual difference, queerness, and LGBTQ+ characters directly. This chapter considers how Altman's presentation of the "gay condition," to use his term, presents uneven social progress at best through tracing key markers in Altman's films in the 1970s and 1980s. Further, through sketching the trajectory of Altman's career through the decades, his attitude towards sexuality will be identified as a significant element for understanding Altman's auteurism.

BACKGROUND: PERIPHERAL STATUS FOR SEXUAL OUTLAWS IN THE 1970S

The period of the New Hollywood, or the Hollywood Renaissance, encompasses dramatic shifts in cinematic storytelling and subject matter for the films of the 1970s. Indeed, an early film text by Seth Cagin and Philip Dray is titled *Hollywood Films of the Seventies: Sex, Drugs, Violence, Rock 'n' Roll and Politics*. It's hardly coincidental that sex is listed as the first topic in the subheading. Exploring sexuality was a consistent thread for cinema of this era. In this decade of increasing feminist and gay visibility, Altman resorts to two approaches when addressing those on the sexual margins: everyday casual slurs and a comic curiosity factor. Certainly the slurs could be justified as merely representing a backlash against the greater visibility, but it is strange that many of these moments are not sewn into the narrative. They are most often extraneous to the story and used to get a quick laugh from viewers. The curiosity factor centers on a sexual representation that is then humiliated or maligned within the film. Altman's curiosity over sexuality is based on his larger embrace of the absurd; as Altman collaborator Anne Rapp comments, "Altman loved absurdity, and you can find it everywhere."² For Altman, exceptions to sexual norms are worth showing simply because they illuminate people and practices that are, by definition, marginal. Altman is not particularly interested in social evolution but he is clearly in favor of representing marginalized sexuality for comic effect. To put it another way, Altman finds these sexualities as just another absurdity in his films. Rather than argue for sexual freedom, Altman seems intent on showing the price people pay for their sexual "transgressions."

The connection to sexuality is evident even in the beginning of Altman's film career. His 1970 breakthrough hit *M*A*S*H* is remembered for its irreverent attitude toward the military, medicine, and American society. Some would also recall the ways that *M*A*S*H* presents gayness and feminism as curiosities, ready to be deflated by the acerbic leads. Two of the most vivid incidents in the film convey this unusual (juvenile? iconoclastic?) approach to sexuality. First, the character "Painless Pole" Waldowski (John Schuck), usually a Don Juan, suffers from an intimate "failure" with a visiting nurse which leads him to think he is a latent homosexual. An elaborate "Last Supper" is hosted in which his compatriots eat dinner while Painless Pole lies supine, readying himself for his own suicide. The friends arrange for the subtly labeled "Lt. Dish" (Jo Ann Pflug) to visit Pole in the night, restoring his virility and saving him from death. Second, Margaret "Hot Lips" Houlihan (Sally Kellerman) is physically exposed when her outdoor shower is removed, all to the glee of the gathered doctors and nurses who are eagerly anticipating the humiliation of the rigid, serious nurse. Robert Self sums up the scene as follows, "The fear of homosexuality is one marker of a sense of male inadequacy in *M*A*S*H*."[3] The first incident equates homosexuality with death and the humiliation of "Hot Lips" Houlihan in the shower pushes to the realm of sadism rather than bawdy fun. Robert Niemi accurately sizes up the impact of this disturbing scene: "The shower stunt is self-deconstructing insofar as it comes off as vicious fraternity hazing—not righteous or funny but mean-spirited and misogynistic."[4] Altman's defense seems to dodge personal responsibility in favor of realistic dramatic presentation in the film: "Well, I don't treat women that way. I'm showing you the way that I observed that women were treated."[5]

Even the most sympathetic reading of these incidents would question Altman's treatment of gay people and women. Biographer Patrick McGilligan concludes his analysis with this sentiment: "If Altman did not exactly endear himself to the antiwar movement, neither, beginning with the public clamor for *M*A*S*H*, has the director scored with feminist or gay activists."[6] Most often, Altman uses a simple passing reference on the soundtrack to call out these sexual groups. For instance, in the freewheeling *Brewster McCloud*, common sexual slurs ("faggot" and "pansy"') are offered by the most despicable characters, the ancient tyrant Abraham Wright (Stacy Keach) and the corrupt cop Douglas Breen (Bert Remsen). There are other occasions when Altman uses these insults. In *Nashville*, as several characters are moving around the Deemen's Den nightclub, an unidentified voice (a patron at the bar? a musician off-screen?) proclaims about the film's central political candidate, "Hal Philip Walker has long hair and smokes cigarettes that look funny. I heard that this guy is an admitted homo." Again, a little word designed to complicate our connection to the (unseen) politician. In these cases, the mentions are either assigned to unlikeable characters or tossed off so quickly that they make little long-term impact. It's worth noting that, during an interview with *Nashville* actress Ronee Blakley by critic Vito Russo, Altman is called out for his use of the term "fag" when describing a character in his films.[7]

Both traits, the slurring and the comic curiosity, are evident in *California Split* (1974). Brief slurs are tossed throughout the film, including a gratuitous scene in which a drunken matron tells lead Bill Denny (George Segal) to "fuck off, faggot" with no provocation or explanation. The film also contains a more perplexing scene, definitely on the curious side. Vito Russo, in

Figure 10.1 Helen (Bert Remsen, second from left) is interrogated by a fake vice squad in *California Split*. Courtesy of Special Collections Research Center, University of Michigan Library.

his groundbreaking text *The Celluloid Closet: Homosexuality in the Movies*, characterizes Altman and sexuality in terms of this curiosity factor: "Altman always creates characters who get their rocks off in strange ways, and gays who deny their own sexuality are invisible by choice and present no threat."[8] Russo's assessment is clearly evident in one of the strangest scenes in *California Split*. Two male gambling buddies (George Segal, Elliott Gould) show up unexpectedly one night just as their prostitute friends (Ann Prentiss, Gwen Welles) are getting ready. The men are asked to leave since the women are expecting an important client at any minute. The client is "Helen," a middle-aged cross-dresser played by one of Altman's ensemble players, tough guy Bert Remsen. Clearly wanting just to "pass," Helen seeks the women's approval of her dress. Just when s/he starts to be comfortable, the gambling friends, now posing as the vice squad, raid the house and interrogate the trio. Initially they threaten to arrest one of the women, with their focus on Helen right away. The gamblers/"vice cops" eventually decide to let Helen go. Helen is ushered away, and the two couples spend the night together. The scene is isolated in its treatment of the Helen character who plays no other role in the film. Is this, as Russo suggests, an invisible character posing no threat, or, as Helene Keyssar claims in her analysis of the scene, "a challenge to the rigidity of our perceptions and categorizations of sexuality?"[9] Keyssar's claim is difficult to accept since the Helen character appears so quickly and so randomly in the film. Since Helen has just a fleeting appearance, her impact is primarily visual; in other words, the scene is centered on Helen's cross-dressing as just a way to humiliate the character and to use a sexual outsider as the punch line to an unfunny joke.

Continuing the representation of LGBTQ+ characters as a joke and simply "a freak of nature," *A Wedding* offers the finicky wedding planner Rita Billingsley (Geraldine Chaplin) who, near the end of the film, gives an unexpected open-mouthed kiss to the bride, Muffin (Amy Stryker). Muffin then staggers down the hall to tell her new husband, Dino (Desi Arnaz Jr.). It turns out that he is fully-clothed in the shower with another man. While there is an explanation (the friend is trying to sober up the new husband), Altman sets the scenes together so that a one-two punch of homophobia is leveled at the viewers. One in-the-closet lesbian and one mistaken gay identity combine to produce an elaborate joke at the expense of gay people.

Altman ended the decade with *A Perfect Couple*, featuring a pop group, Keepin' 'Em Off the Streets, set against the unlikely romance between a young pop singer and a middle-aged Greek businessman. Within the pop group, Altman places a lesbian couple raising a baby. Their appearance is very brief, and, to Altman's credit, they simply fit into the fabric of the film. Curiously, in an interview, Altman appears to blame this representation as one of the reasons for the film's commercial failure: "And we had issues like the gay couple having a baby, which at that time was normally dealt with as a joke."[10] So the progressive image of the gay family is blamed for film's failure, with Altman suggesting that turning the gay family into a gag would have made the film more acceptable to audiences.

SEXUALITY IN FOCUS: THE 1980S THEATRICAL ADAPTATIONS

After the weak box office of his five Twentieth Century Fox films through the late 1970s (*3 Women*, *A Wedding*, *Quintet*, *A Perfect Couple*, *HealtH*) and the perceived commercial failure of *Popeye* in 1980, Altman worked in exile from Hollywood for much of the 1980s. Adjusting to the leaner financial circumstances, Altman became known for adapting stage plays to the screen. These ran the gamut from brief one-hour treatments—*Rattlesnake in a Cooler* (1982), *The Laundromat* (1985), *The Dumb Waiter* (1987), *The Room* (1987)—to feature length—*Come Back to the 5 & Dime, Jimmy Dean, Jimmy Dean*, *Streamers*, *Fool for Love*, *Beyond Therapy*. Some of these filmed plays were praised for their fluid transition to the screen by Altman. As critic Armond White comments on these productions,

"By breaking through the artifice of theater, Altman, the great atmospheric filmmaker of the Seventies, becomes our great expressionist."[11]

While sexuality tended to be of secondary importance to his 1970s films, in several of these adaptations, sexuality, especially beyond heteronormative parameters, becomes the central focus. Two of these films (*Come Back to the 5 & Dime, Jimmy Dean, Jimmy Dean*, *Streamers*) hew very closely to the original play texts. Both films are shaped considerably though by Altman's staging and the seamless cinematography of Pierre Mignot. Altman's adaptation of the Christopher Durang play *Beyond Therapy* offers a greater departure, inspired mainly by Altman's screenplay of the play (it should be noted that the final writing credits for the film list the screenplay by Christopher Durang and Robert Altman, based on the play by Christopher Durang). Altman's adaptation took playwright Durang by surprise; as Durang explains the circumstances, "Altman wrote his own adaptation of the play before I even started to write mine—which certainly wasn't the agreement. Then I wrote mine, which he pretty much ignored. And he was hurt I didn't like his version."[12] Considering all three of these theatrical adaptations clarifies how Altman approaches sexual outlaws, suggesting that all of the marginal references in his earlier films actually betray a conservative perspective on sexuality that is at odds with much of the more progressive material in his films and their marketing/messaging.

Writing in 1986, Robin Wood labeled the 1980s theatrical adaptations as "Altman's new found interest in sex and gender ambiguity."[13] Indeed, this sweeping description does capture much of Altman's work in the 1980s. The thematic ties between *Come Back to the 5 & Dime, Jimmy Dean, Jimmy Dean* and *Streamers* are very strong. *Come Back to the 5 & Dime, Jimmy Dean, Jimmy Dean* concerns the James Dean fan club in two time periods: 1955 (when Dean was filming *Giant* in the town of Marfa, Texas) and 1975 (for the reunion of the fan club at the local discount store). The film jumps between the two time periods, juxtaposing the naïve teenagers and the jaded, willfully misguided adults. The female teens are joined by a single boy, Joe, who eagerly joins in the dancing and singing with the girls. In 1975, on the day of the fan club's reunion, Joe does not appear but a mysterious upscale lady, Joanne (Karen Black), arrives at the five-and-dime. After an undue amount of questioning and guessing, Joanne is revealed as the post-operative trans version of Joe. Joe/Joanne's presence serves to destabilize the enabling fictions of the other women.

The presentation of sexuality and sexual roles in the film is complicated. In an adjoining chapter, Sarah E. Sinwell builds a convincing argument that Altman offers a positive trans image through Karen Black's performance as Joanne. Certainly, as Sinwell suggests, Joanne is created as feminine, elegant, and straight-shooting, especially given how Black chooses to play the character. My own concern is that Black's performance (and the trans representation) feel at odds with the character in Ed Graczyk's play and film script. Despite just being set in the Southern-adjacent Texas, *Come Back to the 5 & Dime, Jimmy Dean, Jimmy Dean* sticks closely to the traits of the Southern Gothic text. R. Bruce Brasell identifies queerness as a key element of the Southern Gothic. As he concludes on the disruptive nature of the genre, "Southern gothic is ultimately not about exceeding the normal but perverting it."[14] As part of this mission, the Southern Gothic employs sexuality as a key way to interrupt social norms and institutions. *Come Back to the 5 & Dime, Jimmy Dean, Jimmy Dean*'s plot mirrors this framework clearly: Joe/Joanna returns after twenty years to expose and dismantle the various falsehoods bolstering the small group of Jimmy Dean fans. Graczyk uses the physical transformation of Sissy (a double mastectomy) and Joe (sex reassignment surgery) for their ability to shock and confuse the status quo. In this way, Joanna is less a complex, psychologically realized character than a change agent designed to move the plot forward. Consequently, through falling into the narrative patterns of the Southern Gothic, Joanne is more of a cipher.

Joanne's function is to be a "truth teller," breaking the composure of the other women. As Ken Anderson describes the process, "In true Southern Gothic tradition, her presence incites the unearthing of secrets and the head-on confrontation of several dark and powerful truths."[15] Secrets, big and small, are revealed, and the characters are forced to accept the realities of their circumstances. The one exception is Mona (Sandy Dennis), who claims to have borne James Dean's son despite clear evidence that Joe was the father. For Mona, the fabrication is just too central to her daily life and she cannot shake her false belief.

Joanne visits the five-and-dime to break illusions and lies, albeit in a friendly and non-threatening manner. As she insists that the women come to terms with their circumstances, it is worth noting that Graczyk fails to offer a happy ending for Joanne. When asked if she regrets the sex change, Joanne replies curtly, "Only when I think about it." Joanne has dignity but remains tormented by her decision to change gender. Rather than offer a favorable depiction of Joanne, Graczyk and Altman undercut the character with this offhand remark suggesting regret and turmoil rather than peaceful self-acceptance.

Based on David Rabe's play, *Streamers* takes place in an army barracks right before deployment to Vietnam. With the exception of the credits sequence, the filmed play has a single set with Mignot's moving camera and lighting effects giving the movie some needed momentum. Unlike the female group and the outsider in *Come Back to the 5 & Dime, Jimmy Dean, Jimmy Dean*, *Streamers* posits a male group with an outsider. Richie (Mitchell Lichtenstein) flirts ambiguously with fellow recruit Billy (Matthew Modine). Billy steadfastly believes that Richie is merely joking and defends him to the other recruits. The games turn serious, however, when a visiting African American recruit Carlyle (Michael Wright) senses that Richie is, in fact, gay. Carlyle makes a serious advance on Richie which causes the tension in the barracks to erupt.

Figure 10.2 In *Streamers*, the flirtation between Richie (Michael Wright, top) and Carlyle (Mitchell Lichtenstein, bottom) destabilizes the power dynamic in the barracks. Courtesy of Special Collections Research Center, University of Michigan Library.

Two characters die while Richie is left sobbing, admitting that he is a "queer" to the senior officer. Richie, the outsider due to his sexual orientation, has destabilized the social order. In Rabe's play, Richie the outsider is the catalyst to igniting both racial and sexual tension in the barracks. The environment cannot contain the threat of homosexuality and apparently miscegenation.

Rather than hiding gayness in the margins, these two filmed plays suggest that gays simply cannot be integrated into the larger group: in *Come Back to the 5 & Dime, Jimmy Dean, Jimmy Dean*, the character of Joe cannot peacefully exist in the society after a cross-dressing incident leads to his gang rape in a cemetery; in *Streamers*, more simply, gayness just leads to death. The narrative parallels between the two films are striking. Both are structured around the same basic issue: a LGBTQ+ person whose presence upsets a social group leading to estrangement, expulsion, or even death. The homophobia connects with the military culture for *Streamers* and the small-town culture of the 1950s in *Come Back to the 5 & Dime, Jimmy Dean, Jimmy Dean*. Both contexts are used to give license to the extreme homophobia as the logical state of being. Threats to heteronormative behavior are eliminated quickly and completely. While the narrative remains intact from the original play, Altman's staging certainly draws attention to the more salacious details, such as Joe being brutally raped.[16] As Vito Russo comments so perceptively on Altman's dramatization of these filmed plays, he is not sure "if hysteria resides in the material or Altman's response to it."[17] In many ways, both textual and stylistic choices tend to work together in sketching sexuality on the margins in these films. Recall that some of Altman's salient stylistic choices, such as the zoom shot, a moving camera, and the comprehensive aural landscape, also deliberately and specifically draw the viewer's attention to key textual moments within the films. Overall, the narratives suggest that sexual transgression is met strongly by forces that are designed to eradicate it.

Derided for being fast and loose with a script, these filmed plays were, in fact, very close to the original texts. Collaborator Allan F. Nicholls believes that Altman's intent with these adaptations was to show Hollywood that he was capable of following a script closely.[18] As Altman commented on the adaptations: "For *Streamers* or *Jimmy Dean* or *Secret Honor* there was never a screenplay written. We took the Samuel French copy of the play, and it was in my hip pocket, and it was done . . ."[19] This fidelity served two purposes: demonstrating that Altman could indeed be faithful to an author's intentions and that he could direct under a battery of restrictions, from a low budget to a single set and a small cast. It would be tough to assert that Altman had much control over the narrative content, perhaps only to the extent that these particular plays spoke to him and were capable of being funded.

The story of Altman's filmed plays and sexuality becomes more interesting with his 1987 adaptation of the Christopher Durang play *Beyond Therapy*. The play was produced on Broadway in 1982 with John Lithgow and Dianne Wiest in the leading roles. *Beyond Therapy* centers on Bruce and Prudence who meet for dinner after responding to a personal ad in the *New York Review of Books*. The encounter is complicated substantially with Bruce talking of his male lover and admitting to bisexuality. The disastrous date is discussed and analyzed by the therapists of Bruce and Prudence. One of the central conceits of the play is that the therapists are openly unhinged. This leads to escalating hysteria and complications making this farce simultaneously absurd and, with a focus on word play and cultural references, sophisticated. Therapy, dating, and existential crises are the main topics for this dark comedy. Susan Abbotson explains the play's ambitions in this way: "The play questions psychiatry by presenting therapists who are crazier than their patients, explores complex issues of sexuality, and the limitations of rationality, all in the guise of screwball comedy."[20]

Well documented in the Altman archive at the University of Michigan, Altman was first approached in 1985 by the cable network Showtime about a variety of potential filmed plays. Showtime executive Julia Chasman indicates that the network wanted to produce a version of *Beyond Therapy* starring John Lithgow and Sigourney Weaver. By September 1985, Altman was in talks with the independent distributor Atlantic Releasing Corporation. Eventually a deal was struck with another independent, New World Pictures, founded by Roger Corman and his brother Gene and known for a mix of exploitation fare and imported art house films. By February 1987, the company was more reliant on low budget horror and action films: immediately preceding the release of *Beyond Therapy* were *Return to Horror High* (Bill Froehlich, 1987) and *Death Before Dishonor* (Terry Leonard, 1987).

Unlike *Come Back to the 5 & Dime, Jimmy Dean, Jimmy Dean* and *Streamers*, Altman was actively involved with reshaping the play for the screen. In fact, despite initial claims to Durang that he would treat the play in the same manner as his previous adaptations, with minimal adjustment to the text, Altman proceeded to draft his own version of the script.[21] Correspondence between Durang and Altman reveals that Altman drafted a script to be used to help determine a budget for the film. Keep in mind that Altman had agreed beforehand that Durang would draft the script from his play. Altman's "budgetary script" became the inspiration for a nine-page letter from Durang to Altman. The dense correspondence identifies Durang's dissatisfactions with the Altman screenplay, with Durang hoping and pleading for Altman to return to the original text. Twelve days after this letter, Durang sends Altman his own screenplay, incorporating some of Altman's draft; as Durang describes it, "I've ended up using a fair amount of the ideas and structure that were in your version, the first scene particularly."[22]

The finished film ended up much closer to the Altman screenplay than to either the original play or the Durang's own screenplay draft. Structurally, Durang makes it clear to Altman that the film needs to introduce Bruce and Prudence first, followed by an introduction to the two therapists, Stuart and Charlotte. This order, while simple, creates a foundation for the play's central premise (i.e., the therapists are damaging their clients and impacting their behavior). Altman undoes this by introducing many of the film's characters, including the male lover Bob's mother and the therapist Charlotte's son, in the first restaurant scene. Attention is drawn away from the Bruce and Prudence exchange to a flurry of activity across two levels of the restaurant. Much of Durang's dialogue is lost or placed over other elements on the soundtrack. Even more troubling though is the lack of a connection to the lead characters and their search for romance.

Durang's play depends on a certain level of realism, both within the setting and the psychology of the characters. This component is necessary for the audience to connect to the characters and their dramatic situation. So, for instance, Bruce and Prudence's desire to seek a romantic relationship, even within the confines of Bruce's bisexuality, needs to be seen as valid. Altman loses this level of realism by breaking the structure of the original play, eliminating much of the careful and precise dialogue choices, and especially by exaggerating the sexual stereotypes of many of the central characters. For Durang, this loss of verisimilitude devalues the play measurably: "Some of the opening up, and some of the adjustments made in lines and events, have, I feel, lost the core story of Prudence and Bruce desperately seeking a relationship, and each other."[23]

One consequence of diminishing the reality of the situation and the characters is a greater emphasis on all aspects sexual. Whereas the characters in the play do embody different sexual orientations, as Durang points out in his memo, this is based in a psychological realism and truth behind the characters. Without this foundation, Altman creates a narrative where sexuality runs rampant, without much causation or explanation. So, for instance, Altman adds a new scene of Bruce sucking on Prudence's toes while in the French restaurant for lunch. Just as curiously, Altman adds a "rendez-vous" room between the offices of the two therapists. This room is used for a quick copulation for the therapists between patient visits. Durang describes in his letter how this new development strains the farce even further: "I don't believe that two therapists would have a secret room where they 'fucked' for 2 seconds . . . there's nothing in either character that actually supports this idea. Do they actually know one another? How did it begin? Why don't they speak? Oh, etc. etc. I must be honest and tell you I don't find it in any way funny."[24] Altman's changes to Durang's play recall the ways that Altman approached sexual transgression in his 1970s films, with the comic curiosity of sexuality weighing somewhat more heavily than the casual slurs against the sexual outlaws in *Beyond Therapy*.

Not surprisingly the film failed to find support with either critics or audiences. Some critics singled out the narrative changes as a reason for the film's disappointments; in *The New York Times*, for instance, Vincent Canby notes, "It's Mr. Altman's production 'improvements' which only get in the way of the straight and narrow farcical narrative line."[25] Others noted that the film relied on portraying sexual stereotypes as a way to make to make its satirical points.[26] Altman's talking point about the film in later years is that *Beyond Therapy* was simply a case of bad timing: "So AIDS opened too, and that finished the film because of the bisexual attitude in the play. It was about a bisexual guy in love with the guy he lives with and a girl who comes into his life."[27] Altman's attribution of the film's failure to the AIDS global epidemic seems curious. It assumes that the film is advocating bisexuality which it really does not in any substantial way. Further, even by the time of *Beyond Therapy*'s release, film (*Parting Glances*, Bill Sherwood, 1986) and television (*An Early Frost*, John Erman, 1985) had addressed AIDS openly and with candor. To suggest that bisexuality alone would be the reason for the commercial failure places an unfair burden on how bisexuality is presented within the film and perhaps indicates a lack of comfort with sexuality in general.

IMPOSSIBLE ANGELS AND THE IDEOLOGICAL LIMITS OF NEW HOLLYWOOD

So we move from sexuality in the margins for the 1970s Altman films to sexuality becoming a primary subject matter in the 1980s theatrical adaptations.

With two narratives highlighting the impossibility of a sexual outsider existing in a larger social group and the third pushing sexual alternatives into the realm of the ridiculous, an argument could be made that Altman simply does not accept or even represent in any plausible way characters who fall outside heterosexuality.[28]

Given this track record, it was surprising that Altman was selected by Tony Kushner to direct a screen version of the two plays composing *Angels in America: A Gay Fantasia on National Themes*. Kushner's groundbreaking work addresses AIDS, gay history, and complicity of American political and social institutions in finding a cure for AIDS. At once incredibly intimate and breathtakingly broad in its canvas of gay American life, the plays created a national dialogue on the topic of AIDS that was unprecedented. Kushner selected Altman for his ability to paint a large social landscape cinematically. As Kushner commented on his decision, "It's not only structured like a movie—it's literally structured like an Altman movie. Quite literally, the form is stolen from *Nashville*."[29] Altman planned to shoot two separate films based on the plays for Fine Line/New Line Cinema.

From 1992 to 1996, Altman was attached to the project, with Kushner drafting several versions of the screenplays. Eventually the project simply lost momentum, due to several factors: Altman's inability to conceive of the project as a single film, the higher costs of shooting two films simultaneously, Fine Line executive (and advocate for the *Angels in America* films), Ira Deutchman, leaving the company, and, perhaps most distressingly, Altman's own lack of initiative. In interviews, Altman pivoted to talk about the Reagan-era political background of the film as his main interest. Interestingly, Altman described exploring new territory about "the social phenomenon of the acceptance of the gay condition."[30] This phrase, both clinical and depressing, illustrates Altman's precarious engagement with the topic of gayness yet again. Later, in the same interview, contrary to Tony Kushner's wishes, Altman diminishes the role of sexual expression in the film:

> Sexuality, in general, can make for an uncomfortable situation on film, and we want to make a film that an audience will sit and experience. I don't know what I'm going to do. I will deal with it as it arises.[31]

In a letter from Kushner to Altman dated 13 February 1996, Kushner makes it clear that Altman needs to either move forward with the film or drop it entirely:

> At the risk of sounding too servile, I want this to be guided and driven by you. I'd be available for discussion and work, of course, but finally if you don't have a strong take for the film version of *Angels* the films are going to fail.[32]

Altman and distributor New Line/Fine Line left the proposed films soon after. Producer Cary Brokaw stayed with the project which grew into a six-hour mini-series for HBO in 2003 under Mike Nichols's direction.[33]

So the path of Altman's sexual outlaws travels from staying in the margins and on the periphery in the '70s films to receiving harsh payback for sexual expression in the '80s adaptations and the open admission that sexuality is tough to portray on-screen while flirting with the screen version of *Angels in America*. At best, you could characterize Altman's attitude toward alternative sexuality on film as conservative. This assessment though does not account for the more prurient, judgmental, and even juvenile representations in many of these films. Looked at across the body of Altman's work, sexuality, instead of being a positive force for social change, is often seen as a means to humiliate, ridicule, and marginalize.

This damning message is most often represented by those falling outside the conventional sexual labels in the Altman films. Heterosexuality fares slightly better in the Altman oeuvre. There are positive yet realistic representations of heterosexuality in Altman's tender noir *Thieves Like Us* (1974) and his romantic comedy *A Perfect Couple*. More often Altman presents heterosexual couples as challenged; think, for example, of the twisted relationship between Frances and the boy in *That Cold Day in the Park* (1969), the tentative and awkward relationship between John McCabe and Constance Miller in *McCabe & Mrs. Miller*, or the compulsive gamblers with their prostitute sidekicks in *California Split*. Even in these troubled examples, the idea of a heterosexual pairing operates as a possible goal. The characters are not defined and demeaned by their sexuality as the LGBTQ+ characters so often are in other Altman films. Heterosexuality is seen as the comfort zone for the troubled characters. For those outside the heterosexual boundaries, Altman's films largely fail to offer this potential for happiness and contentment.

This attitude across the films matched with the omission of non-heteronormative behavior feels more like a missed opportunity for Altman. It's useful to consider Sara Ahmed's work in *Queer Phenomenology* as a way to appreciate this loss. Ahmed ideates around the concept of "orientation"; she describes this process of thinking of queerness and straightness in terms of spatial orientation: "The concept of 'orientation' allows us then to rethink the phenomenality of space—that is, how space is dependent on bodily inheritance."[34] The normalization of heterosexuality as an orientation leads adherents to follow a straight line which also includes a cluster of other behaviors (including being decent, conventional, direct, and honest).[35] Ahmed sees a queer orientation, a disorientation, as those moments when things become distant, oblique and "slip away."[36]

It is this conceptualization—the disorientation—and the transitory nature of our engagement with so much in life that appears to dovetail so well with

Altman's aesthetic. Inversions, unexpected developments, and fleeting glances all embody Altman's style, especially in terms of the soundtrack and his narrative "snapshots" of a group in our society. Robert Kolker describes a very similar process in terms of how the Altman films function: "Altman insisted upon positioning the viewer within the process of narrative, requesting that she or he observe and comprehend the interacting details that cohere in sometimes non-directed ways."[37] Altman is able to make his viewer more attentive to the individual moment in life and to appreciate, as his 2006 Oscar presenters Meryl Streep and Lily Tomlin commented, that life is many things at once.

This appreciation for the richness and texture of life often comes from disorientation as Ahmed has defined it. As a consequence, Altman's aesthetic of disorientation would seem to be a good fit for exploring beyond the boundaries of heteronormativity; sexuality goes beyond the binary definition and the role it plays in defining us ebbs and flows throughout our lives. So Altman's blind spot on the issue is simply a way in which a more complete vision of our social landscape could have been investigated, but is shut down instead. This doesn't invalidate the films. Altman's omission just means that these films fail to embrace one of the key ways that we define ourselves. We are left with Altman's definition of sexuality instead, firmly in line with a pre-Stonewall sensibility and staunch Midwestern values and beliefs. Interestingly, some of the mainstream (and academic) writing (e.g. Peter Biskind's *Easy Riders, Raging Bulls: How the Sex 'n' Drugs 'n' Rock 'n' Roll Generation Saved Hollywood*) on the New Hollywood focuses on the changing ideological lines in American society linking it to the New Hollywood generation of directors. Altman illustrates a conservatism in ideology, even while willfully breaking conventions in genre, storytelling and narration. An account of Altman's auteurism should reflect this social conservatism along with his aesthetic experimentation. Altman's work has altered the shape of Hollywood storytelling with novel uses of sound and innovative storytelling. His contribution, however, to American filmmaking is ultimately restricted by these boundaries on social/sexual representations.

While endless accounts of Altman's production histories include the communal watching of the dailies, the whiskey drinking and pot smoking, and his close bond with his actors and creative crew, his attitudes toward anything outside heteronormative boundaries are much more limited. With few exceptions, Altman's conservative approach to exploring sexuality continues into the 1990s and 2000s. In fact, the Bert Remsen cross-dressing "gag" is replicated on an even larger scale with the Teri Garr/Danny Aiello storyline in Altman's fashion runway comedy, *Prêt-à-Porter*. Despite impressive accomplishments on the level of aesthetics, Altman's social critique needs to be reconsidered given his blind spot on sexuality and especially for those outside the conventional sexual boundaries. His 1980s theatrical adaptations underline this point most of all. Apart from the theatrical adaptations, Altman's films have largely returned to the gay jokes and sneers evident earlier in his career: *O. C. and Stiggs*'s painfully humiliated gay teacher (Louis Nye), the over-the-top, hysterical designers (Forrest Whitaker and Richard E. Grant) with a barely disguised secret liaison in *Prêt-à-Porter*, and the much more hidden tryst between the movie producer (Bob Balaban) and his "valet" (Ryan Phillippe) in *Gosford Park*. Those on the sexual margins remain there, worthy only as the punchline for a joke or a visual gag. This American auteur operates from the sexual definitions and understanding stuck firmly in the 1950s and his conservative Midwestern roots.

CODA: MY INVESTMENT (THANKS TO ALEXANDER DOTY)

Alexander Doty's *Flaming Classics: Queering the Film Canon* begins by questioning the role of the "scholar-fan"; Doty accurately pinpoints how academic writing can "squeeze much of the life out of it in many senses, often relegating our investments in, and enthusiasms for, film and popular culture to the realm of hidden pleasures."[38] Owning his own "embarrassment and vulnerability" over identifying his investment in particular films, Doty demonstrated how context and personal history are so important to understanding our own academic and creative projects, regardless of the stated objectives. To that end, I want to conclude this exploration of Altman's sexual outlaws by situating this essay in my own history, no matter how "cringe-worthy," to invoke Doty's term.

Given a more liberal film classification system in British Columbia, I was able to see Altman's *California Split* and *Nashville* at the tender age of eleven. While *California Split* was fairly easy to categorize as buddy movie—close to *The Sting* (George Roy Hill, 1973) in my mind at that time—*Nashville* was more captivating, from the red, white, and blue color scheme to the landscape of American social classes, *Nashville* drew me back three times in the summer of 1975, at a time when most kids my age were talking about *Jaws* (Steven Spielberg, 1975). As a British/Canadian mutt, I was most fascinated by what the film told me about America: the messiness, fun, silliness, violence and, most of all, the chance to change your fortune overnight. I was dazzled by *Nashville*, the movie, and by several others later that decade (*3 Women*, in particular). As an adolescent coming to terms with my sexual orientation though, Altman's marginal insults and complete exclusion signaled that the closet was the best place to be for a young gay man (keep in mind that we're talking about a time period four decades ago). By the time of 1980s theatrical adaptations, I was not surprised when the punitive space for LGBTQ+ people emerged, whether hiding behind the original stage text or adapting it to minimize the entry point for sexual outlaws.

It would be difficult to claim that Altman's omissions and skewed sexual representation scarred me as an adolescent (I would be more likely to locate that scarring in the daily life of being bullied at my Catholic high school!). In a time when my potential role models were Paul Lynde in the center of *The Hollywood Squares* (Merrill Heatter, Bob Quigley, 1965–80), malcontent critic Rex Reed, or Rip Taylor throwing glitter on *The Gong Show* (Chris Bearde, 1976–80), I was always looking for and hoping to find positive gay representations within the media. Altman did not provide these. Around the same time as my adolescent obsession with Altman films, I did, however, receive just the kind of reference that resonated deeply. In an interview with director Nicolas Roeg for his film *The Man Who Fell to Earth* (1976), Roeg was asked why a supporting character, Farnsworth, a patent attorney played by Buck Henry, was a gay character. The attorney openly lives with another man and the sexual orientation of the character is just another element, like his thick eye glasses. When Buck Henry asked Roeg why his character was gay, Roeg deflated the question immediately by responding, "Why not? There are homosexuals."[39] These simple words normalized being gay for me; Roeg's incidental usage of gayness was perhaps even more empowering (or, to some, threatening) than he ever intended. So, in the end, the British iconoclast Nicolas Roeg proved more significant in building my true self than my favorite American "easy rider, raging bull" Robert Altman.

NOTES

1. See, for example, Robert Kolker's fascinating analysis of social and physical space in 'LA and Paris: The construction of social space in the films of Robert Altman,' in Adrian Danks (ed.), *A Companion to Robert Altman* (Malden, MA: John Wiley & Sons, 2015), pp. 296–320.
2. Interview with Anne Rapp, 21 April 2020.
3. Robert Self, *Robert Altman's Subliminal Reality* (Minneapolis: University of Minnesota, 2000), p. 240.
4. Robert Niemi, *The Cinema of Robert Altman: Hollywood Maverick* (New York: Wallflower Press, 2016), p. 27.
5. Mitchell Zuckoff, *Robert Altman: The Oral Biography* (New York: Alfred A. Knopf, 2009), p. 184.
6. Patrick McGilligan, *Robert Altman: Jumping Off the Cliff* (New York: St. Martin's Press, 1989), p. 314.
7. Vito Russo, "Interview: Ronee Blakley," *The Advocate* (17 December 1975), p. 47.
8. Vito Russo, *The Celluloid Closet: Homosexuality in the Movies*, revised edn (New York: Harper and Row, 1987), p. 159.
9. Helene Keyssar, *Robert Altman's America* (New York and Oxford: Oxford University Press, 1991), p. 130.
10. David Thompson (ed.), *Altman on Altman* (New York: Faber and Faber, 1989), p. 117.
11. Armond White, "Play time," *Film Comment* (January/February 1986), p. 14.
12. *Beyond Therapy* page on christopherdurang.com.

13. Robin Wood, *Hollywood from Vietnam to Reagan* (New York: Columbia University Press, 1986), p. 45.
14. R. Bruce Brasell, "'Mass production of degeneracy': Queer genre-ship and Southern Gothic film," in Tison Pugh (ed.), *Queering the South on Screen* (Athens: University of Georgia Press, 2020), p. 82.
15. Ken Anderson, review of *Come Back to the 5 and Dime, Jimmy Dean, Jimmy Dean*, 2 March 2015 [blog]. Available at <https://lecinemadreams.blogspot.com/2015/03/come-back-to-5-dime-jimmy-dean-jimmy.html>.
16. We hear Joe's recounting of the incident which strongly suggests rape: "They kept punching me then he laid me face down on a gravestone and pulled my overalls down and then Lester T . . ." During the abuse, Joe tells Mona that Lester T. kept calling him "Joanne."
17. Russo, *The Celluloid Closet*, p. 44.
18. Interview with Allan Nicholls, 10 October 2019.
19. Deborah Geis and Steven F. Kruger, *Approaching the Millennium: Essays on Angels in America* (Ann Arbor: University of Michigan Press, 1997), p. 229.
20. Susan C. W. Abbotson, "The deadly seriousness of America's funniest playwright: Christopher Durang," presentation at the William Inge Theatre Festival, 28 April 2008; <http://kuscholarsworks.ku.edu>.
21. Letter from Christopher Durang to Robert Altman, 17 May 1986, 2, Robert Altman Papers, Special Collections Research Center, University of Michigan Library.
22. Letter from Christopher Durang to Robert Altman, 29 May 1986, Robert Altman Papers, Special Collections Research Center, University of Michigan Library.
23. Letter from Christopher Durang to Robert Altman, 17 May 1986, 1, Robert Altman Papers, Special Collections Research Center, University of Michigan Library.
24. Letter from Christopher Durang to Robert Altman, 17 May 1986, 7, Robert Altman Papers, Special Collections Research Center, University of Michigan Library.
25. Vincent Canby, "Film: *Beyond Therapy*, a match made in the ads," *The New York Times*, 27 February 1987. The film's worldwide gross was $1.5 million against a negative cost of $3.5 million.
26. For example, Frank Caso comments on the use of sexual stereotypes in *Beyond Therapy*: "The film's over-the-top farcical nature allows us to poke fun at any and all subjects under the story's purview by playing up the usual stereotypes." See Frank Caso, *Robert Altman in the American Grain* (London: Reaktion Books, 2015), p. 193.
27. Thompson, *Altman on Altman*, p. 142.
28. These three plays/films are most illustrative of Altman's attitude toward sexual outsiders, especially LGBTQ+ populations. Another play/film from that period, *Fool for Love*, similarly explores sexuality from an outsider perspective (in this case, a romance between a brother and half-sister). I am not including this in the current analysis since the characters cannot be labeled at LGBTQ+. Nevertheless, this additional play/film does offer further testament to Altman's interest in sexual issues during this time.
29. Tony Kushner, quoted in "Anxious in America," *New Yorker*, Talk of the Town, 26 December 1994, p. 52.
30. Patrick Pacheco, "Happy? He's really, really trying," *Los Angeles Times*, 31 July 1994, p. 67.
31. Ibid. p. 67.
32. Letter from Tony Kushner to Robert Altman, 13 February 1996, 2, Robert Altman Papers, Special Collections Research Center, University of Michigan Library.
33. It is worth noting that the HBO production cost $60 million compared to the budget of $25 million linked to the two films proposed by Altman. For a comprehensive overview of Altman's involvement with *Angels in America* and the eventual shift to HBO and Mike

Nichols, consult Isaac Butler and Dan Kios, *The Ascent of Angels in America: The World Only Spins Forward* (New York: Bloomsbury USA, 2018), pp. 304–13.
34. Sara Ahmed, *Queer Phenomenology: Orientations, Objects, Others* (Durham, NC: Duke University Press, 2006), p. 6.
35. Ibid. p. 70.
36. Ibid. p. 171.
37. Robert Kolker, *A Cinema of Loneliness: Penn, Stone, Kubrick, Scorsese, Spielberg, Altman* (New York and Oxford: Oxford University Press, 2011), p. 355.
38. Alexander Doty, *Flaming Classics: Queering the Film Canon* (New York: Routledge, 2000), p. 11.
39. Russo, *The Celluloid Closet*, p. 292.

CHAPTER II

The Affection of Death

Robert P. Kolker

I met Robert Altman twice: once in 1975 at a Washington, D.C. screening of *Nashville*. I told him I had just published an article comparing Nick Ray's *They Live by Night* (1948) with *Thieves Like Us*. Altman told me that he had the article, hadn't read it, but was glad it was done. He gave me, for the few moments we interacted, his complete attention, and I recognized how he must have flattered the attention of studio heads and money men, an attention that always seemed to work in getting funding for a new project. The second meeting was a few years later, when Altman was self-distributing *HealtH* by personally taking it around to various venues. This time it was in a Baltimore theater, and as we climbed up to the stage for a Q & A, someone said for us to hear, "I really hate this." We maintained our equanimity. During the session, I asked Altman why so many of his characters died in water. He said he didn't know.

Altman was a consummate artist-naïf. Fully aware, fully intuitive, reluctant to analyze, and always game. Some critics also played naïf, reiterating stories of spontaneous improvisation on the set while disregarding the careful compositions of Altman's images and the artful and purposeful acting of his players. He may have allowed improvisation during rehearsal. Lily Tomlin tells about how she and Meryl Streep improvised a story about Tomlin's mother on the set of *A Prairie Home Companion*: "I heard Altman chuckle when I said that. Of course, when the dailies came, it wasn't in the movie. They never shot it."¹ The precision of the finished film—of any of Altman's films—indicate that great control was exercised during filming. In place of improvisation, we might say *affection*—a great warmth that Altman demonstrated toward his work, toward his actors, toward his cinematography, his editing, toward the concept and execution of the film as a whole. Even toward his fans. This helps account for his extraordinary output, his love of making movies (combined, no doubt, with the

THE AFFECTION OF DEATH 191

Figure 11.1 (From left) John C. Reilly, Woody Harrelson, Kevin Kline, and Robert Altman on the set of *A Prairie Home Companion*. Photo by Melinda Sue Gordon. Courtesy of Special Collections Research Center, University of Michigan Library.

financial need to make them) and his wiliness not only in getting financial backing, but in finding the right venues and outlets to make and distribute them. When opportunities ran out in the US, he moved production to France. When he returned to profitability in the US with *The Player*, he made *Short Cuts*, a three hour misanthropic tour de force that is as alienating as it is impossible to turn away from. Altman needed to make films like he needed to breathe, and he refused to be tied down to any one genre.

His affection for film and all its parts went hand in hand with a playfulness not only within the films but from film to film. From the lyrical tenderness of the early work, his masterpieces, *McCabe & Mrs. Miller* and *The Long Goodbye*, to the operatic multi-character films, *Nashville* and *Short Cuts*, and the silly, somewhat adolescent work of *Brewster McCloud* or *Prêt-à-Porter*, tone kept changing, ironies kept shifting, genres always existed to be bent out of shape. Altman loved to play; he was smitten with performance, whether directing an opera or making a dance film. His camera was a tool for playing with space. His zoom lens worked like an omniscient observer, picking out this or that—and always the right—action or expression. His actors played within that space, seriously or playfully; they perform, *as* performance in *The Company* or in the musical numbers in *Nashville* or *A Prairie Home Companion*, although in that film, the performances are once removed. Instead of performing for us, they are singing as part of the performance of a radio show.

A Prairie Home Companion was a long running Saturday evening radio show on National Public Radio. Its now disgraced MC, Garrison Keillor (he got caught up in the #MeToo movement), presided over skits and musical performances, along with mock commercials, and a general, faux, sometimes forced or smarmy, rustic bonhomie. And while Keillor is credited with the screenplay of the film, and collaborated with Ken LaZebnik on the story, Altman's hand is clearly present in turning the thin plot about the eminent selling and destruction of the show's theater into a lyrical reverie on death. Altman was in fact dying. He had a heart transplant and leukemia. He was in such shaky health that the film's producers insisted that Paul Thomas Anderson—an admirer and early imitator of Altman's—be present as a stand-by director. Altman died five months after the release of the film. The resulting film is about death and joy, about the pleasure of performance and the even greater enjoyment at filming it. Its darkness must peer through the light.

The late, the final works of an artist can take many forms, but often they demonstrate a simplicity and clarity. "The artist's mature subjectivity [is] stripped of hubris and pomposity, unashamed either of its fallibility or of the modest assurance it has gained as a result of age and exile." So wrote Edward Said on "late style."[2] But this applies only so far with Altman. As his body declined, his imagination remained strong, even arrogant, "unashamed." *Kansas City* is as complex a film as any he had made in his prime, its darkness relieved only by the jazz that is performed throughout. He could easily turn to the British Country Estate genre with *Gosford Park*, and do it with a relatively straight face. Altman scrambled across genres, took what he had, and made it his own. He took a radio show and made it a joyous elegy to his own demise.

A Prairie Home Companion is a summary film. It's also a slim film with a lot of performances and one serious bit of content. It is another return to the Midwest, to Altman's own roots as a maker of industrial documentaries in Kansas City. Even more, it is a nod to the past, a savoring of the style that he had perfected over the years. The film begins and ends with an homage to Edward Hopper's *Nighthawks* (1942), the exterior of a diner at night, perhaps the most imitated painting in cinema. (When I wrote about Altman's film *Short Cuts* in *A Cinema of Loneliness*, I pointed out that the film and its source in Raymond Carver's stories had a painterly analogue in Hopper's work. The sense of desolate aloneness and stillness hung over all three.) We are introduced to the narrator of the film, Guy Noir (played by Kevin Kline), a character from the radio show here extracted from one fiction and placed at the head of another. He tells us one direction the film is headed in—the end of the show because the theater has been bought out to be torn down. More significantly, he introduces us to the Lady in White, Lois Peterson, also known as the Angel

Astrophel, the Angel of Death (played by Virginia Madsen). When he first met her, she was looking for the Presbyterian Church, which happens to be the name of the town in *McCabe & Mrs. Miller*. The death in that film was poignant and, in a way, preordained. A Western needs a character to either prevail or be killed. Poor McCabe believed he could win over the bad guys. He couldn't. Death in *A Prairie Home Companion* is less preordained and certainly not poignant. It—she—is simply present and ready.

Her presence is mitigated by the pleasure of the performances by various movie stars—Meryl Streep, Lily Tomlin, Woody Harrelson, and John C. Reilly, among others—playing mostly upbeat music (something like faux folk/faux country). A sense of companionship is shared among the participants. That the camaraderie is tempered by a death of one of the performers, the imminent closure of the Fitzgerald theater (named after the writer) where they perform, and of course, the woman in white who haunts them all doesn't faze the pleasure of their work or Altman's pleasure in filming it.

There is a cinematic energy throughout the film that belies Altman's age and the pall that hangs over it. Altman loved the zoom lens. In his hands and through his eyes, it was an instrument for probing reactions, for picking out the relevant detail, the reflexive motion, the quick glance. Sometimes, as in *The Long Goodbye*, the zoom, in combination with subtle camera movements and the movement of the characters themselves, makes for an unstable *mise-en-scène*, a sense of drift and being unmoored. That instability suited a film about a private investigator whose focus on the world was somewhat compromised and whose moral universe was in a state of flux. In *A Prairie Home Companion* there is hardly a stable shot. The camera moves and zooms softly, perpetually, indicating, perhaps, a world about to end, people about to meet their death. But there is a delicate balance here: the patina of pleasurable performance cannot be entirely undercut by the impending sense of doom. Therefore, the constant motion of the film is so subtle as to be all but unnoticeable, working almost subliminally to cause a disturbance beneath the music and jokes.

The movement is subtle, the use of mirrors is not. The sequences in the Johnson sisters' dressing room is all mirrors—along the wall, on the dressing tables. Mirrors everywhere. Filmmakers are in general in love with mirrors. They reflect the characters to themselves; they open up another screen and add spatial depth. But most of all they present an extra-narrative mystery: how are mirrors set up so that they don't reflect the camera? In the dressing room of *A Prairie Home Companion*, Altman fairly revels in the mystery because the compositions are impossible, there is no way that the camera and lights, indeed the entire apparatus of filmmaking, can't be seen reflected in all those mirrors. But thanks to the wizardry of cinematographer Ed Lachman, they cannot be seen. "Stripped of hubris and pomposity," Altman just takes pleasure in showing off.

In the end, *A Prairie Home Companion* is neither a fitting or unfitting close to Altman's filmmaking career. It is a light entertainment with a strain of darkness and an all too prophetic promise of death. Gone is the lyrical, elegiac tone of the earlier films and, in its stead, is a gathering of friends, the promise of pleasure, a warning of doom. It allows us to remember the high points—*McCabe & Mrs. Miller*, *The Long Goodbye*, *Thieves Like Us*, *Nashville*, *Buffalo Bill and the Indians, or Sitting Bull's History Lesson*, *3 Women*, *HealtH*, and the string of small films that followed up to his return to Hollywood with, among many others, *The Player* and *Kansas City*. It is an eminently forgettable film, remembered only because it is the last, a reminder of the great work of an artist who never gave in or up. "The death of an old man is not a tragedy," says the lady in white. Neither is the loss of an old filmmaker if, for no other reason, we still have the films.

NOTES

1. David Marchese, "It's a tough world. Lily Tomlin has always tried to make it a little more tender," *New York Times Magazine* (5 January 2020), MM13.
2. Edward Said, *On Late Style: Music and Literature Against the Grain* (New York: Pantheon Books, 2006), p. 148.

PART IV

Collaborator Interviews

Figure IV.1 Stephen Rea in *Prêt-à-Porter* as drawn by fashion illustrator Gladys Perint Palmer. Courtesy of Special Collections Research Center, University of Michigan Library.

CHAPTER 12

Allan F. Nicholls

Interviewed by Lisa Dombrowski and Justin Wyatt

Figure 12.1 Allan F. Nicholls and Robert Altman. Courtesy of Allan F. Nicholls.

Allan F. Nicholls began his collaboration with Robert Altman by playing folk singer Bill in *Nashville*. After that time, Nicholls worked in a variety of capacities with Altman. Looking at the period starting with 1980, Nicholls acted as Rough House in *Popeye*, served as music supervisor for *O. C. and Stiggs* and *Prêt-à-Porter*, and worked as either first assistant director or assistant director on many Altman films, including *Streamers*, *Secret Honor*, *The Player*, *Short Cuts*, *Prêt-à-Porter*, and *Tanner on Tanner*. In this interview, Nicholls discusses his collaboration with Altman over three decades, with a particular focus on *Prêt-à-Porter*.

We knew that you worked closely with Altman on a number of films. We were surprised by all the First AD (Assistant Director) work for so many Altman films.
I went to Robert Altman film school as it were! No kidding.

Could you talk about the nature of collaborating with him?
It depended on what specifically I was doing, especially when I wrote with him [on *A Wedding* and *A Perfect Couple*]. It was a different collaboration when I wrote music for his films. But they were all based on—an overused word—a collaborative way of working. He would encourage that too. In my case, he wanted me to give him my own ideas, my own impressions. What did I think? He would then take it from there.

One of the things that stands out to us is the way that you are tied to Altman around the concept of music. Could you talk about how music factored into the projects and pick one, like *Prêt-à-Porter*, to give your answer specificity?
When I first met Bob, I was a musician. I was a performer. He really respected music and performance and he loved everything that went on in *Nashville*, and then that carried through to *3 Women*. For *3 Women*, he was trying to create from source music a kind of country radio sound. He had a whole bunch of popular country and western songs. He had his editor put that country and western music in the radios, the jukebox, and so on. Then when he went to obtain the licenses for the songs, he found out that it was going to cost about $50,000 (I'm just grabbing a number here). I told him that I could write music that sounds like that for much less. Bob said, let's give it a shot. So we did and we went into the studio and I bet I did the music probably for $5,000. I gave him all the songs he needed and station breaks included to make it sound like radio. So we created this country sound of source music coming from radios and jukeboxes. It's really a bunch of country songs that I co-wrote and recorded with some friends.

Now click ahead to *Prêt-à-Porter*. He couldn't use me as a first AD because it didn't work with their union over there. So he brought me over to France as an associate producer and as a video director. I did all the material, all the visual material for the commercials that appeared on the TVs, right.

I also did the music for the fashion shows. Bob said, Well, why don't you do it? Why don't you just choose the music? I did and it was really a great job because I would choose found music like for the Vivienne Westwood stuff, which was one for one with Richard E. Grant's character. For the design of that I used Gilbert and Sullivan music, which was really fun. I took this as a chance to exercise my freedom of choice in music and really step out boldly with the Gilbert and Sullivan. I did some weird music as well. I found an old recording by Bjork ["Ruby Baby"], a jazz version of it. It's a Leiber and Stoller song but it was a jazz version that Bjork did and we used that in one show. I had a blast.

Music is really, really important to so many of his films. He loved music. His biggest frustration in his whole life was that he couldn't play music or sing. He was a great appreciator of music and I actually used one of his songs for a movie. It's called "Let's Begin Again." He wrote the song and we used it. We did a little jazz version of it, and we used it in one of the films. Look on my music CD album. I think it's called "Thick and Thin" and he wrote the lyrics to that. He used to sing it to us, you know, at gatherings and stuff. He had a bunch of songs that he used to sing, but just at family gatherings and wrap parties.

Speaking of family gatherings, it's interesting to read just how many people felt emotionally close to him.
He touched so many, that was the effect he had on people. He seemed like your closest friend. Bob wasn't a father figure for me, but he was just a really great, warm person who liked what I did.

We want to ask you about collaborating with others as part of your own work with Altman. I mean, to what extent are there third parties that are collaborating with him while you're working with him?
Well, Bob had a sort of a group around him when I met him: Bob Eggenweiler, Tommy Thompson, later Scotty Bushnell, and of course, his wife Kathryn. The core group was Tommy Thompson, his first AD and production manager. Eggenweiler was given the title of associate producer or executive producer. I'm not quite sure what his expertise was. Tommy did the budgets and the scheduling. Scotty had expertise with casting. So with everybody's input that was the team. The collaboration was more than that, because he wouldn't say Scotty was just the casting person. She was a producer because first she read the script and would have opinions about who should be cast, but later she would also have opinions about story points and execution or whatever. So, everybody offered an opinion and it was welcomed. Bob's relationship was on-again off-again with this team, depending on the stress and whatever went down on that specific project. There was definitely some in-fighting. Bob just wanted a team that allowed him to create and protected him from the business which he really hated.

So after working with Bob for about five years, they were doing pre-production on the film *Popeye*. I was called to New York, where Bob had returned from Malta in the pre-production phase and asked if I would go over and be an interim Tommy—you know, a production manager—because Tommy had some kind of big fight with Scotty and, after seventeen years, Tommy said that he wasn't going to be involved anymore. He wanted to end the relationship.

So did you fill that gap?
Well, I mean it was big shoes to fill but I tried to. I did my best and it was a tough one. But I hung in there for a while and I did it for decades. Years later, I moved into the freelance world and Bob wasn't needing me as much. I've worked with Tim Robbins for about three of his films. It was a done deal that we would still be friends. When Bob went on, I think with the projects in Texas, he hired Tommy again. He did *Dr. T & the Women* and he did *Cookie's Fortune*. So it was great to have Tommy back in and we were always friends, but I hadn't seen him in years. He passed away suddenly. So, people came and went, you know, it kind of weaves throughout his life. Tommy was probably his most important collaborator, I think, because he was with him from the beginning, from the TV days. Bob really stuck with him. You know, he was a definitely a great guy.

As you know, this book is on the period from 1980 onwards. Which of the movies that you worked on with him after 1980 do you feel closest to?
Okay, that's a good question. It would have to be *Prêt-à-Porter* because he trusted me so much. Well, it's a toss-up between *The Player* and *Prêt-à-Porter*. On *The Player*, he had me doing so much as well. He would say go out and direct some karaoke videos and this was all in pre-production and it was really fun. We would go location scouting together, just the two of us, and we had a blast. So that was a great one but *Prêt-à-Porter* was great in terms of the trust, just the immense trust he showed me. I mean, in *Prêt-à-Porter* he had two cinematographers, Jean Lépine and Pierre Mignot. When one of them wasn't working on a scene, he'd ask me to go direct the scene. I did all the Kitty Potter [Kim Basinger] scenes. I directed them from behind-the-scenes but like it was a TV show. And then I directed all of the Teri Garr shopping spree for her husband, Danny Aiello. I directed all those and I also got to direct a couple of the police announcements. He didn't really want to direct that footage. It was too easy for him. He felt like directing the meat. So I got to do all those.

Can you talk a little bit about the theatrical adaptations because you worked on a lot of those too? Was his method different at all with those?
Well, yes, it was because he stuck to the script. It was kind of Altman's way. It was his "fuck you Hollywood." You know? You haven't liked me. When I improv and you give me shit. I think I'm improving all the time. And it's a loose set. I'll show you. So then he took these scripted plays and filmed them. He filmed them in locations that kept some kind of obscure feeling about them that worked for the play, like *Streamers* being in that claustrophobic barracks or *Come Back to the 5 & Dime, Jimmy Dean, Jimmy Dean* being in that store that had these fascinating lighting effects. It was just really terrific. The films are so cinematic in the way he uses the camera in the space. It's really interesting.

He challenged himself by sticking to the script, the words, and he challenged himself in terms of the casting, the look and the design behind the piece. With him, there was never a dull moment.

When he wanted to go with something, Bob just did it. *Fool for Love* was a good example of that. Bob was at loggerheads with Sam Shepard, because you can't really work with Bob if you think you're as big as him. Sam had a bit of an ego himself. I like Sam, by the way. I didn't understand their relationship. We made the movie happen, though. We filmed it outside of Santa Fe and we built our own motel. That was great.

CHAPTER 13

Alan Rudolph

Interviewed by Lisa Dombrowski and Justin Wyatt

Figure 13.1 Alan Rudolph and Robert Altman on a yacht at the Cannes Film Festival. Photo by Joyce Rudolph. Courtesy of Special Collections Research Center, University of Michigan Library.

Alan Rudolph is the acclaimed writer and director of over twenty feature films, including *Choose Me*, *Trouble in Mind*, and *Mrs. Parker and the Vicious Circle*. He first worked with Robert Altman as the second assistant director on *The Long Goodbye* and *California Split* and assistant director on *Nashville*, and wrote the screenplay for *Buffalo Bill and the Indians, or Sitting Bull's History Lesson*. Altman later produced Rudolph's *Welcome to L.A.*, *Remember My Name*, *Mrs. Parker and the Vicious Circle*, *Afterglow* (1997), and *Trixie*. In this interview, Rudolph discusses Altman as a producer, lessons learned from their work together, and the development of *Mrs. Parker* and the Kurt Vonnegut adaptation *Breakfast of Champions*.

How did Robert Altman first work with you as a producer?
In 1976 Altman produced my first legit film, *Welcome to L.A.* His only dictate beforehand was, "Don't make a car chase movie." He had never produced movies for anyone other than himself and had palpable disdain for producers who tried to interfere—although when he first assumed that position this was his general reference of how a producer behaved. It was a tentative start for us both. We didn't know what roles to play. As an assistant director with knowledge of nuts and bolts, I stubbornly wanted to create my own films my own way (arrogance? survival? Altman influence?). I was self-taught and relatively self-ruling, traits similar to Bob. Except he was a master and I was less than nothing. One week into shooting, we confronted the problem—or more accurately, the problem confronted us. By necessity and through mutual affection, the air was cleared (while hazed with smoke). From that night for the next three decades, he was the best producer I ever worked with.

What is the most important lesson you learned from working with Altman as a producer?
One of Bob's adages was, "The best advice is don't take any." He never taught anyone a single thing. But as an observant student, you learned everything. Casting was the number one key. Actors were your creative partners, not hired hands but reservoirs of talent and substance. With actors and others, unwritten story and character evolution took place. This all made sense to me, something I always thought possible, though I had never seen on the jobs I worked. As assistant director, one of my favorite activities was taking extras and creating behavioral moments in the background with unheard conversations instead of mere screen crosses from point A to B. When I did this for Altman, he put mics on them and used the dialogue. Because I wanted to be a writer and director, Altman's technique informed my primitive concepts and exploded them into my art.

As producer, he opened the cage door and let me fly.

How hands-on was Altman?
Altman the producer never attended production or budget meetings, locations scouts, crew staffing, et al. His first and weightiest major question to me as director was always the same: Who did I see in it? Once that played out, he basically let you alone to follow your own vision, approach, and aspirations. At least he did for me.

"What would Bob think?" was a constant state of mind surrounding my decisions—99 percent of which were never conveyed to him. Because of who and what he was, my bar was innately raised, and results tangibly improved.

Some critics have found similarities between your films and Altman's films. How aware were you of establishing your own voice and style as separate from Altman in your initial films?
Bob and I were rather dissimilar as filmmakers and persons, though we definitely overlapped in many elusive ways. Altman's subject views were

predominately lifelike, large-scale and comprehensive, working their way into stories told through realistic behavioral idiosyncrasy. Mine started with mood or emotional details on their way out to stripped-down, almost fictional worlds.

Bob knew from the beginning of our relationship—the most important non-spouse/family one in my life—that I wanted to make my own kind of European-inspired films. In the late '60s/early '70s, that was an impossible amorphous dream in America with no true path—until I worked with Robert Altman.

When *Welcome to L.A.* became a possibility, then reality, I made a conscious decision to deliberately put on display all the ways Altman influenced my approach and development. I was proud of our association and his impact—running toward it rather than away. I figured if anyone was paying attention or chose to examine beneath the surface, my own voice was indelibly there. Most observers were not paying attention.

For our second film together as director/producer, *Remember My Name*, shot in Los Angeles, Bob was on location in Canada and visited the shooting set once before he left (the same number of set visits he exercised on all our projects). I thought *Remember My Name* was a more evolved and mature film than *Welcome to L.A.* It more comprehensively displayed my own style and perspective; commercial aspects be damned. That was too accurate an assessment as it turned out because the film was barely released and predominately misunderstood—results that have followed my work since. Still, we were both very proud of the film despite its overt commercial failure, an outlook that prevails.

Did Altman offer advice on distribution and marketing as his role as a producer?
Altman was active in marketing his own films, in finished presentations from which he would choose. Multiple ad campaigns were displayed in his office like disposable art for any or all to comment upon. Again, because of his prodigious ability and elevated ideas, his contribution only made things better.

My films beyond Altman have usually been a challenge for distributors to market. They develop artwork for the movie they wish they had instead of the one they have, thereby alienating potential fans and foes alike. For my Altman-produced films, the distributors usually tried to please him and did a better job of it. Bob was somewhat less critical of an ad campaign than me. I'm not sure he thought artwork was all that crucial. He never said that, but he knew every major critic and film festival were going to give his films full attention. That became his primary distribution strategy. To Altman (my opinion), sales tools were ultimately important, but secondary.

The true Altman "marketing" technique for his films, and to a lesser extent for mine, was to constantly screen at every stage—from incomplete sequences to rough cut to finished product. His Rolodex reach was unmatched. When Altman called up people to peek at one of his films as they were being made, they showed up. No one else would expose works-in-progress like Altman.

With my films, I was more cautious but equally eager to screen at various progressions, though to less prominent attendees. No one had to say a thing and you could feel the reaction, sensed what needed fixing or reinforce choices made. Once after a screening of a rough cut of one of his films, an incredulous bigtime director asked Bob why he exposed unfinished film so freely. He answered, "Adulation."

Mrs. Parker and the Vicious Circle was a challenging period piece with a large ensemble cast. Could you talk about how Altman functioned as a producer for this particular film?
Mrs. Parker and the Vicious Circle was the most demanding film experience I had before or since—and that's saying something. Altman and I had not worked together since the late seventies, but always stayed in touch. I was intrigued by the Algonquin Round Table and that era. In the forties, my father worked with Robert Benchley, who gave him every one of his humorous books, each autographed. I read them as a boy—funny stories with drawings a kid could understand. They stuck with me. I decided to craft a screenplay with journalist/novelist Randy Sue Coburn to focus on Dorothy Parker's relationship with Benchley.

During one dinner with Bob around 1993, he asked what I was working on and I told him a script about Dorothy Parker and Robert Benchley. He naturally asked about casting. I had not really given much thought to that yet, and mentioned a few names. He asked about Jennifer Jason Leigh, who was about to be in *Short Cuts*, his next film. The more we spoke, the more he showed interest in the project. We decided then and there to try to get it made together. It was his kind of situation: multiple roles on a wide canvas, production based out of New York, where we both were living at the time.

One of Altman's great qualities, especially as producer, was his optimism and confidence—even against the eternal hopeless odds. He was a committed gambler in art and life. Everything was possible. Because he had proven this to be true time and again, it was the exact attitude needed to persevere with a difficult project.

Once he wanted something to happen, Altman would start the creative machinery working in that direction. Whenever I would present Bob with some important breakthrough, he would light up and say, "Oh, that's the best idea I've ever heard." I knew it wasn't, but coming from him the sentiment would keep me going—even though I'd heard him say that same thing to a variety of people for a variety of ideas over the years.

I was never engaged with financing when Altman was producing my films. Bob would rely on his agent at the time, the legendary and colorful Johnnie

Planco, to selectively do that work with an air of exclusivity. Altman never went out to financers or distributors asking them to become involved as most producers did. Instead, he waited for them to come to him. With a very active social life populated by important people, Bob would casually drop enticing hints of what he was working on, as if he didn't need any help.

Meanwhile, especially on *Mrs. Parker*, I would start prepping as if the project was officially going forward, as per his instruction. Behave as if this were really happening and maybe it would. Because I was as creatively dedicated to getting a film made as he, I efficiently did a variety of necessary work at no cost to keep wheels turning and juices flowing.

Naturally, casting was his main interest and we would schedule actors to visit his impressive, intimidating, intoxicating offices. We behaved with confidence that this film was to be made. All actors were eager to be part of an Altman project, so there was a steady stream of young talent ready to join our growing enterprise—and work for scale. I never liked to consider more than one person per role if possible, which meant roles were filled with regularity. The downside to all this activity and assurance without financing, of course, was the collective heartache if it didn't happen. It could be crushing to a lot of people. This worried me always. Bob never. All part of the game. When Johnnie came around, I'd privately ask how it was going with financing. He would give me uplifting agent-ese, with few or no details. I knew we were in trouble.

Ira Deutchman was head of Fine Line, the distributor of *Short Cuts*, which was gathering huge word-of-mouth before release. Bob and Johnnie had Ira's ear on *Mrs. Parker*, but not his bankable commitment. He had purse-string bosses who didn't share his enthusiasm. Usually, my films are so low budget that someone on the fence with genuine interest could be coaxed over to our side. Unfortunately, because of its multiple time periods, sets, and scope, on location in Montreal (even at rock-bottom costs), *Mrs. Parker* was budgeted at almost $6 million, huge for one of my films. Bob was not fazed.

As dates drew closer, the large cast finalized, production people and sets lined up in Montreal, I was scared to death the whole thing was going to fall apart. Or more accurately, never be built. Bob was steady. Leave for Canada, open offices, start official prep. Which is what I did. We made deals in Montreal but asked to delay payment until the ink was dry. Everyone was so impressed and excited about the project, an Altman project, from construction to costumes to caterers, they agreed. When we needed cash, Bob said to use my personal credit cards as much as possible. Unbeknownst to me, he borrowed money from a bank to seed what I couldn't handle.

We started shooting. Everyone was thrilled with the world and atmosphere we created. We all stayed at a crappy flophouse hotel, which the actors took over and made their own dormitory. Then one day about two weeks into shooting, Altman's production people were constantly on the phone with him in

New York. No one told me why. I hoped it wasn't about financing. While filming one scene in a house, I noticed the actors were summoned to a patio to have discussions with the associate producer and the production manager. When the take was complete, I asked one of the actors what was going on. They told me no one had been paid and were being asked to bear with us. I hadn't been paid either, but assumed it was just me, used to that situation (on *Welcome to L.A.* and *Remember My Name* I had to contribute my salary back to the budget).

The next day, Bob called to say he had secured financing, two weeks into shooting! He created a domestic deal with Fine Line and international sales with their bitter rival the dreaded Miramax, which was making Bob's next film. He used his project as hostage unless they took the foreign on *Mrs. Parker*. Later he told me the arrangement between the two of them was like "forced sex" (no longer a joke in the Weinstein era).

Breakfast of Champions [an adaptation of the novel by Kurt Vonnegut] was announced as a project that Altman would direct from your screenplay in the mid-1970s. Can you describe how the project morphed and developed into your eventual film made in 1999?
Ah yes, *Breakfast of Champions*, one of the most reviled films in modern cinema. And one of my proudest achievements.

In my opinion, although there were exceptions, Altman was not always too eager to work with big name screenwriters. Most were protective of their work with little understanding of how he operated. Although Bob's spontaneous style seemed to preclude the need for a skillful screenplay, in truth, his attitude toward scripts was just the opposite. He was adamant that written material be thoroughly worked out to maximum potential and quality—before it was all subject to change and evolution during prep and especially shooting. He would try to follow the story, not the dictation. Screenplay as blueprint.

For myself, I have always regarded the screenplay as the last best idea before actual filmmaking, which is a living thing and subject to its own free will.

When Altman was first involved with *Breakfast*, a novel deemed impossible to translate into film, instead of finding a seasoned screenwriter, he picked members of his longtime inner circle to crack it. When they couldn't, he turned to me, a newcomer to his world. Why, I have no idea, except perhaps he knew I had writing aspirations and was by nature not one to follow conventional thinking. His only instructions were, "Don't follow the book."

I wrote a draft, filled with spirit of the book's madness but not married to its details. I left out the Vonnegut first-person voice. Altman loved it to everyone's surprise, especially mine, and said this is the script he would shoot. He asked me, a young assistant director at the time, which actor I saw in the lead role of Dwayne Hoover. I had not thought about this. Because the cancer of commercialism was an underlying premise—that and the notion of going sane in an insane world—I said Johnny Carson. Bob immediately sent the script to him. After some flirtation, it predictably didn't work out. Eventually, Altman moved on from the project, as he often did.

Years later, I was informed the book rights were available. With producer David Blocker, we picked them up for a few years (not inexpensive by our standards). That proved fruitless and we also moved on. Over the years, apparently plenty of others tried to adapt the novel with no positive results. Then out of the blue, over twenty-five years after my original script was written, Bruce Willis (with whom I had worked on *Mortal Thoughts* in 1991), called up and said he just secured the rights and financing and wanted to make the movie . . . now. I wasn't sure what I felt. Times and I had changed considerably. But a film bird in the hand . . . I called Bob that day and told him about it. We had recently worked on *Afterglow*, which he produced and was a great experience all the way around. (When he first asked who I wanted to star in that film, I said Nick Nolte and Julie Christie. I saw the light bulb appear above Bob's head, and from that moment on, those two choices were his idea.)

Altman had nothing to do with the filming of *Breakfast of Champions*. He was supportive, but reminded me what a challenge it was. We communicated at regular intervals, and I informed him of its progress. He asked if I met Vonnegut before shooting to discuss the whole thing. I said I had. Kurt told me in no uncertain terms that a film and its source novel were two very separate things. He insisted I should follow my creative instincts and not his book. In other words, keep them separate. Bob asked if I had done that. I said for better or worse, I did.

Once completed, I was eager for Bob to see the film before anyone else. At the very first screening of the finished version (I purposely didn't screen it other than to co-workers during editing), I invited Altman plus a handful of key crew and cast (Bruce was unavailable), plus a major director who asked to see Albert Finney for an important studio film (Albert got the role). When the lights came up, people didn't know what to think.

Bob told me ahead of time he'd be leaving immediately after the screening because of an important prior commitment. (Otherwise we would have gone out and gotten trousered.) Instead, he pulled me aside, hands on my shoulders, stared into my eyes with his x-ray blues, and said in a tone which I had never heard from him, "You have made something truly great. And they're going to kill you for it." It gave me the chills.

At minimum, he was half right.

CHAPTER 14

Ira Deutchman

Interviewed by Lisa Dombrowski and Justin Wyatt

Figure 14.1 Ira Deutchman. Courtesy of Ira Deutchman.

Ira Deutchman is a film producer, director, film executive and a legendary figure in the landscape for independent film over the last four decades. He is also Professor of Professional Film Practice in the School of the Arts at Columbia University. As a co-founder of Cinecom, Deutchman distributed Altman's *Come Back to the 5 & Dime, Jimmy Dean, Jimmy Dean* and *Secret Honor*. As co-founder of Fine Line Features, he distributed Altman's comeback, *The Player*, and *Short Cuts*. Deutchman was Executive Producer on *Mrs. Parker and the Vicious Circle*, an Alan Rudolph film produced by Robert Altman. While at Fine Line, Deutchman shepherded Altman's proposed two-film project based on Tony Kushner's *Angels in America*. In this interview, Deutchman discusses his role as a distributor for several later Altman films, including *Come Back to the 5 & Dime, Jimmy Dean, Jimmy Dean*, *Secret Honor*, *The Player*, and *Short Cuts*.

Can you tell us a little bit about the initial Robert Altman films that made an impression on you? What was it about the film/s that connected to you?
I was in college. I believe that it was my senior year, if I'm remembering this correctly. There was a flurry of Altman films that were released during that time. One of them was *Thieves Like Us*. I think that the others might have been a double feature of *The Long Goodbye* and *California Split*, if that's possible. Altman was now on my radar screen and then I started digging back into earlier Altman films that I had not seen yet. We were bringing them into the college film society, so you know, it was not like all of a sudden he was in my pantheon. There were a lot of interesting filmmakers working at the time that that I was beginning to follow. When I moved to New York, if I'm getting the chronology correct, after college was when *Nashville* opened in New York. I got the job at Cinema V in September of 1975. *Nashville* was playing at Cinema II, and because I was now an employee of Cinema V I was given passes every week. Everybody on the staff was handed four passes every weekend to go see movies. I was using my passes every weekend to go see *Nashville* again. Literally I must have seen it at Cinema II twelve to fourteen times. It was the perfect theater to see the movie in because it was built for widescreen movies.

It was just the zeitgeist at the time that he was just capturing something. I was still finding my own voice as somebody who was not interested in the status quo and was interested in revolutionary ideas. There was something both chaotic and fascinating about the lack of structure in the Altman films.

After *Popeye*, do you feel that the films in the twenty-five years following are significantly different than the '70s films? Was there a shift in his artistry?
I do think that perhaps what it comes down to is that he was working with smaller budgets, without the constraints of the major studios during all those years. I don't think he made a single studio movie, post *Popeye*, if I'm remembering correctly. I think that the pressure was off him. He was able to return to form. There was an aspect of Altman that was anti-authoritarian. He couldn't stand the idea that people would tell him what to do. I think that when he stopped working within the studio system, that pressure just wasn't there anymore. I think it allowed him a certain amount of freedom. That didn't always work. I mean, those movies were still hit or miss. There's a kind of looseness to them. That harkens back to the early Altman before he was under that kind of pressure. One of my favorite things about him was that there was a certain sort of pragmatism about what he did that was self-inflicted. That allowed him to steer things in a different direction. So I don't think necessarily the post-1980 films are any better or any worse.

You worked with him on several films in the '80s and '90s. Did you think of commercial potential for these films? Does that not even enter into the equation?
I always had to think of it that way. I mean, look, it's a business, I either was an employee or a partner in these various companies. I couldn't afford to get involved with movies without thinking about them potentially doing business. What I can tell you is that I thought of Altman as being a brand. You know, the critics certainly and a lot of audience knew who he was. The stakes were much lower, generally speaking, because these were not huge budget films. Certainly, *Come Back to the 5 & Dime, Jimmy Dean, Jimmy Dean* was a very low budget movie. I believe it was made for less than $2 million.

Even *The Player* was not a huge budget movie, if I'm not mistaken, it was done for maybe five and a half or 6 million dollars. The stakes were not that high. In each case, I was evaluating the subject matter and that it was an Altman film in trying to gauge its commerciality versus what I was going to have to pay in order to get the rights and what it was going to cost to market them. So I was, just like any business person, I was doing spreadsheets. I was thinking about whether I could make money on those movies or not. So yes, the commercial aspect was definitely a part of the equation.

Often simply being an Altman film was part of the commercial reality. You know, the sense was *Come Back to the 5 & Dime, Jimmy Dean, Jimmy Dean* was truly a comeback film. He was at the lowest point in his career prior to that film being released. As a marketer, I definitely was thinking, this could be Altman's comeback movie. There was no risk because we didn't pay any money for that film. It was made as a Showtime film, or financed by Showtime as if it was a Showtime film. In Altman's mind, he always thought that he was going to somehow figure out a way to get it into theaters and designed it that way. When it was finished, he then began to shop it to distributors. And you know, I felt incredibly lucky that I already had a relationship with him at that point and that he saw in me a way of achieving his goal, which was to get the film out theatrically. He took a chance, though, Cinecom was a brand new company, and we hadn't released a film yet. He decided that we were going to be the vehicle through which he was going to get the film out to audiences. Then we began the process of trying to get Showtime on board with the idea of allowing a theatrical release. Altman drew us into that process. We went to meetings with the folks at Showtime to talk about why we thought the film could work theatrically, what our plans would be, and how we would market it. Ultimately, the folks at Showtime signed off on us doing it. We ended up making the deal.

Secret Honor was the same thing. That was a project that he did completely on his own. Because of the successes of *Come Back to the 5 & Dime, Jimmy Dean, Jimmy Dean*, he just came to us with it. There was no money involved. We didn't pay anything for it. He just asked us if we would release it, and we agreed. It was one of those rare moments where he was very happy with what happened with *Come Back to the 5 & Dime, Jimmy Dean, Jimmy Dean*. He decided that we could take care of *Secret Honor* for him.

Could you talk a little bit about his second comeback with *The Player*?
I'm a big believer in the fact that Altman's best films were all written by other people or based on material written by others. The ones where he was most involved with it from the concept were less successful. In the case of *The Player*, it was based on a book. The screenplay was really cleverly written by Michael Tolkin, the same person who wrote the book. It was a genre piece in a way. *The Player* performed at a level that was commercial beyond what you would expect from a typical Altman film. It felt very much like an Altman film. I think that the Altman touch is all about the fact that every star in Hollywood wanted to work with Altman. He managed to pack *The Player* full of celebrities, whether they were playing themselves or whether they were playing real roles in the film. Ultimately, when I saw that film, the thing that made it feel commercial to me was the combination of having all those names to help promote the film and that the film was kind of a lark. It was based on poking fun at Hollywood—which was Altman's favorite thing to do anyway. There is a certain slyness to it that I think would not have been there if somebody else had played it more straight. I would say, honestly, *The Player* is among the best movies he's ever made.

The only question mark in my mind in terms of picking it up for distribution for Fine Line was that it was going to be the most expensive film we had ever acquired at that point. My recollection is that we paid about five and a half million dollars for the rights, which was a big leap from anything we had done prior to that. The thing that gave me some confidence in it was all those star names in it. The New Line home video people were giving estimates about the kind of business that they felt like they could do. Remember that the VHS home video business was solely based on star power. The movie had an enormous amount of star power. They were giving us pretty substantial estimates about what they thought the film could do on video. In addition to that, one of the things that Altman always did, which I think really accrued to his benefit over the years, is that he had relationships with certain key critics. This started with Pauline Kael, but also a lot of other critics were kind of in her circle. He would invite a bunch of his friends, as well as potentially cast and crew, to watch rough cuts of movies, and then invite a few of his critic friends. We already had the sense that *The Player* was going to get really good reviews because he had had those kinds of screenings. The only time that I was ever involved with those kinds of screenings was with *Short Cuts*. We were hearing more and more buzz about *The Player* from the screenings and this gave us more confidence with the film.

And it delivered commercially as well?
It was huge. The movie did something like $25–6 million at the box office. That's a solid number for a relatively low budget film with a specialized distributor. *The Player*, ironically, was the biggest film that Fine Line ever released. But, you know, that particular year, it was also the most profitable movie that was anywhere within the New Line family.

***Short Cuts*, even with the success of *The Player*, still must have been a pretty big gamble. One of the things we love seeing in the Criterion edition and the other special editions of *Short Cuts* is all the marketing material that was generated for the film—tons of posters and print ads, and so many ways to position the film. Can you talk a little bit about how you addressed the red flags for *Short Cuts* through your distribution and marketing?**
First of all, *Short Cuts* is a true ensemble movie where there isn't a single character who carries the movie. Those are the hardest movies to market, because the images that you show to people can be confusing. If you look at posters that were done for Hollywood movies like *A Bridge Too Far* [Richard Attenborough, 1977], or other movies where they have the same dilemma, you end up with fifteen faces on the poster. It's just a very difficult message to get across to people. We acquired *The Player* because it had a lot of stars in it. The truth, though, is Tim Robbins was the center of that movie. Everybody else were in smaller roles and, in many cases, cameos. Whereas *Short Cuts* was truly an ensemble piece where there was no central character. Trying to come up with an image that would work to convey the movie was extremely difficult. And conceptually, it was hard to get across, you know, what's funny about it. Structurally it's not that different from something like *Nashville*. There's an important difference, though: *Nashville* had at its center the place and the culture. *Short Cuts* didn't have that. I mean, I guess you could argue that Los Angeles is central to *Short Cuts*, but Los Angeles really wasn't the star of the movie in the same way that Nashville was the star of *Nashville*. Even conceptually, it was a much more difficult sell. It was based on the Raymond Carver short stories, which is a plus and a minus: the plus being that at least from the perspective of critical analysis, some writers might want to write think pieces about it. It was meaningful that there was this kind of union of Altman and Carver. From an audience perspective, most don't know who Carver is and so that doesn't really work in terms of trying to get across to an audience what the film is. So that meant we had to focus on Altman as being the star. We listed off all the names of all the people who are in it to make it star-studded. Most of these actors were stars for an art house market. The artwork that we went with was very representational rather than specific. We tried to highlight the Carver–Altman connection on a certain level. The final poster almost looked like a book cover,

the idea was to make it epic. In movie terms these days if you use the word epic, it's a euphemism for long, which the movie certainly was.

Cary Brokaw, one of the executive producers of *Short Cuts*, insists that the movie would have been way more successful if Altman had cut at least one storyline and streamlined the movie a little bit. I'm not sure that would have made much of a difference, to be honest with you, but it is true that the movie is long. No doubt about it. Ultimately, I think the only reason why the movie never really broke through was because the reviews were just mixed. There were a few horrible reviews, a couple of which hit really quickly up front, that killed the momentum for the film. There were also some really extraordinarily good reviews as well, but they were definitely not uniformly good the way they were for *The Player*.

I remember the opening night of the New York Film Festival. We had a banquet in between the two screenings. We were schmoozing with exhibitors, and press people, the New York glitterati or whatever. Altman was there with the whole cast and it was really quite a wonderful event. Right in the middle, we found out that the *New Yorker* jumped the gun and ran their review early. It was a bad review. What a bummer to have that hit early on when it actually had a kind of ripple effect for some of the reviews that came later. So that was pretty awful. I remember Dave Kehr, from the *New York Daily News*, gave it zero stars. I like Dave and I really respect him as a critic, but I walked up to him at the opening night party. I said "Dave, zero stars?!?"

We want to ask you about *Mrs. Parker and the Vicious Circle*. Both you and Scotty Bushnell were executive producers and Altman was the producer. Can you talk a little bit about how responsibilities were divvied up between the executive producers and the producer?
The traditional formula is that executive producer in the movies—as opposed to television—usually means somebody who has something to do with the money. The money can mean that the executive producer puts up the money, or that the executive producer runs the company that puts up the money. The executive producer might have raised the money or the executive producer might have been the catalyst because of who they are to allow the money to be raised. The producer is usually the person who really wrangled the whole thing together; they may have hired the writers or the director in some cases. What tends to happen is that in any given circumstance, whoever has the most status in the industry is going to end up having the most leverage to get the best credit possible. The credit that everybody craves among all those credits is producer, which is the one where the person goes up and accepts the Academy Award when their movie wins Best Picture. So that's the credit everybody wants. In this particular case, the executive producer of *Mrs. Parker* would be the money, and that would be my role. We were going to pay for half the budget of the film in order to get the domestic rights [for Fine Line] but I also was key in getting Miramax involved to

co-finance the movie. They were the ones who took the foreign rights. There was a moment in time when Miramax and Fine Line were pretty fierce competitors. The idea of us co-financing a movie was fraught, to say the least. The film was already a couple of weeks into production before the financing documents had actually been signed. I actually had to cash flow the movie through Fine Line to bridge the budget so that they didn't have to shut down production. In any case, that's where my executive producer credit comes from.

Scotty Bushnell was always Altman's line producer. She was the one who had worked on so many of Altman's films. In this particular case, Altman didn't have a film in production at the time. And so she came on as the line producer on *Mrs. Parker*. She obviously didn't want to have a line producer credit. The solution was to give her an executive producer credit which was really not the appropriate credit. Calling Altman the producer—I would say that his biggest contribution to the movie was lending his name to it. Because having his name attached gave it cachet coming close on the heels of *The Player*. He added a certain level of commerciality to it that enabled it to get financed. Altman also is the guy who can pick up the phone and get anybody in the world to star in a movie, and I do think he took an active role in helping to get some of the casting for *Mrs. Parker*.

In your blog article (https://iradeutchman.com/indiefilm/altman-remembered/on Altman), we noted how it was clear that your love for Altman as a filmmaker is quite evident. When you worked together, there were certain moments where his behavior was dubious. So for example, you secure the money for the financing of *Streamers* and then you don't have the chance to release it. Altman talks about this "us versus them" situation and characterizes you as a "suit." Do you think he looked upon you always that way or did it change over time?
I honestly do think that he had a certain fondness for me, but that there was a way in which he couldn't reconcile that with his need for the other. He needed an enemy. He thrived in an environment in which he was the rebel through shaking up the institutions. That's who he wanted to be. He was the revolutionary who was doing things within the system, but outside the system. He wanted to be an underdog, you know, rising above the odds with everything that he tried to do. That's what he would want his epitaph to be. I didn't fit that mold. I was somebody who he actually had respect for. We got along really well. The proof is in the pudding because he came back several times to work with me again. I think that's why my relationship with him was complicated: I didn't conform to his image of the typical suit. I know he had a hard time with distributors. I got beyond that barrier. There were times when we were very close. We spent a lot of time together at his Malibu house and his apartment in New York. As I wrote in that blog post, I fell out with Altman without even knowing what I had done. Later at an event his wife pulled me

back into the "inner circle." I was reticent to confront him because I knew that there had been some bad blood and that he wasn't feeling really good about me for a while. It was, however, just like nothing had ever happened. You know, there was definitely an affection there, in spite of all of it.

So do you think that Kathryn continually mended fences for him? Was Kathryn a figure that could step in and deal with these kinds of conflicts and solve them?
Certainly that had been my experience, but that's partially because I got along well with her. I know of other stories that had been told where it's been exactly the opposite, where she's poisoned relationships.

Thinking about the post-1980 films, was there one film that you wish that you had sold or distributed?
Honestly, not that I can think of. There were a couple of films later that were on my radar screen and where I would have been interested in them, even though they didn't appear on the surface to be that commercial. I wanted to just continue the relationship with him. Those are movies where I feel like I kind of dodged a bullet because none of them really worked commercially.

Do you know how *Prêt-à-Porter* ended up at Miramax? Johnnie Planco, who was his agent, was selling *Short Cuts* and *Prêt-à-Porter* simultaneously. He was trying to set up the films back to back. He only talked to [Fine Line] about *Short Cuts* and he only talked to Miramax about *Prêt-à-Porter*. We had just made the deal to finance *Short Cuts*, and then we read in the trades that Altman had made a deal with Miramax for *Prêt-à-Porter*. I've never seen daggers come out of [New Line founder] Bob Shaye's eyes that way before. He looked at me that way because he thought we got screwed because we ended up with the Raymond Carver movie instead of the sexy model movie that ended up at Miramax. He was absolutely convinced that we had gotten the bad end of the deal. As it turns out, we got the better movie and the more successful one even though it wasn't that successful. It was more successful than *Prêt-à-Porter*.

I mean, unless I'm forgetting a movie in there somewhere, I can't think of a movie that came in the later period that I wished I had worked on. Maybe *Gosford Park*. It came out in 2001, though, and I wasn't in distribution at the time.

One thing that we've been trying to figure out is the reason why *Angels in America* with Altman didn't come together at Fine Line. The archival material suggests three possible answers: the budget, insisting on doing two films at once, and your exit from the company. What were the factors that didn't make the stars align for *Angels in America*?
It was all of the above. Altman was insisting that it had to be two films, which meant that the budget was going to be pretty big. He was coming off success. In terms of his reputation, he was not going to compromise on budget. When I left the company, it just kind of got dropped. So it was all of the above. And,

you know, to me the ultimate irony is that Bob Shaye would not go for it being two films, but not long afterwards they committed to three films with *Lord of the Rings* [Peter Jackson, 2001, 2002, 2003]. I would have loved to have seen Altman's version of that movie. I know it would not have been the same as the Mike Nichols version that would ultimately end up on HBO.

Altman's been gone for some time now. What do you see as his long-lasting impact or his legacy?
One of the things that I learned is part of the signature Altman style: long shots of constantly moving cameras. Going from conversation to conversation and all the overlapping dialogue. What I found out is that it was a strategy that was based on trying to make a movie where people couldn't cut out his favorite moments. He made movies where there was virtually no coverage. By having really long tracking shots of things that cover the whole room, it was an aesthetic choice but also, by the way, it was impossible to cut away from that scene.

I've come to think of him as being one of the most successful independent producers of all time. Most people think of him as a director and he has a particular directorial style. I feel like his longest lasting legacy is this idea that, if you want to be the iconoclast, the person who can make these kinds of outsider movies and be stubbornly non-commercial, then you've got to be relentless as a producer. You've got to never take no for an answer. You've got to never let the business wear you down to the point where you no longer have faith in your own abilities to get things done. He never stops for a moment or lets any of the lack of success get in his way. He somehow internalized all of the rejection, rejection by the industry but also rejection by audiences. He internalized that as being part of his identity in a way where he loved it. As a result, he never stopped working. He never stopped. There was always a project if you walked into Altman's office, which I did frequently to talk about future projects. There was never just one project. There were always five projects that he was juggling, not knowing which one was going to appeal to the person he was talking to or which one was more realistic to get made. When you would ask him a question, like, what's the budget of that? His answer would be, what do you want it to be? All he cared about was getting things made. He just loved the work. He loved the interaction. He loved working with actors. He loved the process. I think that it's just that he never stopped working. There was a work ethic there.

CHAPTER 15

Matthew Seig

Interviewed by Lisa Dombrowski and Justin Wyatt

Figure 15.1 Matthew Seig. Courtesy of Matthew Seig.

Matthew Seig first began working for Robert Altman during the production of *Streamers* and continued on a range of projects for the next twenty years. He functioned as an associate producer on *Tanner '88*, a co-producer on *Kansas City*, and a producer on *Tanner on Tanner*. He was also instrumental in maintaining Altman's production archive, and was the editor of *Altman*, written by Kathryn Reed Altman and Giulia D'Agnolo Vallan (Abrams Books, 2014). In this interview, he discusses Altman's theater work in the 1980s, the challenges of completing *Kansas City* and the *Tanner* series, and his view of Altman's legacy.

In his oral biography of Robert Altman, Mitchell Zuckoff describes the 1980s as Altman's time in the wilderness. What is your sense of Altman's attitude towards his work during this period?
Once he decided to do something, that was all he cared about. He was just as enthusiastic about the smallest projects and thought that they were just as great as the largest ones. To have an opera at the University of Michigan was every bit as important as a $20 million *Kansas City* movie.

One area in which he did a lot of work in the 1980s is theater. He's doing opera productions as well. And then he's doing theatrical adaptations. Was this a conscious production strategy on his part? Was it at all related to the background of his producer, Scotty Bushnell, in theater?
It was consciously done to some degree. If you look back in the archives to before his feature films and television work, you'll find a lot of poems, radio plays, plays, little fictional sketches. He painted. He considered himself an artist. There's no getting around that. He considered other art forms very consciously, and was familiar with other artistic disciplines that were given to him in his youth. So I think that he'd had it in his mind that theater was interesting to him and he wanted to give it a try. Sure, it was very convenient that he was working with Scotty, as she had a strong theater background and she was very knowledgeable about actors. But I suspect that he would have entered the theater anyway. As a matter of fact, I don't think he had any particular knowledge or experience in opera, and he suddenly dove into that without a second thought. I would have been petrified, as it seems like a pretty specific art form. But he didn't think twice about it. I didn't know him to listen to opera before that. But he just was inquisitive and confident.

Were you aware of whether the development of the theatrical adaptations was distinctly different than the non-theatrical adaptations?
Yeah, it was. As I recall, it was not necessary to pay for a film script in order to film a play. There was some guild loophole, giving him a lot more flexibility as the director, a window that has since been closed. But at first, I think he had more power over [securing rights], or at least the expense was much less.

On *Secret Honor*, Altman was not only doing another theatrical adaptation, but working with only one actor in a black box environment. Did this radically stripped-down approach open up new aesthetic opportunities?
Altman was known as the master of huge casts, and *Secret Honor* proved that's not all there was to him. He could tell a story with only one person. And he did. I think that was the challenge. He loved the material and he loved what Philip Baker Hall did with it.

Secret Honor **is one of a number of Altman projects, like *Nashville* and the *Tanner* series, that are rooted in politics. And critics have suggested that Altman has been interested in politics throughout his career. Did you see him having a consistent attitude towards American politics that's expressed in his work? If so, how would you describe it?**
Nobody would say that Robert Altman was a political thinker. He was a satirist. He was one of the big American satirists of the second half of the twentieth century, alongside E. L. Doctorow and Kurt Vonnegut. Before long, you'd add Garry Trudeau to that list. All throughout the 1970s, in all of Altman's films, there was that satirical element. Some of his films are interior films, as he called them, Bergman-influenced films that are obviously not satires, but a whole lot of his films, especially the big films, were satires. Satire does not have to be funny.

Is that a way we can also understand his choice to make *O. C. and Stiggs*?
Absolutely, it's a satire. It wasn't effective, but look at it in comparison to what he was known for doing to traditional genre films. And teen films, let's face it, are a genre. Hence, he was doing what he had set out to do in his mind, what he would do with any genre film. It was an unusual film. Some people are crazy about it and they are crazy about the source material. But it certainly hasn't been seen much.

Why was *Kansas City* so challenging to complete? It seemed it required waves of problem solving from start to finish.
It was difficult. Alan Rudolph came on for a while. There were different people trying to solve different problems with the script. But the real problem was, Altman got sick. And the budget, which always had been a problem, became impossible [due to delays]. And I don't think there were many other ways to edit the film because that was all the film there was. There weren't a lot of choices.

It got expensive, and in some situations, maybe the completion bond company would have taken it over. But they never took it over. There was a concern that it would make no sense to do this on a Robert Altman film. The industry knew that if you're going to make an Altman film, it's going to be an Altman film. I think those were really gracious things the completion bond company ended up doing. I don't think they ended up spending any of their own money on it. It went a little over budget, but there was an insurance claim [Altman's health coverage] to cover the costs.

Nevertheless, I think the end result looks great. I think Altman was always happy with it. It's a pretty unusual film. It has a lot to say about America. It is perhaps one of his more politically biting films. More so, I think, than *Secret Honor*. *Secret Honor* wasn't his story. *Kansas City* was really his story from start to finish. It's the story he wanted to tell, with all of its aspects—class, politics, race, and jazz.

The whole subject of the film is democracy. Are we a country of law? Are we a country where everyone is equal, or is something else going on? And if there's any music that represents democracy, it's jazz. We all should be developing our own creativity, our own personality as freely as we like. And then we should all work together as a community, as well. That's the story of jazz. And that should be the story of our democracy.

Speaking of politics and democracy, what was the impetus for *Tanner '88*?
Bob couldn't have been happier to be able to poke fun at an American institution. And especially if that institution happens to be politics itself. That's heaven for Altman.

This was a difficult production to mount. From the condensed time period during which the scripts were written and shot to the way the production was trying to integrate real life with fiction. You were wrangling politicians to perform as themselves. How did this work on a day to day basis?
Bob was an experimenter. He always wanted to try something that nobody else had done. He hated the idea that films are supposed to be made a certain way. Whether it was sound design and inventing new recording technology for multitrack recording, or whether it was dividing the publishing advance for the book version of *Nashville* with all the actors and sending them a check and saying, you helped write this, now you share in the book royalties—he was always out to do things differently. *Tanner '88* opened up a whole new possibility for that. I think he sensed the technology was there to do it, and he gave it a shot. It was grueling. There was a whole lot of relief when it came to an end, although Bob certainly would have liked it to keep going. But it was hard, hard work.

Can you think of any particular examples that illustrate how Altman and the crew were responding in the moment to production challenges?
To my knowledge, the scenes on the floor of the convention were completely improvised, and there were probably situations where the director wasn't even there. That simply had never been done before. Most of the time, the crew was waiting for Garry [Trudeau] to fax script pages based on some new location that might have been told to him the night before, and Garry had to write pages to accommodate this new thing that just popped into his head. But I can't think of any specific instances where the script changed just as a result of any particular news. Generally the shoots were set up so that a party scene or a crowd scene could take advantage of what was in the news.

Did you have someone who was essentially the political wrangler? Who would grab people and pull them into the shots?
Yeah, there were. Bob and Garry had people they had known for years who they reached out to, or who reached out to them. Garry especially knew people that could quickly put together a guest list for a party in Washington, D.C., for

example, or had inside information. At that point everybody in Washington was so into *Tanner '88* that it was easy to get help from people. They wanted to be involved with it.

What do you think was the appeal? Why were people into it?
I think this was an earlier, more naïve time of media and media manipulation. I do think some of the Republican politicians who took part probably felt, this can't hurt. And those who were more liberal felt aligned with Bob and Garry, and they were happy to take part.

These are people who spend their lives trying to get in front of cameras, and Altman has a camera. So it seemed like they should get in front of the camera and say something. It's strange, because I think today people are a little more careful about getting in front of the camera, asking first who's behind the camera and what's it going to be used for? But at that time, nobody would have thought that they would be appearing in a fictional show. I mean, I guess it was clear, but it just didn't seem to be. Nobody saw any danger to it, I don't think.

Some of the most amusing parts of the show are when politicians are simply trying to figure out what is going on.
Well, a lot of it had to do with Michael Murphy [the actor playing Tanner]. He not only looked like a politician, but he looked like someone politicians had seen before. So he's probably a politician, too. I think he was confusing to people. And they just assumed, "Okay, well, I guess he's a politician."

When *Tanner '88* comes out, it's on HBO, and most people don't have HBO. So it ends up being a cult hit that people have heard of, but very few have seen. How does that help create a foundation for when *Tanner on Tanner* is being pitched? Was there a pent-up demand that Altman was able to take advantage of?
Tanner '88 was I think the first or maybe second fictional series that HBO actually produced. They basically presented sports—boxing was their primary form of original programming. *Tanner* helped turn HBO into a fictional television powerhouse. When *Tanner on Tanner* was pitched to the Sundance channel, it too was their first fictional series. They didn't actually produce it, but they did pay for it. And they were involved in the process.

Tanner on Tanner did the same thing for Sundance that *Tanner '88* did for HBO. That's the whole business of sequels. But there are other motivations, and part of that is a heck of a lot of free publicity, millions and millions of dollars worth of free publicity for simply working with Altman and Trudeau.

Are there any aspects of Altman's legacy that you don't think he gets enough credit for?
His effect on television is way more prevalent and more obvious than his effect on movies. Do you remember *Hill Street Blues*? The creator, Steven Bochco, has been very open about acknowledging the influence of *Nashville* on *Hill*

Street Blues. As you know, what Bob was trying to do with *Nashville* and many of his other films, was to formally present the idea of democracy and of jazz and improvisation, everybody getting their say and telling their story, and everyone's story being as important as everybody else's story. That's what *Hill Street Blues* has—multiple storylines, and a big ensemble cast. *Hill Street Blues* changed television. Today everything in the golden age of television is influenced by what *Hill Street Blues* started.

The other influence on television is *Tanner '88*. There were a few people who did political TV shows before but there's been a lot more since then. The most prominent being *K Street* [2003], produced by Steven Soderbergh and George Clooney and featuring James Carville and Mary Matalin playing themselves. All of the cast and crew of *K Street* were expected to see *Tanner '88*. Few people know *Tanner '88*, but everybody knows *K Street*, and *K Street* led to all of the political programming that we have had since then.

Both of these are big changes in television. And Robert Altman influenced them both, enabling television to get to the point where it's considered better than movies, as they're allowed to fully develop characters and have multiple storylines running at the same time. That's Robert Altman. That's *Nashville*. So I think it's entirely fair to say that his influence on television has been bigger than movies, because Hollywood will never move to that formula.

Also, what Giulia D'Agnolo Vallan [who co-wrote *Altman* with Kathryn Reed Altman] explained to me, which I hadn't really thought of, was that in Europe, they have a tradition of public intellectuals. They are not necessarily academics, but come from other parts of social life and culture. And that's what she considered Bob, a "public intellectual."

I think it's a really interesting way of looking at him. Here is a great example of a person who is not a politician and not a traditional intellectual, but who was able to say something that reached a lot of people. The media liked to hear his opinion, which was usually pretty colorful and sort of radical. He always had a way of saying things that was pure Altman. He usually spoke out only when he had a movie to be publicized, and at first he was known for being critical of Hollywood and getting into angry fights with executives, but eventually he expanded into all aspects of culture and politics. That's why I don't really lump him together with a lot of other filmmakers, and think that the category of satirist is where he belongs. He was a public commentator who used film to convey his ideas about life, commerce, politics, art, and "reality."

An example of that are his critical comments about the second Iraq war while he was promoting *Gosford Park*. Some people thought he made it more challenging for the film to receive the Best Picture Oscar simply because he was openly critical.

There was a big backlash. I think the phone had to be turned off in the office in New York. They were getting threats and had to get security at the door. It was pretty nasty.

The Dixie Chicks got it too, didn't they.
Exactly. But whereas the Dixie Chicks basically had their thing, that was Bob's whole career, you know, sticking people in the eye. He just liked to do that and the media loved to cover him doing that.

CHAPTER 16

Wren Arthur

Interviewed by Lisa Dombrowski and Justin Wyatt

Figure 16.1 Producers Wren Arthur and David Levy on the set of *A Prairie Home Companion*. Photo by Melinda Sue Gordon. Courtesy of Special Collections Research Center, University of Michigan Library.

Wren Arthur began working for Altman as a personal assistant in 1996 and worked her way up to serving as producer on *Tanner on Tanner* and *A Prairie Home Companion*. In this interview, she discusses a day in the life of Sandcastle 5, Altman's production company, and how he developed and marketed his films.

What was an average day like at Sandcastle 5?
Our offices were connected to one another, in the Altmans' old New York apartment that they revamped to make a very lovely, cozy office. The main room had Bob's desk and a TV and awards and a big couch and a bar, and then across from it were two French doors. I was in the smaller room with my desk and books and awards, and then there was a kitchen, and when you first walked in, there was another room where Danielle Sotet [Altman's accountant] and Josh Astrachan [a production assistant and producer] and other people would work when they came in.

A lot of Bob's work was whatever was going on in his mind at the moment and who had his ear and what tickled his fancy. If we weren't in production, he would wake up and roll in anywhere between ten a.m. and noon. I would say, "I read a script, I like this about it, I like that," and he would sometimes read it or want me to tell him everything about it. He'd answer mail. So many people were endlessly knocking on the door and wanting to reconnect or give him books to read that should be made into movies. And if there was an idea brewing or a script that he liked, he'd make phone calls and talk to agents and talk to financiers and talk with actors. He was old school, so you didn't have to go through seventeen people to get to him. If someone called, especially in the beginning, I would go, "So and so's on the phone" and he'd just pick it up. And then I realized at some point, he shouldn't actually pick up every phone call. If we were in pre-production, I would make casting lists and he would talk to casting director Pam Dixon.

I became very close with Bob and very, very close with Kathryn, his wife. They were very familial. So the moment that they felt really comfortable with me, I was invited to everything. I did dinners at Elaine's. I was invited to dinner at their house. They were very generous and they loved to have interesting people of all ages, shapes, and sizes around.

How would you describe Kathryn's role in Altman's life and career?
His life was able to be his life because she managed everything. She facilitated a world where he could get up and do what he had to do. She made everybody feel comfortable. And she mended fences. She was the great connector. You'd go to their house and everybody knew who everybody was and there was backstory when she introduced anybody. She really was the ringleader. She didn't step in his territory, meaning I'm 99 percent sure that she didn't look at a script until he had called "action"—which is wise because films collapse pretty easily and regularly. Her life was devoted to making sure that his life could be about making movies.

What factors was Altman considering as he developed projects? Was he ever thinking about their commercial viability?
He knew that there's no recipe. There was a part of him that was mercurial. In a way, the films that were produced were what landed in front of him at the

right moment or what went through his brain that he was passionate about or what script had an actor attached. There were some projects that were dear to his heart that he held on to for years before I ever got there. There was a Mata Hari story, there was an Amos 'n' Andy project that predated me and then for a few minutes bubbled back up again with Harry Belafonte. So he had projects that had been on the back burner for years. But he also was very interested in whatever just flew in. He never made a film about a subject that he wasn't curious about. I think someone might say to him, "This has commercial potential," but I don't know that I ever heard him talk that way. There are films that are not going to be deeply commercial, and then there are other ones that surprise you because they were or they weren't.

How involved was Altman in the marketing of his films?
I'll talk about *A Prairie Home Companion* because it was the last thing that we did together. We went into the offices of Picturehouse [the distributor] and had meetings regularly looking at the one sheets, the small mock-ups of the poster, and he would pull them apart. Then he would weigh in very definitively about where the film was opening first and how they were going to move it out. He was on every big marketing call with every film. He weighed in on every logline and every bit of poster art and made the distributors keep going until they got it to his liking.

He had a really keen sense of how to market something and where you should aim it, and would be furious if people didn't do it right. There were many times when he was absolutely right, especially with *Kansas City*. I think he really felt that Fine Line missed opportunities for the broad audience that the movie could have had. It got pigeon-holed into being this small, personal story about his childhood, when the music and the world was so rich.

How did Altman work with his publicists?
Lois Smith was his American publicist. And Denise Breton was the French publicist. Denise had a relationship with all of the foreign markets because she was a preeminent publicist in Europe, she went to every festival, and she was an extraordinary cinephile. To be a publicist, especially an old-school publicist, you have to be able to suffer foolishness. And you also have to be able to push and steer people around without them feeling pushed and steered. And she was very good at that. You could say the same about Lois, because they had to be pushy with him and shove him around and make him do interviews and make him sit down with people who pissed him off before and not talk about the thing that pissed him off. That is the job of a publicist—to make everything work well and give everyone their time. There could be tussles, but nothing outrageous.

How effective was Altman in interviews or when talking with an audience?
On a good day, Bob was like the cat that ate the canary. He just had that grin. He loved an audience. He was funny and charming, and he had long fingers

that ran around, and he took great deep pauses before answering questions. For those of us who knew him well, there were moments where we would be on the edge of our seats, waiting for, "How is he going to answer that one?" And then you can get an unexpected answer and you're like, "Oh god, did he just say that? Are we in trouble now? What are we going to have to fend off?" But he was the best at it because he was a real salesman.

Until the very end, he was surprising and funny. And he was a provocateur. He could be incredibly tempestuous and drive you crazy. But people wanted to be in a room talking to him because he spoke his mind. He pretty much always said exactly what was on his mind. And if he was pissed off at someone or something, you're going to hear it.

How do you account for Altman's productivity, especially so late in his career when he was not always in the best health?
He taught me as a producer, if you put all your eggs in one basket, you're screwed, because every burner on the stove should have a pot on it and whichever one boils first is the one that you're serving up. He moved at a breakneck pace when he wanted to get something made, and you had to keep up. If you were two minutes behind, he would lose it. On *A Prairie Home Companion*, he had chemo on Thursdays so that he could shoot on Fridays and could collapse on Saturday and Sunday. He was truly amazing and inspirational in ways that I can't fully express. He walked off this planet with his boots on.

CHAPTER 17

Joshua Astrachan

Interviewed by Lisa Dombrowski and Justin Wyatt

Figure 17.1 Joshua Astrachan at the Berlin Film Festival press conference following the premiere of *A Prairie Home Companion*. Courtesy of Joshua Astrachan.

Joshua Astrachan began working with Robert Altman in 1996 as an administrative jack-of-all-trades and served as an associate producer on *Dr. T & the Women*, co-producer on *Gosford Park*, and producer on *The Company* and *A Prairie Home Companion*. In this interview, he discusses casting, financing, and Altman's career trajectory, utilizing examples from Altman's final three pictures.

How do you explain Altman's productivity during his late years?
Bob loved actors, and actors loved Bob—and actors are one of the essentials to getting films greenlit. That was certainly one of the keys to Bob's sorcery.

Because Bob didn't, for the most part, talk to agents, he had a casting director—Pam Dixon worked with Bob in that capacity for the time that I was with Bob—with one notable exception that I'll explain in a moment.

Pam would get Bob directly on the phone with an actor. He'd talk to the actor about the film and cast his spell and essentially say, "Come play," and most actors said *yes*—yes to something that they hoped would be outside of the norm, yes to something that sounded like fun and yes to something that might even be exquisite. This was one of Bob's entirely open secrets.

The remarkable Mary Selway was Bob's British casting director for *Gosford Park*. Pam worked with us on that film too, but Mary assembled that brilliant British cast—and kept all of those actors orbiting around us over the not-insignificant time that it took to put the financing together.

And the actors were key to securing the financing for *Gosford Park*.
That cast is amazing, but it's not, at least by the standards typically used by financiers and studios, a cast of movie stars. It's a cast entirely of brilliant British actors. Just to note: Clive Owen wasn't quite the star he would soon become after *Children of Men* [Alfonso Cuaron, 2006]. Maggie Smith, eternally a genius, had not yet been in the *Harry Potter* films [2001–11].

Originally, Jude Law was supposed to play the Ryan Phillippe role [Denton, an American actor pretending to be a Scottish valet]. And what a different picture that would have been! The contours of the film would have been changed both by having a young star of Jude Law's wattage in the film and by having a British actor in the role. Ryan Phillippe pretending to be a Scotsman is wonderful—and, at least arguably, was a more perfect fit [given the size of the role within the larger ensemble].

But we lost Jude Law to *Road to Perdition* [Sam Mendes, 2002], which he had already committed to, as our schedule at last came into focus. And when we lost Law, as I remember it, we lost something like $3 million of estimated foreign sales value. And the commencement of principal photography was looming closer and closer.

We held it together by bringing the budget down, by cutting a scene or two and a location or two—and, I have to now imagine, by getting a few other sales in place to offset what we'd lost in estimates.

Meanwhile, the role eventually played by Bob Balaban [Weissman, an American film producer who is Jewish] remained uncast. Bob Balaban is a genius in that role—but he didn't want to act in the film. He really wanted to be just a producer on *Gosford Park*, the idea for which had hatched out of a cocktail party conversation between the two Bobs. Capitol Films [the British sales company that financed the picture] wanted a star in the role to make up for the loss of Jude Law. But a SAG strike was looming and as a result, every actor in the world was working except, as I remember it, Pierce Brosnan—then internationally known as James Bond and an unlikely fit for Weissman—and Kevin Costner. Bob allowed that if Capitol was going to insist that Kevin play the role of Weissman, then Kevin could direct the film too—because Bob would no longer do so.

We didn't close the financing until the second week of principal photography, which is a very painful timetable to work on. That is, alas, not at all unusual with independent films. Someone keeps bridging you enough money to continue and you make your cash flow as skinny as possible—where you're not paying for anything today that you can possibly pay for tomorrow. And you hope that your financier will keep you alive from week to week. But it is quite a high wire act and a terrifying way to work.

We still hadn't re-cast the Weissman role, but in the first week of our shoot, Bob Altman shot a body double for Bob Balaban getting out of the car [as Balaban's character and Jeremy Northam's character arrive at the estate in one of the first scenes of the film]. There were still bells being rung telling us that we had to get an actor of more "value" because we'd lost Jude Law. But without Bob Balaban being with us, Bob Altman essentially established him in the film. And of course, Balaban is brilliant in the picture—which couldn't have been more successful and which was an enormous feather in Capitol's cap—so this worked out happily for all parties.

It seems like having a big-name actor in that role would have completely unbalanced the movie.
Because Balaban had said that he didn't want to play the role, Bob [Altman] had talked to George Clooney about it. And had talked to Philip Seymour Hoffman about it. And had talked to Stanley Tucci about it. I think that's expressive of Bob's responsiveness to actors and his faith that the fabric of his films could be tailored—and re-tailored—to accommodate them.

Arguably Phil or Stanley or George Clooney would have done a wonderful job. There were also other actors that Bob talked to. He did try to bolster the star power—respecting the directive of the financier—and did not want to lose the picture. And because the role is a fish out of water, *maybe* the star power wouldn't have thrown things off. It's perhaps harder to think of Jude Law in the Ryan Phillippe role.

I have a hard time thinking of Jude Law downstairs. He's playing the Pope now, isn't he?
The Pope definitely lives upstairs.

How key were foreign pre-sales for Altman?
I would say they were critical, certainly, in the time that I was around Bob. Part of the reason they were critical is that Bob did not want to have a studio boss.

So how do you stay independent? One of the ways you do that is by selling a film territory by territory. That way, nobody is fully financing —because every distributor of the film is partially financing.

When you make a film with a studio, they typically have their own in-house foreign sales division or their own foreign distribution in place. They have recipes or algorithms that they use where they apportion X million dollars against the world, either in gross terms or against the world, territory by territory. By doing that independently—i.e. through a foreign sales company—Bob, and his agent Sam Cohn, were protecting Bob's autonomy and his independence.

What other ways did Altman secure financing?
With *A Prairie Home Companion*, we didn't pre-sell the world. I'm sure we had estimates and likely those estimates came from Capitol [which handled international sales on *A Prairie Home Companion*], but *A Prairie Home Companion* was financed by River Road—Bill Pohlad's company [Pohlad is a Minnesota native]—and GreeneStreet Films, a New York independent film production and finance company. They each put $2 million into that film and said that if you raise the other three, we can make the film for $7 million.

That was our budget on *A Prairie Home Companion*. A lawyer in Minneapolis named John Stout, who wanted to be a part of this adventure and knew Bill Pohlad—and knew all the players in the Twin Cities—raised $3 million—in incredibly modest increments, primarily from a wonderful, large entourage of people in Minneapolis and St. Paul who could afford to invest. They were investing because it was the franchise of favorite son Garrison Keillor and because it was an Altman film—and because, once again, of the magnificent cast, including Meryl Streep, Lily Tomlin, Tommy Lee Jones, Kevin Kline, Maya Rudolph, Woody Harrelson, John C. Reilly, Virginia Madsen, Garrison Keillor himself, and Lindsay Lohan.

And possibly they invested because it might be the last Altman film. Bob was eighty years old when he made that movie.

John Stout, God bless him, I don't know how he did it, somehow he put together $3 million from those relatively small investors, with a few bigger investors coming in and acting as superheroes. And it all worked. And I love that movie. It's such a sweet film for a last film. An upbeat mortality tale. And we had such a sweet time making it.

The other famous story on *A Prairie Home Companion* is we couldn't insure Bob. Bob's health had grown increasingly frail in the years between *Gosford Park* and *A Prairie Home Companion*, but very shortly before we were to commence principal photography on *A Prairie Home Companion*, Bob found out that he had cancer. When we couldn't insure him, we had to get a standby director.

On *Gosford Park*, we had also needed a standby director, but Bob was healthier and younger, and Stephen Frears had to only sign a piece of paper—saying that he was on call in the event that Bob couldn't finish the picture—

and be approved by the financiers and the bond company in order to serve as stand-by director.

With *A Prairie Home Companion*, we needed somebody not only to be approved by the financiers and the bond company but also to be on set. We asked PTA [Paul Thomas Anderson], "Would you come?" *A Prairie Home Companion* had that incredible, large cast who were all coming and going over the course of our brief shoot—we filmed *A Prairie Home Companion* in twenty-three days. The bond company allowed that Paul would need to be with us in St. Paul to pick up the pieces should anything happen to Bob. Maya [Rudolph, Anderson's partner] was already cast in the film. And when we explained to Paul that we needed him to be with us in St. Paul, he said, "Well, I was going to be there anyway." Maya was pregnant with their first child at the time. Paul sat in a director's chair next to Bob that said *pinch hitter* on the back of it. He really saved our lives—and made the film possible. What a phenomenal gift that was to us and to Bob.

What kind of role did Anderson have on set?
Bob directed the picture but Paul was always there. All but one day on the film was shot in the Fitzgerald Theater, where Garrison Keillor did the radio show. Bob had a god mike [a microphone that everyone on set can hear], but he would sometimes lean over and whisper something to Paul and Paul would run down and talk to an actor—when Bob didn't want to give direction over the god mike.

And Paul had Bob's ear. Paul could say things to him that his producers could not say to him. And Bob could hear those things because he respected Paul so deeply—artist-to-artist—and would never think that a note from Paul was grounded in a concern about budget.

Honestly, I don't think I ever gave Bob a note based on budget. And I don't think I ever said, "Bob, we've got to wrap this up." But that was still Bob's worry and his instinct: to be at least a little wary of us producer types—even though he was also very generous to me and open with me. He was emotionally frank with everyone who worked with him: you always felt how deeply he cared—and it made you care just as much.

On *Gosford Park*, where I got to have a much more meaningful role than I had on *Dr. T & the Women*—and was really the producer on through all of post-production—Bob said to me, "You know, you thought of things I never would have thought of." And I was proud of that; I took it as a high compliment.

How would you describe the trajectory of Altman's career during his late period?
A famously observed fact of life—that was certainly true for Bob when I was around—is that on the heels of a film that didn't work so well, either commercially or critically, the world demanded more of Bob's next picture— i.e. the

script had to be better, the cast had to be even more incredible, the plan had to be better. And those pictures tended to be better films as a result.

It created a kind of sine curve. After *Cookie's Fortune*—which was more successful than perhaps had been expected and had wonderful strengths—Bob got more money to make *Dr. T & the Women*. That's the first film I was on with Bob, so it's incredibly dear to me, but I don't think it's regarded as one of Bob's best pictures.

In response, the world was much harder on Bob—and much more demanding—and he made . . . *Gosford Park*. Many more elements had to be in place, the script had to sing, the cast had to be even more remarkable.

On the heels of the success of *Gosford Park*, we got to make *The Company*—which again I love because of my involvement in it, but which I know does not measure up to *Gosford Park*. And on *The Company*, Bob was unhappy while we were making it because I think he didn't quite know what the picture was. He finally discovered it in the last few weeks of the shoot—when, at last, we were filming the dance footage on a stage in Chicago. That's what he loved. And that's what he shot best.

And then, the pattern continued: *The Company* was tough . . . and *A Prairie Home Companion* was the more successful film.

As we've been conducting interviews, other people have offered their own versions of your sine curve theory. Ira Deutchman focused on the significance of the script, and certainly from *Kansas City* to *A Prairie Home Companion*, your sine curve theory is perfectly aligned with his script theory.
Bob would be forced to wait for the script to be better when the market demanded. The script for *The Company* was an entirely astonishing research document. Barbara Turner had thrown herself into it and she was passionate and adept. She fell in love with the subjects that she was writing about—and allowed us all to follow her, in turn. But we did not shoot a lot of that script.

Altman was always quick to acknowledge how fortunate he was to have the career that he had, to have the chance to keep making movies.
Yes, he did say that often and I think he at least half meant it. He would say something like, "Nobody's had a better shake than me, because I got to keep making the films I wanted to make." And that is true. Every one of them—even the stinkers—are Altman films.

I'm a long-time fan of the film writer and critic David Thompson. We used to give his *Biographical Dictionary of Film* to our interns at Sandcastle 5 Productions [Altman's production company] as a thank you gift.

In 2006, Bob stayed in California for much of the year because his health was so poor [the Sandcastle office was in New York]. But Bob came back to

New York that summer—after *A Prairie Home Companion*'s premiere in June. It was our intern's last day. The *Biographical Dictionary of Film* was on the glass top table in the office, where we often ate lunch. Bob came in and sat down at the table and I thought, "Please don't look yourself up in the book, Bob. Please don't look yourself up." Because Thompson is admiring of Bob, but he is also sharp and sometimes acidic.

Bob opened the book to his page and read the last lines of the then-existing Altman biography, which said, "Of all American directors, there's probably no one more capable of a masterpiece—or a flop."

And Bob looked up and said, "Yep," closed the book, and slid it back across the table.

CHAPTER 18

Anne Rapp

Interviewed by Lisa Dombrowski and Justin Wyatt

Figure 18.1 Anne Rapp on the set of *Cookie's Fortune*. Photo by Joyce Rudolph. Courtesy of Special Collections Research Center, University of Michigan Library.

Anne Rapp wrote two features for Altman: *Cookie's Fortune* and *Dr. T & the Women*. In addition, she wrote the script for the "All the President's Women" episode of the limited Altman series *Gun* (1997). Anne Rapp also has a lengthy career as a script supervisor on many films, including *Tender Mercies* (Bruce Beresford, 1983), *The Color Purple* (Steven Spielberg, 1985), *The Accidental Tourist* (Lawrence Kasdan, 1988), *The Firm* (Sydney Pollack, 1993), *That Thing You Do!* (Tom Hanks, 1996), and *Marvin's Room* (Jerry Zaks, 1996). In this interview, Rapp discusses her collaboration with Altman on *Cookie's Fortune* and *Dr. T & the Women*.

You knew Robert Altman through your ex-husband, Ned Dowd. At that time in the 1970s, when you weren't working professionally with Altman, but you knew of his work, what did an Altman film mean to you?
He's always new and often each film has its own style. There aren't many filmmakers where you could just watch a film and not ever see any credits and go, I know who directed that film. I mean, it's the same thing with Woody Allen, for example, the same thing with the Coen Brothers. Altman's films had that quality where you were almost like a bug in the room, just drifting around watching. He had a way of filming something to make it look like it was a real-life situation. People were talking over each other and it has a real-life, rambling quality to it that wasn't staged in any way. That's what I always thought of the Altman films—that they were a little loosey-goosey that way. They also all have an absurdity to them. He loved the absurd side of anything, whether it was a dramatic moment or a comedic moment.

So, for those early films, the ones in the '70s, I saw *M*A*S*H* and just thought it was the funniest thing I've ever seen. For other '70s films, I liked *Nashville* and *McCabe & Mrs. Miller*. *M*A*S*H* was still my favorite. It made me laugh so much and I took all of our friends to it as well.

You made a transition from script supervisor to screenwriter. What does your work as a script supervisor give you in terms of screenwriting? What does it teach you regarding how to write a screenplay or a story?
There are things about that job that helped me and there are things about that job that didn't help me at all. They were just completely different. In terms of where it helped me, there are two things I can say. Number one, I was so comfortable with the format. I've had other people's scripts in my lap, treating them as the Bible for nearly fifteen years. So I was just totally comfortable with the script format. I knew how to do a transition and, for example, how important transitions from one scene are to the next. I had that ability later when I was a writer to go in there and understand the repercussions in changing an element of a scene: I've got to change this in the script so I've either got to take it out so that we don't have time to shoot it, or I have to change something. Our stories tend to be very tapestry. You know, they're not just these real solid, straight storylines, where you can just pull something out. It affects a lot of other things in the script. If you're a script supervisor, you develop that kind of brain.

Could you tell us a little bit about how you collaborated with Altman? Did the collaboration differ by the project (the *Gun* TV show versus *Cookie's Fortune* versus *Dr. T & the Women*)? Did the collaboration change over time?
Well, you know, my collaboration with him was different on every one of those. The one thing all of them had in common was that each one was based on a

short story that I had written that he liked a lot. *Cookie's Fortune* was actually a short story that was in progress. Once I told him the idea, Altman was wildly excited about that story. He wanted me to dump the short story and write a script instead. And so I did. Probably the greatest thing anybody's ever said to me was Altman, when he first hired me, telling me that he loved the way I write. He didn't ever want to change that. With everything I wrote, he would just let me go down my path with it.

With *Cookie's Fortune* I was on the set every day, all day. Bob wanted me there in Mississippi. That's a movie where he really stuck to the script. Most people often think he just throws the script out the window. He doesn't necessarily do that. He will go in and tell actors from the very beginning, day one, when they first come in: "You can do anything you want. You can do the script. You can throw the script out and do whatever you want to do. I hired you and trust you as this character." The good thing for me with *Cookie's Fortune* was all the actors wanted to do the script. That's not to say that Julianne Moore wouldn't add some wonderful little touch to the scene or somebody would come up with another little tweak. They didn't change the story, though. It was a really tightly woven little tale, and they wanted to stick to it.

Bob was constantly having me cut the script down. It was always a little bit too long. He was constantly having me shave dialogue out of the Patricia Neal and Charles Dutton scenes. There was all this dialogue before she shoots herself. I was like, "No, I don't want to cut that out," but he was having me do it. I was still little by little wiggling in some of my best moments in the scene. One day Patricia Neal came in and Altman tells her she can do anything she wants with the script. And she said, "Well, I do want to do something different. I want to go back to the first script you sent me. I didn't like that you cut all that stuff out." So Patricia Neal ended up doing the original script. All that stuff we cut out went back in.

My experience on *Dr. T & the Women* was completely different, because Altman had an idea in his head that he wanted to make *Dr. T & the Women* about him with just a parody of Dallas women. He didn't advocate for the short story I wrote that was about the character, Dr. T, and how he was just swimming and almost drowning in this sea of women. It looks kind of like the perfect life, but it really isn't, you know? And so, what happened with that one was, I got my first draft done. I felt like Dr. T was developed, but none of the women were even halfway developed. I kept trying to go in and say, "Bob, these women are terrible. I've got to wrangle them and give them a better fit." He said that you're not writing anymore. This is all I want. All I want is the blueprint.

He said *Cookie's Fortune* was your movie. This one's my movie. That's basically what he said to me. And he would not let me write anymore. So all of the women in *Dr. T & the Women* just did ad libs. The funny thing is, Richard Gere did the opposite thing. He was the only one who stuck to the script. Altman's not going to bullshit you; he's upfront with you. I knew from the very beginning that he was going to treat that script in a much different way than *Cookie's Fortune*. I knew not to expect that it would be the same experience. *Cookie's Fortune* was a dream for me. I'm certainly proud of *Dr. T & the Women*. I'm certainly happy we did it. The only thing I felt like I really influenced in that script was the Dr. T character.

Were there times when you and Altman were at odds with what you would put down on paper and what he wanted to shoot?
On *Cookie's Fortune*, Bob called me up one day early. We hadn't gotten to Mississippi yet. I was still in LA. He said, "Listen, I was in New Orleans last night and I met Chris O'Donnell, the actor. I want him in the movie, and I'm going to give him the role of the young cop." He was a much more minor character. I always thought Bob would just cast that part locally. I told Bob that character is so small, and he goes, "That's what I'm telling you: Chris O'Donnell will be the young cop. I need you to write that character bigger." I was kind of battling with him a bit and I didn't battle very much. Usually I would just go with it, especially that early in the game. Okay, so I went in there, pushed up my sleeves and I rewrote. I started at the beginning and I thought, okay, now, I'm going to make him a character that Liv Tyler's character had a relationship with and she just kind of abandoned him. Back then he wasn't even a cop. And then she comes back and she finds out that he's now a cop. That character turned out to be one of my favorite things in the script. Chris O'Donnell was great. He delighted me with every scene he was in. No one even knew at the time that Chris O'Donnell could do comedy because he'd only done dramas. That was one of Altman's brilliant things. That's an example of how you collaborate.

So sometimes I would dig in my heels and be stubborn. I would say that almost always, when Altman would push me down the road, I didn't want to go down. If I went down it, it made the movie better. He said, when I push you down that road, you still go down *your* way.

With *Dr. T & the Women*, all his effort went to the ensemble cast of women and that's what the movie was going to be about. I was hardly ever on the set. Everybody was always really nice to me, though. I loved Richard Gere, and all those women too. They're all wonderful, everyone. But it was awkward for me. They weren't doing lines I wrote. Richard was, but the women were allowed to adapt the lines I wrote. I would go up and visit the shooting in Dallas about once every two weeks. But I wasn't really a part of making the film.

Altman's style was so different than the style in which I wrote, so it's really odd that we actually ever came together. I thought, you know, I'm one for two with him. That's good enough. He gave me my movie, and so I gave him a blueprint for his. I was never angry about it.

When *Dr. T & the Women* was happening, my reign was pretty much over with him. I knew that was the end because he had only put me under contract to write for him for a year, and it turned into three years, and we did those three projects. And I knew when *Dr. T & the Women* was over, he was done with his Southern Texas phase. He was off to go do something that was completely different than what I wrote.

So one of the things you mentioned is the Southern feel of these movies. We're just so struck by how you create an environment for these characters, and you really get a sense of Mississippi versus Texas.
Altman loved absurdity, and you can find it everywhere. It is on the surface in the south. People don't hide it. People are wacko. Word is a mark of honor in the south. In other parts of the country, they'll hide their absurdities. Whereas in the south, it's all out in the open. I think that's one thing that Altman liked about the south, the absurd way that people carry on their lives.

He loved going to Mississippi to shoot *Cookie's Fortune*. He just loved that world. Texas is the bookend of the south. I don't think of Texas as the south because it's half west—it's where the south meets the west, really. Dallas is right in the center line. His parody of Dallas women, it wasn't my choice. I would have given them different kinds of strings, you know? Yes, Dallas women dress like that. Yes, Dallas women are outlandish. And yes, you know, he captured a lot of truth. But he missed the whole level with those Dallas women that I would have preferred to capture.

Here's something Bob was smart about. For *Cookie's Fortune*, he hired a Japanese director of photography [Toyomichi Kurita] who didn't speak English. We all thought, well, Bob, that's an interesting choice. He said, "Let me tell you something, if I hired an American to go into Mississippi, they're going to automatically see stereotypes. The Japanese guy is not going to see all stereotypes of the south." He was right, you know, and he often avoids stereotypes. He doesn't do the typical casting.

He cast Liv Tyler in a role that was written for a girl who was a real rebel. I would have never thought of Liv: she's so soft and soft spoken and kind of timid and shy. You know, she comes across that way on-screen a lot of times. I thought that was kind of strange casting. I love her in the role though, because she didn't overdo the rebel child thing. She's perfect in the movie.

How would you describe the role played by Kathryn Reed Altman on your films? What did she add to the productions?
I knew Bob and Kathryn socially through my ex-husband Ned [Dowd]. We would all go to the race track. You soon realized that Kathryn was part of the deal with a Bob Altman film. She set up show wherever he was filming, and she set up a house as well. Bob and Kathryn, their attitude was that we are all a big, happy family. If she saw you going by, Kathryn would say come in here and invite you

into their home. She became everyone's mother, and, you know what, she was great at it! Kathryn was a big part of the filmmaking, and she was a rock for him. When you call wrap on the set, Kathryn takes over and you would just socialize and hang out. It happened a lot with dailies each night too. Kathryn would be at dailies too. There was lots of socializing after wrap and on the weekends.

So one of the things we want to talk to you about is Altman and women. There have been critiques of how Altman presented women in his films. This is complicated by the fact that he collaborated with many creative women in the making of his films.
He basically told me that he was raised by all women, and he was always more comfortable around women. He just loved being around women. So, you know, there were times where people thought in his films that he treated his characters in a misogynistic way. But I can tell you he had great respect for them. Altman was very female-influenced in a way. I think he just portrayed women across the board the way he saw them. Again, he went for the absurdities and sometimes he maybe would go a little overboard for critics. He never forced any actress ever in a film to do something that they didn't want to do. In *Dr. T & the Women*, Farrah Fawcett takes her clothes off and gets in the fountain. Farrah wanted to do that, you know? I'm sure that Julianne Moore in *Short Cuts*, when she's standing there ironing naked from the waist down, it was Julianne's decision. Julianne Moore is not going to do that if she doesn't think that it makes a point, you know? A lot of people took issue with stuff like that.

Critics have also commented on his representation of gay people. We were impressed by how the DeeDee and Marilyn relationship [in *Dr. T & the Women*] is presented in a very positive light.
That was one of those roads Altman pushed me down that I didn't want to go. After submitting my script, there were a couple of things that he wanted me to go back and do over. He wanted me to do different things with a couple of these characters, especially the sister who is a Dallas Cowboys cheerleader. He said I want you to make her a lesbian. I said that wasn't in my original game plan at all. I'm the one that balked at it at first. He wouldn't push me too far down that road because he wasn't going to let me overdevelop that character. He just had to have her about to marry somebody, but she was in love with a woman and they run off at the end. It's not my experience. I just had to kind of write them on the surface in the script. So that's what I did. They developed that whole relationship. That was Altman's idea.

Looking at your work with Altman, we are struck by the ways that traditional dividers between people, such as gender, ethnicity, and class affiliation, are ultimately shown to matter little. The way that you

engage with race in *Cookie' Fortune* is particularly interesting. Could you talk about how your perception of racial (and other) barriers impacted the development of *Cookie's Fortune*?

I was writing the script while he was off doing *The Gingerbread Man*. He didn't change a whole lot in the script. The structure and basics stayed the same. I felt that it was never about race. It's not a film that addresses race. Mississippi movies always have a racial factor in them. I had lived and studied in Oxford, Mississippi for more than two years. Frankly, I've seen more racism in my home state of Texas or in Los Angeles than I saw in Mississippi. Rather than conceive it as dealing with race, I thought of it as a comedy about family pride. Family pride can be a good thing or a destructive thing. If the movie offers a critique it's about the downside of family pride. It could save you, but it can also hurt you or destroy you. I think that Mississippi has gotten a worse rap than it should have. Nobody wants to see another Mississippi race story. What means more to me than any of the good reviews was getting letters from the people in Mississippi. I heard, "Thank you for making the movie. You got us right." That meant the world to me.

Did you work on any potential projects with Altman after *Dr. T & the Women*? If so, what happened to the project/s? Did you decide to focus your talents in another direction?

There were two different occasions. The first was the strangest experience. Bob was toying with the idea of working with Garrison Keillor on *A Prairie Home Companion*. He was clearly an amazing writer, but Garrison Keillor has to write his own material. He has a uniqueness to him. He's a strange bird too. It's hard to get in his head. So Bob sent me to St. Paul to spend time with Garrison Keillor. I returned and told Bob, "There's only one person who can write this script, and it's Garrison Keillor." The second time was when Bob asked me to write a draft for the *Hands on a Hard Body* project. He had already gone through several writers. I even knew someone in Austin who did another script for it. There was a lot going on with that one. I think it even continued after Bob died.

CHAPTER 19

Andrew Dunn

Interviewed by Lisa Dombrowski and Justin Wyatt

Figure 19.1 Andrew Dunn on the set of *Gosford Park*. Photo by Mark Tillie. Courtesy of Special Collections Research Center, University of Michigan Library.

Andrew Dunn trained at the BBC as an editor before becoming a camera operator and cinematographer. A member of the British Society of Cinematographers, he has shot more than fifty features and twenty-five television dramas and has won three BAFTA awards. He was the director of photography on *Gosford Park* and *The Company*. In this interview, he discusses his working relationship with Robert Altman and how they prepared and shot *Gosford Park* and *The Company*.

What about Altman's career made you interested in working with him? And do you have any thoughts on what might have made him interested in working with you?
Well, he was just one of those people that I grew up with in my formative film-watching life. I'd watch his films, go to them with friends, other students and also lovers, and I'd get a kick out of the way he approached subjects, the overlapping dialogue and the style of shooting. It always seemed a big challenge for any cinematographer to achieve what he wanted to achieve and still have some cinematic style.

I could recognize the delight in the challenge of working with him. His maverick and his anti-establishment approach to things, fighting with the system and sometimes from within the system. There was always a part of him that came through his work. Just like a glass sculpture, a painting, or a story, his art reveals an author.

And as far as his interest in me, I think there were some people he knew who knew me and my approach and my willingness to be able to adapt, to go with his approach and not be too conservative. He could see that I was willing to go to a place that he might want to go to that didn't necessarily have to do with my taste or the photographic or cinematic thing but had to do with storytelling and the characters. I've always loved getting the camera inside someone's head and inside a character.

Before I met him, I had a catalogue of different styles. I think maybe the recurring thread was that I love the camera to delve into character. The casting and the performances are always paramount to me and if I can, within that, create something that's worth looking at again in five, ten years' time, I'll be happy.

And Bob would have known that I originally came from an editing background. Maybe when I met him, he could see that despite my being a cameraman, I could understand what's necessary to make the film as a whole in post-production. It's not all about what happens on set with the camera and the shots. It's about the whole.

What was the pre-production process like when you were working with Altman on *Gosford Park*? Did you discuss important visual influences?
The sound mixer [Peter Glossop] and I had not worked together before. So during pre-production the three of us and Steve [Altman], our production designer, considered how to create this space and light and shoot it in such a way that we would have choices in post-production for multi-layer mixing.

Bob knew there were different, interesting directors who had adopted similar aesthetics. I remember we looked at *The Long Good Friday* [John Mackenzie, 1980]. The use of zooms and camera movements. Somewhere in *Gosford Park* there is *The Long Good Friday*. We talked about how every shot should be moving. In *Gosford Park* there is not one static shot. We also used zooms. Hopefully they're fairly hard to spot, because in *The Long Good Friday* they are a lot that are more obvious, like in the '60s French New Wave cinema. There is no sign of that in *Gosford Park*. The other film we looked at was Jean Renoir's *The Rules of the Game* [1939]. I think the seed of *Gosford Park* started quite early with its help. These were the two main influences.

Altman is known for being open to changing the script during shooting. On *Gosford Park*, did that lead to a lot of takes?
I think sometimes he just changed the shot, you know? After we did something initially, perhaps the actors wanted to make a little change to the dialogue, and we just did another take. How many takes of the same shot were ever the same? Because the two cameras were moving all the time, and that is going to create its own serendipity. And I think Bob loved the serendipitous nature of film-making. He created this arena, this space to get people together and to see what would happen.

There was one thing that I remember him saying very clearly, which is that you cast actors as they are going to be in the film. And then you don't necessarily have to direct them because they are those characters. It's not meant to be demeaning, but you don't tell actors of that class what to do.

Basically, he would leave them alone to do what they are going to be doing as those characters. And instead he might cross the room to talk to a background actor about what they are doing, because he understood that background actors and the extras were super important to any storytelling; whereas he went straight past the group of principal actors because they were who they were going to be and he trusted them.

He trusted the commitment of each artist. And he would ask the artist to help him create his artistic vision. He was like an orchestra conductor. I just adored him and hoped I understood him, but I did witness once or twice when he was with people he didn't like or didn't trust or whatever. It wasn't a pretty sight. It's such a subtle control, I think. When it's time to prep or just spend time with us, he wouldn't say very much. He was a great reader of people. I am lucky that I got on with him quite well. He understood what artists want to have. He gave you the freedom to do what you felt was right.

On *Gosford Park*, you were shooting in historic homes with big casts and multiple cameras, doing long takes. How did you choreograph the cameras from shot to shot? What kinds of strategies did you develop on a day-to-day basis that would help create order out of what could potentially be incredibly chaotic?
What Bob described to us was that we would put actors into space, just like doing stage work, then we would choose somewhere in that room where the camera, and the audience, has to be observing. Therefore, we need a space, a

corner inside the room, from which to watch the coverage. And that was generally the day to day approach.

Then, we obviously moved around for other people and things, and if it didn't quite work from that corner, we would move into another corner. That time in the morning was very, very important. I think actually a lot of directors are quite scared of actors. But Bob wasn't, he loved them and he knew they loved him. They could plan a scene and allow it to develop. And I would have my camera team and the lighting teams and other groups of people set up and give them the freedom to do what they wanted to do. The actors gave us the space and we gave them space.

Sometimes we got equipment or lights ready in place and he understood when he saw the room that some cables were coming in a particular window or a door or something that he needed in the shot. And he knew that if we had to move certain things, that's gonna cost him at the end of the day, that's gonna cost him thirty, forty-five minutes on his day and therefore he may lose a take or a shot. He had been doing this for a long time, so he understood the artistic, aesthetic needs on the technical side. But if he wanted to shoot in a way that gravitates towards this window, say, then we would note it is going to cost lead time. And fortunately, with our planning, we could try and make it work.

Actors loved him. But he also had a real affinity for the crew. They could recognize him as a demanding character, but he was also considerate and understanding of the work. Directors of that caliber know that when all those crew people, probably 600 people, when they see this film in time, they want them to say they were proud to be a part of it. Bob really understood that everyone's life plan was not just about going home with a paycheck.

I actually remember one night, we scheduled for a 6:00 p.m. wrap, but we went home at 6:20 p.m. I remember him telling us that he would give the time back to us. And, just for twenty minutes, he did. And that has to do a lot with the crew. He understood that everybody was important.

So on *Gosford Park* the blocking and the camera movement were really being worked out organically once everybody was on the set. How did the two camera operators choreograph their movements?
I operated one camera. I developed a shorthand from being with Bob, rooted in my understanding of who he was and what he was trying to achieve. Those weeks of prep create a shorthand that runs right through to the days of shooting. Therefore, when he said something, I could interpret it into something he might wish for and then we could achieve it.

Yes, absolutely. But then you are, in some way, also describing the film as a musical piece. There was a moment when Eileen Atkins's character was sitting on the staircase listening to Ivor Novello sing upstairs. And I think we just made it up in the moment. It's a magic moment. We captured magic moments.

That definitely is one. It's one of the most memorable shots of the film. How did the wide screen format shape the look of the film?
What the wide screen allows is to capture a wide landscape and open spaces. But of course there can be diversity to it, because you can use the format to show different people thinking and doing different things within the same frame. That is the beauty of it. You might not think it's so good for stately homes or anywhere with very high ceilings. But, the wide screen, contrary to belief, can be used for intimacy. I fought for that.

***Gosford Park* is a master class in terms of wide screen. You were able to utilize it to tell a multiplicity of stories unfolding at the same time, to give significance to the background as well as the foreground. And there is also lateral depth across the frame. Even in those moments where you have fewer figures in the frame, say for instance, some of the more intimate moments downstairs where you only have two characters in a room together, the frame is still able to bring in the servants' environment which is so much a part of their identities.**
Quite. And the other thing is that the actors, of course they know if they are near the camera and there is an eyeline there for them, but generally, they wouldn't know all the time if they were on camera or not or if they were going to be on camera. So they were always acting. Therefore in that widescreen format, with two cameras going, cross-shooting sometimes, actors were always on for you to catch these little moments, a little flick of an eye, a downward glance. They were always doing something.

A story Bob told me is that, he'd ask a friend to go see a film and they'd say, I've already seen that, and Bob would say, well, if you listen to a favorite piece of music a hundred times, a thousand times, you know your experience of it has changed, therefore you can go and see a film again to see what has changed. One of his hopes, wishes, and dreams was that people would revisit his films. With their multi-layered sounds and images, you have to watch them a few times to make sure you've got it all. They can be confusing the first time, but you go back for the extra layers. You can catch a glimpse of something in the background when you're reviewing his films. He was a master of layers, audio and visual and acting layers.

That is very true. It took us many viewings of *Gosford Park* before we felt like we really got it because of the wide array of characters and their individual stories and motivations. It's one of those films where you can have a successful first screening experience, but the subsequent screenings really do enrich your understanding of the characters and their world.
Yes, exactly. When you first watch it, you just feel like going along with it, and later viewings invite other enrichments.

Let's discuss *The Company*. What was distinct about its pre-production?
We were like a traveling group of tightly knit players because, apart from the local crew, we were all on location in Chicago together. And there was a semi-derelict building which we used as a base. The offices were there, the art department, and we got a couple of sets in the building. And then obviously we also went to the Opera House to shoot.

When I first arrived, I got off the plane on a Sunday after finishing on another film in London on Friday. I set my bags down in the hotel room, then the phone rang. It was Bob. He said to come over to his hotel room. And that's the way it was, we started discussing things and we watched American football together. That's the beauty of him. Making a film with him is like a social occasion.

We had a little talk before about, what should we shoot this on? And he said it was up to me and he didn't mind. But he clearly had a mind to push it into an area which hadn't really been done before. So we talked about digital, which was still fairly primitive at that stage. We wanted to do widescreen and there were only three or so other films that had gone from digital to widescreen at that point. And we saw about thirty cameras that week. I am not sure if there were any 8 mm cameras but certainly we had 16 and 35 mm, different digital cameras. And based on those tests we decided to shoot on hi-def digital. Hi-def digital cameras suited him beautifully because instead of having to reload at the end of nine minutes or ten minutes, we could keep rolling. So that is an advantage of shooting digital.

The downside of digital is that at that time there were a lot of cables. So moving to another location—like we want to rehearse in the building and then the same afternoon we go out to another area—it was quite cumbersome.

Was the decision to use digital made because Altman wanted to explore this new technology, or was there something about it that he thought would be useful for this particular project?
I think he basically wanted to explore the technology. I think he wanted to be at the cutting edge of things. I think he would have probably heard about it, read about it, from mixing with other directors, writers, and people he knew. He knew this was the new thing.

Did the choice to use digital shape anything regarding the look or the feel of the film?
The Company has an observational, documentary feel to it. What we really wanted to get across was those times when the dance company is together within the main rehearsal space. To focus on their commitments, their depth of feeling, when there is pain and the fear of blood seeping through their ballet shoes, because that is what happened. Sometimes the ballet dancers got crippled. That was a line we wanted to pursue. The idea was to get inside them and look at the pain that drives people when they do ballet at a high level, what

it takes to get through the physical pain, and the emotional and artistic pain, of striving to get where they want to go, in terms of the dance.

Whether the use of digital high-def cameras at that stage in their development allowed us to get to the part of the film that was literally under the skin and the intimacy is a question. I think it may not have been quite as intimate as we would have hoped. It is different now, but back then we couldn't get a crazy amount of detail on digital. If we could have shot it on 16 mm film, the camera could have been much more free-roaming.

But the thing is, every day in my working life, I think, "what if we'd done this or done that," and I think that's true for all artists in practice. You gotta just accept. Altman gave me this quote from Picasso, that one of his secrets was "knowing when to stop." Watching him while we were shooting, he knew when he had it, when he had this beautiful thing. The way he looked at the actors. The actors just adored him, they would do anything for him. And he had a way of looking at them, and smiling. He knew when he had it, and he recognized that, he could smell it and see it and taste it.

Oh, another thing about digital is in post, we could play around with it quite a lot, the look. You know, it definitely was a different experience. I would give my eye teeth for those times again.

How did you plan the dance sequences? Was that done during pre-production because of the intricacy of the dances or was that an organic process as on *Gosford Park* **where you were working it out on the day of the shoot?**

It was mostly organic. We would have space. On the stage we talked to the choreographers the previous day so we could actually see what the dance is like when everything is laid out. The dance company people were fantastic. They were so thrilled to have us and they would do anything for us, work with us and adapt their lighting to create what we needed. So at the end of the previous day or perhaps, if possible, during the weekend mornings, we would look at what we needed to do or where we were. We had two or three cameras at that point and a dolly and a crane out in front of the stage. It was an observational approach, allowing the dancers space, because it was their space.

We were entering their world, you know. Whether it was James Franco or Neve Campbell, or people from the Joffrey Ballet, we were being approved to enter their world, which actually is the way that Bob would approach filmmaking. We were privileged to enter these people's lives. Actors created lives, and we were there to observe, to be absorbed into their world, but not by objectively observing. It was a kind of subjective observation.

The camera is a voyeur. But the camera has to be a character in the story. Therefore the audience is entering the story world as an individual, as a participant and a character. And that's very much Bob's perception of movie storytelling, that the audience is invited into the environment as well. And we are privileged to enjoy it with these people, with the Joffrey Ballet, to get up close and personal. That was his way of working.

One reason we find the dance sequences so dynamic is that they provide a multiplicity of perspectives. In some moments of a dance, we're in the audience. In other moments, we're on the stage with the dancers, or we're in the wings with the crew or the other dancers who are waiting to go on. Were you thinking about editing or post-production, how all the shots would fit together, when you were shooting the dances?
Editing is always important to consider because we're being allowed in this world to record it and share it. You are in this space with these people who are in their world. You then choose angles so we can have a camera in the wings observing what's happening there but also see what is on the stage in the background. And then it really is going to be an immersion.

Tied in with that, as we are shooting it is necessary to have a range of shots in the editing process to have enough choices. We knew and Bob knew that we wanted to see what the audience might see from the balcony or the stalls. What we do with the cameras and lenses is to hone in on an individual to see the expression on their face or their feet or whatever. But you still have to pull back and see the whole stage because the company designs and choreographs and performs for the whole on the stage. We love to go in there with a scalpel and see a detail up close. The audience desires intimacy, but they also desire to see the dance as a whole.

One thing that Altman is often associated with is a kind of realism, an emotional or psychological or sociological realism. And one of the things that is so palpable in *The Company* is the desire to provide a sense of what the lives of these dancers are really like. In the dance sequences, the shots into the wings, or lighting hotspots in the frame, remind us that this is all being staged. The wide shots remind us of the perfection of the dance, and other shots from the stage or into the wings remind us of the work that goes into creating this image of perfection.
Yes, we were creating imperfections to provide a sense of realism. From the audience's perspective, what the dancers are creating is perfect. But then we are privileged to see other things, the combination of blood, sweat, and tears the dancers go through together.

The Joffrey Ballet lighting people worked very closely with us, quite generously. They were keen to make it work for us, to push the lighting a bit further than they might have done. We took out some of the original lighting created for the dances and added other hotspots to provide a more dramatic storytelling point of view for cinema. And for me the extra challenge was that this was my first foray into digital filmmaking. At that point I knew on film what we could do, now I needed to know on digital what we could do.

How did your experience working with Altman shape or alter your perception of him as a filmmaker?
I always had a deep understanding of his heart, his emotion because of the stories down the years of this firebrand. This maverick person who was in battles with studio heads and other people. When someone is one of your gods or heroes, every story you hear is apocryphal and may not be true. Once you work with someone they become your friend.

I think afterwards I sort of understood this person, this man. And Kathryn, who is this woman who knows him deeply. When my wife met them, she said, "These people are deeply in love." Since 1959, or whatever it was. You would hear the stories of Altman, the firebrand, drunk in the drink and all of the rest of it. And actually, he had such a deep understanding of the human condition. After all this time, my eyes are welling up just saying that to you.

Many directors are scared of actors. They get scared of the process of directing. And he just grabbed it with a huge heart. Grab this toy, he would often call filmmaking that, and invited all his friends to come play with it. To create magic, you know.

CHAPTER 20

Mitchell Zuckoff

Interviewed by Lisa Dombrowski and Justin Wyatt

Figure 20.1 Mitchell Zuckoff. Courtesy of Mitchell Zuckoff.

Mitchell Zuckoff is currently the Sumner M. Redstone Professor of Narrative Studies at Boston University. Zuckoff has published several best-selling books including *13 Hours: The Inside Account of What Really Happened in Benghazi*, *Frozen in Time: An Epic Story of Survival and a Modern Quest for Lost Heroes of World War II*, and *Lost in Shangri-La: A True Story of Survival, Adventure, and the Most Incredible Rescue Mission of World War II*. Knopf published Zuckoff's *Robert Altman: The Oral Biography* in 2009. *The New York Times Book Review* praised Zuckoff's book as, "Scrupulously intelligent and entertaining . . . Noisy, funny, slightly ill considered, a bit chaotic, and wholly believable. In short, Altmanesque." *Robert Altman: The Oral Biography* is now recognized as a key text for understanding Altman and his creative work. In this interview, Zuckoff recounts the history behind the oral biography of Altman, his collaboration with Altman, and his special appreciation for *Short Cuts*.

Tell me a little bit about why Altman is a focus for you. What was the connection? What were your impressions of Altman before you started the project?
I would see anything he would make. It just had a different feel to it. I accepted the fact that I wouldn't love everything because I just knew it would be different.

I was not a film buff. I was not a film academic by any means or a scholar. I was just a fan who thought everything Altman does is interesting and different and grown up. You know the feeling of walking out of a theater and saying, "I'm not exactly sure what happened, but let me think about it for the next two weeks." As opposed to the Chinese food feeling that was, "I enjoyed that" and I forget about it immediately. That's most Hollywood movies for me.

In terms of the Altman movies, my list is a little bit boring because it's predictable. You know, *McCabe & Mrs. Miller* was really special to me. It is frankly my number one. I love *Nashville*. I think the first movie that made me aware of him was *M*A*S*H*. I was changed by *Short Cuts*. That reordered my brain on how you could tell stories. I thought *Short Cuts* was brilliant.

So tell us, how did the oral biography come together as a project?
There's no reason why I should have been the one chosen for this. That's not false modesty. I had done a book with the editor who signed up Bob to do a book on how he made his movies. I was put on a list of people to consider partly because I was somebody who had experience as an interviewer. I think they probably thought it made sense for somebody who Bob could relate to for some reason. They would like somebody who Bob's going to hang around with for a while. So I was one of I don't know how many people he was going to talk to about the book. I got a call from my agent saying, "Bob Altman is looking for a collaborator to do a book." My agent knew that I was a great Altman fan. But again, I was not somebody you would think of. I hadn't written about Bob.

I think there were two, maybe three, reasons Bob chose me. I got there and I was really dressed up. I was dressed in my best suit because I had had to go to a funeral that morning. I told him an incredibly dark true story, which is it was a funeral for my uncle. My uncle was living in Florida with my aunt. He backed up his car and accidentally hit her and killed her. It's horrible. He died two months later. He just was so broken by it. I came into Altman's offices and they asked, why are you so dressed up? I told him the story. I think Bob found it amusing. You know, it's dark as hell and messy, but it's life. If you wrote it in a screenplay it would probably be too on the nose. But it's what actually happens sometimes in life. The second reason is much simpler, which is, we were talking baseball. I knew that he was a Kansas City fan and, at the time, I had Red Sox season tickets. We both hated the Yankees. There you go. I made the first cut. The second meeting was at his apartment. I think the real reason was for me to meet Kathryn. Kathryn was so central to everything. Bob did have a bit of a cold and Kathryn was serving him tea or soup and we just sort of sat around and talked for a couple of hours. I went back to Boston and I got a call. I think Bob was the decider, but Kathryn ratified it.

I honestly don't think Bob cared that much. Bob knew that his legacy was his movies. He wasn't insecure. He wasn't worried that, oh, this guy might screw up a book about me. I think the stakes were incredibly low for Bob.

What was the working project going to be like?
I'm going to interview him on filmmaking, on his approach to actors, on his approach to sound and so on. You know, it's a little bit like *Altman on Altman*, but it was going to be even more in his voice. It was not going to be about him or his personal life or his family. I think I allude to that in the prologue to the oral biography. These limits were more trouble the more I got to know him as a man. He was pretty determined, especially in the first month or two, to keep them separate. So that was hard.

Did you have the sense that he was analytical when talking about the films? Did he want to break them down in terms of technique and story?
Certainly not. You know, that was just anathema to him. I think he was right. As soon as he applied a meaning, as soon as he applied a frame to the work, it foreclosed or made it harder for other people to find other meanings in it. He rejected that kind of search for meaning utterly. We were having lunch in Malibu and somebody came up to Altman and started talking about what *The Player* meant to them personally. I don't remember the details of what this person said. The person was so sincere and so passionate and so certain that's what that movie spoke to him about. Bob was charmed by it.

Do you see any differences between the films of Altman's "golden period" of the 1970s and those he made after 1980?
I know you're focused on the post-1980 period. I kind of love that because I think it's a fascinating period. I really do. The younger Bob in the 1970s is angry in a lot of ways—for good reason given the state of the world. From the '80s on, there's something I see about the human condition. He's kind of understanding that he's going to be an artist and what that really means. As high as he lived, he understood he needed to keep working. He had to stay true to who he was, who he wants to be, and what he wants to convey. I'll just see something in his later movies and say, okay. I know why he left that in. It was about something that had happened in his life or something he wanted to say about the human condition.

I want to make it explicit. Thinking about *Short Cuts*, which you've mentioned already, how do you feel it spoke to Altman's sense of the human condition?
I mean the baker's story and the concept of loss and healing—juxtaposed with a murder—life and death are extraordinary. Those two pieces of it are the things that speak to me most of all. They are sort of small-scale tableaus, these are not in the world. These are examinations of character in human behavior that are, at once, micro and actually universal. Those are two pieces that I think are the work of much of a more mature artist than his work in the '70s.

Short Cuts haunted me after I saw it. I think it's sometimes hard for me to articulate why I had that reaction. There was something about the messiness of life in the moment and the relationships of people with each other. I do believe it's a meditation on death. I'm sure Bob would smack me in the back of the head for reducing it that way. It was more than that, you know, but that's what I got from it.

Did you get a sense of how Altman viewed his relationship with critics and journalists?
I would separate those two categories. I think, with journalists, he knew how charming he was. He knew how charismatic he was. And he could, if he was sitting down with a journalist, always be truthful. He has a bit of an alpha male quality, sort of bearish. He was a big guy, and suddenly you're out drinking or you're out smoking a joint with Bob Altman. So he will enlist you in that way.

Now with critics, he couldn't do it quite so much because he was not in their presence. It could be a little bit more of a fraught relationship. He had different relationships with different critics. He loved Roger Ebert. He had a special relationship with Pauline Kael. So there was a variety and so only after he read their work would he meet some of them. If they got him, he would seek them out. He would call them, he would talk to them, he would see them at a film festival. The journalists were often focused on the man. The critics were focused more on the work. Altman hated the idea of control or of controlling other people, but he was, in my estimation, often in control. That's why, you know, he was the director. So he could direct with journalists, in a way he couldn't direct with critics.

Could you tell us a little more about how you collaborated with Altman? Were there mainly times of uninterrupted conversation in person or by phone? Did Altman prioritize the dialogue?
It was a little bit of everything. I would go out to Malibu for a week and hang out for a day. He was always sort of in between stuff. I'm thinking of one time in particular. We're at his place in Malibu and I guess Stephen [Altman] was

there and Kathryn was in and out, and Wren Arthur was on the phone calling in. They were planning *Hands on a Hard Body*. There was a big whiteboard with the cast, and you could see who was in and who they were thinking about. It wasn't like he didn't have a million other things going on. He was about to go film a commercial he was planning. I just had to sort of be around and then grab him for an hour or say, "Hey, Bob, can we just talk about this for a little while before dinner?"

More often than not it was in person. But there were also times when I could say, "I'm just trying to close a loop on this one thing. Can I get an hour on the phone?" This went on for about four or five months. I guess I met with him first in February [2006] or maybe it was longer, actually, what am I saying? The full-time work was four months. He died that November. So I guess it was nine months all told. The real work was a focused four-month period of that.

We were talking before then. He was getting comfortable with me. Early on I went out to Malibu to talk with Bob. Kathryn was having a problem with the garage in their Malibu house. I had to be the one who called the garage door guy. I think that during the entire trip to California that was the only thing I accomplished: I got the garage door fixed. It was ridiculous. So that was maybe three days in April. I think it was just a test. Is Mitch going to be part of the mix? Will he be a pain in the ass, or is he going to pitch in? It took us a while to get really rolling.

Did your relationship with him change over that core four-month period?
Very much so in my eyes. I know Kathryn came to like me. I felt it. By the late summer and into early fall, the conversations deepened. They were more relaxed. It wasn't that it didn't feel like work. I would get invited along to things that were just fun. Suddenly I'd be out on the balcony looking over the ocean having a glass of wine or smoking a joint with Bob. It did deepen the relationship and there was a trust that was developing. I wouldn't say it was completely developed, but it was it was definitely developing.

You talked about this in the introduction to your book, but it was a seismic shift after Altman passed on. What were your thoughts about the project moving forward at that point?
Well, I got screwed. There were all kinds of lawyers involved with the contract before Bob died. The contract wasn't finished, and the work wasn't finished. The publisher said, "Hey, Chief, thanks, but we're not going to do the book." I knew that, in the book contract, there was an expense piece. I figured I'd get paid back my travel costs. I had been keeping really close records of my travels [flying to Los Angeles to work with Altman]. That didn't happen. And I was screwed. It all just kind of fell apart. A couple of months later I got a call that there was this plan to do an Altman biography.

Kathryn, who I love and who I actually became closer to after Bob died, stayed in very close touch and I saw her regularly and spent time with her in New York. She told the agent who was putting this project together that Bob already picked his biographer. Knopf had somebody else in mind. Kathryn basically laid down in front of a train for me. Wow. She said, if Mitch isn't on the book, the family won't cooperate. Bob picked Mitch. I couldn't believe she was doing this for me. That's all Kathryn and I love it forever, for it speaks to her amazing integrity.

So continue, tell us what else happened and how you proceeded at that point.
I knew that I had these last interviews, and I knew they weren't enough for a book. It just made more sense to have overlapping voices tell the tale of Bob Altman. It had to be a little bit messy. I think I put up a yellow sticky above my writing desk: Keep it messy. Yeah. If it was too neat, if it was too orderly, that wouldn't work. I felt I needed to follow the life story.

A major portion of the book is interweaving these other interviews with Altman's interviews. Could you talk about how that developed?
It started with me making an Excel spreadsheet with the help of a grad assistant listing everybody from different points of view. Obviously we wanted to have a lot of actors, but also people who were in costumes, in music, and other crafts. Frankly, talking a lot with Kathryn helped enormously. She never was seeking approval for the interviews. It was sort of like, "Oh, don't forget this person who really had a take on Bob." Kathryn was fantastic on that.

Matthew Seig was great as well. Matthew was a bit of a historian and he was so generous in talking with me about who I needed to go see or talk to. He was just never subtracting names, but adding names. I was always just amazed by his generosity. He wanted the book to be as good as it could be. So the process became me calling people up or, with the more famous ones, reaching out through the lawyers.

I had some amazing people for these interviews like Tim Robbins who just couldn't not talk. He's like, "When you get to be in New York, come on down." We talked for hours. I was in his apartment and in his place, and he was fantastic. He was still with Susan Sarandon at the time. Susan came in and, and then he's like, "Let's call Kathryn and take her to Elaine's tonight!"

Now when the project was conceived originally, it was just about the films and not his personal life, correct?
That was the hardest part because I was growing close to Kathryn and a real friendship developed there. I knew that it had to be more than the films if we're going to do an autobiography. The hardest one was Faye Dunaway [who had an affair with Altman]. Getting Kathryn to understand that I needed to talk to

Faye Dunaway and include her took months. Ultimately to her lasting credit, Kathryn understood that was part of the big, messy, complicated life that she had lived with Bob. The whole credit goes to Kathryn as she said it was okay and that I should go ahead and talk to Faye. To me, it just pops. It just makes the book real and legitimate. I really felt my reputation was at stake as a journalist. If I'm going to do an oral biography that is so sanitized, what's the point?

Did you send the finished manuscript to Kathryn before it was published?
I was very determined to not let Katherine control it in a certain way. As I recall, I sent it to my editors at Knopf, my agent, and Kathryn at the same time. I thought that was the right way to do it, which was nobody gets it first. Everybody gets it at the same time.

And what was her response?
She came to love the book. I think she loved most of it on a first read. The infidelity stuff was hard for her to know that that would be part of his legacy. You never know how a book is going to be received. She really wanted this book to frame his legacy outside of the films. Within a matter of months after publication, she was singing its praises. She was in love with the book. She sponsored the party for it at Elaine's. The book party was held at Elaine's and she was the hostess of the party. Once Kathryn embraced it, I thought that my work is done now.

Could you talk about other noteworthy reactions to the book?
Wes Anderson, of all people, reached out to say how much he loved it. A number of the people who I spoke to reacted to the book: Michael Murphy, who became a friend, Elliott Gould, and Sally Kellerman all shared their reactions. Michael was great about it because he was just really thoughtful about it, he read it really closely. That was meaningful to me. In the ten years since it was published, when I would go out to LA I would sometimes see with Konni [Corriere], his stepdaughter, for lunch or, and again, I always saw Kathryn when I was ever in New York. That to me was the only reception that mattered.

What do you hope people take away about Altman or his filmmaking from reading your oral biography?
I hope they see that he was a genuine artist. For all of the discussion of the maverick, all these words that people want to apply to him. That to me is the word that's most meaningful. He was absolutely determined to make art on his own terms. It's just the hardest thing because it's such a collaborative medium. It is so dependent upon money. For forty years, he fought to make art that was different than anybody else's. And I've taken inspiration from that, and I hope other people will do as well.

Index

3 *Women* (1977), 1, 2, 93, 176, 186, 194, 198

Academy Awards, The, 132, 151, 214, 223
Afterglow (1997), 202, 208
Ahmed, Sara, 184, 185
Aiello, Danny, 185, 200
All That Jazz (1979), 103, 104, 107, 111 113
Altman (2014), 3–4, 8
Altman (book), 218, 223
Altman, John, 53, 54–5
Altman, Kathryn Reed, 4, 7, 8, 9, 47–9,
    51–7, 59–62, 66, 72, 142, 199, 216, 218,
    223, 226, 240–1, 251, 254, 256
  homemaking, 51–5
  labor, 52, 55–6, 60–2
  and *Robert Altman: The Oral Biography*,
    257, 258
  role in production, 52–5, 241
Altman, Rick, 16, 24, 111, 116
Altman, Robert, 120, 122, 123, 124, 125,
    126, 128, 129, 130, 132, 143, 191,
    197, 202
  1980s career, 3, 117–19, 123–7, 138, 143,
    151–2, 173, 176–82, 185–6, 211–12, 218
  1990s career resurgence, 3, 7, 117, 118, 119,
    127–33, 138, 142, 146, 152
  and actors, 125, 126, 127, 212, 230–1, 238,
    245, 246, 249, 251
  and *Afterglow*, 208
  and Altman, Kathryn Reed, 226, 240–1
  and *Angels in America*, 216

as anti-Hollywood, 6, 124, 138, 139, 140,
    151, 200, 212, 223
archival papers of, ix, 4, 5, 15, 81, 82, 86,
    87, 180
artistic vision, 1, 5, 7, 8, 9, 10, 19–20, 23,
    49–50, 59–60, 137–8, 146, 148, 191,
    200, 204, 217, 219, 221, 237, 244, 245,
    247, 248, 249–50, 254–5, 258–9
brand, 7, 9, 137–53, 211
and *Breakfast of Champions*, 207–8
as businessperson, 7, 9, 10, 152, 217, 226
casting, 125, 203, 206, 230, 240, 244
cinematography, 33, 36, 39, 159, 161,
    167, 168
as collaborator, 7–8, 10, 198, 200, 201, 253
and commercials, 3, 9, 198, 256
and critics, 2, 3, 22, 27, 65, 85, 88, 118, 122,
    124, 126, 127, 128, 130, 131, 132–3, 138,
    140–1, 145–6, 148, 149, 150–1, 152, 159,
    162, 165, 182, 190, 203, 204, 211, 212,
    220, 227–8, 241, 255
daily planner, 83, 92–3
development process, 9, 81, 82, 85, 86,
    94, 226–7, 228, 230–1, 233, 234,
    242, 256
editing, 31, 37, 39, 40, 190, 208, 244, 250
and European support, 137, 138, 143, 152–3
exile from Hollywood, 2, 3, 123, 125,
    126–7, 151–2, 176, 192
and family, 47, 51, 52–6, 61–2, 199, 240,
    254, 257

Altman, Robert (*cont.*)
   and film festivals, 43, 128, 130, 140, 141, 144, 148, 150, 152, 159, 202, 204, 214, 229, 255
   financing process, 133, 138, 139, 143, 148, 152, 153, 206, 207, 208, 215, 230, 231, 232
   and genre, 2, 5, 6, 10, 34, 70, 73–7, 111–14, 129, 130, 131, 141, 148, 149, 150, 151, 172, 185, 191, 192, 212, 220
   health, 8, 9, 83, 88, 90, 92–3, 143, 147, 192, 228, 232, 234, 220
   and Hollywood Renaissance, 1, 6, 118–19, 120, 121
   improvisation, 8, 20, 22, 25, 27, 67, 83, 129, 190, 223
   and independent film discourses/discourses of independence, 118, 125
   interest in the art world, 87–8, 89, 141
   legacy, 7–10, 61, 118, 119, 150, 217, 218, 222–3, 254, 258–9
   locations, use of, 49–52, 54–5, 59–60, 66, 88, 148, 152, 200
   marketing, 7, 106, 126, 130–1, 132, 137, 139–40, 144, 145, 150, 152, 204, 213, 227
   and *Mrs. Parker and the Vicious Circle*, 205–7, 209, 215
   and music, 99, 110, 111, 112, 117, 198–9, 201, 247
   and opera, 3, 9, 139, 191, 219
   and parties, 47, 53–5, 57, 59, 62, 199
   and pre-release screenings, 205, 212–13
   as producer, 65–6, 203–8, 217
   production practices, 5, 8, 10, 13, 15, 19–27, 56–60, 137, 149, 190–1, 198, 199, 200, 201, 203, 231, 233, 238, 239, 240, 245–6, 248, 249–50, 251
   as public intellectual, 223
   and *Remember My Name*, 204
   and representation of gay people in 1970s films, 172–6
   and *Robert Altman: The Oral Biography*, 253–6, 257
   and satire, 3, 5, 10, 36, 42, 44, 84, 87, 88, 130, 144, 145, 220
   and screenwriters, 5, 7, 13–27, 85, 94, 144, 207, 212, 237–40, 241, 242
   and sexual outsiders, 176–82, 183, 184–5, 241
   sound editing, 39–40
   soundtracks, 20, 23–26, 99–100, 101, 103–4, 106–13, 145, 174, 181, 185
   and studio executives, 1, 2, 138, 190, 210, 215–16, 223, 231, 251
   and television, 1, 9, 30–45, 87, 88, 117, 118, 123, 139, 147, 219, 222–3
   and theater, 3, 9, 150, 219
   and theatrical adaptations, 3, 6, 71, 125, 177, 180, 200–1, 219
   unproduced projects, 5, 81–2, 94–5; *Amos 'n' Andy*, 227; *Hands on a Hard Body*, 83, 90–4, 242, 256; *Mata Hari*, 83–7, 227; *Paint*, 82, 83, 87–90; *Ultraviolet*, 82, 87
   use of windows and mirrors, 160, 161, 162, 168
   and *Welcome to L.A.*, 203, 204
Altman, Stephen, 8, 55, 59, 88, 244, 256
Altmanesque, 8, 47, 78, 90, 94, 129, 135, 150, 151, 252
American Film Market, 142, 154
Amos 'n' Andy (n.p.), 227
Anderson, Paul Thomas, 8, 78, 92, 120, 121, 192, 233
Anderson, Wes, 258
Angels in America (n.p.), 183–4, 209, 216–17
Animation sound, 24
Annie (1982), 24
   and *Annie* musical, 13, 14
Aria (1987), 123
Arthur, Wren, 7, 87, 88, 225, 256
   interview with, 225–8
   and *Kansas City*, 227
   and *Prairie Home Companion, A*, 227, 228
   and unproduced Altman projects, 227
Artisan Entertainment, 133
Astrachan, Joshua, 7, 9, 88–9, 226, 229
   and *Company, The*, 234
   and *Cookie's Fortune*, 234
   and *Dr. T & the Women*, 233, 234
   and *Gosford Park*, 230–2, 233, 234
   interview with, 229–35
   and *Prairie Home Companion, A*, 232, 233, 234
Atkins, Eileen, 148, 246
Attenborough, David, 150
Avenue Pictures, 128, 132

BAFTA Awards, The, 151, 243
Balaban, Bob, 147, 148, 149, 186, 230, 231

Basements (1987), 139
Basinger, Kim, 125, 200
Bates, Alan, 148
Bates, Kathy, 125, 161
Bee Gees, 101
Belafonte, Harry, 77, 227
Belbo Films, 139
Benchley, Robert, 205
Berlin Film Festival, 150, 229
Beyond Therapy (1987), 3, 123, 125, 126, 127, 176, 180–2
   adaptation of play, 177, 180
   budgetary script, 181
   release during AIDS era, 182
   sexual representations, 182
Biographical Dictionary of Film, The, 234–5
Biskind, Peter, 120, 121, 122, 185
Bjork, 198, 199
Black, Jack, 92
Black, Karen, 125, 166, 167, 169, 177
Blakley, Ronee, 174
Blanchett, Cate, 84
Blockbuster films, 6, 13, 19, 27, 100–5, 108–10, 112, 118, 122, 126
Blocker, David, 208
Boardwalk Records, 107–8, 112, 115–16
Bochco, Steven, 87, 222–3
Boeken, Ludi, 139
Bogart, Neil, 107–8, 112
Bond, Sudie, 161
Boys Don't Cry (1999), 164, 165, 169
Breakfast of Champions (1999), 7, 202, 203
   adaptation, 207–8
   development, 208
   production, 208
   reception, 208
Breton, Denise, 144, 227
Brewster McCloud (1970), 2, 74, 174, 191
Brokaw, Cary, 128, 129, 132, 184, 214
Brown, David, 84–5, 128
Broyles Harper, Patti, 53
Buck, Kelvin, 57
Buena Vista International, 145
Buffalo Bill and the Indians, or Sitting Bull's History Lesson (1976), 2, 71, 72, 73, 84, 194, 202
Bushnell, Scotty, 199, 214, 215, 219

Caine Mutiny Court-Martial, The (1988), 139
California Split (1974), 174–6, 184, 186, 202, 210

Campbell, Neve, 249
Canby, Vincent, 125, 127, 182
Cane, Marvin, 106–7
Cannes Film Festival, 130, 140, 144, 202
Cannon Films, 119, 123, 125
Capitol Films, 87, 148, 151, 230, 231, 232
Carpenter, Lucy, 57
Carver, Raymond, 192, 213, 216
Casablanca records, 107–9, 115
CBS records, 107–8, 112, 115
   and CBS-Boardwalk distribution deal, 112, 115
César Awards, 145
Cher, 125, 159, 161, 167
Chicago International Film Festival, 159
Choose Me (1984), 74, 75, 78, 80n, 202
Christensen, Helena, 144
Christie, Agatha, 74, 147
Christie, Julie, 208
CiBy 2000, 147
Cinecom Pictures, 119, 123, 125, 131, 159, 209, 211
Classical Hollywood paradigm, 16, 24–6, 119, 125
Coburn, Randy Sue, 205
Cohn, Sam, 93, 232
Columbia Pictures, 1
Come Back to the 5 & Dime, Jimmy Dean, Jimmy Dean (1982), 3, 6, 93, 123, 124, 126, 127, 200, 209, 210, 212
   character of Joe/Joanne, 177–8, 179
   distribution, 211
   and fandom, 159–71
   and representations of sexuality, 176–81
Comic book superheroes, 16
Comic strip modes of drawing, 20–1
Company, The (2003), 3, 87, 133, 191, 229, 243
   cinematography, 248–51
   production, 234, 248–50
   script, 234
   themes, 248, 249
Connors, Deke, 34–5, 36
Cookie's Fortune (1999), 3, 4, 7, 47, 51, 61, 62, 133, 200, 234, 236, 237
   casting, 240
   development, 238
   production, 56–60, 238, 240
   script, 238, 239, 242
   themes, 242
Coppola, Francis Ford, 1

Corriere, Konni, 258
Criterion Collection, 213
Crying Game, The (1992), 164, 165, 169

Daly, John, 139
Danish Girl, The (2015), 164, 165, 169
Danson, Ted, 92
Dean, James, 159–71
Demarchelier, Patrick, 144
Democratic Party, 30–1
Dennis, Sandy, 125, 161, 178
DePalma, Brian, 1
Deutchman, Ira, 7, 9, 206, 234
    and acquiring Altman films, 211
    and *Angels in America*, 183, 216–17
    and *Come Back to the 5 & Dime, Jimmy Dean, Jimmy Dean*, 211, 212
    and early Altman films, 210
    and Fine Line, 210
    interview with, 209–17
    and *Mrs. Parker and the Vicious Circle*, 214–15
    and *Player, The*, 131, 132, 212–13
    and relationship with Robert Altman, 215–16, 217
    and *Secret Honor*, 212
    and *Short Cuts*, 213–14
DeVault, Marjorie L., 61
Disney, 105, 113–14, 133
Dixon, Pam, 92, 226, 230
Do-it-yourself (DIY) filmmaking, 41–5
Doctorow, E. L., 220
Doty, Alexander, 186
Dowd, Ned, 237, 240
Downton Abbey (2010–15), 151
Dr. T & the Women (2000), 3, 7, 98, 148, 158, 200, 229, 233, 234, 236, 237, 242
    distribution, 133
    production, 239, 240
    script, 238–40, 241
Dukakis, Michael, 31, 37, 38
Dumb Waiter, The, (1987), 176
Dunaway, Faye, 257, 258
Dunn, Andrew, 7
    and *Company, The*, 248–51
    and *Gosford Park*, 243, 244–7, 249
    interview with, 243–51
Durang, Christopher, 124, 177, 180–2
Dutton, Charles, 58, 238
Duvall, Shelley, 99, 102, 104, 109–10, 112–13

Ebert, Roger, 74, 75, 78, 100, 114, 255
Eggenweiler, Bob, 199
Elaine's, 226, 257, 258
Elektra Records, 115
EMI Films, 108
Evans, Robert, 6, 13–14, 16, 19, 99, 101–2, 104–5, 113
Exploitation filmmaking, 117, 121, 122, 123, 126, 180

Famous Music Publishing, 106–7, 115
Fawcett, Farrah, 241
Feiffer, Jules, 5, 13, 14–19, 20–3, 25–7, 113
Fellini, Federico, 78, 113, 139
Fellowes, Julian, 147, 148, 151
Fine Line Features, 131, 132, 133, 137, 183, 184, 206, 207, 209, 212, 213, 214, 215, 216, 227
Finney, Albert, 208
Fitzgerald Theater, 193, 233
Flash Gordon (1980), 14, 106, 108, 113
Flash Gordon comic strip, 21
Fool for Love (1985), 3, 123, 124, 125, 127, 176, 188n, 201
Foote, Horton, 93
Forman, Milos, 108
Fosse, Bob, 103, 113
Franco, James, 87, 92, 249
Frears, Stephen, 232
Freed, Donald, 71
Fry, Stephen, 151

Gallagher, Peter, 129
Garr, Teri, 185, 200
Gaumont, 145
Gere, Richard, 238, 239
Giant (1956), 162, 163, 177
Gilbert and Sullivan, 198–9
Gill, Mark, 142
Gingerbread Man, The (1998), 3, 67, 80n, 133, 242
Glossop, Peter, 244
Goldblum, Jeff, 125
Golden Globes, The, 151, 159
Gore, Al, 31, 41–2
Gosford Park (2001), 3, 6, 10, 49, 81, 93, 148, 186, 216, 223, 229, 233, 234, 243, 249
    awards, 151
    box office, 138, 151

casting, 148, 230–1
cinematography, 244–7
development, 147–9, 230
distribution, 133, 148, 151
and film festivals, 150
financing, 148–9, 152, 230–1
genre, 67, 74–5, 148, 149, 150, 151, 192
marketing, 149, 150
production, 148–9, 152, 231, 232, 245–6
reception, 138, 148, 150–1, 152
and Robert Altman's brand, 148–51, 152
Gosling, Ryan, 92
Gould, Elliott, 92, 175, 258
Graczyk, Ed, 159, 177, 178
Grant, Richard E., 129, 139, 144, 186, 198
Gray, Jonathan, 34, 41
Grease (1978), 101–4, 108, 111, 114
GreeneStreet, 232
Gun (1997), 236, 237

Halberstam, Jack, 165, 166, 170n
Haldman, Myron, 24
Hall, Philip Baker, 72, 73, 125, 219
Hands on a Hard Body (n.p.), 83, 242, 256
development, 90–4
Hari, Mata, 82–6; see also Zelle, Margareetha Geertruida
Harlow, Jean, 76–7
Harrelson, Woody, 191, 193, 232
Harrigan, Stephen, 91
Hayek, Salma, 87, 89, 92
HBO (Home Box Office), 30–1, 33, 71, 84, 139, 142, 184, 188n, 217, 222
HealtH (1980), 1, 2, 71, 130, 176, 190, 194
Heflin, Marta, 161
Hemdale, 123, 127, 128, 139, 142
Hemingway, Ernest, 67
Henley, Beth, 91
Henry, Buck, 187
High concept filmmaking, 102–6, 114–15, 118, 122, 126
Hill Street Blues (1981–7), 87, 222–3
Hillier, Jim, 121
Holly Springs, Mississippi, 56–60, 62
Hollywood musical, 13, 14, 16–17, 20, 23, 24–7, 111
Hollywood Renaissance, 1, 6, 13, 27, 117, 118, 119, 120, 121, 122, 123, 133, 173; see also New Hollywood

Images (1972), 139
Independent Feature Project/West, 128, 133
Independent Spirit Award, 132, 133
Independent cinema, 3, 6, 7, 43, 117, 124, 128, 131, 132, 153
of the 1980s, 125
and academic film criticism, 121, 133
and aesthetic experimentation, 119
and audience demographics, 126
and authorship, 126, 127
as brand identity, 123
and exploitation genre, 123
and genre experimentation, 126, 127, 129
and Hollywood Renaissance, 118, 119, 120, 121, 122
and marketing, 126, 127
and popular criticism, 120, 133
and stars, 126, 127, 129
Insdorf, Annette, 124, 125, 126
International Creative Management, 92, 133
Island World
and Island/Alive, 128

Jackson, Jesse, 31, 37–8
Jacobi, Derek, 148
Joffrey Ballet, 249, 250
Johnson, Dwayne, 92
Jones, Tommy Lee, 92, 232

Kael, Pauline, 65, 212, 255
Kansas City (1996), 7, 50, 66, 67, 71, 92, 133, 147, 192, 194, 218, 219, 234
genre, 75–7
marketing, 227
production, 220
themes, 220
Kaplan, Mike, 140
Kehr, Dave, 214
Keillor, Garrison, 92, 192, 232, 233, 242
Kellerman, Sally, 174, 258
Kerry, Alexandra, 43–4
Kerry, John, 42, 43
Kessler, Kelly, 111
Keyssar, Helene, 162, 165, 167, 175–6
Kline, Kevin, 191, 192, 232
Kolker, Robert 163, 165, 185
Kuhn, Annette, 55–6
Kurita, Toyomichi, 240
Kushner, Tony, 183, 209

Lachman, Ed, 193
Ladd, Alan Jr., 1, 2
Lagerfeld, Karl, 144, 145, 146
Lane, Diane, 92
Laundromat, The (1985), 176
Law, Jude, 230, 231
LaZebnik, Ken, 192
Leary, Timothy, 71–3
Leiber and Stoller, 198–9
Leigh, Jennifer Jason, 75, 205
Lemper, Ute, 83
Lépine, Jean, 68–9, 200
Lerner, Sammy, 106, 115n
Levy, David, 81, 83, 85, 88, 89, 225
   and the three C's of independent
      filmmaking, 83, 86, 95
Lewis, Jeffrey, 87–9
Lichtenstein, Mitchell, 178, 179
Liddy, G. Gordon, 71–3
Lion's Gate, 19, 23, 140
Lohan, Lindsay, 232
Lombardo, Tony, 22
London Film Festival, 150
Long Good Friday, The (1980), 244–5
Long Goodbye, The (1973), 13, 49, 74, 129,
   140, 191, 193, 194, 202, 210
Loren, Sophia, 74
Los Angeles Actors' Theater, The, 125
Love at Large (1990), 67, 75
Lovett, Lyle, 8
Lucas, George, 1
Lumet, Sidney, 93, 108, 129

M*A*S*H (1970), 1, 2, 84, 118, 129, 145, 172,
   173, 174, 237, 253
Made in Heaven (1987), 74, 75
Madsen, Virginia, 193, 232
Man Who Fell to Earth, The (1976), 187
Mann, Ron, 3–4, 8
Mastroianni, Marcello, 74
Mata Hari (n.p.), 82–7
McBride, Joseph, 140
McCabe & Mrs. Miller (1971), 2, 74, 118, 129,
   140, 184, 191, 193, 194, 237, 253
McGilligan, Patrick, 15, 174
Mead Products, 105
Mercer, Jack, 22–3
Merchant-Ivory, 148, 151
Metro-Goldwyn-Mayer (MGM), 1
Midnight Cowboy (1969), 101

Mignot, Pierre, 8, 177, 200
Millar, Mark, 57
Miramax, 132, 142, 144, 145, 147, 207, 215, 216
Mirren, Helen, 148
Mitchell, Robert, 145
Mockumentary, 30, 32–3, 41–5
Moderns, The (1988), 67–70
Modine, Matthew, 125, 178
Moore, Julianne, 92, 93, 238, 241
Mortal Thoughts (1991), 67, 74, 208
Mrs. Parker and the Vicious Circle (1994), 7,
   71, 78, 133, 202, 207, 209, 214
   credits, 215
   development, 205–7
   financing, 205–6, 215
Murphy, Michael, 8, 40, 222, 258

Nashville (1975), 1, 2, 65, 70, 93, 111, 145, 146,
   150, 151, 172, 174, 183, 186, 197, 198,
   202, 210, 220, 221, 237, 253
   locations in, 49, 50, 66
   plot structure, 183, 213, 222–3
Neal, Patricia, 238
New Hollywood, 13, 27, 118, 119, 120, 121;
   see also Hollywood Renaissance
New Line Cinema, 126, 132, 183, 184, 212, 213
New World Pictures, 123, 125, 126, 180–1
New York Film Festival, 214
Newman, Randy, 108
Newman, Robert, 93
Nicholls, Allan F., 7, 8, 180, 197
   and *3 Women*, 198
   and *Come Back to the 5 & Dime, Jimmy
      Dean, Jimmy Dean*, 200
   and *Fool for Love*, 201
   interview with, 197–201
   and *Nashville*, 198
   and *Perfect Couple, A*, 198
   and *Player, The*, 200
   and *Popeye*, 199–200
   and *Prêt-à-Porter*, 198–9, 200
   and *Streamers*, 200
   and *Wedding, A*, 198
Nichols, Mike, 217
Nilsson, Harry, 6, 13, 25–6, 99–101, 104,
   110–13
Nixon, Richard, 71–3
Northam, Jeremy, 231
Nostalgia Press, 15, 17
Novello, Ivor, 246

O. C. and Stiggs (1985), 79n, 117, 186, 197, 220
O'Donnell, Chris, 239
October Films, 128
Oursler, Tony, 89–90
Owen, Clive, 230

Padva, Gilad, 161–2
Paint (n.p.), 80n, 82, 83, 87–90; see also
    Ultraviolet (n.p.)
Palmer, Gladys Perint, 196
Paramount Pictures, 1, 13–14, 19
Parker, Dorothy, 205
Parks, Van Dyke 110, 112
Patton, Mark, 161
Pavlounis, Dimitrios, 118
Pelosi, Alexandra, 41
Perfect Couple, A (1979), 1, 2, 176, 184, 198
Perkins, Claire, 121
Peroni, Geraldine, 8
Phillippe, Ryan, 230, 231
Picturehouse, 133, 227
Planco, Johnnie, 205–6, 216
Player, The (1992), 3, 6, 66, 70, 73, 74, 83,
    84, 85, 117, 123, 127, 138, 142, 144, 145,
    146, 150, 152, 191, 194, 197, 200, 209,
    211, 215, 254
    adaptation, 212
    as "Altmanesque," 129
    and audience demographics, 130–1, 132
    box office, 213
    casting, 129, 131, 212
    financing, 128
    genre, 130, 131
    as indie cinema, 130–1, 132
    reception, 131, 213
Pohlad, Bill, 232
Polygram Films, 133
Popeye (1980), 2, 5, 6, 9, 10, 117, 123, 142, 152,
    176, 197, 199, 210
    and blockbuster musicals, 99–107, 109–11,
        113–14
    and "I'm Popeye the Sailor Man" song,
        14, 24, 27
    and Popeye the Sailor Man animated
        series (Fleischer Studios), 13, 14–15,
        16, 19, 22–4, 26–7
    and Popeye Story, The, 13, 14, 15, 20–1,
        22–3, 99
    reception, 99–100
    soundtrack, 101, 104, 106–9, 111, 112

and Thimble Theatre comic strips (E. C.
    Segar), 13, 14–19, 20–2, 25, 27, 101, 113
and transpositional poetics, 13–27
Prairie Home Companion, A (2006), 3, 7, 8,
    79n, 92, 133, 225, 228, 229, 234
    cinematography, 193
    development, 192
    financing, 232
    marketing, 227
    mise-en-scène, 193
    music, 193
    performances, 191
    production, 190, 232–3
    themes, 192–3
Prêt-à-Porter (1994), 3, 6, 74, 86, 118, 132,
    133, 185, 186, 191, 196, 197, 200
    box office, 138, 143, 146–7, 152
    development, 142–3
    distribution, 142, 144–5
    and fashion world, 142, 144, 145
    financing, 142, 216
    marketing, 144–5, 147, 152
    publicity, 138, 143–4, 152
    reception, 138, 142, 143, 145–6, 148,
        149, 152
Prêt-à-Porter (cont.)
    and Robert Altman's brand, 143–4,
        146, 147, 152
    title, 144
Prince Vince, 38–9

Queer death drive, 168
Quintet (1979), 1, 2, 130, 176

Rabe, David, 124, 178
Rainer, Peter, 66, 77
Rapp, Anne, 7, 91, 93, 94, 173, 236
    and Cookie's Fortune, 238, 237, 239, 240,
        241, 242
    and Dr. T & the Women, 238–40, 241, 242
    and Gun, 237
    and Hands on a Hard Body, 242
    interview with, 236–42
    and M*A*S*H, 237
    and McCabe & Mrs. Miller, 237
    and Nashville, 237
    and Prairie Home Companion, A, 242
Rattlesnake in a Cooler (1982), 176
Ray, Bingham, 128
Rea, Stephen, 196

Reality television, 42–3
Redford, Robert 43
Reed Altman, Robert, 49, 54
Reilly, John C., 92, 191, 193, 232
Remember My Name (1978), 67, 202, 204, 207
Remsen, Bert, 174, 175, 185
Renoir, Jean, 245
Return Engagement (1983), 67, 71–3
Rhys, Paul, 68
River Road, 232
Roadie (1980), 75, 79n
Robbins, Tim, 129, 130, 200, 213, 257
Robert Altman: The Oral Biography
    development, 253–4, 256–7
    reception, 258
    writing process, 254, 257–8
Robertson, Pat, 32, 35–6
Rock, Chris, 92
Roeg, Nicolas, 187
Room, The (1987), 176
Rose, Charlie, 88, 94
Rossini, Gioachino, 139
Roth, Tim, 68, 127
Rudolph, Alan, 5, 7, 50, 54, 55, 133, 209
    and *Afterglow*, 202
    and *Breakfast of Champions*, 202, 203, 207–8
    and *Buffalo Bill and the Indians, or Sitting Bull's History Lesson*, 202
    and *California Split*, 202
    and *Choose Me*, 202
    contrasted with Robert Altman, 66–7, 69–70, 77–9
    interview with, 202–8
    and *Kansas City*, 220
    and *Long Goodbye, The*, 202
    and *Mrs. Parker and the Vicious Circle*, 202, 205–7
    and *Nashville*, 202
    and *Remember My Name*, 202, 204
    and *Return Engagement*, 71–3
    and *The Moderns*, 67–70
    and *Trixie*, 202
    and *Trouble in Mind*, 75–7, 202
    and *Welcome to L.A.*, 65, 202, 203, 204
Rudolph, Maya, 232, 233
Rules of the Game, The (1939), 245
Russo, Vito, 174–5, 179–80
Rybin, Steven, 69–70, 78
Rykiel, Sonia, 142

Sallitt, Dan, 65, 66
Sandcastle 5 Productions, 7, 225, 226, 234
Sarandon, Susan, 257
Sarnoff, Dorothy, 37
Saturday Night Fever (1977), 101, 102, 103, 108, 111
Sayles, John, 118, 126
Schulgasser, Barbara, 144
Scorsese, Martin, 1, 120
Secret Honor (1984), 3, 67, 71–3, 93, 123, 125, 127, 180, 197, 209, 211–12, 219, 220
Segal, George, 88, 174, 175
Seig, Matthew, 7, 52, 59, 62, 87, 88–9, 218, 257
    interview with, 218–24
    and *Kansas City*, 219, 220–1
    and *O.C. and Stiggs*, 220
    and *Secret Honor*, 219, 220
    and *Tanner '88*, 221–2, 223
    and *Tanner on Tanner*, 222
Self, Robert, 47, 88, 161, 165, 168–9, 174
Selway, Mary, 230
sex, lies, and videotape (1989), 126, 127
Shaye, Bob, 216, 217
Shepard, Sam, 124, 125, 127, 201
Shipton, Alyn, 110–11
Short Cuts (1993), 3, 80n, 118, 142, 144, 145, 172, 191, 192, 197, 205, 206, 209, 212, 241, 253
    box office, 133, 214
    financing, 132, 216
    marketing, 213–14
    reception, 214
    themes, 255
Smith, Lois, 227
Smith, Maggie, 148, 230
Soderbergh, Steven, 121, 133
Solomon, Matthew, 82, 83, 94
Songwriter (1985), 74, 75
Sony Pictures Classics, 133
Sotet, Danielle, 226
Steenburgen, Mary, 92
Stockwell, Dean, 129
Stone, Arnold M., 71
Stout, John, 232
Streamers (1983), 3, 93, 123, 124, 125, 127, 176, 177, 178–80, 181, 197, 200, 215, 218
Streep, Meryl, 92, 185, 232

Sundance Channel, 41, 222
Swank, Hillary, 92

Tanner '88 (1988), 3, 5, 7, 30–41, 45, 67, 71, 87, 123, 218, 220
   cameos in, 31, 35–6, 42
   casting, 221–2
   improvisation in, 221
   legacy, 223
   pilot episode, 34–6
   production, 221–2
   reception, 222
Tanner on Tanner (2004), 3, 5, 7, 30, 32, 41–5, 197, 218, 220, 222, 225
Tarantino, Quentin, 120, 121, 126, 133
Terry, Bridget, 13, 14, 15, 20–1, 22–3
That Cold Day in the Park (1969), 184
Thieves Like Us (1974), 184, 190, 194, 210
Thompson, David, 234–5
Thompson, Tommy, 199, 200
Thornton, Billy Bob, 92
Tolkin, Michael, 128, 212
Tomlin, Lily, 8, 92, 185, 232
Toronto Film Festival, 141
Transmedia, 13, 14, 15–19, 20–2, 27
Travolta, John, 101, 103, 111
Trixie (2000), 67, 75, 202
Trouble in Mind (1985), 66, 67, 75–7, 78, 202
Trudeau, Garry, 5, 30–3, 45, 220, 221–2
Tucci, Stanley, 231
Turner, Barbara, 234
Twentieth Century Fox, 1, 2, 87, 144
Tyler, Liv, 239, 240

UK Film Council, 148
Ullman, Tracey, 144
Ultraviolet (n.p.), 82, 87; *see also Paint* (n.p.)
United Artists, 1
United Artists Classics, 119, 123, 125, 131
Urban Cowboy (1980), 101, 102, 111
USA Films, 133

Vallan, Giulia D'Agnolo, 3, 66, 72, 218, 223
van Gogh, Theo, 139
van Gogh, Vincent, 67, 88, 139, 140, 141
van Sant, Gus, 128, 133
Venice Film Festival, 144

Vincent & Theo (1990), 3, 6, 88, 117, 123, 128, 148
   box office, 141–2
   development, 139
   distribution, 139, 141, 152
   financing, 123, 139, 152
   marketing, 139, 140
   production, 139, 149, 152
   reception, 138, 140–1, 144, 146, 152
   and Robert Altman's brand, 139–40, 141, 142, 147, 152
   themes, 67–70
Vonnegut, Kurt, 202, 207, 208, 220

Walston, Ray, 104, 113
Warner Bros., 1
Waxman, Sharon, 120, 121, 122
Wechsler, Nick, 128
Wedding, A (1978), 1, 2, 172, 176, 198
Weinstein, Harvey, 147, 207
Welcome to L.A. (1976), 65–6, 75, 202, 203, 204, 207
William Morris Agency, 129, 132, 133
Williams, Robin, 13, 18, 22–3, 24, 27, 99, 101, 102, 106, 112, 113
Williamson, David, 85–6
Willis, Bruce, 208
Witherspoon, Reese, 92
Wood, Robin, 1, 2, 10, 177
Wright, Michael, 178, 179
Wyatt, Justin, 102–3, 106, 114–15, 121, 138, 159, 186–7

Yesterday, Today, and Tomorrow (1963), 74

Zaharoff, Basil, 85–6
Zelle, Margareetha Geertruida, 84; *see also* Hari, Mata
Zuckoff, Mitchell, 3, 7, 50–1, 94, 219, 252
   and *Hands on a Hard Body*, 256
   interview with, 252–8
   and *M*A*S*H*, 253
   and *McCabe & Mrs. Miller*, 253
   and *Nashville*, 253
   and *Player, The*, 254
   and *Robert Altman: The Oral Biography*, 253–4, 256–8
   and *Short Cuts*, 253, 255

EU representative:
Easy Access System Europe
Mustamäe tee 50, 10621 Tallinn, Estonia
Gpsr.requests@easproject.com

www.ingramcontent.com/pod-product-compliance
Lightning Source LLC
Chambersburg PA
CBHW050212240426
43671CB00013B/2311